Patton's Pawns

Other Books by the Author

The Battle of Berlin 1945
Berlin: Then and Now
Farewell to Spandau
Zhukov at the Oder: The Decisive Battle for Berlin
Race for the Reichstag: The 1945 Battle for Berlin
With Our Backs to Berlin: The German Army in Retreat, 1945
Death Was Our Companion: The Final Days of the Third Reich
The Third Reich: Then and Now
Slaughter at Halbe: Hitler's Ninth Army in the Spreewald Pocket, April 1945

Translation
Helmut Altner's *Berlin Dance of Death*

Patton's Pawns

The 94th US Infantry Division at the Siegfried Line

TONY LE TISSIER

THE UNIVERSITY OF ALABAMA PRESS
Tuscaloosa

Typeface: ACaslon and Gill Sans

∞

The paper on which this book is printed meets the minimum requirements of
American National Standard for Information Sciences–Permanence of Paper for
Printed Library Materials, ANSI Z39.48-1984.

Library of Congress Cataloging-in-Publication Data

Le Tissier, Tony, 1932–
Patton's pawns : the 94th US Infantry Division at the Siegfried Line /
Tony Le Tissier.
p. cm.
Includes bibliographical references and index.
ISBN-13: 978-0-8173-1557-3 (cloth : alk. paper)
ISBN-10: 0-8173-1557-8 (alk. paper)
1. United States. Army. Infantry Division, 94th. 2. World War, 1939–1945—
Regimental histories—United States. 3. World War, 1939–1945—
Campaigns—Germany. 4. Siegfried Line (Germany) I. Title.
D769.394th .L4 2007
940.54′21342—dc22

2006029217

Photo credits: 1–27 courtesy of US Army, 28–33 are used by
the permission of the author.

Contents

List of Illustrations   vii

Preface   ix

1. The Division Moves into the Line   1

2. The Division Goes into Action   14

3. Disaster at Orscholz   51

4. Action on the Left Flank   64

5. The Second Battle of Sinz   93

6. The Division Unleashed   117

7. Clearing the Triangle   134

8. Crossing the Saar   147

9. Establishing the Bridgehead   190

10. Developing the Bridgehead   217

11. Taking Trier   240

12. The Battle of Lampaden Ridge   264

13. The Race for the Rhine   290

Epilogue   297

Appendix A: HQ 94th Infantry Division   305

Appendix B: 301st Infantry Regiment   307

Appendix C: 302nd Infantry Regiment   309

Appendix D: 376th Infantry Regiment   311

Appendix E: Selected Telephone Conversations between
HQ XX Corps and HQ 94th Infantry Division   313

Notes   329

Bibliography   341

Index   345

Armed Forces Index   359

Photographs to follow page   176

Illustrations

MAPS AND DRAWINGS

1. Some Westwall Pillboxes & Bunkers   8–9

2. The Area of Operations—7 Jan/21 Feb 45   10

3. The German Defenses on the West Flank
   of the Orscholz Switch   17

4. Battle of Tettingen-Butzdorf—15 Jan 45   19

5. The Nennig-Berg-Wies Battleground   29

6. Battle of Tettingen-Butzdorf—18 Jan 45   39

7. Disaster at Orscholz   56

8. The Sinz Battleground—26/28 Jan 45   75

9. The Campholz Woods Complex   88

10. The Sinz and Bannholz Woods Battleground—7/11 Feb 45   95

11. Break-Out—19/21 Feb 45   119

12. Beyond Münzingen Ridge   127

13. The Serrig Bridgehead—Night 22 Feb 45   166

14. The Ayl Bridgehead—Night 23 Feb 45   193

15. German Fortress Engineers' Design
    for the Ockfen-Irsch Defenses   198

16. The Serrig Bridgehead—Night 23 Feb 45   200

17. The Ayl Bridgehead—Night 24 Feb 45   207

18. The Serrig Bridgehead—Night 24 Feb 45   211

19. The Combined Bridgehead—Night 25 Feb 45   224

20. The Southern Flank—25/26 Feb 45   229

21. Area of Operations—376th Infantry Regiment—26/28 Feb 45   236

22. The Advance on Zerf—26 Feb 45   238

23. Redeployment—27 Feb/2 Mar 45   243

24. The Taking of Trier by the
10th Armored Division—26 Feb/1 Mar 45   252

25. The Battle of Lampaden Ridge—3/7 Mar 45   269

26. Race for the Rhine   292

Photographs Following Page   176

Preface

In entering into this project, I was fully aware that I was treading on ground already well covered by Nathan N. Prefer (*Patton's Ghost Corps*) and the official *History of the 94th Infantry Division* by Lt. Laurence G. Byrnes. Nevertheless, I believed that the story of the 94th U.S. Infantry Division's role in World War II was worth investigating further, that any new book could only help promote fresh interest in this historical event, and that this book might even throw some new light on the subject.

Some may think it odd that I, as a British military historian specializing in the battle of Berlin, should interest myself in such a theme. My fascination with the 94th Infantry Division's efforts at the Siegfried Line came about as a result of my work in Berlin conducting city and battlefield tours, which in 1999 brought me into contact with American veterans associations and the invitation to lead veterans of the 94th on a visit to their old stomping grounds. This was followed by a repeat performance in 2001 as well as one veteran's private family tour in 2000. The spectacular terrain of the Saar-Moselle Triangle seen in summertime, veterans' accounts of their experiences, and the extremely friendly reception given by the local inhabitants, who used the term "liberators" for the invaders and conquerors, were all intriguing.

My efforts have been greatly encouraged by veterans Robert P. Kingsbury (E376) and Robert E. Trefzger (C376) (both gave invaluable help in correcting the text) and Sgt. Robert K. Adair (I376), for their most generous contributions of material, as well as William A. Foley Jr. (G302), T. Jerome French (B376), and Jim Burns (E302), editor of *The 94 Attack,* the 94th Infantry Division Association's official publication. Thanks are also due to

Dr. Gilbert E. Kinyon (F302), Maj. Albert R. Hoffman (Engrs), my long-time friend Oberst (Colonel) Dr. Winfried Heinemann of the Federal German Military Archives in Potsdam for assistance with my research, Ernst J. Kronenberger of Halfway House for background information on that part of the Saarland and its inhabitants, and Werner Kortenhaus for material on the 21st Panzer Division.

I would also like to thank the 94th Infantry Division Association for permission to quote several witness statements from Lt. Lawrence Byrnes's *The History of the 94th Infantry Division in World War II;* Robin Neillands for permission to quote a statement from his book, *The Conquest of the Reich;* Charles Whiting for permission to quote a statement from his book, *The West Wall: The Battle for Hitler's Siegfried Line;* Ernst Heinkel for permission to use his account of the fall of Schloss Thorn; Nathan N. Prefer, PhD, for his encouragement and assistance; and my friend Col. Dr. Steve Bowman (U.S. Army Ret.) for his advice.

I owe special thanks to Jürgen Ludwig of the Landesamt für Kataster-, Vermessungs- und Kartenwesen (State Cartography Office) in Saarbrücken, who most generously provided copies of overlaid maps showing the German defenses that were discovered during a postwar survey of the Orscholz Switch area. Unfortunately, the other map office concerned, the Landesamt für Vermessung und Geobasisinformation Rheinland-Pfalz (State Cartography Office), in Koblenz, was unable to provide similar maps covering the main defenses of the Westwall along the Saar River. Nevertheless, the maps covering the Orscholz Switch area are still not 100 percent reliable, as they omit items such as antitank ditches and bunkers that were not found at the time of the survey, and some of the woodland shown as minefields turns out not to be completely so from the survivors' accounts. Consequently, I have had to guess the location of the first antitank ditch at the western end of the Unterste Büsch Woods. Sebastian Kirch also kindly provided a map showing some of the Orscholz Switch defenses, as did British historian Neil Short. My overlays incorporate all the available information, including that obtained from the sketches in the division's official history.

The reader is reminded that the contours on the current German maps of 1945 used as a background for my drawings relate to meters rather than feet. The scale is shown by the one-kilometer squares of the grid. Surprisingly, the grids on the Rheinland-Pflaz and Saar maps do not coincide, and the grid references given in some quotations in the text, using the Allied forces' system, do not correspond with those on the maps I have used, so I have not attempted to include them.

A visit to the battlefield today provides some fantastic, spectacular scenery. There have been some changes, of course, but none sufficient to mar the historically oriented visitor's quest. The Saar River now has low dams with navigation locks near Hamm and Schoden, slowing down the pace of the raging river of 1945, and a broad highway now runs along the eastern bank, with a new bridge at the Taben crossing point and another connecting with Ayl farther north. The heights of Hocker Hill and the Auf der Hütte cliffs remain as awe-inspiring as ever.

What the men of the 94th achieved under the appalling conditions of that winter of early 1945 hardly seems credible today, and I have great admiration for them. The unique Peace Monument, on the B 406 (E 29) highway where it crosses the Münzingen Ridge between Sinz and Oberleuken, serves as a fitting memorial to all the men in the 94th Infantry Division.

I have concluded this presentation with what became an award-winning address by the association's chaplain, the Reverend Charles H. Manning (H301), to their 47th Annual Memorial Service in 1996. Having had the pleasure of meeting him on the 1999 and 2001 tours, it was hard to imagine that this man, who now has difficulty with breathing and walking, was a company runner in 1945, but his spirit outshone his difficulties, and his style of address could not have been more apt for his audience. It is only right that he should have the last word.

Tony Le Tissier
Lymington, U.K.
June 2006

Patton's Pawns

I

The Division Moves
into the Line

In Belgium's Ardennes region the Battle of the Bulge was in full spate, and all attention and resources were focused in that direction when the 94th U.S. Infantry Division arrived at the front to relieve the more experienced 90th Infantry Division.[1]

Between January 7 and 10, 1945, the 94th Infantry Division moved out of France into the southwest corner of Germany and deployed in the forward line of the XX Corps of Gen. George S. Patton Jr.'s Third Army. The sector assigned to it was the base of the Saar-Moselle Triangle on the left flank of Maj. Gen. Walton H. Walker's XX Corps, whose front extended eastward beyond Saarlautern.

The Saar-Moselle Triangle was formed by the confluence of Germany's Saar and Moselle Rivers immediately south of the important communications center of the ancient city of Trier, the east-west base of the triangle being about thirteen miles long and the distance from base to tip about sixteen miles. The main German line of defense, the Westwall, was known to the Western Allies as the Siegfried Line. This line followed the east bank of the Saar River to the Moselle, from where it continued northward along the east bank of the Sauer River. As an additional protective belt for Trier, the Germans had built a spur of the main defensive line, known as the Orscholz Switch, across the base of the triangle, which abutted the independent country of Luxembourg, occupied at the time by the 2nd Cavalry Group of the American XII Corps.

The 94th had been activated at Fort Custer in Battle Creek, Michigan, on September 15, 1942, as part of the massive expansion of the United States armed forces to meet the requirements of World War II. With such vast growth, it was inevitable that some of those men who were given command appointments would prove inadequate to the task and that this evolution would lead to frequent changes in personnel.

The entire enlisted and officer cadres below regimental rank for the 94th came from the 77th U.S. Infantry Division at Fort Jackson, South Carolina, and the junior officer strength was topped off with Reserve Officer Training Corps lieutenants and newly commissioned Officer Candidate School graduates from Fort Benning, Georgia. All would have completed special-to-arms courses, the enlisted men having gone through up to seventeen weeks of basic training at a Replacement Training Center. According to the program laid down by the War Department, the division then had one year to prepare itself for active service. The guidelines allowed thirteen weeks for individual training, five weeks for unit training, four weeks for combined training, seven weeks for maneuvers, and a further six weeks for post-maneuver training, with proficiency tests being carried out at every stage.

Because Fort Custer proved inadequate for its requirements, in November 1942 the 94th Infantry Division moved to Camp Phillips, Kansas, where training was conducted in extreme climatic conditions of snow, mud, and dust storms throughout the ensuing winter, spring, and summer of 1943. Then, at the end of August 1943, the division moved again to the Army Maneuver Area in central Tennessee, where it was immediately drained of fifteen hundred personnel who were urgently required as overseas replacements.[2] That November there was another move to Camp Forrest, near Tullahoma, Tennessee, where the division lost one hundred men from each of its battalions and much of its equipment to the 8th Infantry Division, which had been alerted for a move overseas, before moving again at the end of the month to complete its training at Fort McCain in Grenada, Mississippi. Shortly afterward the 94th was brought up to full strength after the collapse of the Army Specialized Training Program. Draftees with an adequate educational background had been able to apply for the program upon completion of their thirteen-week basic infantry training. This entailed attending intensified university courses in certain subjects under military supervision before resuming their military training for commissioned or specialized roles. However, the program came to an abrupt end when Gen. Dwight D. Eisenhower asked for an extra fifty-five thousand troops for the invasion of Europe, and the 94th Infantry Division was one of those whose ranks were boosted by the intake of these better-than-average-educated soldiers in February 1944.

The 94th Infantry Division was eventually alerted for overseas service on May 26, 1944, by which time the standards of training achieved were such that despite the constant upheaval of personnel and equipment changes, the following day several of its units were awarded Expert Infantry Company streamers, and the following month the 376th Infantry Regiment qualified as the first Expert Infantry Regiment in the U.S. Army, with the 94th Infantry Division qualifying as the first Expert Infantry Division. Sadly, these standards were later allowed to slip, and every soldier who survived training camp was given the qualification badge.

The division then moved to Fort Shanks, New York, to prepare for embarking for overseas service, and on August 5 they were taken aboard the RMS *Queen Elizabeth* for a fast voyage to Greenock, near Glasgow, Scotland. The men were then moved down by rail to Wiltshire, where the units were accommodated within the Devizes-Melksham-Trowbridge area while awaiting transfer to France. Here the division drew its establishment of vehicles and was joined by an air support group, a photo interpretation team, a prisoner-of-war interrogation team, a military intelligence interpretation group, an Order of Battle team, and a civil affairs section. The division then sailed in several small ships from Southampton and landed on Utah Beach on September 6, appropriately ninety-four days after D-Day.[3]

On September 12, 1944, the division took over from the 10th Armored Division the task of containing the German units that were in the separate pocket at Lorient in southern Brittany defending their submarine bases. The orders from VIII Corps, Ninth Army, to which the 94th Infantry Division was now assigned, were specifically to contain, not attack, the enemy, for the corps' previous assault on Brest with three divisions had proved far too expensive in terms of casualties. The enemy garrison at Lorient was estimated as being between twenty-one and twenty-five thousand troops. Shortly afterward the 94th's responsibility was extended to include the Saint Nazaire pocket with an additional thirty-five thousand enemy troops, and it took over from the 83rd Infantry Division in that area. Consequently, the 94th's experience in Brittany was mainly that of skirmishing, except for one attack organized by Brig. Gen. Louis J. Fortier, the divisional artillery commander, on December 8, using the 3rd Battalion, 301st Infantry, together with engineers and artillery to capture nine bunkers among the defenses covering the foot of the Quiberon Peninsula and taking fifty-nine prisoners with minimal casualties.[4] Frustrated as he was by his division's role in Brittany, Maj. Gen. Harry J. Malony used the chance to practice elements of the division in patrolling, infantry-tank cooperation, infantry-artillery cooperation, and battle indoctrination in general.

On Christmas Eve the torpedoing of a transport carrying elements of the 66th U.S. Infantry Division across the English Channel led to the sad loss of 14 officers and 784 enlisted men. This division was already scheduled to relieve the 94th Infantry Division for more active duty on the Western Front, where the Battle of the Bulge was pressing. Fortunately, by this time most of the containment of the enemy garrisons was in the hands of French Forces of the Interior units under the control of the 94th, so it was still practical to have the depleted 66th take over as planned.[5]

Handover was completed on New Year's Day, and the 94th set off by rail for the Reims staging area to become the SHAEF (Supreme Headquarters Allied Expeditionary Forces) Reserve, but this was changed to the division being reassigned to the Third Army while it was still on the move.

During its spell of duty in Brittany, the 94th could claim to have successfully contained a force of some 60,000 enemy troops, inflicting some 2,700 casualties and capturing 566 prisoners, for a loss of 100 dead, 618 wounded, and one man missing in action.[6]

Like other U.S. Army infantry divisions of World War II, the 94th was designed as the smallest military formation capable of operating independently, although it could detach one of its regiments with appropriate supporting elements as a task force. Triangular in structure and dispensing with the intermediary brigade level, the division consisted of three rifle regiments (the 301st, 302nd, and 376th Infantry), each consisting of three battalions, and each of those including three rifle companies, as well as additional heavy weapons companies at regimental and battalion level. The division also comprised an artillery element of one medium (390th) and three light field artillery battalions (301st, 356th, and 919th), with a light aircraft air-spotter section, the 319th Medical Battalion, the 319th Engineer Combat Battalion, the 94th Signal Company, the 94th Ordnance Light Maintenance Company, the 94th Quartermaster Company, the 94th Reconnaissance Troop, and a military police platoon. The overall strength was set at 14,253. Additional units, such as antiaircraft artillery, tank, tank destroyer, and chemical warfare battalions, could be attached when appropriate, bringing the command to well over 15,000 men. The additional units, as of January 7, 1945, consisted of the 774th Tank Destroyer and the 465th AAA Automatic Weapons Battalions. The 778th Tank Battalion was to be attached on February 16 and the 704th Tank Destroyer Battalion on January 23 until replaced by the 691st Tank Destroyer Battalion on March 4.[7]

Upon assignment to XX Corps, the 94th Division, under Maj. Gen. Harry J. Malony, was augmented by the attachment of the 607th Tank Destroyer Battalion and the 81st Chemical Warfare Mortar Battalion, which was in fact a heavy mortar battalion equipped with 4.2-inch mortars. It should be noted here that the standard tank destroyer was the M18 Hellcat, which was armed with a 76.2-mm gun and usually supplemented by a .50-caliber machine gun mounted on the open turret, which left it vulnerable to snipers in built-up areas. The M18 Hellcat had the same hull and engine as the standard Sherman tank in its M4A1 through M4A4 versions, which were armed with either a 75- or 76-mm gun and .30-caliber machine guns, also with a .50-caliber machine gun mounted externally on the turret. Both vehicles had five-man crews. The Sherman was mechanically reliable, but its gasoline engine made it highly inflammable. Neither its armor nor its firepower matched that of the German Mark IVs, Panthers, and Tigers, but it remained highly successful in the close infantry support role.

The initial orders for the 94th Infantry Division were to "prepare a plan for limited-objective attacks in battalion strength to shorten and straighten division front lines." The stated purpose of this plan makes little sense when one considers that the division was confronted with a well-established fortified line of defense in depth. However, further orders arrived on January 12 for "a series of limited-objective attacks involving not more than one battalion."[8]

With the Battle of the Bulge still the center of attention and drawing all available resources, little could be spared for this sector of the front. While this situation continued, the role of XX Corps was to keep the Germans tied down and prevent them from switching resources to the densely forested Ardennes. However, the limited scale of the American attacks would mean that the Germans could counter them individually with more powerful reserves, against which the Americans would have to rely on their artillery, providing sufficient ammunition was available.

Although Walker and Malony had been classmates at West Point in 1908, there was little rapport between them. Previously in his career, Malony had held posts senior to Walker, but in the spring of 1942 Malony had apparently fallen foul of his superiors on the Munitions Assignments Board of the Combined Chiefs of Staff and had been given command of the 94th Infantry Division as a way out of the predicament. So now the senior position was held by Walker, who was a fervent disciple of General Patton and his aggressive style of waging war.[9]

During the "Phony War" period of 1939–1940, before the Germans invaded Western Europe, the German defenses along the country's western border had been dubbed the "Siegfried Line" by the British, who disparaged it with the popular ditty:

> We're gonna hang out the washing on the Siegfried Line,
> Have you any dirty washing, mother dear?
> We're gonna hang out the washing on the Siegfried Line,
> 'cos the washing day is here.
> Whether the weather may be wet or fine,
> We'll rub along without a care.
> We're gonna hang out the washing on the Siegfried Line,
> If the Siegfried Line's still there.

However, the Siegfried Line was no joking matter and was very much still there. Designated the Westwall by the Germans, it had been constructed between 1938 and 1940 as a counter to the formidable French Maginot and Belgian Wegand Lines and extended some 630 kilometers from the Swiss border opposite Basel in the south to just beyond Aachen in the north. It had cost 3.5 billion reichsmarks and consumed 4.5 million reichsmarks of materials to build fourteen thousand bunkers, fighting positions, shelters, and antitank defenses.[10]

The German concept of defense was entirely different from that of their neighbors. The Westwall was not intended as a fortress as such, but was meant to provide a defensive position that could be manned by normal field formations as a temporary measure until a counterthrust could be mounted. According to the nature of the terrain, the line was apportioned into sectors designated "fortified" (*Festungsbau*), where a strong defense was necessary;

"defended" (*Stellungsbau*), where an interlocking net of machine-gun posts would suffice; and "barricaded" (*Sperrbau*), where an antitank ditch or dragon's teeth (*Höckerlinie*) served as the prime defensive measure.

The small corps of German fortress engineers produced standard patterns for the various installations to be built and supervised their siting and construction. The majority, 93 percent, of these installations fell into the three B subcategories that were capable of withstanding bombardment by anything between 105-mm and 210-mm artillery, or direct hits from heavier guns, and had walls and ceilings of between 0.8 and 2 meters of reinforced concrete. Another 2 percent of the A category had walls and ceilings that were 2 meters thick and could withstand even heavier punishment, while the remaining 5 percent of the C and D categories were meant to be only splinter or machine-gun proof. In every case, the actual firing position was protected by a thick steel plate.

Bunker models 502 and 504 were particularly predominant on the Orscholz Switch, as were shelter bunker models 51, 51a, and 395. Some installations were entered by way of a gas-proof lock that incorporated a decontamination niche where a dry toilet could be installed. The gas-proofing was further backed by an air conditioning plant that also helped force out fumes from the machine guns. The entrances to these bunkers were often covered both internally and externally by firing slits, and in some of the structures there was also an escape route that the occupants could dig out in an emergency. Other variations incorporated steel turrets with either three or six loopholes for a machine-gun mounting, and some models were equipped with the all-around 50-mm M-19 automatic fortress mortar (50- to 600-meter range, up to 120 rounds per minute) or flamethrowers (75-meter range), while others were equipped as artillery observation posts.

The layout of these installations met the deployment requirements of a standard infantry division of three regiments, each of three battalions, and was fully linked by underground telephone cable systems. The exposed earth from the excavations was then concealed from the air by planting bushes and other vegetation with the advice of landscape gardeners.

Finally, the dragon's teeth obstacle consisted of rows of teethlike projections from a concrete base. These pyramid-shaped fortifications were lower at the front than at the rear and were intended to cause a tank attempting to cross to rear up and shed its tracks, thus immobilizing it.[11]

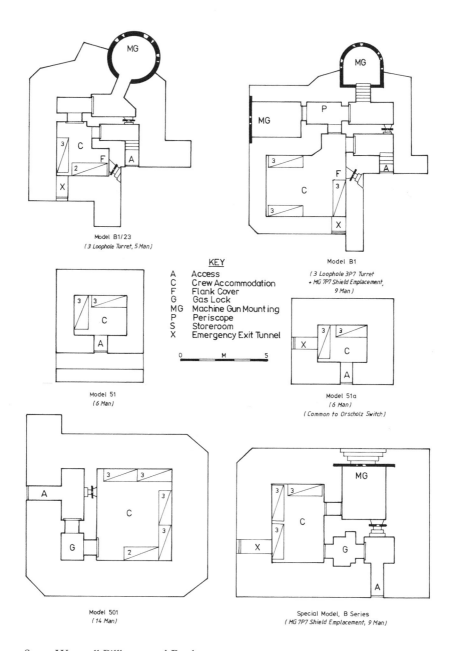

Model B1/23
(3 Loophole Turret, 5 Man)

KEY

A   Access
C   Crew Accommodation
F   Flank Cover
G   Gas Lock
MG Machine Gun Mounting
P   Periscope
S   Storeroom
X   Emergency Exit Tunnel

Model B1

(3 Loophole 3P7 Turret
+ MG 7P7 Shield Emplacement,
9 Man)

0   M   5

Model 51
(6 Man)

Model 51a
(6 Man)
(Common to Orscholz Switch)

Model 501
(14 Man)

Special Model, B Series
(MG 7P7 Shield Emplacement, 9 Man)

Some Westwall Pillboxes and Bunkers

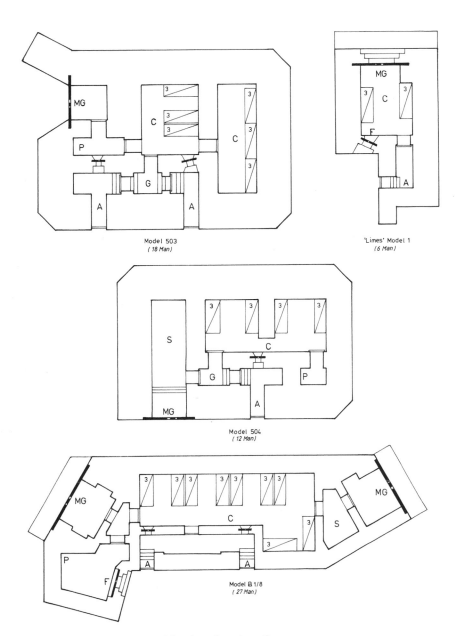

Model 503
(18 Man)

'Limes' Model 1
(6 Man)

Model 504
(12 Man)

Model B 1/8
(27 Man)

Some Westwall Pillboxes and Bunkers (continued)

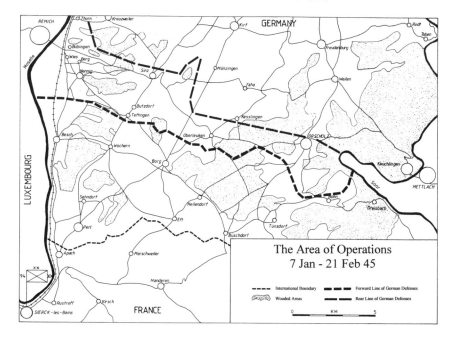

The Area of Operations
7 Jan - 21 Feb 45

After the collapse of the German front in Normandy, Hitler ordered a survey of the Westwall, which revealed how it had declined through neglect during the past four years. In some cases fields of fire had been obstructed, and mines and barbed wire had been removed. Then, on September 1, 1944, Hitler issued the following specific orders for the preparation and use of the Westwall:

1. All fighting bunkers that are not equipped with their own fortress weapons must be provided with suitable weapons of the troops' own. The bunkers will have a commander, who together with his deputy will only use reliable soldiers to man the loophole covering the bunker exit. In an emergency, any soldier can become commander of the bunker, including the deputy.

2. All the fighting bunkers of the Westwall are to be defended by the crew until the last breath. When this is not possible from a loophole, the fight must be continued from outside the bunker.

3. Every fighting bunker is to be surrounded by a protective position. This is to be laid out so that an enemy attack from the front or flanks

can be engaged, and an enemy attempt to bypass or attack the flanks and rear of the bunker can be repelled. The protective position is to be at least a hand grenade throw from the bunker and protected with it by barbed wire entanglements.

4. The bunker defense will include a specific team to defend the bunker as a strong point to the last bullet.

5. Those soldiers not required as members of the fighting bunker crew or the defensive system will conduct the defensive battle from field positions. These will be dug between the foremost fighting bunkers and in the depth of the main fighting area, and linked to each other by trenches.

6. Fighting bunkers and bunkers without fighting positions can be used by occupants of the defensive and field positions for shelter from enemy artillery or air attacks. The observation of enemy measures and quick alerting must be assured. Here the artillery observers have an especially great responsibility.

7. Communication trenches are to be dug to enable the occupants of the field positions to take cover in the bunkers when under enemy fire.

8. In combat casualties are to be replaced regularly in order to maintain the defensive strength. Withdrawal is out of the question.

9. Regimental and battalion command posts will use existing positions and telephone connections laid out thickly enough on the front to be able to have an immediate influence on the fighting troops.[12]

All of this, the German forces found, was easier said than done. Above all, men and equipment were lacking, and the increasing Allied domination of the air hindered the regular supply of vital items for rearming the bunkers and completing obstacles. Nevertheless, a massive construction program was implemented, with the introduction of positions of a more modern pattern, including the concrete-lined Tobruk foxhole and the use of tank turrets, while Hitler ordered the German forces in the west to "deny every inch of ground with the enemy by stubborn delaying action."

But problems remained in that the basic regimental structure had been changed to one of only two battalions. Some of the weapons, such as the MG 42, no longer fitted the prewar mountings, and many of the new artillery and antitank pieces were too large for the bunkers. Despite these problems, the Westwall was still highly effective, as was demonstrated all too well with the horrific casualties inflicted upon the Americans in the Hürt-gen Forest during September 1944.[13]

The Orscholz Switch had been attacked first on November 21, 1944, by Combat Command A of Gen. William H. H. Morris Jr.'s 10th Armored Division while General Patton's costly battle for the city of Metz was still in progress.[14] Virtually nothing was known of the Switch at the time, and the division's armored infantry had to locate the individual pillboxes by exposing themselves to the inevitable crossfire coming from them while at the same time being heavily bombarded by the German artillery. Dragon's teeth hampered support from the tanks in some places, and one task force could not even cross its line of departure for the attack. After two days, only a single breach had been achieved in the enemy lines at considerable cost in men and armor.

Nevertheless, this attack was seen as a potential threat to the city of Trier and caused some alarm at Field Marshal Gerd von Rundstedt's headquarters. Reinforcements in the form of the 404th Volks Artillery Corps, 21st Panzer Division, and 719th Infantry Division were consequently ordered to the immediate support of the 416th Infantry Division, which was responsible for the defense of the Orscholz Switch.[15]

General Walker had then attached the 358th Infantry Regiment of the 90th Infantry Division to General Morris's command and ordered single battalion attacks on Tettingen and Borg. Consequently, on the morning of November 23, in dense fog, which prevented air support but served to screen the attacking forces, the 3rd/358th launched an attack on Campholz Woods that achieved complete surprise. When the troops came up against an antitank ditch, General Morris had a bulldozer brought up to bridge it, and it was not until the men entered the woods that they encountered enemy fire. Coordination proved difficult in the fog and dense woods, but the leading I and K Companies took eighty-four prisoners that day. Next morning the Germans counterattacked with about forty troops, only to lose eighteen as prisoners. K and I Companies were then directed upon Butz-dorf and Tettingen respectively. I Company made a successful pell-mell dash to get through the enemy machine-gun and artillery fire to get into Butzdorf, but K Company came up against a number of pillboxes that delayed their penetration of Tettingen until nightfall.

Meanwhile, as the 2nd Battalion headed uphill in its approach to Borg, it had encountered deep mud, bogging down its supporting armor, and consequently made little progress on November 23. Then it took most of the next day to reduce a large bunker, only to have the battalion checked yet again when it came under heavy artillery fire from the direction of Oberleuken. The 1st Battalion was then committed in support and fought its way into the village, where fighting continued throughout the night.

Back in Tettingen, where K Company came under heavy counterattack and was closely surrounded in three houses by enemy infantry and tanks using machine guns and flamethrowers, the fighting continued all night long, during which the company commander was killed and one of the houses lost. At dawn I Company directed artillery fire on the houses in Tettingen that were not occupied by K Company, and charged down from Butzdorf to join the K Company survivors in Tettingen under cover of smoke. L Company was then ordered in to reinforce Tettingen and retake Butzdorf.

This second attack on Butzdorf by one platoon of L Company was massively supported by fighter-bombers of the XIXth Tactical Air Force and artillery from both the 90th Infantry and 10th Armored Divisions, plus two tanks from the latter's Combat Command A. The platoon took 21 German prisoners and recovered 4 men of K Company previously taken by them. Meanwhile, the 35 survivors of I and K Companies joined in clearing Tettingen, and the commander had the remains of his battalion deploy to cover the two villages until it could be relieved by armored infantry at dawn the next day, the twenty-sixth. This action had cost the 3rd/358th 7 officers and 148 enlisted men, and earned three Distinguished Service Crosses.

German counterattacks against the armored infantry of Combat Command A forced a gradual withdrawal, and by December 18, when the 10th Armored and 90th Infantry Divisions were diverted to deal with the German offensive in the Ardennes, the American front line had reverted to where it had been a month earlier. However, the bunkers that covered the dragon's teeth on the approach to Tettingen were destroyed before the American soldiers left.[16]

While the Battle of the Bulge raged, the 3rd Cavalry Group had the task of holding the line facing the Orscholz Switch with its 3rd and 43rd Reconnaissance Squadrons until the 94th Infantry Division took over on the left of the corps' line.[17]

2
The Division Goes
into Action

The 94th Infantry Division settled into its new role by sending out probing patrols to learn something of the terrain in which it was to operate. It had yet to receive any winter warfare clothing to counter the bitter cold, and the men had to improvise snowsuits from sheets and tablecloths taken from German homes.[1]

Robert Adair of the 2nd Platoon, I Company, 376th Infantry Regiment, described how he survived the conditions:

> Like the rest of the company, we lost men to the savage conditions. During this time, the temperature ranged from as low as zero one night to as much as 40 degrees during the day. At times we faced rain and wet snow in our face from the north. With the constant shellfire, we were forced to stay in the trenches where the low spots were always filled with water, iced over sometimes during the day and always at night.
>
> However, I made out rather well. I gathered pine boughs and filled the bottom of my six feet or so of trench with the boughs and stood and slept insulated a bit from the ice and frozen earth. By then I had begun the procedures I practiced until the end of my infantry career. I carried extra socks stuffed under my shirt[,] and regularly, I took off my shoes, took off the three—later more—pairs of socks, and replaced the innermost layer with a warm dry set from my chest store. When possible, I tried to dry my shoes over tiny fires of paraffin tablets given us to heat our C-rations. Since we had to be prepared for

an attack at any time, we couldn't remove our shoes to sleep. I also was dressed warmly, and differently than many, as I wore five sets of winter underwear tops—later seven!—almost like light sweat shirts, below my wool OD [olive drab] shirt, a heavy sweater, and my quilted field jacket, and I kept a warm knitted cap on my head. I used my overcoat only as a mattress, the warmth-to-weight ratio for the overcoat was inadequate. So I was only mildly miserable when others suffered severely—particularly with trench foot.[2]

Col. Earle A. Johnson's 302nd Infantry Regiment, as corps reserve, reconnoitered the whole of the corps sector against the possibility of a German attack, and even prepared five lines of defense in the rear of the 94th Division's sector to meet such an eventuality. Minefields were laid across possible tank approach routes, bridges were prepared for demolition, and trees were dropped across roads to act as barriers.[3]

Manning the Germans' Orscholz Switch defenses opposite the 94th was Lt. Gen. Kurt Pflieger's 416th Infantry Division, with its headquarters in Mettlach-Keuchingen, the suburb on the west bank of the Saar. The division consisted of Lieutenant Colonel Hoelscher's Grenadier Regiment 712, Colonel Hachenberger's Grenadier Regiment 713, Major Kraft's Field Training and Replacement Battalion 416, Fusilier Company 416, and Major Albrecht's Artillery Regiment 416, which had been brought up to 60 percent effective strength at the beginning of January by the transfer of Luftwaffe personnel into its ranks. Only its engineer, assault gun, and antiaircraft units were at full strength. However, as a result of having been employed on garrison duty in Denmark for most of the war, the divisional components were rated by their superior LXXXII Corps as only "conditionally fit for combat." The average age for the men was between thirty-two and thirty-four, and many of them were convalescents or subject to stomach complaints.

Upon arrival in the Triangle at the beginning of October 1944, the 416th Infantry Division was reinforced by Major Knadt's Grenadier Regiment 714, consisting of a Luftwaffe parachute battalion, Major Friedrich's Fortress Infantry Battalion "Merzig," and Fortress Artillery Battalions 1024 and 1025, bringing the division's total strength to nine thousand men.

In taking over this sector of the Westwall, the 416th Infantry Division had to man a predetermined system of defense that failed to match either its structure or some of its weaponry. The east bank of the Orscholz Switch was securely based on the sheer cliffs of the Saar River at the Saarschleuse bend. However, the west flank, on the Moselle River opposite Luxembourg, was already outflanked by American troops, albeit few in number.[4]

Dragon's teeth in open terrain and an antitank ditch in the wooded areas, being extensively supported by minefields, generally delineated the forward line of defense. In the center, the Münzingen Ridge provided a dominating overview of the Switch. Other antitank ditches that were set at right angles to the main line of defense appeared to be intended to split the more obvious lines of approach, compartmentalizing the battlefield, while the main road between Remich in Luxembourg and Mettlach on the Saar provided the necessary lateral maneuverability for the defense. A cluster of shelter bunkers in the Unter den Eichen Woods between Oberleuken and Orscholz appear to have been intended to accommodate a reserve force.

TETTINGEN-BUTZDORF

General Malony decided to employ Lt. Col. Russell M. Miner's 1st Battalion, 376th Infantry, for the first attack, which would take place at 0730 on January 14. For assistance, Miner was allocated a platoon each from B Company, 607th Tank Destroyer Battalion, and C Company, 81st Chemical Warfare Mortar Battalion, which fired a 4.2-inch round, heavier than the standard infantry mortar, and he could also call on support from the regiment's heavy weapons.

Prior reconnaissance revealed the presence of extensive minefields, both German and American, and antitank obstacles in the form of either ditches or dragon's teeth backed by pillboxes, bunkers, and entrenchments in depth. There was more than a foot of snow covering the ground, completely concealing all trace of the antipersonnel mines, the most common of which, the Schü-mine, had a wooden casing that was impervious to metal mine detectors.

The plan was for Capt. Carl J. Shetler's A Company and Capt. Edwin F. Duckworth's C Company to lead the attack, passing through the lines of B Company, which would then follow up as battalion reserve. The 3rd Battalion would then take over the 1st Battalion's defensive positions.[5]

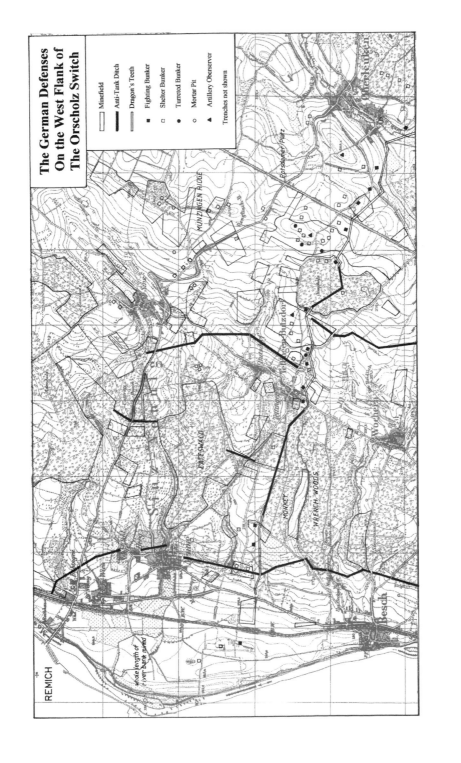

The German Defenses
On the West Flank of
The Orscholz Switch

	▢	Minefield
	▬	Anti-Tank Ditch
	▭	Dragon's Teeth
■		Fighting Bunker
▫		Shelter Bunker
●		Turreted Bunker
○		Mortar Pit
▲		Artillery Oberserver
		Trenches not shown

The 919th Field Artillery Battalion commenced laying a twenty-minute bombardment at 0700 before the infantry advanced with A Company on the right and C Company on the left. At the same time, Lt. Claude W. Baker's heavy machine-gun platoon sprayed Campholz Woods and the pillboxes in the high ground east of the village from the forward edge of Der Heidlich Hill. The antitank dragon's teeth were crossed quickly, with Company A losing some casualties to mortar fire. The troops entered Tettingen and deployed according to plan. The companies spread out, hand-grenading the individual buildings before clearing them out, and capturing twenty-three prisoners in the process. By 0815 hours the village was secure, and Company A then sent a squad out on the east flank to reconnoiter the hillside. These men found several skillfully camouflaged pillboxes and bunkers, one of which was detected only when they heard voices coming from beneath them, but they had neither the equipment nor the numbers to tackle them.

From the observation post on Der Heidlich Hill, east of Wochern, Brig. Gen. Henry B. Cheadle, the assistant division commander, accompanied by the divisional G-2 (staff officer for intelligence), Lt. Col. Robert L. Love; the divisional G-3 (staff officer for operations), Lt. Col. Rollin B. Durbin; and the divisional engineer, Lt. Col. Noel H. Ellis, together with Col. Harold C. McClune of the 376th, had watched the successful attack and decided on the spur of the moment that it should be pursued by taking Butzdorf.

Lieutenant Colonel Miner was informed at 0840, and Captain Shetler's A Company was detailed for the task. His artillery liaison officer, Capt. Larry A. Blakely, then arranged for a ten-minute barrage by the 919th Field Artillery Battalion at 0950 to precede the infantry attack at 1000, and Miner moved his battalion command post forward into a house opposite the church in Tettingen, where he was followed by Lieutenant Baker and his machine-gun platoon.[6]

Meanwhile, supported by a battery of 81-mm mortars near Sinz, a battery of 88-mm dual-purpose antiaircraft/antitank guns, and reinforced by men from a fortress battalion, Major Becker commanding the Germans' five-hundred-strong 1st Battalion, Grenadier Regiment 713, was already planning the obligatory counterattack in accordance with standard German battlefield practice. Mortar and artillery fire was pouring in on Tettingen, and American casualties were mounting.[7]

Battle of Tettingen-Butzdorf - 15 Jan 45

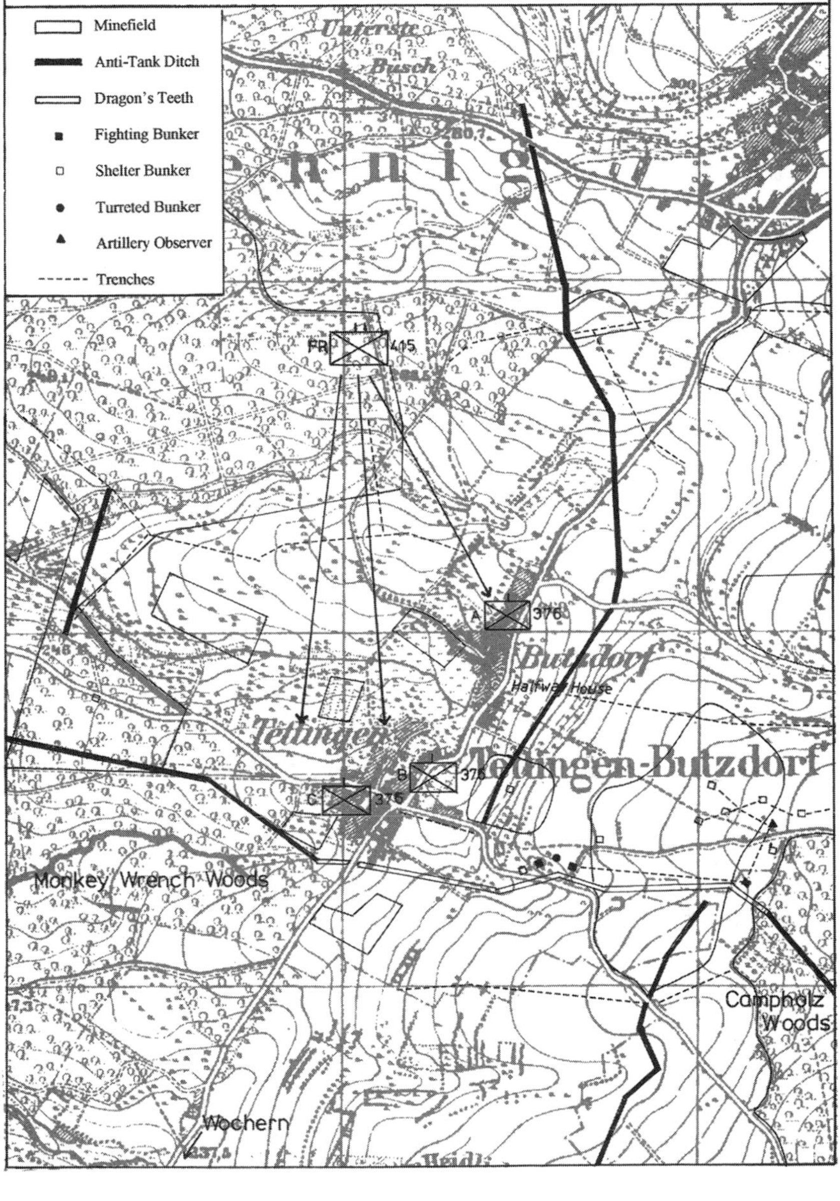

Minefield
Anti-Tank Ditch
Dragon's Teeth
Fighting Bunker
Shelter Bunker
Turreted Bunker
Artillery Observer
Trenches
FR
415
A
376
Butzdorf
Halfway House
Tettingen
B
376
C
376
Tettingen-Butzdorf
Monkey Wrench Woods
Campholz Woods
Wochern

Captain Shetler recalled his reconnaissance patrol and prepared his platoon commanders for the forthcoming attack. Lt. Tom Hodges's platoon would lead and seize the prominent house halfway between the two villages on the right-hand side of the road, thereafter known as Halfway House, while Lt. Richard L. Creighton's platoon would advance on the left. Lt. George L. Dumville's platoon would provide support from the northern edge of Tettingen. As Lieutenant Baker's machine-gun platoon from D Company was unable to find suitable covering positions for the advance, it was ordered to follow Hodges's platoon into Butzdorf.

The reconnaissance patrol reported that the pillboxes east of the villages could bring in enfilade fire on any advance and would need to be reduced if the attack were to succeed. Enemy fire on Tettingen was now so fierce that Captain Shetler requested a postponement of the attack. Lieutenant Colonel Miner denied his request, and with only five minutes to go, Shetler detailed Lieutenant Creighton as to his platoon's role in the attack.

Meanwhile, Lt. Ben R. Chalkley's support platoon from C Company moved forward to take over the defense of the northeast sector of Tettingen, and Sergeants Kornistan and Douglas, along with six riflemen and four engineers carrying explosives, set off to deal with the nearby pillboxes.

It was 1007 before Lieutenant Hodges could get his men moving. Enemy artillery and mortar fire was still falling heavily on the area, but the small-arms fire coming from Butzdorf had been all but silenced by the American bombardment. Hodges's platoon had already gone about two hundred yards before Lieutenant Creighton's platoon set off. Captain Shetler and his radio operator and messengers then followed behind Hodges's platoon and had reached just beyond Halfway House when an artillery strike descended on the advancing troops. Captain Shetler and fifteen others were hit by enemy artillery fire, but Creighton's platoon charged forward into the comparative shelter of the village, followed by the survivors of Hodges's platoon.[8]

1st Lt. David F. Stafford, the company executive officer, immediately came forward and took over the command. The company's radio operator had been killed and his set smashed, and communication with the battalion could now be conducted only by runner. The forward artillery observation officer, Lt. William C. Woodward, had remained in his observation post in Tettingen, so Stafford had no means of calling for direct artillery support. Meanwhile, medical aid men moved the wounded into Halfway House, and by 1113 the 1st and 2nd Platoons had cleared Butzdorf of the enemy and taken a few prisoners.

Lieutenant Dumville's platoon was then ordered to occupy Halfway House and a row of buildings on the southern edge of Butzdorf, while Lieutenant Baker sited his machine guns to cover likely avenues of attack. However, the position remained vulnerable, for this reinforced company now found itself isolated one thousand meters into the enemy defenses.

At approximately 1300 a group of about fifty German soldiers were seen leaving Campholz Woods in column of twos. At first they were taken to be prisoners of C Company, but when it was discovered that they were instead free German soldiers, this counterattack was driven back by artillery fire and ten of the enemy were killed. Another counterattack from Campholz Woods occurred shortly afterward, this time in V formation and led by an officer in a light-colored coat, but this too was driven back.

At 1335 hours Lieutenant Colonel Miner called forward B Company from where it had been waiting in Wochern. As the company marched up to Tettingen, it came under sporadic artillery and mortar fire. The bulk of the company then took up positions in Tettingen, while the 1st Platoon went on to reinforce the troops in Butzdorf.[9]

Apart from enemy artillery and mortar fire, the afternoon passed uneventfully, but serious trouble was in store. Gen. Wend von Wietersheim's 11th Panzer Division had been on the move from Trier to the Rhine when the attack on Butzdorf occurred and was identified as a direct threat to Trier. The division was promptly diverted to the Saar-Moselle Triangle with orders to restore the original line of defense at any price. It had just been refitted in the Bitburg area, and its Panzer Regiment 15 now had nearly one hundred tanks, the 1st Battalion having four companies of Panthers and the 2nd Battalion four companies of Mark IVs, but the division was so desperately short of fuel that it had to leave fifty Panthers behind. Panzergrenadier Regiment 110, which had suffered heavy casualties in the battle for Metz, had been brought back up to strength, as had Panzergrenadier Regiment 111.

The other units in the division were Panzer Reconnaissance Battalion 11, Panzer Artillery Regiment 119 (three battalions), Army Flak Battalion 277 (three batteries), Panzer Signals Battalion 89, Panzer Engineer Battalion 209, Tank Hunting Battalion 61, and Panzer Field Training and Replacement Battalion 61 (six companies).[10]

The 11th Panzer Division's historian commented:

Divisional Headquarters did all it could to prevent being engaged here against all arguments. It was unfortunately unsuccessful and was placed under LXXXII Corps, which had no understanding about the use of armored troops, and whose inflexibility led to an especially unpleasant combat situation with little success. The division, which was unusually well refreshed for this period, could have achieved a great deal under the right conditions, but this tried and tested formation was to lose many men, especially in the panzergrenadier regiments.

The terrain in the Saar-Moselle-Orscholz Switch Triangle was strongly cut up, and in any weather the roads and tracks, bridges and ditches became badly affected, so that even good reconnaissance was soon outdated. The Orscholz Switch was only of value as long as its right flank rested against a neutral Luxembourg, but now the Americans were occupying the heights on the west bank of the Moselle and outflanked any attack to the southwest with good observation opportunities.

The shattered 416th Division, which was supporting us, was of no real value in the attack that had been ordered. There was only one bridge across the Saar for supplies, upon which and from which everything depended, and should it be destroyed by the overwhelming enemy air force, the fate of the whole division would be linked to this single, narrow escape route.[11]

The 416th Infantry Division responded to the situation by bringing forward Grenadier Regiment 714, which had been manning the main Westwall defenses on the far side of the Saar, to assist Grenadier Regiments 712 and 713 in the defense of the Triangle. In addition, Major Kraft's Field Replacement and Training Battalion 416 was dispatched to assist Major Becker's 1st Battalion at Tettingen.

During the night the wounded were evacuated from Halfway House and supplies brought forward to Butzdorf, while patrols checked the surrounding area. The German mortar teams that had been operating east of Butzdorf appeared to have withdrawn, but considerable activity was reported in the woods to the northwest of the village.

The German artillery preparation (artillery fired before an attack to interrupt communications and muddle the enemy's defense) began at 0440 on January 15 and was followed by a company of Major Kraft's battalion charging downhill into the villages from the woods, where its presence had been detected earlier on. Butzdorf was surrounded and penetrations were made into Tettingen despite all the artillery, mortar, machine-gun, and small-arms fire the Americans could raise. After two hours of this firefight, the machine-gun ammunition was running so low that Cpl. Donald W. Krieger, the transportation NCO (noncommissioned officer) of D Company, volunteered to run back to Wochern to collect some more. He returned safely with sixty-four thousand rounds loaded on his vehicle, being the first soldier to make the journey between the two villages on a road presumably now clear of mines.

The firing eased off with daybreak, by which time the supporting mortars in Wochern had fired off four thousand rounds, and by 0755 all firing had ceased. The snow around the villages was dotted with the bodies of dead and wounded. Medical aid man Pvt. Milton A. Welsch went forward to investigate and found some thirty to thirty-five German soldiers still alive but bleeding and freezing to death. These men were hastily evacuated for treatment. Patrols then rounded up another sixty prisoners from the surrounding area. It was estimated that the German battalion had lost three-quarters of its strength in the attack.[12]

C Company veterans then-Privates First Class Robert Trefzger of the 3rd Platoon and Herman Thornton of the 4th Platoon later put together the following account of their part in this action at the western end of Tettingen. Bob Trefzger starts off:

> The attack on Tettingen on January 14, 1945, by the 1st Battalion of the 376th Infantry Regiment found the town to be virtually undefended. There were very few casualties.
>
> The west end of Tettingen consisted of a single road along a very broad-crested, east-west trending ridge. There were houses on both sides of the road[,] and the 3d Squad was assigned to occupy and defend the last house at the west end of town, a short distance from the northeast corner of the woods (Monkey Wrench Woods). Like most of the houses in Tettingen, it was a two-storey, stone masonry farmhouse with space for farm equipment and stable/barn areas for farm animals on the ground floor. Everything had been removed, in-

cluding the windows and the wooden window frames. Only the rectangular window openings in the masonry walls remained.

Inside the house we all felt pretty secure, as it was like a two-storey fort, and it would have taken a direct hit for artillery to hurt us. We had a great view of the snowy fields to the south, to the dragon's teeth and the woods beyond. Across the road to the northeast we could see the southeast corner of a large apple orchard, which extended at least a few hundred feet to the north and west. Beyond the orchard, to the north and northwest, we could see open, snow-covered fields, and beyond the fields was a large clump of woods, about 1,000 yards to the north-northwest.

A light machine-gun squad from the 4th Platoon then took up position on the eastern edge of the northern part of the apple orchard, about sixty feet west of one of the houses fronting a north-trending side road. Herman Thornton, who was in the 4th Platoon's light machine-gun section, takes up the tale:

Sergeant Wiser got us started digging in as quickly as possible, but we soon realized that it wouldn't be an easy job. The ground was frozen solid. As soon as we could chip through a little of the surface of the ground, we started to employ our blocks of TNT, extras of which had been brought forward in anticipation of the problem. Every few minutes someone would give the shout: "Fire in the hole!" that was required before setting off a charge. The deeper we got[,] the more effective each half-pound block was. We didn't need anyone to prod us on, as just after we started digging, mortar fire and 88-mm artillery started raining down on the town. The 88s came in rapidly and could be heard coming, but the mortar shells gave no warning until, just before impacting, a slight whishing sound could be heard. Most shells were directed into the town, but a few hit among our positions. One or two guys received wounds, but in most respects, we got through the day pretty well. We were in the back yard of a farmhouse protected from view by the apple orchard to the west and a row of trees to the north. The east side was protected from view by the closeness of the houses. By late afternoon we had our positions dug and prepared, as we were told to expect a counterattack that night.

The night was cold out in our positions, but the weather remained partially cloudy with no new snow anticipated. We were able to change off once in a while and go back for a little warmth into the cellar of a house about 60 feet back from our foxhole. About 4 a.m. we were driven to alertness by a massive artillery and mortar attack on our positions and the town. The expected counterattack had begun.

Bob Trefzger, who was sound asleep in the farm equipment storage area on the ground floor of the house, continues:

Suddenly there was a burst of very nearby gunfire, presumably from the 3d Squad GIs guarding the front (north side) of the house. Instantly wide awake, I grabbed my M-1 rifle and hurried up the nearby stairs leading to the second storey rooms. A lot of shooting could be heard some distance away. As I entered the northwest room, I could see bright pink (friendly) tracer bullets from a machine gun going from right to left across the orchard. It was soon obvious that the tracers were coming from the east edge of the orchard at the location where I had seen some GIs digging in the previous morning. The tracers were going several hundred feet across the orchard in a north-westerly direction, apparently without hitting anything—"grazing fire" I thought.

Herman Thornton continues: "Firing began from positions to our left, and in a few moments we saw shadowy movements in the orchard to our front. Directly to the north the ground dropped off quite steeply, providing pretty good protection from that direction, but the orchard tapered off gradually to lower ground."

Bob Trefzger resumes the account:

On reaching the window opening, I looked out and to my amazement could clearly see an enemy soldat [soldier] lying in the snow about 30 feet from our 3d Squad house. There was a bipod-mounted MG-42 in front of him, pointed at the house. As he was not firing or moving, it seemed probable that he had been shot by our 3d Squad guards—probably the nearby firing that had awakened me.

The enemy attack plan at western Tettingen appear[s] to have been to very quietly approach the town from the north across the snow-covered orchard in order to surprise the defenders. Unfortunately for the soldaten, the machine gunner, pushing his MG-42 ahead of him, had crawled in the snow hundreds of feet ahead of the other attackers to within 30 feet of the Third Squad house. The initial burst of small arms fire apparently caused the remaining soldaten to get up on their feet and attempt to charge toward the houses at the top of the apple orchard slope. They were immediately fired on by the heavy machine gun (D376) near the southeast corner of the orchard and the light machine gun further to the northeast (Herman Thornton's location).

Herman Thornton goes on with the story: "Within a few moments all hell had broken loose from our line. The machine gun with all of the ammunition we had brought forward was in front and to the left of my foxhole; therefore, all I had to do was to make use of my carbine. I fired at shadowy figures that appeared from behind a log of an old apple tree that was about 15 yards away."

Bob Trefzger once again picks up the account:

Soon artillery and mortar shells began exploding in the central part of the orchard. The smaller shell-bursts, the mortar shells, traversed back and forth, methodically decimating the enemy soldaten. As the friendly machine-gun fire was often nearly continuous and of long duration, I concluded that it must be a water-cooled, heavy machine gun from Company D.

The machine-gun fire and shelling by the mortars and artillery continued off and on until it started to become light. It seemed like a very long time.

When it had become quite light and visibility was good, our squad was ordered to abandon our house and go to the 3d Platoon command post in the next house to the east. We did not ask why, we just followed orders and ran to the command post. We were ordered to leave the house because someone (we never learned who) thought they saw enemy soldaten approaching from the woods west of the house. As there were no west-facing windows, the defenders (us) could not see them coming.

After a while we were ordered to retake the abandoned house. The few enemy soldaten in the house did not fight, but willingly surrendered; lucky for us! I especially remember the first live soldat I ever saw. He was quite short, wearing a paratrooper's jumpsuit and a white paratroopers helmet. He and the others looked pretty scared, since they were not sure that we would not shoot them in cold blood.

When we looked out from the second floor of the recaptured house, we could see that some of the wounded or half-frozen soldaten in the orchard indicated that they wanted to surrender. Our medics cautiously went into the orchard and tended to them. The walking wounded were helped out of the orchard; the more seriously wounded were carried out on litters.

Herman Thornton concludes the account:

When we looked out in front of us as daylight came to the area, we saw a terrible sight. Bodies were strewn all over the place. When it was quite evident that it was safe to leave our holes, we walked out into the orchard. Medics were on the scene administering to the wounded and taking them to the rear. That was probably the reason the enemy threw no artillery at us while in the orchard. There were very few who were just wounded. Most of the attackers had died with the possibility of a few escaping back to their own lines.

By the time I got out there, the bodies had already frozen in that miserably cold weather and had taken on the appearance of wax dummies. Those who checked the bodies discovered that most them had schnapps instead of water in their canteens.[13]

The day continued with the usual enemy artillery and mortar fire ensuring that the men of the 1st Battalion kept under cover, although it was found possible to distribute ten-meals-in-one ration packs for the first time since they had crossed the English Channel. The isolated detachment in Butzdorf improved its position by blowing mouse holes (passages) between adjoining buildings, but found that the only water available was from melting snow.[14]

NENNIG, BERG, WIES

Meanwhile, the previous afternoon, January 14, Lt. Col. Benjamin E. Thurston's 3rd/376th had received orders to prepare to take the village of Nennig and the hamlets of Berg and Wies that lay in a corner of lower ground of the Moselle valley and to secure the western end of the Orscholz Switch.

Thurston was able to make a brief reconnaissance late that afternoon from an observation post in the riverside village of Besch, where a lieutenant of the 3rd Cavalry Group, which was responsible for the surveillance of this area, informed him that the German soldiers across the way numbered about four hundred and showed no inclination to patrol aggressively but responded quickly with artillery and mortars to any sign of movement. The double-track railroad and highway running toward Thurston's objectives were known to be mined and covered by enemy fire from five pillboxes located some seven hundred yards south of Nennig at a point where a previous American attack had been checked.

The original proposal was to attack from the east, but Thurston decided there were too many unknown factors on that flank and decided instead to attack from the west. An alternative approach route was chosen across the open expanse to the railroad tracks opposite Nennig that would form the line of departure, the whole route being covered by smoke to avoid the troops being exposed against the snow-covered ground. This route started northwest to intersect the Moselle River opposite Nennig, then doubled back south and east to meet the railroad tracks across from the village. To clear and mark this almost two-mile approach to his objectives, which would have to be traversed in single file, Thurston sent forward Lt. Charles R. Palmer of the 319th Engineer Combat Battalion with a mine-clearing team at 0300 on January 15. Another engineer team laid antitank mines across the Besch-Nennig road to prevent any armored counterattack on this route.

The battalion assembled in Besch during the night along with a platoon of the 774th Tank Destroyer Battalion and Company A, 81st Chemical Warfare Mortar Battalion, that were under command for the operation. Lt. Inman E. Mallard and Staff Sergeant (SSgt.) Gladwin J. Flory, the battalion intelligence sergeant, crossed the Moselle on a ferry operated by the divisional engineers below Besch and set up an observation post in Remich for Sergeant Flory to man. The high ground there gave good observation

THE NENNIG-BERG-WIES BATTLEGROUND

☐	Minefield
▬▬	Anti-Tank Ditch
▭	Dragon's Teeth
⊠	Strongpoint
■	Fighting Bunker
☐	Shelter Bunker
– – –	Communication Trenches

of the ground from Schloss Thorn, the castle on the German west flank, across to Sinz and down to Tettingen, with all movement in Nennig being clearly visible. This post proved invaluable for collecting intelligence and directing artillery fire over the next few days.

The task of clearing and marking the battalion route had taken longer than expected, delaying the launching of the attack by thirty minutes. The news came through too late to withhold the accompanying artillery preparation, which the artillery was unable to extend due to a shortage of ammunition. Fortunately, the chemical warfare mortar platoon offered to take up the preparation when the artillery ceased, and there was no shortage of shells for their 4.2-inch mortars, which had an even heavier impact than the shellfire.

Capt. Julian M. Way's K Company, with a platoon of heavy machine guns and a mortar section from M Company, led the way at 0745 with the task of taking Nennig. They were followed by Capt. William A. Brightman's L Company, with the other heavy machine-gun platoon, which was to bypass Nennig and go on to take Wies, while I Company remained in Besch as battalion reserve. The approach march between the engineers' tape was hampered by subzero temperatures, ice, and a snowstorm and was made even more unpleasant by the men's having to wade through several streams, the circumstances eventually leading to several cases of frostbite and trench foot.

The smoke covering the advance was so dense that some of the troops became confused. Some of K Company, including Lt. Dwight M. Morse's 2nd Platoon and a section of mortars from M Company, missed Nennig altogether and went on to Wies, while Captain Way eventually found himself approaching his objective from the north instead of the west as he had intended. Nevertheless, the Germans were taken completely by surprise, and K Company was able to take the village in barely twenty minutes for only three casualties, including the fatally injured Lt. James H. McCoy of the 3rd Platoon, who had been the first to cross the line of departure. The enemy survivors fled toward Sinz, leaving twenty-three prisoners and ninety-five casualties behind. It appeared that the Germans were confused by the smoke and thought the attack was coming from across the Moselle, because at 0900 they launched a massive and futile barrage on both banks of the river opposite Berg.[15]

The troops approaching Wies were not so lucky. Machine guns concealed in the hamlet pinned the men down before they could get anywhere near. Some members of the 2nd Platoon attempted an outflanking maneuver, but when they were caught out on an open hillside in a clear killing ground from machine guns located in a line of buildings on the Remich-Sinz road that included Schloss Bübingen, they started taking heavy casualties. An attempt by the mortar team to cover the men with smoke failed because of an adverse wind, and mortaring proved to have no effect on the volume of fire being directed at them.

Captain Brightman then arrived to assess the situation before deploying his company. He sent Lt. William M. Goldensweig's platoon to relieve the trapped troops, but the platoon was driven back by the Germans, who had no intention of letting their prey get away. Eventually a German officer, accompanied by a medical aid man, appeared under a Red Cross flag and offered to let the wounded be returned to the American lines if the others would surrender. The men on the ground agreed to the plan, and American medical aid men were then able to retrieve the wounded, while the others were led off into captivity. Battalion was informed at 1530 that part of K Company's 2nd Platoon had been captured.[16]

Lt. Raymond G. Fox of I Company was sent forward with his platoon to reinforce K Company during the course of the morning. He was then instructed to take a patrol and establish contact with the 1st Battalion on the right. The patrol was joined by Lt. Thomas A. Daly, who wanted to reconnoiter the terrain over which his platoon on the eastern side of Nennig might be attacked. The patrol followed the course of a stream to the higher ground north of Lateswald Wood, where it encountered a group of about fifty Germans and exchanged fire. Daly crawled forward along a shallow ditch to tackle one of the two machine guns the Germans were using and managed to wipe out the crew with a grenade and his pistol before returning to the patrol with the captured machine gun. Contact with the enemy was then broken off and the incident reported to Captain Way, who ordered the patrol to return. (Lieutenant Daly was later awarded a Silver Star for his part in this action.)[17]

Meanwhile, a specific time and location for making contact with the 1st Battalion had been received, and that afternoon Technical Sergeant (TSgt.) Frank M. Fields led a patrol to the rendezvous, which was near a German pillbox about halfway between Nennig and Tettingen. However, the patrol came under fire from the pillbox and there was no sign of the 1st Battalion contact, so Fields brought his men back. The ten-man patrol sent by C Company to meet them had encountered enemy machine-gun fire twice on the way and had been obliged to make detours, but they got to within fifty yards of the designated pillbox when it came under intense mortar fire and finally withdrew, unaware that Sergeant Field's patrol was so close.

Lieutenant Fox made another attempt to break through to the pillbox, but his platoon became involved in a thirty-minute exchange of fire without making any headway before he was recalled to Nennig.[18]

Late in the afternoon a platoon from Company L secured the hamlet of Berg together with its fortified medieval castle (Schloss Berg) about six hundred yards north of Nennig. Wies was also eventually secured, despite the constant harassing machine-gun fire that had decimated the 2nd Platoon earlier in the day.[19]

The 3rd Battalion's objectives remained under constant artillery, mortar, and machine-gun fire, and in Nennig they continued house-to-house fighting, which K Company was not strong enough to control by itself. The wires for the field telephones, upon which the bulk of communication depended, were constantly being cut by shellfire.

The remainder of I Company, which had been held back in reserve at Besch, was ordered forward at 2130 and arrived soon after dusk, taking over the defense of the southern and western parts of the village.

Lieutenant Colonel Thurston then led into Nennig a forty-man team carrying supplies to sustain his unit. Later he reported the battalion's casualties for that day as eight dead and twelve seriously wounded, but he did not mention the Red Cross incident in his account of this action.

There was a curious event in Nennig that night when a group of Germans rushed in noisily to where SSgt. Fred Grossi was on guard duty with a machine gun. His gun jammed after firing only two shots, so he used his rifle, and some others joined in with their rifles. Next morning it was discovered that fourteen Germans had been killed in this confrontation, twelve of whom were officers. (Grossi was later awarded the Distinguished Service Cross for this action.)[20]

It was discovered that the German prisoners taken at Nennig that day were not from the 416th Infantry Division as expected, but from Maj. Gen. Gerhard Franz's 256th Volksgrenadier Division. This was a new formation that had been raised the previous summer to replace the former and now extinct 256th Infantry Division. The division consisted of the two-battalion

Grenadier Regiments 456, 457, and 458; the four-battalion Artillery Regiment 256; Fusilier Company 256; Engineer Battalion 256; Field Training and Replacement Battalion 256; and Tank Hunting Battalion 256, which in turn consisted of a motorized antiaircraft artillery battery, a motorized tank-hunting battery, and an assault gun battery.[21]

Early the next morning, January 16, the Germans launched an attack on Schloss Berg, where one of the heavy machine guns attached to 2nd Lt. Dale E. Bowyer's platoon was lost and a rifle squad was captured. However, this squad later escaped unharmed, and the Germans were beaten back, with sixty of their men dead.

A German attack on Nennig followed an hour later, after being preceded by a heavy mortar and artillery concentration, and came down the draw from Sinz, the same route that Lieutenant Daly had reconnoitered the previous day. Daly's men were prepared for the attack, opening fire only at the last minute, and Lieutenant King blocked the enemy escape route with a mortar concentration. Those Germans that survived then surrendered.

Another attack on Nennig came from the same direction shortly after daybreak, again preceded by a heavy mortar and artillery concentration, but the gunners were spotted by both Staff Sergeant Flory in his observation post across the river at Remich and SSgt. Leroy McPherson's heavy machine-gun section from its position on the high ground north of the village. The heavy machine guns succeeded in breaking up the attack and drove the survivors into the cover of Lateswald Wood. However, one enemy machine-gun team managed to break into the village and got to within fifty yards of the battalion command post, firing down the main street. Lieutenant Colonel Thurston killed the machine gunner with his M1 and also wounded a German soldier, who was armed with a Panzerfaust and was trying to get at one of the two tank destroyers that had moved up to join the defense during the night.[22]

MONKEY WRENCH WOODS

Orders were then received from Regiment on January 15 for Lt. Col. Olivius C. Martin's 2nd Battalion to clear the woods southwest of Tettingen, known to the troops as Monkey Wrench Woods because of their shape on the map, and thus connect the two narrow breaches in the Orscholz Switch that had already been established by the 1st and 3rd Battalions at Tettingen and Nennig. The 3rd Battalion was ordered to extend its right flank eastward to link up with the 2nd Battalion, so I Company left Nennig at 1330 and started occupying the German communication trenches extending in that direction with Lieutenant Fox's 3rd Platoon on the far flank digging into an orchard about halfway between the two villages. However, there were still some enemy-occupied pillboxes to the rear of I Company, which began taking casualties from shellfire that was clearly directed from these pillboxes. Meanwhile, the 2nd Battalion's attack, with F and G Companies leading, made good progress through the densely wooded, rough terrain, and by noon most of the area had been cleared of the enemy.[23]

Capt. George P. Whitman of F Company described in his memoirs how the previous day Lieutenant Colonel Martin had briefed him on an attack on the woods just northwest of Tettingen that Martin's company was to make at 0700 hours on January 16. By this time both men were aware that the 1st Battalion of the 376th Infantry Regiment had made the initial penetration of the German defensive line at Tettingen and Butzdorf and had been fighting for two days to hold their position. The woods northwest of and adjacent to Tettingen posed a danger to their left flank and had to be taken, which was F Company's mission. Whitman was also told that Lt. Thomas Fairchild of Company G would be making a preliminary reconnaissance of the area and would report to him upon his arrival in Wochern.

The company executive officer, Lt. Richard A. Hawley, had the task of guiding the company from Perl, but lost his way in the knee-high snow, and the company arrived dead tired late in the afternoon. Meanwhile, Captain Whitman had driven forward in his jeep to find Lieutenant Fairchild, who reported that there was an antitank ditch, ten feet wide by ten feet deep, in Monkey Wrench Woods.

Next morning at 0700 hours, F Company set off through the woods beyond Perl. The 1st Platoon, under Lt. Wilfred Wilson, came to the deep antitank ditch, which the Germans used in wooded areas instead of the cement dragon's teeth they used in open areas. Captain Whitman sent Lt. Stanley C. Mason and his 3rd Platoon to follow the ditch and cross it when they could. Lt. Gordon A. Weston's 2nd Platoon was sent after them in support.

The 1st Platoon crossed the ditch in single file with Captain Whitman following. On the other side they came to a minefield in which antipersonnel mines were attached to every tree with trip wires just one inch above the snow. The lead scout, Sgt. Michael Alba, called forward Captain Whitman and quietly pointed out the moving head of a German soldier reading a book. They had stumbled upon the German command post. Whitman then worked his way back to the rear, carefully stepping over the trip wires, to brief Lieutenant Wilson on his plan of attack.

The Germans were caught completely by surprise in one of the most successful engagements in the attempts to breach the Orscholz Switch. Many Germans were killed, sixty-two were taken prisoner, twelve machine-gun nests were reduced, and a three-story hospital bunker was captured. American casualties amounted to four men killed and a few wounded.

One of the Americans killed was eighteen-year-old medical aid William L. Cleary, who, despite his clearly marked helmet, was shot while attending to a wounded man. This so incensed Captain Whitman that he had Cleary's body left there for several hours so that every man in the company could appreciate what they were up against. Sgt. William D. Van Dusen, one of the squad leaders, saw Cleary lying dead, turned to find two Germans approaching to surrender with their hands above their heads, and killed them both. (Sergeant Van Dusen was himself to be killed three weeks later in Bannholz Woods.)[24]

Allen Howenstine of Michigan City, Indiana, also took part in this attack. His account mistakenly gives the date as January 14, when it was in fact January 16:

> At this time I was twenty years old, a mortar gunner in H Company, 2d Battalion, 376th Infantry Regiment, 94th Infantry Division. On the morning of 14 January 1945, the 2d Battalion of the 376th jumped off from Wochern in Germany into the Siegfried Switch, a very well fortified part of the Siegfried Line. My assignment was to order fire for our two 81-mm mortars, and I traveled with a rifle platoon of F Company.
>
> Late in the day of the 14th, the rifle company had pretty well cleared Monkey-Wrench Woods, so called because its shape resembled the well-known wrench with its jaws open. A squad of German soldiers

came out of a pillbox and our machine-gunner decimated them. Four were killed outright and five or six more were wounded, and I think a couple got away across the draw, which separated Monkey-Wrench Woods from a wood which the Germans still controlled.

We gathered the wounded and took them back to the pillbox, which we immediately took over as our headquarters; a place to get warm. The pillbox, as I recall, was about fifteen to twenty feet underground. It was equipped as a hospital bunker, with probably twenty to thirty bunks built into the walls. When the first guys got into the pillbox they discovered a German doctor there. He had medicine and instruments in his pack, and a Red Cross armband. He had evidently been getting ready to depart when we came in but immediately began to assist the wounded. One German was critically wounded, shot through the upper body and lungs, and died during the night.

We probably should have carried the wounded German back to our battalion aid station, about two miles to the rear, but by the time we were in a position to do so it was dark, we weren't absolutely sure the woods were cleared, and the area was heavily mined. No one was willing to run the risk of injury or death for a wounded enemy. Also, the Germans had not endeared themselves to us. Earlier in the afternoon Jamie, one of my friends, was taking two German prisoners to the rear when one kicked the trip wire of a booby trap or mine. Both Germans hit the ground, the mine went off and wounded the guard. Jamie was only superficially wounded and was able to shoot both the Germans as they attempted to escape.

The German doctor, who could speak fairly fluent English, did what he could to make his patients comfortable. The next morning the wounded prisoners were taken to the rear, and the German doctor put on his pack and indicated that he was going to rejoin his comrades in the wooded area across the draw from where the pillbox was located. He said that according to international law we had no right to hold him and that he was free to go. A few rifles pointed in his direction changed his mind, and he was taken to the rear.[25]

Contact was eventually established between the battalions during the afternoon when a member of G Company crawled into Lieutenant Fox's position in the orchard.[26]

TETTINGEN-BUTZDORF

The Germans made two small-scale attacks on Lieutenant Colonel Miner's 1st/376th during the evening of January 15. The first, against B Company, involved about fifty enemy soldiers and was repulsed without difficulty. The second, against C Company, was supported by four Mark IV tanks, two of which were damaged by bazookas and withdrew on fire, while the other pair withdrew when they lost their escorting infantry to American fire.

That night Lieutenant Chalkley sent out a patrol under Sergeant Soka to check out the area east of his position. The patrol found some bunkers and a pillbox covering Butzdorf, all of which were occupied, so Lt. James W. Cornelius took out a patrol with Sgt. Jesse R. Towers of the 319th Field Engineers to destroy them. They found the pillbox unoccupied and demolished it with explosives. Only one of the bunkers was now found to be occupied, and the door of that was blown off with a satchel charge, but the patrol then came under intense mortar fire and was obliged to withdraw.[27] Next morning a German medical aid man and another soldier appeared under a white flag, requesting permission to remove the wounded. This was granted, but the medical aid man's companion was detained. Shortly afterward a German halftrack came down the hill and removed seven wounded from the bunker.[28]

About noon on January 16, Capt. Harry C. Bowden's B Company left Tettingen and relieved F Company in the woods west of the village. The company now had a one-thousand-yard front with all the platoons deployed in line. Fifteen hundred yards off to the left were the five pillboxes still occupied by the enemy, while about five hundred yards to the northwest Lieutenant Fox's platoon of I Company was still holding the orchard.[29]

Elements of the 11th Panzer Division were now known to be in the vicinity, for aerial reconnaissance had picked up traces of the armor crossing at Saarburg and alerted the 94th Infantry. Poor weather prevented further reconnaissance, but now the tanks could be heard all along the 376th's front. More bazooka ammunition was brought forward and issued out, while Lieutenant Palmer and his engineers laid mines on the road leading into Butzdorf from Sinz and also laid a belt of them along the eastern edge of Tettingen. Pole and satchel charges, as well as daisy chains, were prepared to meet an armored attack.

Tanks were heard in Campholz Woods at about midnight, and at 0300 on January 18 a patrol from A Company returned with two prisoners who were readily identified as belonging to the 11th Panzer Division.[30] In fact, General Wietersheim's 11th Panzer Division had assumed command of the Orscholz Switch sector late on January 14, relieving the 416th Infantry Division but retaining the fortress machine-gun battalion. In addition, Lieutenant Reudiger's 2nd Battalion of Grenadier Regiment 714 had been brought forward across the Saar and occupied the ridge south of Sinz. General Wietersheim intended to clear Butzdorf and Tettingen with Panzergrenadier Regiment 110 and to clear Wies and Nennig with Panzergrenadier Regiment 111, both regiments having been recently brought back up to strength. They would be supported by the full weight of the divisional and corps artillery.[31]

Dawn of January 18 brought an extremely heavy bombardment on Butzdorf, Tettingen, and Wochern. At 0740 the din of the German artillery preparation subsided to be replaced by that of approaching tanks. The 1st Battalion of Panzergrenadier Regiment 110, led by its 10th Engineer Company mounted on halftracks, swarmed down the valley from Sinz. The attack was supported by four self-propelled 75-mm assault guns of Tank Hunting Battalion 61 and several tanks of the 7th Company, Panzer Regiment 15. The Germans advanced in a wide arc in the face of the American defensive barrage with their right flank on Butzdorf and their left on Tettingen.

It appears that the Germans must have bridged or filled in the antitank trench across the Sinz road to make this advance, for the accompanying map shows that their approach was seriously hampered by the static obstacles of minefields and this trench, which only had a gap on the track leading eastward out of Butzdorf up to the Münzingen Ridge.

An assault gun hit a mine just outside Butzdorf and stopped there. Two halftracks loaded with infantry tried to bypass it and were knocked out by bazookas as First Lieutenant Stafford's A Company went into action. Another assault gun pushed its muzzle into a building and was knocked out. The crew was then captured and bundled into a cellar. However, German infantry managed to occupy two buildings in the village.

Captain Duckworth's C Company in Tettingen was the next to go into action as two tanks, an assault gun, and four halftracks approached its position. One of the halftracks hit a mine, and although one of the tanks was disabled by a bazooka hitting its tracks, it was able to continue to use its

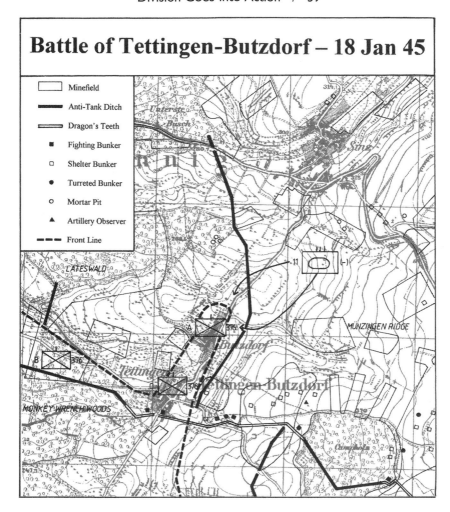

gun. The other tank took shelter behind the church, then blasted a hole through to fire on the buildings beyond. The approaching halftracks were fired on by bazookas, none of which exploded, and then stopped broadside opposite the American positions, from where Pvt. James C. Hobbs and Pvt. Charles F. Croan opened up their heavy machine guns with devastating effect as the German infantry dismounted.

Fire from the disabled tank forced Lieutenant Chalkley and his messenger to quit their command post and reestablish themselves in a barn across the street, only to come under fire from the second tank behind the church.

Lieutenant Peters and his platoon sergeant, Joseph J. Quentz, were wounded by an 88-mm gun and had to be evacuated. Sgt. Charles Foxgrover then had his antitank gun crew get their 57-mm gun firing on the tank behind the church at a range of three hundred yards, and they succeeded in knocking it out before it could turn its turret. However, a mortar shell then hit the crew as they were changing position, wounding most of the men and jamming the trails of the gun.

Meanwhile, German infantry had taken the Halfway House between the villages and also three or four buildings in Tettingen. German tanks had penetrated Butzdorf and were firing at point-blank range into the buildings still occupied by A Company, which was engaging them separately with satchel charges and bazookas while blasting away with small-arms fire. Pfc. Richard J. Kamins, a bazooka man of the 2nd Platoon, gives the following account of this action:

> I stood in the doorway and saw the first tank go by me. I fired at the second and yelled, "I got the sonuvabitch!" [Pfc.] Lindsay reloaded. The next tank came down the street toward me. I hit him in the track. He saw me. I turned and ran down the hall. A spray of machine-gun bullets chased me, ricocheting from where I'd been standing at the door. After that I fired from a window.
>
> A fourth came and a fifth. It was too dark to use my sights but I couldn't miss. They were only 50 yards away. I hit them in the tracks but still they kept coming. I hit one on the turret and the round bounced off like a tennis ball. I set one on fire and he withdrew in a sheet of flame.
>
> Pop Houston crouched in a doorway. Some concrete dust blasted from the walls got in his eyes. Nevertheless, old Pop fired every rifle grenade he had. He hit tank after tank and watched rounds glance off. His language was lovely to hear.
>
> The 1st Squad was across the street. Jack Zebin and Wylie of the 3d Platoon were attached to them as a bazooka team. Zebin had a tank graveyard in front of his position. He got credit for five. Dick Schweig and Whiz Wicentowski were to my left and "The Reverend" [SSgt. W. T.] Pillow and Howard Curler were down to my right. We had a nice box formation. One tank that I'd hit in the tread went down to be mousetrapped by Pillow. Pillow scared him back to me.

He was in reverse swinging his gun toward the 1st Squad's building. Simultaneously, Zebin and I shot him. My round tore a three-by-four hole in the rear armor. It was a long-range shot . . . all of five yards. The driver and gunner lay dead in the tank. A third was hanging out of the turret like a tablecloth. A fourth had started to run. Crossfire from three buildings hit him. With every burst his body would jump, making us think he was still alive. Other bursts followed. McIntyre came running up with a satchel charge and dropped it in the tank. The explosion was terrific. Later we examined the smoking hulk. There was no sign of any bodies.[32]

Soon after 0900 the attack petered out. The German infantry withdrew to reorganize but had considerable difficulty in doing so because of the harassing fire from several American artillery battalions. An attempt at a repeat attack by the 2nd Battalion, Panzergrenadier Regiment 110, at 1045 was stopped dead in its tracks by artillery fire, and the 7th Company, Panzer Regiment 15, was held in check by the 105- and 155-mm guns for the rest of the day. During the pause in the fighting, A Company recovered all the buildings it had lost in Butzdorf, and C Company retook Halfway House, taking sixteen prisoners.

The second major attack took place at 1130 when the 2nd Company of Panzer Regiment 15, which had about ten Panthers, swept down from Sinz. Four tanks took up positions behind the trees and haystacks opposite Butzdorf and began pounding the buildings with high-explosive and armor-piercing shells while the rest of the tanks assumed hull-down positions for the same purpose opposite Tettingen.

In Butzdorf, A Company kept one man in each building on watch above, while the remainder took shelter in the cellars. The American artillery brought down defensive fire, joined by Lieutenant Nielson's cannon company from Tettingen, which alone fired nineteen tons of shells that day. Lt. Col. George F. Miller tried to get his supporting tank destroyers into more effective firing positions, but sniper fire, the narrow streets, and low silhouettes of the targets seriously diminished their effectiveness.

The third and final major attack of the day came at 1430, when the 1st and 2nd Battalions of Panzergrenadier Regiment 110 and Field Replacement and Training Battalion 256, supported by the 2nd Company, Panzer Regiment 15, converged on Butzdorf. Led by infantry on foot backed by fifteen widely dispersed halftracks, the attack was met by a defensive barrage when the men were still two hundred yards from the village, but although many casualties were inflicted, it did not stop the advance. The infantry in the halftracks dismounted and joined in the assault until the murderous small-arms fire drove them to take cover behind their vehicles once more, the performance being repeated several times. Meanwhile, tanks drove into the village, firing into the various buildings at point-blank range, but they failed to quell the resistance. Private Kamins resumes his account:

> We were lucky. Zinny and Craig had blasted holes in the walls of every building in our block. We could withdraw without going into the open. One "Tiger" fired two rounds at us. The living room became unfit to live in, but no one was hurt. We ran across the street to the platoon CP [command post]. Joe DeLibero was the last man in. A piece of shrapnel tore his thigh. Two men dragged him inside.
>
> Two machine-gun squads set up in the barn. "The Reverend" Pillow was giving the boys hell. Never have I seen more inspiring leadership. He talked like a movie hero, only he meant it. Pillow's loader, Howard Curler, was pretty comical. His glasses were broken and he was using binoculars in their stead. He'd squint in myopic glory through the field glasses at tanks that were no more than 150 yards away. To everyone but Curler their 88s looked like telephone poles.
>
> Over in the 1st Platoon, Tom Wilson was pretty comical too. His squad leader pointed to a tank about 15 yards away with its gun leveled at their building and asked, "What do you think of that?" Laconically Wilson replied, "Dirty bore."
>
> Then came the order for us to withdraw as best as we could. Speaking as though he were talking about the weather, Joe DeLibero asked Smith, our acting platoon sergeant, if he was to be left behind. Smitty and Peck, the platoon runner, were the last men to leave the building. They had Joe with them. We all took off like birds.
>
> At the company CP a machine gun was set up in each door. We counted noses. In the 1st Squad only one man was uninjured. Klein was gone, Walters gone, Derickson gone, Burdzy gone. Kovac was hit in the thigh, but continued to laugh and hobble around. Fite got a nasty piece of shrapnel through his hand. Joe DeLibero lay looking up at the ceiling. Some guys stepped on him; he didn't say anything.[33]

While these actions were going on, three men of D Company volunteered to take supplies to Butzdorf in a jeep. With the driver, Pfc. Virgil E. Hamilton, were Cpl. Bernie H. Heck, the company transportation NCO, and Cpl. Earl N. Vulgamore, the mail clerk. Halfway along they had to hide behind a barn to avoid some approaching enemy tanks. Although none of them had ever handled a bazooka before, they decided to try to use one that they had brought in the jeep for A Company. With Hamilton aiming and the other two men loading, they succeeded in setting the first tank on fire, then by chance got their second round into the opening hatch of the second tank. The third tank took five rounds to knock out, by which time the fourth tank was beating a retreat, but was eliminated in turn at a range of 150 yards.

The struggle for possession of Butzdorf continued all afternoon. Sgt. William McQuade of D Company destroyed a tank with a pole charge, and when three tanks tried to converge on the remaining heavy machine-gun section, Cpl. Earle F. Mousaw, despite being wounded, managed to fend them off with a bazooka. But by 1700 First Lieutenant Stafford's A Company was reduced to holding only five buildings in the southern part of the village, and a Panther was parked right outside his command post. They were out of bazooka ammunition and other antitank devices, and only one heavy machine gun of Lieutenant Baker's platoon was still operating. He had thirty wounded in his command post, as well as a number of prisoners, and his only means of communication was Lieutenant Morrison's artillery radio, which could send but no longer receive.[34]

From Tettingen, Lieutenant Colonel Miner could see the enemy tanks patrolling the streets of Butzdorf, but at least part of A Company still seemed to be holding out. He then received word that the 2nd Battalion would relieve him that night, and shortly afterward Lieutenant Colonel Martin arrived with F Company following close behind.

Brigadier General Cheadle was monitoring the situation for General Malony and reported to him that between twelve and eighteen tanks were coming in from all sides of Butzdorf and that A Company had been overrun by them. Malony passed this information on to XX Corps before going forward to see for himself. He then saw that A Company was still engaged in Butzdorf and corrected his previous message to XX Corps. A light tank company of the 3rd Cavalry Group that had been brought forward to support the defense was then sent back, since it would be of little use in such a situation. Malony decided that Butzdorf would have to be evacuated that night.

While the two battalion commanders discussed the handover, Lieutenant Chalkley was instructed to take some men of F Company and clear Butzdorf of snipers. Then at about 1700 two squads under Sergeant Soka and Sgt. Harold B. Price stormed the building on the eastern edge of Butzdorf that had previously housed the command post and recovered Sergeant Dury and several other men who had been wounded and taken prisoner. Two other squads retook the building next door.

With the village cleared of snipers, the tank destroyers were better able to engage the enemy. An assault gun near Butzdorf was hit and blew up in a spectacular display. Two tanks northeast of that village were set on fire, and at least one of the hull-down tanks on the ridge was damaged. In addition, three Panthers were hit while attempting to cross the antitank ditch east of Tettingen. Later, under cover of darkness, German recovery vehicles managed to tow away three of the damaged tanks before they could be set alight.

The evacuation of Butzdorf then began in conditions of intense darkness and falling sleet. With the aid of Lieutenant Morrison and his one-way radio, Lieutenant Chalkley called for fire support, which was provided by the 248th and 919th Field Artilleries. House doors were ripped off to serve as litters for the wounded. Checking his men by touch, Lt. Tom Hodges discovered a fully armed German unwittingly lined up among them. The enemy soldier was promptly disarmed and taken prisoner.

By 2200 on January 18 the whole of the 1st Battalion, less B Company, was back in Wochern. Captain Bowden's company had to spend another miserable night in the sleet and mud of the woods, during which a forty-strong German patrol penetrated its lines and was driven out only at daybreak, leaving behind fifteen dead. B Company was relieved the night of January 19 and rejoined the battalion in its reserve location at Veckring.[35]

The performance of Lieutenant Colonel Miner's 1st Battalion in the fighting for Tettingen and Butzdorf between January 14 and January 18, 1945, was recognized one year later with the sole Battle Honor award being made to a unit of the 94th Infantry Division. In the citation the battalion was credited with having "killed approximately 850 Germans and captured 150, and destroyed 8 tanks and 11 half-tracks. The unconquerable spirit displayed by these men in the face of superior odds, and their self-sacrificing devotion to duty are worthy of the highest emulation."[36]

NENNIG, BERG, WIES

Meanwhile, the heavy machine guns that had been dug in on the ridge north of Nennig were receiving considerable attention from the enemy artillery and came under infantry attack on six occasions, each time proving able to drive the Germans back.

There were problems with communications back to Regiment, so SSgt. James L. Jennings took a wire team from Perl to lay a cable across the river south of Besch at the ferry point and up the western bank to opposite Nennig, where the engineers ferried them back to the east bank under fire. The line was successfully connected, but by the time the wire team returned to Perl the next morning, it had been cut again. SSgt. Delbert A. Larson and Technician Fourth Grade (Tech-4) Mervin L. Moore then tried laying a line straight up the railroad tracks with the rails protecting the line from the constant mortar and shellfire, a technique that proved successful.

On January 17, Lieutenant Colonel Thurston's 3rd/376th received orders to eliminate the enemy positions that were still operating behind I Company. Lt. Pablo Arenaz's 2nd Platoon was detailed, but after an initial reconnaissance, he reported that his platoon, now down to only eighteen men, was inadequate for the task, so the assignment was given to Lt. Ravnel V. Burgamy's 1st Platoon. The platoon set off at 2030 having been split into two assault groups and given all the flamethrowers and pole and satchel charges available. Having successfully traversed some eight hundred yards of open ground to reach a deep draw one hundred yards short of the pillbox, the troops then discovered that their light machine guns had iced up and the only automatic weapon still functioning was a Browning automatic rifle (BAR). Lieutenant Burgamy and Pfc. John Mauro Jr. went on alone toward the pillbox until the sight of trip wires made them stop. The rest of the platoon opened fire as planned, and their fire was returned from men in several positions around the pillbox, who sent up signal flares calling down artillery and mortar fire on the platoon's position. The platoon then withdrew, covered by Pfc. Ray Sweeney's BAR. After investigating the matter, Lieutenant Colonel Thurston instructed Lieutenant Burgamy to pursue the pillbox no further.

Enemy patrols remained active along the 3rd Battalion's front all night, and an attack on Berg just before midnight was checked with artillery assistance, killing twenty of the enemy.

At about 0500 on January 17, a large patrol coming from the northeast attempted to enter Berg but was stopped by Lieutenant Bowyer's platoon.

Early in the morning an enemy column was spotted approaching in twos across some open ground in front of Lieutenant Fox's orchard, seemingly on the way to the positions behind and unaware of the American presence. The 3rd Platoon withheld fire until the Germans were within fifty yards, then opened fire with devastating effect. The Germans reacted with a frontal assault that cost them even more casualties. They then began a series of assaults with about twenty-five men at a time, simply varying the line of approach, that went on until 1100 the next day, but failed to get within grenade range. Some Germans infiltrated through the thin strip of woods between the 3rd and neighboring 4th Platoons, setting up machine guns to blast away at Lieutenant Fox's men, effectively isolating them. Their telephone line was cut, and one man was killed and another was injured in an ineffectual attempt at repair. Then late in the afternoon, Lieutenant Colonel Thurston and his driver, Technician Fifth Grade (Tech-5) Thomas M. Clausi, crawled in dragging a half-filled box of C rations. Thurston told Fox that under no circumstances was he to yield his position to the enemy, and gave him his bandolier of spare ammunition before leaving.[37]

There was another attack on Nennig at about 1000 with some twenty Germans coming down the usual draw from the northeast. Lieutenant Colonel Thurston described the draw as being the bed of a long dried-up stream that had cut a channel with almost vertical sides through the chalk up to fifteen feet deep, so that access and exit were possible only at either end, making it an ideal trap. On this occasion the German advance was stopped by Lieutenant Daly's platoon yet again, but some Germans managed to get into a couple of unoccupied buildings until one of the tank destroyers forced them out again by firing at point-blank range. Thurston eventually had one of the tank destroyers posted at the near end of the draw, for the Germans persisted in using it.

Aggressive enemy patrolling, particularly at night, together with frequent artillery and mortar bombardment, continued to harass the American defense of the Nennig sector. In Wies, Captain Brightman ordered his men to stay indoors at night so that any movement outside could be clearly identified as that of the enemy. In Nennig the number of German dead accumulating was proving quite a problem. There was no means of evacuating them, so they were collected and laid out neatly in one of the barns. (This was later to prove a bit of an embarrassment when the Germans recaptured the village and in their reports their propaganda ministry increased the number of dead found fourfold, ascribing their deaths to murder. "Berlin Sally," broadcasting in English, dubbed the 94th "Roosevelt's Butchers.")[38]

On the night of January 17 the weather changed to near-freezing rain and a sharp wind, bringing out enemy patrols all along the battalion front. It was particularly miserable for the men of I Company, who occupied the water-filled communication trench and foxholes.

On January 18 Lt. Edward G. Litka led an eighteen-man assault team from G Company to tackle two of the pillboxes that had checked I Company. An antitank ditch enabled the men to get within a hundred yards of their objectives unseen, then two light machine guns and the BARs were set up on the edge of the ditch to provide covering fire as two of the men carrying satchel charges moved forward. However, they had gone only twenty-five yards when extremely accurate heavy mortar fire crashed down all around them and in the antitank ditch, forcing an immediate withdrawal and killing one man as well as wounding nine others.

Reports kept coming in during the day of tanks being in the area, and the observation post in Remich reported the presence of large numbers of troops to the north. They had also spotted wire parties laying line to observation posts from pillboxes.

Then at about 1430 Wies and Berg were hit by an artillery concentration that was estimated as being fired from at least four battalions. This was followed by a battalion-sized attack on the two villages. Because all lines had been cut and the artillery observer's radio had been destroyed, Captain Brightman used an SCR-300 radio to communicate his artillery requirements to the Remich observation post for relay to the artillery liaison officer in Besch. This method was so effective that the Germans were cut down in large numbers and the immediate defense was able to deal with the survivors. In his after-action report, Lieutenant Colonel Thurston said: "By 1700 the last living German had loped back across the ridges and the attack had failed . . . some three hundred dead or wounded remained on the snow-covered fields when the last shot had been fired. Moans and cries of the wounded were plainly audible from both towns."[39]

Sgt. Bob Adair, who was with the 2nd Platoon of I Company, reported:

"The very cold evening of the 18th, I was sent into Nennig as a kind of one-man contact patrol with information for Battalion Headquarters there. I was depressed by Nennig. Dead bodies were stacked neatly on one side of the snow-covered main street. There must have been well over a hundred, all frozen. Most were German[,] but I thought (perhaps incorrectly) that American dead were also laid out there. Curiously, [as I was] cold myself, it bothered me that they were cold. Even death had not been an escape from the cold."[40]

By nightfall it seemed that both sides were equally exhausted. The 3rd Battalion was reaching the end of its endurance; the men were exhausted, and many were suffering from either frostbite or trench foot. Evacuation of the wounded to Besch proved so slow that Capt. John J. Ryan, the battalion surgeon, moved an aid station into Nennig. That night the first truck to use the road from Besch arrived with ammunition and was loaded with wounded for the return journey. Others were carried on litters as far as the river and then pushed back to Besch on wheeled litters along the track the battalion had originally used. They were evacuated by road to the collecting station in Sierck, then on to the casualty clearing company in Veckring.[41]

The 11th Panzer Division's historian wrote about this period of time from the German perspective: "The fighting began on January 18, 1945, under the unfavorable circumstances described, bringing some local successes at first, but the operation goal of Perl could not be reached. The division's main fighting force, the tank regiment, was only partly available due to lack of fuel, and this part got stuck in a German antitank ditch. Now the division, under strict orders from Corps, became engaged in expensive infantry operations. Schloss Berg changed hands several times. Some parts of the Orscholz Switch were taken, only to be lost once more."[42]

Meanwhile, General Malony had become convinced that the division was wasting its time with battalion-sized attacks. He therefore asked General Walker for permission to "exploit what he had gained." Walker said he would ask General Patton's permission to increase the size of the attacks in the Triangle and would also ask for some assistance for the division. However, shortly afterward Walker's chief of staff complained to Col. Earl C. Bergquist, the division's chief of staff, about the amount of ammunition the division was consuming. Bergquist countered that the division had just had to repel five enemy counterattacks but would be more careful about its ammunition expenditure in the future. General Walker later telephoned back to say that he had spoken to General Patton, who had given preliminary permission for an increase in the size of attacks, and pending formal approval from the Third Army, Walker authorized Maloney to "shoot the works."

Patton decided to release one of the combat commands of Maj. Gen. John M. Devine's newly arrived 8th Armored Division from his army reserve to enable it to get some practical combat training, but the other two combat commands of this division were to remain intact in reserve. Consequently, General Devine saw the chief of staff of XX Corps, Brig. Gen. William A. Collier, on January 18 and was briefed on General Patton's instructions. Devine then detailed Brig. Gen. Charles R. Colson's Combat Command A for temporary attachment to the 94th Infantry Division, and that same night Colson reported in to General Malony.

By this time Malony had had second thoughts on increasing the size of his attacks, but General Walker told him: "Its your show and I am going to leave it to you," giving him formal permission to use up to a regiment at a time with a combat command in support.

Next day, January 19, General Devine called on General Malony and discussed the use of Combat Team A with him, although it would not arrive until January 21 or 22. The icy roads made conditions for tanks extremely difficult, but if the Germans could use theirs, so could the Americans. Nevertheless, Malony was not impressed with the idea of indoctrinating this unit "in one of the most strongly fortified areas in the theater and under such weather conditions."[43]

On the night of January 18, the 302nd Infantry changed status from corps reserve to division reserve, and Lt. Col. Silas W. Hosea's 1st Battalion moved up to Perl in anticipation of the regiment relieving the 376th.

Then, early on the afternoon of January 19, Capt. Altus L. Woods Jr.'s B Company launched an attack on the five enemy pillboxes commanding the Besch-Nennig road from south of Nennig. The first pillbox had been taken, together with twelve prisoners, when it was discovered that the accompanying tank destroyer had run out of ammunition and the troops had insufficient demolition material to continue. The company was obliged to withdraw.

The attack was repeated the next day, for Division was anxious to have this enemy position eliminated without further delay, especially because a counterattack on Nennig on the scale already experienced at Tettingen-Butzdorf was expected. The B Company assault group was augmented by two platoons from B Company of the 319th Engineer Combat Battalion, a section of tank destroyers from the 607th Tank Destroyer Battalion, and an improvised heavy machine-gun section. To ensure that the ammunition did not run out this time, A Company provided two platoons as carrying parties as well as a third platoon to cover the right flank.

The attack began at 0912 on two of the German pillboxes, while the rest were blanketed with fire from the supporting weapons. The enemy troops responded with intense artillery and mortar fire, but the first two boxes were taken with the aid of flamethrowers manned by the engineers. Immediate interrogation of the prisoners taken by Pfc. Morris H. Wasserman of the battalion intelligence section revealed that there were several enemy artillery emplacements south of Schloss Thorn, and these positions were then subjected to counter-battery fire.

The assault on the remaining pillboxes continued, each being packed with explosives and destroyed as they were taken. Heavy enemy artillery fire continued throughout the operation and inflicted many casualties, but by 1405 the last of the pillboxes had been taken, together with 108 prisoners.

A and B Companies then turned to clearing Monkey Wrench Woods as the engineers finished demolishing the pillboxes. Capt. Robert A. Woodburn's A Company tackled the northern section, while B Company cleared the southern part. They then returned to Besch as instructed.

The following morning, January 21, when B Company returned to take up positions in the woods, they were met with a hail of fire coming from the area of the demolished pillboxes and sustained heavy casualties. The Germans had infiltrated back during the night and set up machine guns in the ruins. The men of B Company were so badly hit that they had to return to Besch. A Company took over and assumed positions in the southwest corner of the upper jaw of Monkey Wrench Woods.

On January 22 B Company took over A Company's positions, and the latter used an artillery concentration to help clear the upper jaw before assuming a defensive position across the northern edge of the woods. B Company came under heavy shellfire all through the night of January 22–23, then found the next morning that the German machine gunners had retreated from the demolished pillboxes. That night A Company moved forward to the line of the antitank ditch.[44]

3
Disaster at Orscholz

Within the limitations imposed on him, Major General Malony decided that his basic strategy would now be a double envelopment of the Orscholz Switch. Operations on the left flank had gone reasonably well, despite the fierce reaction experienced at Tettingen with the arrival of the 11th Panzer Division, and now he turned his attention to the right flank and the small town of Orscholz, nominating the 301st Infantry for the task.

Immediately east of Orscholz the cliffs dropped a sheer seven hundred feet to a hairpin bend in the Saar River below, providing a view of astonishing beauty. Just south of this bend a deep cleft or ravine cut across to a point due south of the town at the hamlet of Steinmühle. There a curve of dragon's teeth backed by a formidable array of pillboxes and bunkers barred the gently sloping, open southern approaches as far as the dense Schwarzbruch part of the Saarburg State Forest, sometimes referred to as the Forêt de Saarburg.

Col. Roy N. Hagerty's 301st Infantry started their initiative by sending reconnaissance patrols drawn from the regimental intelligence and reconnaissance section and Lt. Col. George F. Miller's 1st Battalion into the Schwarzbruch to search for enemy installations. Although some exchanges of fire occurred, nothing of significance was discovered. Some patrols reached as far as the antitank ditch without being detected. As a precaution, no further patrols were sent beyond the ditch until two days before the assault, when a small, carefully selected group was dispatched to try to determine the strength of the enemy in Orscholz. The men in this group were never seen again.

In preparation for the attack, the division's right boundary was altered to come into line with the hairpin bend in the Saar, releasing the 3rd Battalion, which then took over the 1st Battalion's front as the 3rd Cavalry Group moved up to fill the gap, and the 2nd Battalion covered the regiment's left flank. The 301st Field Artillery was detailed to provide fire support, and A Company of the 319th Engineers was to check the trails through the woods for mines.

On the night of January 19–20 the 1st Battalion set off from Ober-Tünsdorf in single file at 2400. It was bitterly cold with over a foot of snow on the ground and more falling thickly in what was to become a blinding snowstorm. TSgt. Ernest W. Halle of the regimental intelligence and reconnaissance platoon led the way for the battalion, which moved along behind in the following order: Capt. Herman C. Straub's B Company, Lt. Robert W. Jonscher's 1st Platoon of D Company, Capt. Charles B. Colgan's A Company, D Company's 2nd Platoon, Lieutenant Colonel Miller and his battalion headquarters group, Capt. Gilbert S. Woodrill of D Company with the mortar platoon, and Capt. Cleo B. Smith's C Company as battalion reserve.

The troops had four thousand yards to go to reach the line of departure. It was difficult going for the heavily laden men, and frequent rest halts had to be made. Pvt. A. Cleveland Harrison, a former Army Specialized Training Program man serving as a rifleman with B Company, described his experiences in his book *Unsung Valor.* Carrying extra ammunition on a backpack under his improvised camouflage cape, he had the impression that their route through the woods in the dark was uncertain, often changing course and even doubling back on itself. However, by 0330 the head of the column had reached the forward assembly area within a few hundred yards of the line of departure, where H-hour (when the attack would begin) was set for 0600. Patrols and listening posts were sent out to protect the assembly area, while Captains Straub and Colgan made a last-minute reconnaissance.

The Merlbach, a small stream running just behind a row of dragon's teeth, had been designated as the line of departure. Just behind this was a small clump of buildings that were thought to be camouflaged pillboxes, so the leaders of A Company had organized a special assault squad to precede them and deal with this problem. At the point where the stream crossed under the Oberleuken-Orscholz road, the dragon's teeth changed to an antitank ditch running through the woods south of the road as far as Ober-leuken.

At 0500 A and B Companies moved forward from the assembly area to the line of departure, but visibility and conditions were so bad that they soon lost contact with each other, and Lieutenant Colonel Miller decided to delay the attack. It was 0725 before contact was reestablished and the attack could be launched. No artillery preparation was used.

Harrison reports that the long single file of his company extended for several hundred yards ahead of him. As the troops left the woods and discerned a gravel track under the snow beneath them, the head of the column had reached the intersection with the main road when suddenly some 88-mm shells burst overhead. The soldiers had in fact successfully penetrated the lines of the Germans' 2nd Battalion, Grenadier Regiment 712. The column then split, taking cover on either side of the road. Harrison saw Lieutenant Colonel Miller and an aide hurry past toward the intersection, and the head of the column began turning right onto the road leading to Orscholz. To the left of the road was a steep, heavily wooded slope, and on the right was a fairly level open field with dragon's teeth just visible against the undergrowth at the far end. German artillery fire intensified as Harrison approached the intersection, and machine-gun fire from bunkers hidden in the trees started sweeping the open ground, forcing the men to scatter. There was no cover to be had; it was a perfect killing ground. It was only by being assumed already dead that Harrison and fourteen others were able to survive the day without being seriously wounded.

Meanwhile, the head of the column overran some enemy machine-gun positions, killing some of the enemy and taking others prisoner. Having reached the edge of the woods leading to Orscholz, Captain Straub's group settled down to await the arrival of the rest of the battalion for the planned left-hook assault on Orscholz.

However, no sooner than A Company had moved beyond the dragon's teeth, the right-hand platoon found itself in an antipersonnel minefield, with the Schü-mines and tangles of barbed wire concealed by the snow leading to heavy casualties. An attempt to veer to the right brought about further explosions. Only a few men got through the dragon's teeth unscathed.

Back at the line of departure, the remainder of the battalion began moving through the dragon's teeth on B Company's route, but as soon as the leading elements crossed half of the open ground beyond, they came under withering machine-gun fire. The 1st Platoon of A Company, which had yet to cross the dragon's teeth, then provided covering fire to allow the others to withdraw. Clearly the Germans were now fully alerted to the American incursion. The artillery troops were now called to bring down fire on the German positions in the woods, which were skillfully concealed under tangles of felled trees. German artillery then joined in to add to the carnage.

Lieutenant Colonel Miller came forward to try to resolve the situation, but was killed outright by shellfire, as was Lt. Adrian B. DePutron shortly after. Maj. Arthur W. Hodges, the battalion executive officer, took over command and withdrew the survivors deeper into the woods to prepare for another attack.

Informed of the situation, Regiment sent forward I Company as reinforcements at 1000. The attack was renewed at 1500 with the aid of a heavy artillery preparation, but again it foundered on hidden antipersonnel mines and machine-gun fire coming from concealed pillboxes. Casualties mounted to such an extent, one company sustaining sixty casualties from mines alone, that the battalion was again obliged to withdraw.

Regiment then sent Lt. Col. Donald C. Hardin, who had previously commanded the battalion, to take over temporary command, and at 1755, shortly before nightfall, he launched another attack farther to the left than had previously been made in a vain attempt to avoid the antipersonnel minefields. But the battalion ended up being badly mauled and was forced to withdraw yet again. B Company remained isolated and unreachable.

In the meantime, Lieutenant General Pflieger, commanding the Germans' 416th Infantry Division, had rallied all available troops, including the divisional battle school at Trassem and the regimental signal and engineer companies of Grenadier Regiment 712, to surround the American penetration and prevent a breach developing in his lines.

Early on January 20, as the 1st Battalion attacked, the 2nd Battalion had wheeled right into the woods toward the attack with a view to preventing enemy interference from Oberleuken. With the 2nd Battalion went A Company of the 748th Tank Battalion, which was prepared to join in the assault on Orscholz once the antitank ditch had been cleared and bridged, but the opportunity failed to arise.

Meanwhile, Captain Straub's group was coming under increasing enemy attention and moved back south of the road to adopt a position of all-around defense. Forward observers from the 301st Field Artillery and the regimental cannon company ensured that a ring of protective fire was brought down when required.

With dusk, the fifteen or so survivors around Harrison got together and discussed what to do. One of the soldiers, Pvt. George Holbrook, said he thought he knew how to get back through the minefield, and eight men elected to go with him. By treading carefully in one another's footsteps they managed to get through, but Harrison stumbled and set off a mine that wounded him and several others, although he managed to stay upright by using his rifle as a crutch. They found the area beyond the minefield deserted, and it took them another eight and a half hours to reach the regiment's lines.

Enemy artillery fire pounded the troops in the woods throughout the night of January 20–21, with treetop bursts adding to the lethal explosions, and casualties continued to mount. Attempts to recover the wounded from the open ground were repeatedly driven back by enemy machine-gun fire. Patrols were sent forward to try to find a way through to B Company, but their efforts proved unsuccessful. Finally, Lieutenant Colonel Hardin informed Colonel Hagerty that it would take at least a regiment to force a way through, whereupon Hagerty reluctantly gave permission to abandon the attack on Orscholz.

After conferring with Lt. Col. Samuel L. Morrow of the 301st Field Artillery on January 21, Colonel Hagerty decided to lay a smoke screen between Orscholz and the Forêt de Saarburg to provide cover for B Company's withdrawal. Hagerty then went up to the battalion's forward positions to brief Captain Straub on this plan by radio, but Straub told him that the plan would be impossible to execute: his men's ammunition was almost exhausted, they themselves were exhausted and freezing to death, their location was known to the enemy, and the only way back was through minefields. For the sake of his surviving men, Straub would have to surrender. However, when the smoke arrived, he passed the word for the men to try to break out by mingling with their prisoners in order to confuse the enemy. One group reached a pillbox, where they found the frozen bodies of several of their comrades who had died during the night and six or eight badly wounded men lying on the cold concrete floor, but there was no escape— there were Germans all around them. When the men learned that Lieutenant Jonscher had been killed in the trench, they opted to surrender. In all, 10 officers and 230 men were reported to have gone into German captivity.

The 1st Battalion then pulled back through the woods that afternoon. They recovered and evacuated as many of the wounded as they could under cover of smoke. The 2nd Battalion covered the withdrawal, the regiment returning to its original lines with the shattered 1st Battalion going into reserve.

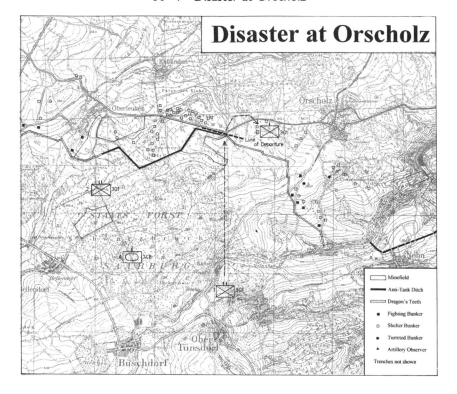

Of the nearly 1,000 men with whom the 1st Battalion had started the attack on Orscholz, only 19 officers and 415 enlisted men remained. Major Hodges was now formally appointed battalion commander, with Maj. William E. McBride as his executive officer, and Lt. Joseph E. Cancilla was appointed commander of B Company, which he would have to rebuild from scratch.

This attack on Orscholz had proved a sorry affair, and when General Patton eventually learned about it, he expressed his anger about the conduct of the attack and the surrender of B Company in no uncertain terms.[1]

NENNIG, BERG, WIES

On January 19, Lt. Col. Otto B. Cloudt Jr.'s 3rd Battalion of the 302nd Infantry received orders to relieve the 3rd/376th on the division's left flank, so he and his officers down to platoon level drove by jeep to a point midway between Besch and Nennig, from where they had to walk and crawl their way forward. They came under mortar and machine-gun fire near the railroad but sustained no casualties. They were then briefed on the situation by Lieutenant Colonel Thurston and his staff. Thurston was not impressed by Cloudt and his team, whom he regarded as dangerously careless and sloppy in their attitude.

Cloudt assigned Capt. Allan R. Williams's I Company to Wies and Berg, and Lt. Carl W. Seeby's K Company to the defense of Nennig. Capt. John N. Smith's L Company was to take over the right flank positions extending some fifteen hundred yards east of the village. As usual, Capt. Francis M. Hurst's M Company was divided, with one heavy machine-gun platoon each going to I and K Companies, while Lt. Douglas LaRue Smith's mortar platoon was to cross the Moselle and provide covering fire from the higher ground in Luxembourg.

Later in the afternoon the battalion executive officer, Maj. Earl L. Myers, brought the rest of the battalion up from Sierck to the woods north of Perl. He then had Lt. Robert A. Edwards, the executive officer of I Company, lead I and K Companies with the 1st Platoon of L Company under cover of darkness to Besch, where they were picked up by a guide from the 3rd/376th, who took them on to Nennig. The company commanders were waiting for them at the railroad tracks west of Nennig to lead them to their assigned locations. It was a cold, clear night and the handover went without a hitch.

The 3rd/376th assembled in Besch, where the battalion had arranged warm rooms and hot meals for the troops coming out of the line. Once they were refreshed, they were taken by truck to the little French village of Monneren for a well-earned rest. However, they lost the valued services of Captain Ryan, the battalion surgeon, who had to be evacuated after suffering from extreme fatigue.

By midnight I Company had taken over Wies, and Lt. William J. Doherty's 2nd Platoon had taken over Berg. One heavy machine-gun section went to Wies and the other went into Schloss Berg with two rifle squads, while the third rifle squad was placed in a house in Berg overlooking a draw that approached the hamlet from the east.

Lieutenant Seeby deployed the 1st and part of the 2nd Platoons to defend the village but had TSgt. Frank O'Hara's 3rd Platoon and the attached heavy machine-gun platoon occupy the communication trenches at the edge of the woods on the ridge overlooking Nennig. There they were joined by the forward artillery observer from the 356th Field Artillery. Extending this line of defense along the communication trenches came L Company and elements of K Company, with Lt. John R. Travers's 1st Platoon relieving Lieutenant Fox in the orchard. Fox and his men left, carrying their dead with them.

Sergeant O'Hara's platoon and the neighboring squad from L Company were fiercely attacked soon after they had moved into their positions and were forced back into Nennig. When they tried to regain their positions, they were repulsed by heavy fire. Lieutenant Seeby then ordered the men back onto the ridge to the right of Lt. Henry J. Fink's 2nd Platoon, which was defending the eastern edge of the village.

Meanwhile, the rest of L Company moved out westward from Tettingen to fill the gap to the east of the orchard. TSgt. Chester E. Markowski's 3rd Platoon occupied the area north of the Nennig-Tettingen road next to Lieutenant Travers's men in the orchard, while TSgt. John Karl's 2nd Platoon took position on the extreme right between Markowski and Tettingen in a series of communication trenches south of the road. The weapons platoon was divided between them.

Lieutenant Travers's men first made contact with the enemy at 0400 the next day, January 20, when a three-man patrol entered their lines and was shot down. Two hours later a forty-man German patrol approached the orchard in column of twos and stopped for a break only fifty yards away. The 1st Platoon opened fire, killing and wounding about half of the patrol as the rest scattered. Later, enemy activity heard in the area indicated that the platoon was being surrounded.

With daylight a heavy artillery concentration on the 2nd and 3rd Platoons heralded an attack by Panzergrenadier Regiment 111, which drove back Sergeant Karl's men to the firing trench at the rear of their position. Sergeant Markowski's men held fast but were in danger of being out-flanked. Lt. William Burke, forward observer from the 356th Field Artillery, had joined the 3rd Platoon during the night and was now able to arrange fire support through the use of Captain Smith's SCR-300 radio, which was used to make contact with the 2nd Battalion's command post in Wochern. Captain Smith then had to rely on runners getting messages through to Wochern for relay to his own battalion's command post in Besch. He ordered the 2nd Platoon to attack and regain their old positions immediately, but the understrength platoon encountered such heavy infantry fire that the men were forced back to the communication trench. They were later joined by five men who had managed to work their way back from the 3rd Platoon's position having run out of ammunition after killing twenty-five of the enemy. They had no idea what had happened to the rest of their platoon.

Captain Smith sent a messenger to Wochern to report the situation, and to request reinforcements and another radio, but the messenger returned with a patrol from F Company led by Lt. Joe D. Alvarado, who had been tasked with establishing contact with the 1st Battalion troops working on the pillboxes south of the Nennig-Tettingen road. Smith then sent Lt. Anthony Czerboskas of L Company to Wochern to emphasize the seriousness of the situation. Smith was down to forty men and was receiving constant heavy rocket and artillery fire. He expected to be overrun at any moment.

Meanwhile, it became obvious to Lieutenant Travers that the Germans had bypassed his position in the orchard and were now at his rear. He had no radio, so with two volunteers he set off to inform the battalion. As the battalion command post was located in Besch, Travers first headed due south, avoiding interception and enemy minefields. Reaching the Nennig-Tettingen road, he was surprised to encounter Lt. Col. John W. Gaddis, the regimental executive officer, at the northern edge of Monkey Wrench Woods. Gaddis took Travers on to the battalion command post in Besch and then to the regimental command post in Perl to make his report. But by now the whole of the regimental front was under heavy attack and there were no reserves available.[2]

TETTINGEN-BUTZDORF

On the night of January 19, Lt. Col. Frank B. Norman's 2nd Battalion began relieving the 2nd/376th, which had replaced the 1st/376th at Tettingen the day before. Capt. James W. Butler's E Company moved into Borg, Capt. James W. Griffin's G Company took over Tettingen, and Capt. Herman Kops Jr.'s F Company occupied Wochern and Der Heidlich Hill. Capt. Orville M. Owings had his H Company 81-mm mortar platoon deploy in the cemetery west of Wochern and sent one machine gun to Wochern and the other to Borg.

At 2000 the next day, January 20, G Company in Tettingen came under attack from three sides by what appeared to be a reinforced company. After three hours of hard fighting, the Germans were driven back.[3]

MONKEY WRENCH WOODS

On that same day Lieutenant Colonel Hosea's 1st/302nd, less C Company, were employed in clearing five pillboxes that dominated the supply route into Nennig from Besch but that the 376th had had neither the time nor resources to clear. The task was given to Captain Woods's B Company, supported by a Hellcat. One pillbox was taken, together with a dozen prisoners, before the Hellcat exhausted its ammunition and the explosives needed for tackling the remaining pillboxes. Attempts to resupply the company proved unsuccessful, and the attack had to be called off. However, it was resumed the next day, with B Company being substantially reinforced by A Company, a heavy machine-gun section, two platoons of B Company, the 319th Engineers, and several tank destroyers of the 607th Tank Destroyer Battalion with 90-mm guns. It still took six hours of intense fighting to subdue the remaining pillboxes, which yielded another 108 prisoners. During this action A Company was mainly employed in carrying parties to keep the attacking troops fully supplied with ammunition and explosives.

Meanwhile, Capt. Norman C. Marek's C Company had moved into Wochern as regimental reserve, and Marek took his platoon commanders forward on reconnaissance, calling on Captain Smith for a briefing. While they were together, a radio message was received from Lieutenant Colonel Norman assigning Captain Marek's company, which had been briefly attached to the 2nd Battalion, to Captain Smith's command, which had also come under Norman's control. Marek sent for his men and along with Smith decided they should mount an immediate counterattack to restore L Company's original line and reestablish contact with the 3rd Platoon. Captain Smith then promoted Sergeant Karl to first sergeant and gave the command of the 2nd Platoon to SSgt. Anthony S. Ewasko.

As C Company arrived the men were deployed in the firing trench occupied by L Company's 2nd Platoon, only to be greeted by a heavy artillery barrage on their positions. Lt. Johan A. Wilson, the 356th Field Artillery observer with C Company, then arranged a five-minute preparation on the woods in front of them, after which the troops moved forward to the antitank ditch and slid down its sides. The ice in the bottom of the ditch broke, immersing the men almost hip-deep. Lt. Donald L. Renck's platoon was momentarily delayed by this turn of events, but Sergeant Ewasko's and Lt. Carl D. Richards's platoons went on. A burst of machine-gun fire from the wooden bunker that had previously been used by Captain Smith as his command post killed Lieutenant Renck and injured several others as they emerged from the antitank ditch. The rest of the platoon managed to overwhelm the Germans who were defending this bunker, capturing twelve prisoners and two machine guns. The position then came under rocket and artillery fire, as well as machine-gun fire from pillboxes north of the Nennig-Tettingen road, pinning down the troops, and only those on the right flank were able to reach the old positions.

Following close behind the attacking platoons, Captains Smith and Marek encountered several Germans, killing two and capturing eight, thus encouraging other Germans to surrender in turn. Because the area was far from being cleared, Captain Smith sent a runner to find the left-hand platoon, but the runner returned saying he had been unable to find anyone. Captain Smith went himself and found the platoon close to the antitank ditch, where it had been pinned down, and reorganized the survivors under SSgt. Francis J. Kelly, the platoon guide. Captain Marek meanwhile took a small group to eliminate the machine gun that had been causing the trouble. The combined forces then dug in facing the Nennig-Tettingen road and the two pillboxes that had checked their advance. The enemy kept the men under heavy rocket and artillery fire all night, inflicting many casualties. Technician 3rd Grade (Tech-3) John F. Risky, a medical aid man attached to L Company, worked day and night tending the wounded. He ignored automatic fire and bombardments and stayed behind with the wounded when the unit was forced to withdraw, thus earning a Distinguished Service Cross for his outstanding efforts.

Freezing conditions added to the toll, with fifteen casualties from trench foot and frostbite, so that by the time all the casualties had been evacuated, L Company was down to eighteen men, and when Lieutenant Colonel Norman came to visit the unit at 1000 next day, he ordered Captain Smith and his remaining men back into reserve at Wochern.

Captain Marek remained with his C Company and that afternoon of January 21 was joined by a patrol from A Company, which had worked its way east along the northern jaw of Monkey Wrench Woods, thus establishing a tenuous link with the main line of resistance. There was still no sign of L Company's missing platoon.[4]

On January 22 the skies were at last clear enough for flying activity, and German 120-mm mortar and artillery positions in the villages of Kreuzweiler and Beuren were bombed by eighteen B-24 Liberators "with good effect." The following day three flights of P-47 Thunderbolts bombed and strafed the village of Sinz and Bannholz Woods beyond, where enemy armor was known to be sheltering. Numerous fires indicated some success from this mission.[5]

On the morning of January 23, Lieutenant Colonel Norman and his G-3 (staff officer for operations), Capt. Burgess G. Hodges, reported to regimental headquarters and were ordered by Colonel Johnson to take the pillboxes that had stopped the combined attacks of C and L Companies and had previously been captured by F Company but retaken by the Germans. Lieutenant Colonel Norman then called his executive officer, Maj. Harold V. Maixner, and ordered him to have the elements of F Company holding Der Heidlich Hill relieved by the remnants of L Company and then form two assault teams from F Company. A squad of engineers equipped with satchel charges, flamethrowers, and explosives was attached to F Company to assist with the task, and Captain Marek was told that his C Company would be responsible for securing F Company's left flank as it attacked. F Company then formed up for the attack behind C Company, which was expected to move forward afterward to occupy the new line.

The attack was launched at 1645 after a brief artillery preparation, and a diversionary attack was also made on Campholz Woods, but to no apparent effect. As the company advanced it was met by a devastating barrage of rockets and artillery fire, with intense and accurate automatic fire cutting in from the flank. The number of casualties rapidly increased. What happened next is best described in TSgt. Nicholas Oresko's citation for the Medal of Honor:

Master Sergeant Nicholas Oresko (then Technical Sergeant) was platoon leader with Company C, 302d Infantry, on 23 January 1945 near Tettingen, Germany, in an attack against strong enemy positions. Deadly automatic fire from the flanks pinned down his unit. Realizing that a machine gun in a nearby bunker must be eliminated, he swiftly worked ahead alone, braving bullets which struck him, until close enough to throw a grenade into the German position. He rushed the bunker and, with point-blank rifle fire, killed all the hostile occupants who survived the grenade blast. Another machine gun opened up on him, knocking him down and seriously wounding him in the hip. Refusing to withdraw from battle, he placed himself at the head of his platoon to continue the assault. As withering machine-gun and rifle fire swept the area, he struck out alone in advance of his men to a second bunker. With a grenade, he crippled the dug-in machine gun defending this position and then wiped out the troops manning it with his rifle, completing his second self-imposed, one-man attack. Although weak from loss of blood, he refused to be evacuated until assured the mission was successfully accomplished. Through quick thinking, indomitable courage and unswerving devotion to the attack in the face of bitter resistance and while wounded, Sergeant Oresko killed twelve Germans, prevented a delay in the assault and made it possible for Company C to obtain its objective with minimum casualties.[6]

Pvt. James F. Cousineau also distinguished himself in this action by charging a German machine-gun position, knocking it out with grenades and then cutting down eleven of the enemy with his M1 rifle. Later on, while trying to evacuate wounded comrades from in front of the firing line, he and another soldier were surrounded by Germans but managed to fight their way back to the company. (For these actions Cousineau was later awarded the Distinguished Service Cross.)

Despite all of their efforts, the continuous hail of ear-splitting rockets and artillery fire on the position rendered it untenable, and at 1730 Lieutenant Colonel Norman ordered the remaining men of F Company back into Wochern.[7]

4
Action on the Left Flank

NENNIG, BERG, WIES

Lieutenant Colonel Cloudt's 3rd/302nd was now drawing considerable attention from the 11th Panzer Division. At about 1000 on January 20, five German tanks loaded with infantry tried to storm Nennig from the north and were beaten back by intense small-arms fire and a defensive artillery barrage. A few enemy soldiers managed to get into the village but were soon eliminated.

The tanks were heard again that evening at 2045, and soon afterward an attack came from a hill to the east of the village. The American 60-mm mortars fired illuminating shells to expose hordes of infantry, supported by four tanks, sweeping down on the village. Lt. David H. Devonald's K Company stood its ground, beating off the enemy, and again those few Germans who managed to get as far as the village were soon eliminated.

The next day, an intensely cold one, passed relatively quietly, apart from the usual harassing rocket, mortar, and artillery fire. Suddenly, at 2100 the Germans laid a terrific artillery preparation on the northern part of the village, then switched to battering Wies and Besch. Again tanks and infantry swarmed down on Nennig, but the guns of the 356th Field Artillery laid down their own barrage and were joined by other artillery battalions within range, as did M Company's mortars from across the Moselle, paying no attention to ammunition expenditure limitations. The Germans, too, pushed on regardless and took several buildings. One German tank fought its way through to the command post in the center of the village, knocking out a

57-mm gun and two machine guns. By midnight the situation within the village was utterly chaotic.

Using the artillery radio, Lieutenant Seeby summoned Lieutenant Fink, whose platoon was occupying an open position on a ridge east of the village, and had him report back to the command post. Upon arrival Fink was given fifteen men and told to clear the enemy out of the buildings they had occupied. The men cleared the enemy soldiers out of the church but were then held up by fire coming from a former observation post. Appreciating that they were not really strong enough for their task, the men reported back to the company command post.

Meanwhile, Lieutenant Carpenter and some men of the 1st Platoon had become isolated in a house on the northeast corner of Nennig. A German tank commander called on them to surrender, a suggestion they rejected, so the commander laid siege to the building. Carpenter and his men continued to hold out (as we shall see later).

By morning the enemy had driven K Company back to the southern edge of Nennig, where the company now had three tanks. They launched a bitter counterattack on the Germans at 0800 and regained some ground, but the overall pressure was too great and Lieutenant Seeby ordered a withdrawal to the line of the small stream running east to west in the southern part of the village.

At the same time, Schloss Berg was also under siege. The open ground between the Schloss and the rest of I Company in Wies was swept by machine-gun fire, making it impossible to cross in daylight, but after dark on January 20, Pfc. James V. Collins, a 2nd Platoon runner, got through to Wies and reported to Captain Williams that enemy tanks were firing through holes that they had blasted in the Schloss at point-blank range and were giving the defense a hard time. Bazooka rounds, the only means the troops had of holding the tanks off, were running out, and more were urgently needed. A carrying party was quickly formed with Private Collins to lead it back to the Schloss, but the men repeatedly came under enemy fire and were unable to get through. A six-man combat patrol was then formed to fight their way through, but they abandoned the attempt after four of them had been killed.

Inevitably, the gallant defense of Schloss Berg, consisting of two squads of the 2nd Platoon and a machine-gun section, succumbed to the enemy assault, one of the captured machine guns later being turned against the Americans. The remaining squad under SSgt. Thomas W. Fontaine found itself cut off from both its platoon and company, so Sergeant Fontaine led his men by a circuitous route to Besch and then back to Wies.[1]

On the morning of January 22 the Germans began infiltrating the southern part of Nennig, despite all attempts by Lieutenant Seeby's men to drive them back. General Malony called XX Corps and told Brigadier General Collier, the chief of staff, "We are having a helluva time holding Nennig this morning." Collier offered Malony the use of the 8th Armored Division's Combat Command A, which had yet to experience combat, but only for two days.

Brigadier General Cheadle brought the combat command's commander, Brigadier General Colson, to have a look at the terrain, which Colson declared unsuitable for armor. Nevertheless, General Malony was determined to use the armor without delay. The original intention was for the armor to provide support for an attack by the 2nd/376th, but Lieutenant Colonel Martin protested that his men were exhausted and the battalion far too understrength to be able to accomplish the task, so with Malony's approval it was decided to use the 7th Armored Infantry Battalion instead.

Colson's command was split into two task forces. He ordered Task Force Poinier, under Lt. Col. Arthur D. Poinier, with his 7th Armored Infantry Battalion, C Company of the 18th Tank Battalion, and a detachment from A Troop, 88th Calvary Reconnaissance Squadron, to seize and hold Nennig.

Capt. Joseph Finlay's A Company of the 7th Armored Infantry, supported by an assault gun platoon, was then ordered to assist the 302nd's K Company in clearing the northern part of the village. Outside on the ridge Lieutenant Fink's men were also recalled to assist in this operation. Slow but steady progress was made through the village, and a machine gun taken by the Germans from Schloss Berg was recaptured; however, much of the village still remained in German hands as the fighting continued at nightfall. A German counterattack then drove the Americans back to their start point, eliminating all the gains of the day, and some of A Company were left behind hiding under the altar in the village church. While this was going on, a sixteen-man carrying party under Lieutenant Edwards, the executive officer of I Company, 3rd/302nd, arrived from Wies, having followed the railroad tracks to a point south of Nennig, and reported to Lieutenant Colonel Cloudt at his command post in the village.

General Malony reported to XX Corps that the situation was "red hot" in Nennig and at last told Corps the bad news of the 301st Infantry's debacle at Orscholz two days earlier.[2]

The fighting on January 22 had also cost the Germans' 3rd Battalion, Panzergrenadier Regiment 110, dearly. The battalion had sustained so many casualties that it was disbanded and the survivors distributed among the other battalions of the regiment.

Lieutenant Reudiger's 1st Battalion, Grenadier Regiment 714, was also brought in from across the Saar to reinforce the German counterattack. By this time Panzer Regiment 15 was desperately short of fuel. Against its operational requirement of ninety-one cubic meters of fuel per day, it was receiving only twelve.[3]

By the morning of January 23 the situation had deteriorated to the extent that Lieutenant Colonel Martin's 2nd/376th had to be called forward from its reserve position in Monneren. It was another bitterly cold day with blinding snowstorms.

The 2nd Battalion, led by Capt. Simon D. Darrah's E Company, moved up along the railroad to a point opposite Nennig, which was again used as the line of departure for an attack on Nennig and Berg. After a strong artillery preparation, the company attacked with the 2nd Platoon heading for Berg, only to be pinned down by heavy machine-gun fire coming from three directions within the first three hundred yards.

Lt. Gus E. Wilkins's 1st Platoon, together with SSgt. David H. Godfrey's 60-mm mortar squad, pushed into the northwestern corner of Nennig, encountering little resistance, and had taken four houses and twenty-seven prisoners when three German Mark IV tanks appeared. TSgt. Nathaniel Isaacman and Pvt. John F. Pietrzah climbed up to the rooftops and made their way forward under sniper fire until Pietrzah could fire his bazooka at the leading tank. With his second round he scored a direct hit and the tank burst into flames. He then engaged the last tank and set it on fire with a single round, trapping the second tank, which was then put out of action with a rifle grenade fired by Pvt. Albert J. Beardsley. The tankers trying to escape on foot from this carnage were cut down by rifle fire.

By noon E Company's 1st Platoon was in possession of several buildings in Nennig, but the 2nd Platoon was still pinned down only three hundred yards from its line of departure. Lt. Bernard F. Simuro's 3rd Platoon, which had been providing infantry escort for some supporting tanks, all but one of which had been knocked out during the attack, was now split between the other two platoons with the task of silencing the machine guns in the cemetery midway between Nennig and Wies. A squad under SSgt. Anthony S. Rao accomplished this task, but accurate mortar and artillery fire soon drove them out again.

Capt. John D. Heath's G Company moved through Wies and on to the northeast as far as the antitank ditch, where machine-gun fire from Schloss Berg forced the troops to retire. F Company was then inserted between G and E Companies to prevent any enemy infiltration. Late that afternoon Captain Darrah worked his way from Wies to Nennig and reestablished contact with his 1st Platoon. At 2000 the rest of E Company moved into Nennig to reinforce the defense.

During the night Lieutenant Colonel Cloudt and Lieutenant Fink worked their way forward to within twenty-five yards of the building in which Lieutenant Carpenter and his men were still isolated, but enemy machine guns still prevented closer access to them. However, the two lieutenants managed to shout messages of encouragement to the trapped men, promising an early release.

Again the Germans had suffered badly that day. Five Mark IV tanks had been knocked out in Nennig in the assaults conducted by the 1st and 2nd Battalions, Panzergrenadier Regiment 111, and also later by the 1st Battalion, Panzergrenadier Regiment 110. Both regiments were reduced to half the strength with which they had entered the Saar-Moselle Triangle. With orders to take Nennig at all costs, they had singularly failed.

At 0700 on January 24, the 1st Platoon of E Company and a composite platoon from the 3rd Battalion made a concerted attack to clear the last buildings that were still in German hands, and by 1030 Lieutenant Carpenter and his men had been released and the entire village was back in American hands.

The next objective was the hamlet of Berg, particularly Schloss Berg, whose commanding position still held as much value as when it had been built in medieval times. An attack was planned by which G Company would advance southeast from Wies while F Company thrust north from Nennig. At 1330 a Hellcat fired several rounds into the nearest building in Berg as Lieutenant Simuro's 3rd Platoon dashed toward it across the intervening one hundred yards of open ground. Simuro was wounded in the charge but continued to lead his men. Just as he and his men got inside, a Mark IV tank opened fire on them as the enemy started concentrating mortar, artillery, and machine-gun fire on them.

Trying to relieve the pressure, a squad of the 2nd Platoon under Sgt. Ray Ketner then seized a second building in the hamlet, and one of the supporting tank destroyers knocked out the Mark IV tank. The fire concentration was so intense that Captain Darrah ordered his men to withdraw. Only seventeen of the forty men who were involved in the assault made it back.

G Company, on the right flank, also ran into trouble. Racing toward Schloss Berg across open ground, the 3rd Platoon was raked with machine-gun fire from the castle and hit by mortar fire. The troops took cover in the antitank ditch one hundred yards short of the castle, where they found themselves in a most uncomfortable trap. The ice in the ditch broke under their weight, soaking them in icy water up to their hips, as machine-gun fire clipped the edges of the trench, which was impassable in one direction and led deep into the enemy lines in the other. A radioed appeal for help led to the 1st Platoon, on the right, making another attempt to break into Berg, but this was checked by artillery and machine-gun fire. Back in the ditch it was so cold that the men's canteens and their radio froze. At nightfall the aid man decided to attempt the evacuation of one of the wounded and managed to reach Wies. He returned an hour later with the news that a smoke screen was about to be laid to cover their withdrawal to Wies. As soon as the smoke arrived, the men made off.[4]

With the attachment of the 8th Armored Division's Combat Command A limited to only forty-eight hours, General Malony was eager to make the most of this opportunity. He therefore proposed a combined attack to clear the Nennig-Berg-Wies area once and for all, and to create a strong defense to ensure that he could retain his gains. As a diversion and an attempt to exploit any weakness in the enemy that might arise out of the main attack, he also proposed a combined attack on Butzdorf and Sinz.

Consequently, on the evening of January 24 Brigadier General Cheadle, the assistant divisional commander of the 94th, and Brigadier General Colson of Combat Command A, visited the command post of the 2nd/376th in Wies, where Cheadle told Lieutenant Colonel Martin, "I have orders that our battalion will attack at 0300 to establish a bridgehead for the armor, which will then pass through you and continue the attack." Martin replied that his men were exhausted and far too understrength to carry out such a task. While Martin was prepared to obey the order if so demanded, he suggested that a fresh battalion be employed in a night attack. After some discussion, the matter was raised with Division, where it was decided that the 7th Armored Infantry Battalion would carry out this attack at 0600.

Under cover of darkness Lieutenant Colonel Poinier sent Lt. James P. A. Carr's platoon of the 88th Cavalry Reconnaissance Squadron to protect A Company of the 53rd Armored Engineer Battalion as the latter attempted to make three breaches in the antitank ditch that previously had prevented the American armor from supporting the infantry. The men of Combat Command A, experiencing their first night under combat conditions, were subjected to the usual harassment from "Screaming Meemies" (German rockets) and artillery fire.

The attack went ahead according to schedule and was observed by Major Generals Malony and Devine. The armored infantry had no winter camouflage outfits and stood out in their olive drab against the snow, making easy targets. As the daylong battle relentlessly continued, the 7th Armored Infantry and supporting C Company, 18th Tank Battalion, suffered severe casualties. The tank company commander and most of his platoon commanders fell, and the battalion operations officer took over briefly before he was killed himself. Lieutenant Colonel Poinier was wounded by mortar fire, as was his executive officer, Maj. Richard Moushegian, leaving the battalion intelligence officer, Capt. Harry Craddock, to take over the command. Major General Devine and Brigadier General Colson went forward to encourage their men during the battle, and Colson had a very close call when he lost the star from his helmet by artillery fire. Capt. Grover B. Herman's B Company, supported by the tanks of the 3rd Platoon of C Company, 18th Tank Battalion, bypassed Schloss Berg and reached the high ground behind, but in attacking the last enemy position Captain Herman was killed and 2nd Lt. Arthur J. Fisher, the last officer remaining, led the final assault.

Despite these heavy losses, leaving private soldiers to lead squads, and in some cases platoons, Berg was cleared by midday. Only the castle remained in enemy hands, seemingly impervious to everything thrown at it. Brigadier General Colson now ordered Lt. Andrew T. Boggs's 3rd Platoon, supported by Lt. John D. Stinson's assault gun platoon, to move forward and fire directly on the castle. The 105-mm guns of the assault gun platoon, with the cooperation of the 390th Field Artillery Battalion, brought about some slackening of fire from the castle, and B Company of the 7th Armored Infantry advanced as far as the antitank ditch surrounding the building, where they were obliged to take cover from machine-gun fire, only to find themselves hopelessly up to their hips in freezing water as their predecessors of the 94th had done, and rapidly withdrew.

Another attempt was made on the castle that afternoon by Lt. Peter F. Godwin's platoon of A Troop, 88th Cavalry Reconnaissance Squadron. This time the attempt was successful; the platoon stormed the castle and took thirty-three prisoners. Once inside they realized why the position had been held so strongly, as the garrison had warm rooms, food, and liquor— unbelievable luxuries for troops used to existing for days on C rations that were so frozen that only the biscuits and candy were edible.

Task Force Poinier had destroyed five Mark IV tanks and taken seventy-two prisoners for a loss of three M-4 tanks and four halftracks, but casualties on both sides had been severe.[5]

Throughout the day Major General Malony had been under pressure for a speedy result from XX Corps, where Major General Walker reflected the impatience of his superior, General Patton, who was hoping for a quick breakthrough somewhere on his front. Now that the Battle of the Bulge was over, Patton was losing experienced formations such as the 101st Airborne and 10th Armored Divisions to the Sixth Army Group, which was having problems to the south, and receiving instead combat-weary formations in what he vaingloriously believed was a plot to deprive him of his rightful place in the forefront of a victorious campaign.

However, Walker told Malony that he was lifting all restrictions off the use of the 94th's resources and attached units, but before Malony could make use of this, Schloss Berg was reported to be in American hands. Other good news that day was the reported arrival of shoepacs (felt-lined, waterproof boots) for the troops, as frostbite and trench foot were continuing to exact a heavy toll.[6]

In anticipation of the relief of its 1st Battalion by the 1st/376th on the night of January 25, and its 2nd Battalion by its 1st Battalion early on January 26, some readjustment took place within the 302nd Infantry on the morning of January 24. L Company was returned to the 3rd Battalion and C Company to the 1st Battalion. One platoon from F Company took over Der Heidlich Hill, while the other two moved briefly into the line west of C Company before being replaced by A and B Companies.[7]

THE FIRST BATTLE OF SINZ

On the morning of January 25 General Malony issued his orders for the attack on Sinz, about a mile up the road from Butzdorf, so as to relieve the pressure on the Nennig-Berg area. To accomplish such relief, he needed to control both the village of Sinz and the Münzingen Ridge.

Colonel Hagerty's 301st Infantry, less the 3rd Battalion, were to support this operation from their position on the division's right flank while maintaining contact with the 3rd Cavalry Group on the right and the 1st/302nd on the left. The latter unit was placed under divisional control and tasked with providing direct support for the main assault. This was to be conducted by Colonel McClune's 376th Infantry, who were to seize and hold the objective while maintaining contact with the 1st/302nd before being relieved by the 2nd/302nd. Meanwhile, the men of Colonel Johnson's 302nd Infantry were to launch an attack on the left flank to clear a bridgehead for Combat Command A while covering the division's left flank on the Moselle and maintaining contact with both the 376th Infantry on the right and the 2nd Cavalry of XII Corps across the river. The armor was to pass through the 302nd Infantry and destroy all enemy tanks and installations on its way to Sinz while being prepared to repel counterattacks from the north and east. Lt. Col. William A. McNulty's 3rd/301st was to be motorized and held in reserve to meet any counterattacks.

To conduct the main assault, Colonel McClune would have his own 1st and 3rd Battalions of the 376th, plus the 2nd/302nd after their relief that night. He explained to his battalion commanders that his plan was to push through the clearing and woods to the northwest of Butzdorf with the 2nd/302nd on the right, the 3rd/376th on the left, and the 1st/376th in reserve in Monkey Wrench Woods. Lieutenant Colonel Norman's 2nd/302nd was to take Sinz, while Lieutenant Colonel Thurston's 3rd/376th crossed the Remich-Sinz highway and secured the woods of Unterste Büsch (misspelled "Untersie Busch" in most accounts) and the high ground of Rosenberg Hill beyond.

Lieutenant Colonel Miner then had his 1st/376th company commanders reconnoiter Monkey Wrench Woods and the antitank ditch just north of the upper jaw, where B and C Companies were to line up that night, while A Company occupied the southwest corner of the lower jaw. At dusk the battalion executive officer, Maj. Benjamin S. Roper, brought the troops by truck up to Besch, from where they moved off into the woods. The two assault battalions then moved into the upper jaw of Monkey Wrench Woods behind B and C Companies. During the course of the day, General Malony modified his orders for the assault, changing the objective from Sinz to the edge of the woods immediately south of the Remich-Sinz road.

The attack on Sinz was launched in a blizzard at daybreak on January 26. A platoon of the 81st Chemical Warfare Mortar Battalion laid smoke on Campholz Woods, the Butzdorf-Sinz road, and Sinz itself. Lieutenant Colonel Thurston's 3rd/376th launched its attack from the line of an antitank ditch. The engineers were supposed to have supplied ladders for the men to negotiate the ditch during the night, but neither had appeared, so the men improvised their own means with timber taken from nearby buildings. The battalion advanced in order of companies, L, K, and I. The leading elements encountered some searching artillery and mortar fire, but it was not sufficient to impede their advance. Then, as they crossed the brow of some high ground about half a mile from the line of departure, they came across a dense minefield of Schü-mines extending right across their front and flanks and were attacked by machine-gun fire that scattered the men, detonating some of the mines. The Germans then began a systematic artillery bombardment of the exposed battalion. SSgt. Salvatore Vastola selected a small team of men to accompany him as he crawled forward through the minefield to deal with a troublesome machine gun and succeeded in destroying it.

Second Lieutenant Bowyer, leading his 3rd Platoon of I Company, headed Lieutenant Colonel Thurston's 3rd/376th on the left flank. As he reached the first phase line, there was a violent explosion and he fell, having lost both feet. When others rushed to take care of him, the movement set off more Schü-mines, blowing off the men's feet or badly injuring them. Lt. Joseph Klutsch of the 2nd Platoon was similarly injured. Both officers then refused aid and directed the evacuation of the wounded from where they lay, then crawled out of the minefield and back to the forward aid station in the antitank ditch. (Bowyer was subsequently awarded the Distinguished Service Cross.)

Mine detectors and Primacord detonating cord were used unsuccessfully in an attempt to find a way through, but the battalion was trapped. A request to Regiment for tanks to clear a way through for the infantry could not be met, but Colonel McClune accepted the situation and ordered the battalion to reassemble in an area about half a mile behind its line of departure, where it would form the regimental reserve.

Lieutenant Colonel Norman's 2nd/302nd, on the right flank, attacked with E Company on the right and F Company on the left, and G Company followed six hundred yards behind. E Company's advance was slowed by machine-gun and rifle fire coming from the woods in front but, using marching fire (a continual firing of rifles as troops advance), was the first to reach the first phase line. F Company ran into the same minefield as their neighbors and experienced some casualties. The company executive officer, Lt. Maurice S. Dodge, came forward to see what was holding them up, only to step on a mine himself. Pvt. Jennings B. Petry, approaching with a prisoner, tried to rescue Dodge but detonated another mine, which temporarily blinded him, killed the German prisoner, and mortally wounded Dodge.

The engineers then brought up some Primacord to blast a way through the minefield. F Company reorganized and moved on to draw up alongside E Company, which had already reached the far edge of the woods. Artillery, mortar, and small-arms fire was now falling on the advancing troops, so the regimental cannon company was ordered to bombard the pillboxes northwest of Campholz Woods once every five minutes, as long-range automatic fire and artillery fire was clearly being directed from these positions.

As E Company drew up to the second phase line, it was ordered to dig in and await the rest of the battalion. Marching fire had proved most effective in its advance, and the woods behind were strewn with dead Germans. The rest of the battalion soon caught up and began digging positions in the frozen ground. Lieutenant Colonel Norman tried to contact the armor by radio, but failed to do so.

The blocking of the 3rd/376th's advance by the minefield had dangerously exposed the 2nd/302nd's left flank, so Lieutenant Colonel Miner's 1st/376th was ordered to take over the left flank, going through or past Lieutenant Colonel Thurston's battalion. As it approached the minefield, the 1st/376th came under heavy artillery fire, causing the men to veer off to the right and follow the 2nd/302nd's route.

Meanwhile, E and F Companies of the 2nd/302nd had spread out

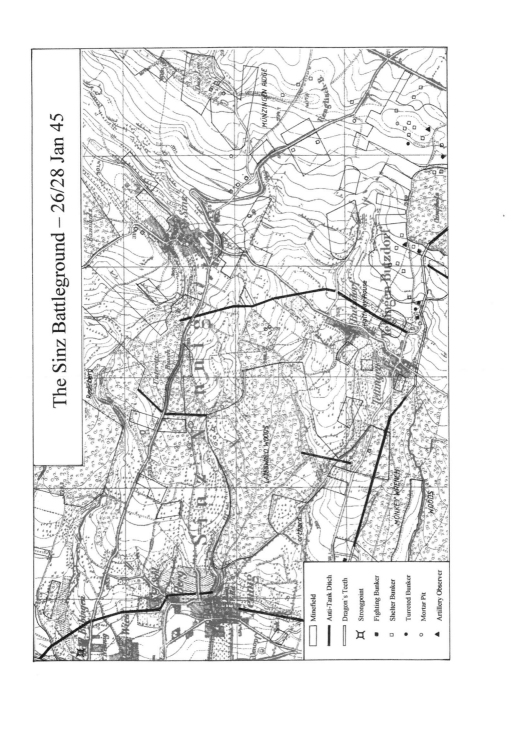

The Sinz Battleground – 26/28 Jan 45

Minefield
Anti-Tank Ditch
Dragon's Teeth
Strongpoint
Fighting Bunker
Shelter Bunker
Turreted Bunker
Mortar Pit
Artillery Observer

through the woods facing Sinz to await the arrival of the others. When three tanks were seen approaching, the poor visibility caused by the snow and undergrowth led the men to assume they were American, and the tanks were nearly on top of them before it was realized that they were German. The tanks opened fire and infantry were seen advancing with them, so the American troops pulled back to the reverse slope to avoid the direct fire. Sgt. Gilbert E. Kinyon of F Company remained, however, and fired his carbine at the leading tank. The tank operators buttoned up, thus limiting their vision, which allowed Pfc. Laverne Sinclair of E Company to disable one of its tracks with a single round at a range of twenty-five yards.

Tanks were seen in Sinz at dusk and the word was passed back. When it was confirmed that no American tanks had reached that far, the full weight of the divisional artillery was directed on the village.

Captain Griffin ran up to find his G Company withdrawing, so he ordered his men to hold their ground and sent for his bazooka teams. He then directed the fire of these teams, which resulted in one of the tanks catching fire and the third withdrawing. Artillery fire helped disperse the German infantry. The companies had to dig in under the trees, where German artillery fire brought many casualties from tree bursts.[8]

The retaking of Butzdorf was part of the overall plan and was conducted by A Company of the 1st/302nd with the support of tank destroyers. The attack was launched from the woods southwest of Tettingen and proved costly across the clear ground in full view of the German pillboxes up on Münzingen Ridge. Fire also came from Halfway House until the tank destroyers intervened with high explosive and white phosphorous shells. Lt. Samuel G. Norquist, the company's acting executive officer, greatly distinguished himself by his disregard for personal safety in the conduct of this attack and was subsequently awarded a Silver Star. Lieutenant Colonel Love, the divisional G-2, and Capt. Luis J. Flanagan, the battalion S-3 (staff officer for operations), were both wounded in front of the company command post.[9]

During these attacks, Capt. Chester B. Dadisman's A Company of the 1st/376th remained in reserve in the antitank ditch in Monkey Wrench Woods. With a view to establishing a satisfactory supply and evacuation route for his battalion, Dadisman sent out a patrol consisting of Sgt. Joseph

Sanniac and four men to check the Nennig-Tettingen road for mines. Sergeant Sanniac spotted several figures in GI overcoats on the north side of the road and sent Pfc. K. O. Kettler across a gully and into a clearing beyond to investigate. When Kettler called out, "Who is it?" the reply came back, "L Company! Get out—Germans are on three sides!" The patrol withdrew and the matter was reported to the battalion S-3, Capt. Frank Malinski, with the result that a stronger patrol was organized, accompanied by Capt. Edwin Brehio. Having identified the men through binoculars as Americans, four BAR men went forward to cover their withdrawal. Four of the L Company men had to be carried. Back at A Company, the L Company men were fed and then sent on to the aid station in Besch.

TSgt. Arnold A. Petry recounted what had happened in the seven days since Lieutenant Travers had left the orchard for Besch on the twentieth to obtain aid. The men of L Company had soon realized that Lieutenant Travers could not have made it through, but were firmly resolved not to give in, despite their hunger and thirst and constant harassment, including mortar and shellfire. The men had just one can of C rations each, the only additional food found being a thick slice of black bread, a bag of biscuits, and a can of meat taken from two dead Germans. The only way the men could obtain water was by sitting on a helmet full of snow until it melted or by moving in small groups at night to refill their water bottles at a nearby brook. Pfc. Earl Freeman had been killed by shellfire on one such detail.

They held a council of war on the third night, deciding on a breakout attempt toward Nennig. The two scouts, Pfcs. Johan A. Dresser and James E. Meneses, repeatedly came up against German outposts, so finally the group returned to its position in the orchard. Thereafter three-man patrols were sent out every night to try to find a way out, but without success. (Sergeant Petry was subsequently awarded a Silver Star.)[10]

The attack on the left flank on January 26 was launched at 0700 by Colonel Johnson's 302nd Infantry, which had only its 3rd Battalion and the 2nd/376th under command. They were supported by Task Force Goodrich, consisting of the remains of the 7th Armored Infantry and Capt. Odin Brendengen's A Company of the 18th Tank Battalion. During the night A Company of the 53rd Armored Engineer Battalion, supported by A Troop of the 88th Reconnaissance Squadron, had gone forward to bridge two identified anti-tank ditches that lay across the line of advance and to clear mines on the approach route. Only the first ditch had been bridged and the route to it cleared before the attack began. Consequently, when Task Force Goodrich attacked, its advance was held up by the second antitank ditch and forced to halt under heavy artillery and mortar fire along with Lieutenant Colonel Cloudt's accompanying 3rd/302nd.

After repelling a brief counterattack by enemy tanks, Task Force Goodrich withdrew at nightfall to Nennig for the tanks to replenish their supplies of fuel and ammunition in preparation for resuming the attack the next morning, leaving the 3rd/302nd to hold the line. Meanwhile, Lieutenant Colonel Martin's 2nd/376th attacked from the line of Wies-Berg to the Remich-Sinz highway, but Captain Heath's G Company, on the far left, was checked by heavy fire coming from the direction of Schloss Bübingen and forced back into Wies. Captain Darrah's E Company, on the battalion's right, hit an antipersonnel minefield after progressing only one hundred yards. When his men hesitated, Lt. Arthur Dodson called on them to follow him and led them through safely. As E Company approached an open-topped hill, it came under fire from several machine guns, forcing the company to halt with both flanks exposed. Sgt. Gerald W. Jende spotted another machine-gun team setting up behind them and killed both gunners with two well-aimed shots from his rifle. E Company remained pinned down until Lieutenant Colonel Cloudt's 3rd/302nd, which had had a difficult time breaking through heavy enemy resistance east of Nennig, caught up on E Company's right and came under the same machine-gun fire. E Company then made a desperate and costly rush for the enemy positions ahead of it, which resulted in the capture of two machine guns and twenty-nine prisoners.

As E Company reached the Remich-Sinz road, three German tanks appeared, prompting the company to drop back 150 yards to line up with the 3rd/302nd. Artillery support was called for but fell on the American positions in error, resulting in many casualties. The troops were then told to dig in for the night.[11]

In Colonel McClune's 376th Infantry's central sector on January 27, Lieutenant Colonel Miner's 1st/376th attacked in conjunction with Lieutenant Colonel Norman's 2nd/302nd to occupy the Unterste Büsch Woods and the high ground around it. As B and C Companies of the 1st/376th moved off, A Company occupied their vacated positions to protect the attack's left flank. E and G Companies of the 2nd/302nd bypassed F Company and pushed forward to the far edge of the woods, where they came under enemy sniper and artillery fire, which took a heavy toll.

Lieutenant Thurston's 3rd/376th moved up to an alert position behind their 1st Battalion. The battalion then deployed into three separate company locations in such a way as to be able to meet enemy attacks from any direction. While occupying these positions, and during the coldest night they had experienced, the battalion was instructed to absorb one hundred replacements who were already on their way. Thurston protested at the impracticality of taking on these men in such circumstances but was overruled. Within thirty-six hours all but forty of them had been either killed or evacuated for various reasons.

Meanwhile, B and C Companies of the 1st/376th came up to some barbed-wire entanglements two hundred yards south of the Remich-Sinz highway. Lieutenant Colonel Miner then realized that the assault companies of Lieutenant Colonel Norman's 2nd/302nd had yet to appear, leaving his right flank exposed. Miner therefore ordered Captain Dadisman to bring his A Company up to the right rear to cover against any possible counterattack from that direction as the assault companies continued to work their way forward, mopping up as they went.

When the assault companies reached the highway, they each delegated a squad to go forward into Unterste Büsch Woods, where they were met by ferocious enemy fire coming from three concealed tanks and their escorting infantry. Lt. William Bendure of B Company and Sergeant Ackerman of C Company were hit. One squad got so close to a concealed tank that it could not depress its main gun sufficiently to engage them. Lt. William Ring, also with the leading troops, fired six bazooka rounds at one tank, all of which were deflected by the dense undergrowth. The survivors were obliged to withdraw across the road, and the companies pulled back behind a slight fold in the ground that provided them with some protection from the automatic fire, but not from the heavy mortar, rocket, and artillery fire that was directed on them as they awaited the arrival of the tanks from Nennig. Lieutenant Cornelius took over B Company when Captain Duckworth was hit.[12]

The attack from Nennig was launched at 0915 that day (January 27), with Lt. Col. William A. McNulty's 3rd/301st passing through Lieutenant Colonel Cloudt's 3rd/302nd in a vigorous attack backed by Capt. Russell D. Miller's B Company of the 18th Tank Battalion. The engineers had erected a bridge across the second antitank ditch during the night, but the Germans had placed an antitank gun to block it. The first tank to approach the bridge was knocked out by this 88-mm gun, and another got stuck in the ditch. When Captain Miller sought an alternate passage, he found fifteen German tanks lying in ambush. A tank battle then ensued in which the novice American tankers knocked out four Mark IV tanks, the antitank gun at the bridge, and an antiaircraft gun engaged against them. By noon the Remich-Sinz highway had been crossed, and the tanks and 7th Armored Infantry of Combat Command A were able to follow through up the main axis on Sinz.

The converging attack on Sinz from the south did not go as planned, as Lieutenant Colonel Miner's 1st/376th clashed with a simultaneous German counterattack, leaving Lieutenant Colonel Norman's 2nd/302nd to go on alone. As they emerged from the woods, Captain Griffin of G Company was hit by enemy shellfire, so the company executive officer, Lt. Peter R. Kelly, took over the command, but was killed almost immediately. Lieutenant Colonel Norman was also wounded and was relieved by his executive officer, Major Maixner. The leading elements paused at the antitank ditch to enable the others to catch up and then continued on using marching fire.

At about 1300 the leading tanks were seen approaching the open ground south of the highway from the woods southwest of Sinz. Lieutenant Colonel Miner then ordered his A Company to move to the left and attack Unterste Büsch Woods and Sinz in conjunction with the tanks. The whole 1st/376th crossed into the Unterste Büsch Woods, where the Germans who were hiding there either surrendered or fled back to Sinz. The battalion then took up a perimeter defense of the woods with C Company on the left and B Company facing Sinz. A Company detached a platoon to C Company to enable the latter to extend their line to Lieutenant Colonel Cloudt's 3rd/302nd on the far side of the clearing from Unterste Büsch Woods, but otherwise remained in reserve in the woods south of the highway.

The order then arrived for the 1st/376th to attack Sinz from their present position in conjunction with an attack from the south by Lieutenant Colonel Norman's 2nd/302nd. Lieutenant Colonel Miner organized his battalion for the forthcoming attack with B Company on the left and A Company on the right and liaised with the tanks.

The attack planned on Sinz was to be given maximum support from the divisional artillery. The high ground of the Münzinger Ridge above the town would be smoked out to deprive the enemy artillery observers and machine gunners of their view, while Sinz and the pillboxes southeast of the village would receive a ten-minute preparation immediately before the attack. A battery would then fire on the pillboxes every two minutes. However, by early afternoon the tanks were running out of ammunition and gasoline, so Colonel Goodrich sent in A Company to take over the battle. A Company pushed forward to the edge of the woods overlooking Sinz and provided supporting fire for the 2nd/302nd's attack, until it too began running out of fuel and ammunition and was replaced by Capt. Paul R. Halderson's D Company.

The Germans counterattacked with tanks and infantry. A and B Companies moved back to the antitank ditch and joined in the heavy fire coming from the Sherman tanks on the highway, eventually forcing the Germans to withdraw. The battalion's next task was to sweep the Unterste Büsch Woods clear of the enemy, which was accomplished without difficulty.

Lt. James P. Bolinger then led D Company of the 18th Tank Battalion into Sinz, where he destroyed a Mark IV tank, only to have his own tank knocked out by a Panzerfaust. He then transferred to another tank to continue the fight. By nightfall the 18th Tank Battalion had had six Shermans destroyed and another four disabled. The men of the 7th Armored Infantry were then called forward to help clear Sinz.

An American tank that had been firing up the main street in Sinz mistook some men of G Company, 2nd/302nd, for the enemy and inflicted several casualties before TSgt. Edward P. Regan could reach the tank and bang on the turret with his rifle butt to attract the crew's attention. Meanwhile, E Company crawled up the ditch alongside the highway to get to suitable positions from where the men could fire on the nearest buildings. Pvt. James Guerrier responded to sniper fire coming from a barn by standing up and firing a light machine gun from the hip, his tracers setting fire to the hay in the barn. When his ammunition ran out, he obtained two more belts from a tank and fired at the Germans who were trying to escape from the burning barn. (Guerrier was later awarded a Silver Star for this exploit.)

A tank hidden inside a haystack held up G Company until Pfc. Edward D. Yewell set the hay on fire with a bazooka round fired at close range. Pvt. Clifford R. Macumber was the first man into Sinz. He tossed a grenade into the nearest house, then took eleven prisoners from it. SSgt. Michael Wichic tackled the second house, using a phosphorous grenade to quell the fire coming from a second-storey window, thus killing one sniper and wounding another. He then led his squad into the village and was killed by a burst of machine-gun fire. (Wichic, too, received a Silver Star.)

Lt. Harry J. Lewies of E Company, 2nd/302nd, took charge in Sinz, but had no radio or wire communication back to the battalion command post, so two volunteers, Pfcs. Mark D. Atchinson and Orleane A. Jacobson, donned snowsuits taken from the prisoners and headed back at dusk, noting the location of the wounded as they went. After reporting on the situation in Sinz, they returned with litter parties and assisted with the evacuation of the wounded, Jacobson himself becoming wounded in the process.

Major Maixner now found that his two companies in Sinz were both down to half strength, and his reserve company had been reduced to sixty effectives (able-bodied soldiers). He reported this to Colonel McClune, who had rifles issued to the regimental antitank company and sent them forward as reinforcements. McClune also sent some halftracks to help evacuate the wounded from Sinz. The news then came through that the 1st/376th would be relieved that evening by Lieutenant Colonel Thurston's 3rd/376th. This relief was completed by 2100, but the 1st/376th came under heavy artillery fire as it moved out and suffered more casualties.

Plans were also under way for the 7th Armored Infantry Battalion, which had been placed under the temporary command of the 376th Infantry, to cooperate with the 2nd Battalion in an attack to secure the whole of Sinz the next day. However, early on January 28 the loan of the 8th Armored Division's Combat Command A to the 94th Infantry Division came to an end and the armor and their escorting infantry were withdrawn.

It was clear that Sinz could not be held without armored support, so Lieutenant Colonel Norman's 2nd/302nd was instructed to pull back into the woods southwest of the village and organize a new defensive position before daybreak. Meanwhile, B Company of the 7th Armored Infantry provided protection for the disabled American armor until it could be recovered from the village, and spent the morning of the twenty-eighth fending off German counterattacks with the 2nd/302nd. In this attack on Sinz Combat Command A had suffered 23 men killed and 268 wounded, most of them from the 7th Armored Infantry, in just two days of combat.[13]

General Walker now ordered the 94th Infantry Division to rest and reorganize, but also to maintain battalion-sized attacks to keep the enemy pinned down. General Malony instructed his regimental commanders to hold and consolidate the ground they had gained while planning how they would continue the offensive once the newly arrived reinforcements had been integrated into their units. He also used the opportunity to untangle the various battalions from attachments to other regiments. So by January 30 the division was redeployed with the 301st Infantry on the left flank and the 302nd on the right, each with its battalions in the order 1st, 3rd, 2nd, and with the 376th Infantry in reserve.

While the division's reshuffle was still incomplete, on January 29 Captain Woods's B Company of the 1st/302nd was ordered to seize the southeastern tip of Campholz Woods. The task was executed by Lt. Edwin R. Bloom's 2nd Platoon without difficulty, and the position, together with Borg, Butzdorf, and Tettingen, was taken over by the 2nd/302nd.[14]

In the meantime, General Patton was going through a period of intense frustration. He was unable to persuade his superiors, Lt. Gen. Omar N. Bradley and Gen. Dwight Eisenhower, of the need to push on despite the fatigue and understrength state of the American ground forces at this stage. In addition, his plan for an attack by XII Corps on Trier in early February was squashed when Bradley refused to provide any armored support. Patton then set off on a tour of his subordinate formations, and on January 30 General Walker told General Malony to get "as many senior officers and unit commanders down to noncoms of each company that could be assembled without too much trouble" at the reserve position in Veckring by 1430 that day.[15]

Patton first called on the division's headquarters in Sierck-les-Bains, France, with Walker and told Malony and his staff that the 94th was the only division in his army whose nonbattle casualties exceeded its battle casualties. This was not in fact correct, and the failure to provide adequate shoepacs and other winter clothing and equipment was the responsibility of his Third Army staff, but these were matters that one could hardly address with Patton in person.

Patton and Walker went on to visit the officers and NCOs assembled at Veckring, where Patton began by complimenting them on doing a good job. However, he then attacked them on the subject of nonbattle casualties and the number of prisoners lost to the enemy, saying, "This division has had the dishonor of having more men surrender than either of the First and

Third Armies which I have commanded." At one point during his visit to the division, Patton threatened General Malony with relieving him of his post, but then, before leaving, he said: "You're doing fine otherwise—but Goddammit, do something about those slackers." Patton also rebuked Lieutenant Colonel Miner for having dirt on the badge of rank on his helmet. (Patton insisted that all officers and NCOs in his army wear badges of rank on their helmets, thus clearly identifying them to enemy snipers.)[16]

Battalion rest areas were now established in order to give the troops a chance to wash and get warm. For example, Pillingerhof, near Borg, was where the 1st/302nd provided a place for its men to relax out of the line, as Lieutenant Colonel Thurston had previously done at Besch. But conditions remained harsh in the line with the continuing cold, wet weather, and the clothing of many of the men was in tatters after so much hard use. The water level was barely three inches below the surface in the sector occupied by the 3rd/301st, so the trenches and foxholes were constantly filling with water. XX Corps now ordered a resumption of limited-objective attacks in which the forces employed were not to exceed one regimental combat team.[17]

SCHLOSS BÜBINGEN

Schloss Bübingen was selected as the first objective under the new rules of engagement. Located close to where the Remich-Sinz highway crossed with the Moselle valley highway immediately north of Wies, the Schloss had long been suspected of providing a major artillery observer post and forming-up position for enemy attacks. The task of taking the castle was given to the reconstituted 1st/301st's A Company, which was given a self-propelled 155-mm gun from XX Corps's 558th Field Artillery Battalion for close support.

After the usual artillery preparation, Lt. Harrison H. Walker led A Company's 2nd Platoon into the attack from Wies. The 155-mm gun advanced to within 150 yards of the castle before beginning to fire at its massive stone walls. Lieutenant Walker took his platoon to assault the castle gate on the right, while TSgt. George Montgomery took the 1st Platoon to the left. Walker and his men were met by a hail of automatic fire, wounding him and holding up most of the platoon, but five men managed to get in and were then trapped in a room by enemy soldiers who were holding the building.

The 1st Platoon also came under heavy machine-gun fire and had to take cover against a blank wall of the castle, which they decided to breach. Explosives were sent for, and while they were waiting the men tried using the satchel charge, two beehive charges,[18] and even a bazooka, but to no effect. Eventually Sgt. Joseph C. Castanzo of A Company, 319th Field Engineers, appeared and supervised the setting of the selected charge. Because this group was under intense fire, it took about four hours before the charge could be detonated. The blast caused the castle wall to buckle and collapse, trapping several enemy soldiers in the castle cellars. Armed respectively with an M1 rifle, a flamethrower, and a BAR, Sgt. Harry Schmidt, Pfc. B. D. Tabel, and Pfc. A. Bullard stormed in, surprising and overwhelming a machine-gun crew. They then moved on from room to room, killing or capturing the enemy as they went. A radio operator was killed at his set and forty-two prisoners were taken. The presence of other Germans in the cellars was then detected, and when they refused to surrender, a bangalore torpedo was thrust through a basement window to finish them off.[19] A Company then secured the castle in anticipation of a counterattack, which came shortly afterward and was repulsed.[20]

CAMPHOLZ WOODS

The next objective was Campholz Woods, whose prominent position on the forward brow of the Münzingen Ridge dominated the front between Tettingen and Oberleuken and the Perl-Saarburg highway and was now occupied by panzergrenadiers of the 11th Panzer Division.

Lt. Col. Francis H. Dohs's 2nd Battalion of the 301st Infantry Regiment now had two platoons of G Company in Butzdorf and its 3rd Platoon in Tettingen, from where they were under close observation from the German pillboxes on the ridge to the northeast and constantly subject to mortar fire. Lt. Richard H. Myers's 1st Platoon was subsequently detailed to destroy these enemy positions. Their first attempt failed when the platoon ran into a minefield in the dark, and Myers and four men were injured. In a second attempt the following night, under TSgt. Tom R. Parkinson, the platoon and some men of A Company, 319th Combat Engineer Battalion, managed to approach the blind side of the main bunker undetected under cover of a mortar bombardment. Once they were in striking distance, they directed machine-gun fire at the bunker's observation slits to keep them closed, while the engineers put a sixty-foot bangalore torpedo into position to clear a path through the minefield. The position was then taken using satchel charges and grenades.

However, the main enemy positions on the Münzingen Ridge in and around Campholz Woods remained a constant threat and obstacle. On the night of January 31 Lt. Joseph E. Glover of the battalion's intelligence and reconnaissance section led a party of eleven men to try to locate the minefields that were known to be contained in that area. They got as far as the antitank ditch running through the center of the woods without encountering any mines, but on their return journey they bumped into an enemy patrol. Tech-5 John J. Centrello was killed and four others were captured before the remaining men were able to disengage and return to their own lines.

Lieutenant Robinson's C Company, which had been resting at Pillingerhof, was then delegated the task of taking Campholz Woods. The company marched to Borg, where the men picked up prepared demolition charges and then set off in single file with Captain Woodburn and 1st Sgt. Jerome Eisler of A Company leading. The company crossed the open ground to the woods without incident and then formed up for the assault with the 2nd Platoon on the left, the light machine-gun section in the center, and the 3rd Platoon on the right, while the 1st Platoon took up the reserve position in the rear.

The company moved off at 0800, and within minutes TSgt. James L. King rounded up five German prisoners, including an officer. This was an artillery observation group that had been occupying a large foxhole and was equipped with two radios. The company soon discovered that the woods were heavily mined and took some casualties. By 1000 the company reached a communication trench running parallel to the track that cut across the center of the woods. Offering the only cover, the trench was only three feet deep and had a foot of water in it. The company then came under a fierce rocket, artillery, and mortar bombardment, which was to continue all day and into the night. Casualties were heavy, especially from tree bursts (shells exploding in treetops), and four men were killed by direct hits. That night B Company arrived and took over the eastern half of the woods south of the communication trench.

It was planned to continue the attack to take the rest of the woods the next morning, February 2, so Lt. Charles F. Ehrenberg of the 301st Field Artillery arranged for a ten-minute preparation on the antitank ditch, beginning at 0850. As the infantry waited for the signal to advance, German mortar and artillery fire continued to fall on and behind them.

The antitank ditch proved a formidable obstacle for the infantry, being about twelve feet across and twenty feet deep, with a muddy bottom. In emerging from the ditch, SSgt. Jack Cox came face-to-face with one of four machine guns that had been hastily set up to confront the attack. He promptly shot one of the machine gunners, wounded another, and took the third one prisoner.

B Company's 3rd Platoon swung to the right to take a large pillbox, then hesitated when the leading NCO was killed. Captain Woods found the platoon deployed around this pillbox but making no headway, so he had the men seal the firing ports and had a beehive charge detonated on one of them. A white phosphorous grenade was then introduced through the hole, and shortly afterward a German captain and the other fifteen occupants surrendered. This six-room pillbox was then taken over as B Company's command post.

The 1st and 3rd Platoons continued their advance to the northern edge of the woods, and SSgt. Stanley K. Jurek's 2nd Platoon was brought up from reserve position to fill the line between them. Meanwhile, as C Company cleared the northwestern portion of the woods, they encountered many antipersonnel mines that slowed progress, but by 1200 the men had taken two pillboxes and seventy-five prisoners to add to the fifty taken by B Company. These prisoners were then used as litter bearers to evacuate the wounded.

A Company moved up under cover of darkness to relieve C Company, a task that was not completed until 0400 on February 3. Because of an oversight, a captured bunker that the Germans had been using as an observation post over the Tettingen-Pillingerhof area was omitted from the handover, and the Germans reoccupied it before daylight.

Lt. Carl J. Baumgaertner and a patrol of four men managed to take another bunker some three hundred yards northwest of the woods during the early hours, tracing it through the fog and darkness by the sound of voices coming from it. The patrol closed up to the bunker and threw a grenade, after which Baumgaertner called out in perfect German to tell the men inside that they were surrounded and should surrender, or a flamethrower

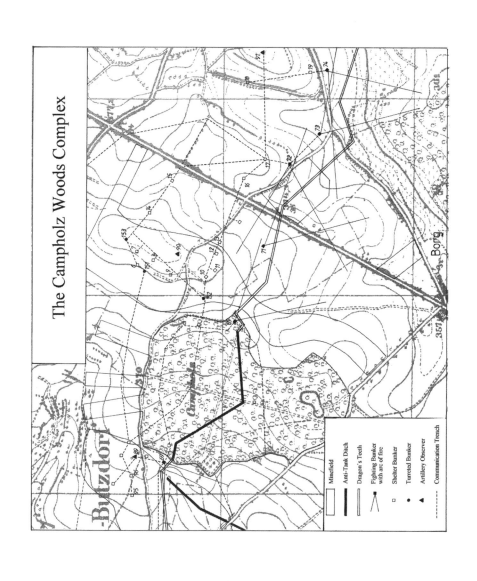

The Campholz Woods Complex

would be used. In fact the patrol had no flamethrower, but thirteen German soldiers surrendered without further ado.

A and B Companies held the position throughout February 3. Captain Wood's command post pillbox was surrounded by mines and was so close to a German mortar position that the Germans lobbed a bomb across every time they heard the metal bunker door being used, on one occasion actually getting a bomb inside. However, the mortar position gave itself away with the muzzle flash and was eliminated by an artillery barrage. On the night of February 3 there was a report of a wounded man in a minefield near the antitank ditch. The soldier sent from the command post to assist the medics in evacuating the wounded man stepped on a Schü-mine and was killed, and the man who was already wounded was injured yet again along with three others. Tech-3 John Asmussen called for more help and managed to get all four wounded to the pillbox, where he treated them by candlelight, saving the lives of the two who were the worst wounded. (Asmussen was later awarded the Silver Star for this action.)

C Company returned to relieve B Company on February 4. Despite the battalion's success in taking Campholz Woods, Lieutenant Colonel Hosea was relieved of his command that day and was replaced by Maj. Warren F. Stanion. Captain Woods became battalion executive officer, and Lt. Joseph Wancio took over B Company.

Lieutenant Baumgaertner was in action again at 2300 that night with a team from A Company to retake the important observation post bunker that the Germans had reoccupied. This bunker was so sited that it was impossible to approach unobserved, and the patrol was easily beaten back. When Baumgaertner returned to report his lack of success, he was informed that he would have to try again at 0400 with his whole platoon, even though the company was due to be relieved that night. The second attack was supported by a heavy artillery preparation, followed by a vicious exchange of hand grenades at ten yards, but the platoon was still unable to break in and had to withdraw with its wounded, leaving the dead behind.

The battalion supply officer, Lt. Joseph F. Concannon, and his assistant, Sgt. Robert H. Fluch, borrowed some halftracks from the 465th Antiaircraft Artillery Battalion to enable them to resupply the forward companies in Campholz Woods from Borg by day. This was risky business, as the route was under enemy observation and fire. At night they used a Weasel (a small tracked supply vehicle) to bring up hot food for the troops.

Another attempt was made on the observation post bunker at 1700 on February 5, this time by C Company after they had exchanged positions with B Company and with the support of some men of B Company, 319th Engineer Combat Battalion. The 301st Field Artillery began by providing a fifteen-minute preparation, but after five minutes this had to be lifted as it was so concentrated and so close to their own attacking troops that it was beginning to affect them. Again the enemy resistance was ferocious, and freshly laid Schü-mines hampered the attack, inflicting so many casualties that the attempt was called off and the men withdrew to the woods.

That night Major Stanion's exhausted 1st/302nd was relieved by Major Maixner's 2nd/302nd, who, after suffering a mauling in the battle for Sinz, had been recuperating on the division's extreme right flank with their command post in Wehingen and companies deployed in the villages of Nohn and Unter-Tünsdorf. From there the battalion's E and G Companies had carried out unsuccessful attempts to take pillboxes in front of Orscholz in such extreme weather conditions that on one occasion their rifles had frozen up and refused to function.

Major Maixner now deployed his battalion, with E Company on the left and G Company on the right. He placed H Company's heavy machine guns in the woods in support of the forward companies and the 81-mm mortars in support of Butzdorf. He also had engineers clear and mark more paths through the woods. His most important task was to secure the observation post bunker that had resisted all previous attempts to retake it. For this he decided to use two assault teams. Lt. Charles A. Hunter of F Company was to take fourteen men and make a feint from Tettingen, while a group from F Company would attack west from the edge of Campholz Woods.

The attack was launched early on February 7, but F Company was immediately checked by a heavy bombardment on its position. Lieutenant Hunter's platoon started off at 0645 in a fast advance that surprised the defenders of the first bunker (see map 9) and took thirty-three prisoners. The prisoners were sent back under guard, and another two men were left to hold the captured bunker as the rest pushed on, only to come up against fierce resistance. When a shell killed two and wounded four of the small group, they decided to withdraw but then stumbled upon another bunker that yielded a further thirteen prisoners.

When Major Maixner, who was in Tettingen with his artillery liaison officer, Capt. Clair H. Stevens, was informed of how the two bunkers had been taken, he ordered part of E Company to leave Campholz Woods and join him in Tettingen as soon as possible. E Company brought their platoons by truck to Wochern and marched the rest of the way. They then worked their platoons forward to the newly captured bunkers. The expected artillery preparation failed to materialize, so they pushed on without it and by nightfall had taken yet another bunker. A patrol was sent back to establish wire communications with Battalion, and they were told they would be relieved by F Company and were then to return to Borg.

The Germans had now been in reoccupation of the observation post bunker for five days, and Division was adamant that it had to be taken at all costs. Major Maixner decided to use C Company for the next attempt, so he relieved them in Campholz Woods, with Lieutenant Lewies's platoon and the battalion ammunition and pioneer platoon armed as riflemen.

Captain James W. Griffin had only thirty-four men left in G Company, but was joined by a few engineers equipped with flamethrowers and demolition charges. Lt. Ralph E. Ginsburg's 1st Platoon was to circle the objective and attack it from the north, while elements of the 2nd Platoon under SSgt. Arthur Ernst were to approach from the east by means of the communication trench that connected the woods with the observation post. The remaining men of the 2nd Platoon, together with the 3rd Platoon, were to move farther west and tackle the other enemy positions supporting the observation post bunker.

Lt. Douglas A. Barrow, commanding the H Company mortar platoon, suggested that he put a two- to three-minute preparation down on the known enemy mortar positions, followed by a one-minute pause and another three-minute preparation, because the enemy were known to take shelter in their bunkers as soon as they were shelled and would return as soon as the shelling ceased. Barrow's suggestion was adopted and used successfully.

G Company's attack went according to plan on February 8. Sgt. James E. Clark led his 1st Platoon in the final rush to take the objective, which yielded only four uninjured prisoners, but the view from the bunker showed how valuable the position had been to the enemy and how important it was to neutralize it. The group operating farther out to the west captured one pillbox without a fight, and the 3rd Platoon's objective turned out to be an unoccupied gun position. Lt. Oliver K. Smith took out a patrol to reconnoiter the area, including the draw to the north that led down toward Butz-dorf, but found no enemy. G Company then dug in and consolidated its position around the captured bunkers.

Lt. James W. Porter of B Company, 319th Combat Engineers, arrived late that afternoon with some of his men to demolish the newly captured positions, but his group stumbled on an antipersonnel minefield and tripped a Schü-mine that injured three of the engineers. Tech-5 Robert Cole led a rescue party to their assistance, and a second mine went off, temporarily blinding Cole and wounding an aid man and Private First Class Curi. When the men called for help, Lieutenant Porter led a second party to their aid and removed three of the wounded from the minefield, including Cole, without further incident. Lieutenant Porter, Pfc. Weldon J. McCormack, and an aid man went back into the minefield in the gathering gloom and placed another wounded man on a litter, but the aid man inadvertently detonated another mine, killing himself and wounding Lieutenant Porter and another man who had volunteered to help. Although he was nearly exhausted, McCormack then carried these two wounded men to safety before going back for Curi and carrying him out some fifty yards to a cleared path where litter bearers were waiting. (McCormack was later awarded a Silver Star for this deed.)

When General Malony informed General Walker that Campholz Woods was now securely in American hands, Walker congratulated him and asked him to "congratulate your people down there for me too."[21]

5
The Second Battle of Sinz

General Malony remained frustrated by the failure to crack the Orscholz Switch, so he called a conference of his staff and regimental commanders on February 3 to discuss plans for future operations within the limitation of regimental size imposed upon him by General Walker. The result of this conference was the issue of Field Order Number 10 (as outlined below). The defeat at Sinz still rankled, so the next objective was set as Sinz and the adjacent Bannholz Woods. If this strike succeeded, it would be followed by another regimental-sized attack on Münzingen Ridge and the hamlet of Münzingen, coupled with an attack on the village of Oberleuken, thus providing an opportunity to roll up the eastern end of the Orscholz Switch. Starting on February 7 the 301st Infantry would take on the Sinz-Bannholz attack, the 376th Infantry would conduct the Münzingen Ridge attack, and the 302nd Infantry would handle the Oberleuken attack.

General Walker visited the 94th Infantry Division headquarters on February 5 and approved the plan. Shortly afterward, however, General Malony discovered that the 704th Tank Destroyer Battalion was being taken from him on February 8, leaving him only the 774th Tank Destroyer Battalion in support and seriously weakening his striking ability for the forthcoming attacks. Checking on this situation, Brigadier General Collier, the XX Corps chief of staff, said that the 704th was being moved on Patton's orders but that its departure could be delayed until February 9 or 10 and that the 748th Tank Destroyer Battalion would be replacing the 704th.

The beginning of February was a particularly miserable time for the troops in the line. It started raining on February 2 and continued doing so for the next ten days, turning their foxholes into icy-cold mud baths. For many their clothes were in tatters, and there was still a dearth of shoepacs, so trench foot was prevalent.

During the period of relative quiet from January 31 to February 6, Colonel Hagerty's 301st Infantry held the line from Schloss Bübingen to Tettingen-Butzdorf and took the opportunity to make a detailed study of the ground in front of the battalion positions for the forthcoming attack on Sinz and Bannholz Woods. Hagerty's plan involved using all three battalions in line for the assault. On the left flank, Major Hodges's 1st Battalion was to seize the high ground seven hundred yards beyond its present position. In the center, Lieutenant Colonel McNulty's 3rd Battalion was to secure the Remich-Sinz highway as the main supply route to Sinz by pushing farther north, while on the right Lieutenant Colonel Dohs's 2nd Battalion was to push through and secure both Sinz and the Bannholz Woods beyond.

Sinz, a village of about one hundred buildings, lay in a hollow below the Münzingen Ridge, with Bannholz Woods crowning the high ground to the immediate north. The nearest covered approaches ended some one thousand yards from the village, either in the Unterste Büsch Woods due west, or southwest in the woods north of Butzdorf. The draw in which the village lay hooked around to the west and north toward Unterste Büsch Woods, where it became marshy with occasional clumps of shrubs, but otherwise the landscape was bare and shorn of cover.

The artillery fire plan for the operation was based on a series of progressive phase lines, on which the forward observers with the infantry could call for fire as they advanced. Once the final phase line had been crossed, the forward observers could call for protective barrages and emergency concentrations.

Lt. Col. Hal S. Whitely's 356th Field Artillery was to cover Sinz and the Remich-Sinz highway, and Lieutenant Colonel Morrow's 301st Field Artillery would be responsible for specifically timed fire on Sinz. Lt. Col. James M. Caviness's 919th Field Artillery was to engage Adenholz Woods, while Lt. Col. Robert G. Crandall's 390th Field Artillery would crater Bannholz Woods with delayed-fuse shells. The 301st Infantry's own cannon company would lay fire on the southern edge of Bannholz Woods, and the 376th's cannon company would engage the pillboxes southeast of Sinz. B Company of the 81st Chemical Warfare Mortar Battalion was to provide smoke south of Bannholz Woods before H-hour, then shift to the north-

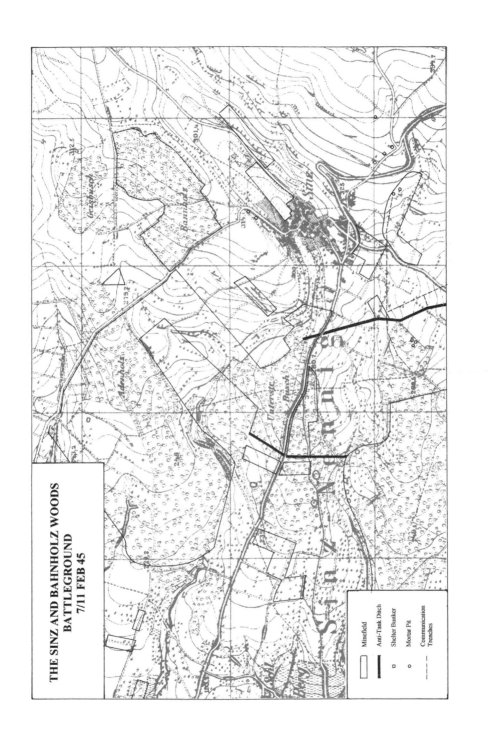

THE SINZ AND BAHNHOLZ WOODS
BATTLEGROUND
7/11 FEB 45

Minefield
Anti-Tank Ditch
Shelter Bunker
Mortar Pit
Communication Trenches

west of the woods. The chemical mortars were also to fire white phosphorus bombs at the Münzingen Ridge east of Sinz.

The 301st Infantry's attack was launched at 0700 on February 7. On the left flank, Major Hodges's 1st Battalion had no problem gaining its objective by 0802, and Lieutenant Colonel McNulty's 3rd Battalion also gained its objective by 0945, despite Capt. Charles W. Donovan's I Company losing some casualties to a minefield. The Remich-Sinz highway was thus secured as the main line of supply and communication. The difficulties arose on the right flank.

Lieutenant Colonel Dohs proposed using F and G Companies for his assault on Sinz and Bannholz Woods, with E Company in reserve. G Company would provide a section of heavy machine guns for each of the assault companies, who would also have the battalion's 81-mm mortars at their disposal. Lt. William W. Schofield's antitank platoon was earmarked for the defense of Bannholz Woods, and a special "commando" team formed from the intelligence and reconnaissance platoon was to assist G Company in clearing up Sinz. E Company would hold itself ready to assist either of the assault companies on order. In addition, a platoon of A Company, 704th Tank Destroyer Battalion, and the 2nd Platoon of the regimental antitank company were available to deal with any enemy armor that might be encountered.

The 2nd/301st had left Wochern early on the morning of February 7 by truck for Nennig via Besch. From there the assault companies marched to their forward assembly areas through a pitch-black night. Capt. Charles H. Sinclair's F Company headed for Unterste Büsch Woods, while Lt. Knox L. Scales's G Company, with part of the Headquarters Company, moved east from Nennig in column of twos along a muddy trail, each man holding on to the person in front of him under a steady fall of rain.

With a misty dawn came the thunderous crash of the artillery preparation, and the infantry moved forward. The engineers had set up two footbridges across the antitank ditch in front of G Company's position. TSgt. Tom Parkinson led his 1st Platoon straight for Sinz, while TSgt. George E. Babcock led his 2nd Platoon north, parallel to the antitank ditch at first, to hit the highway near the first house in the village. Lt. Arthur A. Christiansen's 3rd Platoon followed up in close reserve. These platoons had just crossed the footbridges when a heavy German barrage fell on their line of departure behind them, inflicting numerous casualties on the weapons platoon and the commandos, seven of whom were lost to one tree burst alone.

Sergeant Parkinson's platoon came under fire while still seventy-five yards from the village but continued using marching fire. A minefield was encountered and easily avoided as the mines had been exposed by the rain and thaw. Then came an enemy artillery barrage. The platoon took its first building, but further progress was blocked by heavy machine-gun fire. Sgt. Joseph Rencavage then took his squad in a flanking movement to subdue the machine guns, which was achieved with the use of grenades and bazookas, enabling the platoon to continue its advance.

Sergeant Babcock's platoon moved forward rapidly to reach the village's main street, taking three casualties from a sniper behind them, who was killed soon after by the commandos coming up from the rear. The silencing of the German machine guns enabled the platoon to continue down the left-hand side of the street until two men were killed by submachine-gun fire from across the street and more fire came from a large building in front, checking the advance. Lieutenant Scales then arrived with his artillery forward observer, 2nd Lt. Sylvester M. Beyer of the 356th Field Artillery. Beyer called for a concentration on the building in question, which was then stormed, yielding about thirty prisoners, and its cellar was taken over as the company command post. The accuracy of the American artillery fire was demonstrated here as Lieutenant Beyer stayed up with the infantry, calling for fire on each house in turn as they came to it. The 2nd Platoon went on to clear its section of the village and took another forty prisoners in the process.

Captain Sinclair's F Company, with the 1st and 2nd Platoons leading, moved off on Bannholz Woods at 0700 in order to prevent the enemy from reinforcing Sinz from that direction. As Sinclair's men approached the woods, they came under German artillery fire. The 2nd Platoon, with the attached heavy machine-gun section, took up positions on the western corner of the woods, while the 1st Platoon moved to the eastern flank and the 3rd Platoon, accompanied by Sinclair and Lt. Henry J. Smythe, the forward observer from the 356th Field Artillery, passed through the middle to occupy the northern part. Smythe called for the fire to be lifted on his second phase line, only to be told that it was not his guns that were firing—it was German artillery fire.

Visibility in the woods was poor as a result of the smoke laid by the 81st Chemical Warfare Mortar Battalion coming down off the Münzingen Ridge and filtering through the dense undergrowth. The 3rd Platoon stumbled upon two tanks of the 4th Panzer Company hidden in the undergrowth, and a bazooka team consisting of Pfcs. Curtis C. Darnell and Ernest Atencio worked forward to within thirty yards of the nearest tank before opening fire. The first round was a hit, and the tank started to withdraw. The second round was also a hit, but the tank kept moving, and then the second tank started raking the area with machine-gun fire in support, wounding Atencio in the neck. Pfc. Stanley Bock took his place as loader, and as Darnell aimed at the second tank, the muzzle of the 75-mm assault gun swung toward him. Both Panther and bazooka fired simultaneously. It was again a hit for the bazooka but caused no damage. The tree behind the bazooka team was blown to pieces, showering the men with debris before they withdrew.

The 2nd Platoon and heavy machine-gun section were digging in on the western edge of the woods when the smoke lifted momentarily to reveal a German tank moving through the Adenholz Woods northwest of their position. A second tank appeared, and both tanks moved out into the open ground and began spraying Bannholz Woods with machine-gun fire. The men requested artillery fire, but none was available, since the guns were being engaged in support of G Company in Sinz, so the group moved farther back into the woods.

Panzergrenadiers then appeared in support of the Panthers all along F Company's front, preventing the bazooka teams from getting within range of the advancing tanks and forcing a withdrawal. Lieutenant Smythe could not call for artillery fire on the woods, because it would endanger the American troops as much as the enemy. Captain Sinclair informed Lieutenant Colonel Dohs of the situation by radio and received permission to withdraw to the line of departure. However, the word did not reach the 2nd Platoon and the heavy machine-gun section in the western part of the woods, so they remained in place. Lt. John G. Truels of the weapons platoon, who had been wounded, saw German infantry coming down the road from Adenholz Woods and prepared to engage them with his machine gunners and about thirteen riflemen, but the Germans turned left short of Bannholz Woods to move northeast along a track just outside the woods.

The remainder of the company returned safely to the line of departure and reported that the only Americans remaining in the woods were dead. The divisional artillery then gave a savage pounding to the woods, where twenty-one Americans, three of whom were already wounded, lay in the mud and icy water, not daring to move as the shells crashed down and German tanks and infantry milled around. At one stage some Germans held a conference only fifty yards from them.

The survivors in Bannholz Woods huddled on the wet ground and prayed to survive until nightfall, when they silently and carefully made their way out. To make their escape, they had to abandon their equipment and then crawl past an enemy outpost, but eventually they got back safely to Unterste Büsch Woods.

Lieutenant Colonel Dohs and his G-3, Capt. John Flanagan, had watched the progress of the attack from an observation post on the edge of the Unterste Büsch Woods, then moved the battalion command post from the woods into a cellar in Sinz as soon as G Company had established itself in the village. When F Company withdrew, Dohs ordered up his antitank guns. Lieutenant Schofield then deployed his platoon south of the Remich-Sinz highway, but Lt. James E. Prior's 2nd Platoon of the antitank company had to wait for the engineers to bridge the antitank ditch so as to move its guns forward. Dohs also ordered Capt. Walter J. Stockstad to take his E Company to join up with G Company and resume the attack on Bannholz Woods.

Stockstad's attack had reached a point where E Company's right flank was level with the first buildings in Sinz when it suddenly came under intense mortar and artillery fire coming from the north, and four tanks could be seen on the high ground on the right firing down into the village. Orders then came for the company to assist Lieutenant Scales's G Company, which was having trouble clearing the northern half of the village. Captain Stockstad made his way with difficulty to the battalion command post, where he coordinated plans for clearing the village with Lieutenant Scales and Captain Flanagan, the battalion S-3.

It was about 1100 when E Company's 1st and 2nd Platoons moved into the village. They quickly overcame light resistance from the nearest buildings and took twenty-two prisoners. But when they started on the buildings in the northern part of the village, they came under intensive artillery, mortar, and machine-gun fire and sustained many casualties, including both platoon leaders, Lts. Edmund G. Reuter and John S. Fisher. The remaining men from these two platoons, together with the 3rd and Weapons Platoons, were then pooled and divided into two assault teams, while Lieutenant Scales conferred at the battalion command post. As soon as he returned, the attack was resumed. Again 2nd Lieutenant Beyer of the 356th Field Artillery provided invaluable support by targeting each of his batteries on a separate house and then having the whole battalion fire together for effect.

Captain Stockstad's E Company was the first to arrive at the street junction from where the coordinated attacks were to be launched. His men had suffered so many casualties that he requested a postponement until he could get reinforcements, but Dohs denied his request and the attack went ahead with the 1st Platoon moving down the left side of the street and the 2nd Platoon down the right. The lead scout of the 2nd Platoon was killed by rifle fire, and then from the village outskirts four enemy machine guns started firing on the men, pressing them back against the walls. SSgt. J. W. Green's squad of the 1st Platoon took cover behind a house but found themselves against a blank wall and unable to enter. TSgt. Raymond E. Collins, the acting platoon leader, saw this and sent another squad with a bazooka to assist Green's men. Some twenty bazooka rounds were fired at a house at the end of the street from where machine-gun fire was coming. The house was then sprayed with light machine-gun fire, enabling the two squads to rush it, only to discover that the German machine gunners had left. Meanwhile, TSgt. Elmer W. Griffords's 2nd Platoon had taken all but the last house on the other side of the street. With E Company's task all but complete, the enemy soldiers who were facing G Company surrendered after offering only a token resistance.[1]

During this activity a group from Butzdorf that was taken mainly from the 2nd Platoon, F Company, 2nd/302nd, under Lieutenant Alverado, was supposed to have escorted six combat engineers under the command of Lt. T. J. Wellom to sweep the road of mines between Butzdorf to Sinz that morning to enable armored support to get through safely if necessary. The men tried three times, but were beaten back each time by artillery fire directed from observation posts on Münzingen Ridge. They then decided to wait until late afternoon, when approaching dusk would hamper enemy visibility, and the task was completed just before nightfall.

Lieutenant Prior and his 2nd Platoon from the regimental antitank company arrived before nightfall and deployed in the northern part of Sinz, losing a prime mover and several casualties to enemy artillery fire in the process. They were followed at about 1800 by the battalion antitank platoon, which deployed in the southern part of the village. Further reinforcements arrived in the form of F Company and the remainder of the 2nd Battalion, L Company, on attachment from the 3rd/301st, and a platoon of the 704th Tank Destroyer Battalion. L Company deployed abreast of G Company, while F Company's 1st and 2nd Platoons occupied buildings on the western side of the village. The 3rd Platoon positioned themselves in the woods outside and were eventually joined by those who had been left behind in Bannholz Woods after they had worked their way back under cover of darkness. E Company's 3rd Platoon also dug in outside the village on the high ground above the west side of the draw.

Back in Sinz it was now dark and the last house had still to be taken. Just as the 1st Platoon of E Company was about to assault the building under a hail of fire, the Germans opened heavy fire from it. A panzerfaust crashed through the wall of the American-occupied house into a room, killing three occupants and knocking the remaining six unconscious. Returning with medical help, Sergeant Green met the rest of his platoon as they were leaving the house after being ordered to do so by Lt. Dale Reynolds, who was confident that his heavy machine-gun team could hold it.

Toward midnight the artillery, mortar, and rocket fire on Sinz eased off, with just intermittent fire occurring until 0230, when it resumed with a vengeance until 0400, causing several fires. The American troops used the cellars of the houses to good advantage, but E Company's 3rd Platoon took heavy casualties on the open ground above the village. Urgent orders came for the last German-held house to be taken at all costs, and an attack on it was planned for 0500. A tank destroyer of the 704th Tank Destroyer Battalion was to open the attack by firing several rounds point-blank at it, and the noise of the tank destroyers' approach would be drowned by Lieutenant Reynolds's machine guns and the weapons of E Company's 1st Platoon, who would then carry out the attack. Sergeant Green had only six men left, but they were all armed with BARs, and Lieutenant Reynolds increased their number with five of his own men and a bazooka team. The attack went ahead as planned, but the troops quickly discovered that the enemy soldiers, some fifteen strong, had vacated the house just ten minutes earlier. Sinz was now completely in American hands and had yielded 208 prisoners.[2]

The German positions on the Münzingen Ridge overlooking Sinz remained a problem, so Lieutenant Colonel Dohs assigned Capt. Paul E. Frierson's L Company to eliminate a group of bunkers there that had proved extremely troublesome during the battle. Reconnaissance patrols were sent out during the night to check the terrain, while Frierson and Lt. Glenn H. Gass, commanding the 1st Platoon, studied the aerial photographs of the area in the battalion command post and Lt. Carl Schaefer of the 356th Field Artillery Battalion planned time-fire on the individual bunkers for the assault.

At 0800 Lieutenants Gass and John R. Fraboni led their platoons forward through the eastern part of Sinz. Fraboni had first to eliminate two German machine-gun nests before he could get to the bunkers assigned to him. Using time-fire to keep the enemy machine gunners' heads down, his platoon closed up to them by a route defiladed by BAR fire. Pfc. Eugene Crenshaw circled around and caught the first machine-gun crew by surprise, while Pfc. Warren Dunn eliminated the second crew. Enemy infantry and a panzerfaust team located between these positions were also eliminated.

Lieutenant Gass's platoon's first objective proved to be just a pile of rocks, but Lieutenant Schaefer was with it and adjusted the time-fire accordingly to two known enemy positions. When Lieutenant Fraboni's platoon called on the enemy to surrender at their first objective, thirteen Germans emerged in a frightened state. Before they could be moved to the rear, one of the prisoners was killed by time-fire. At the second objective a hand grenade was dropped down a smoking stovepipe, causing the stove to explode. One of the two engineers with the platoon rushed forward with a satchel charge and blew the bunker door in, which yielded another eighteen prisoners. The last bunker was taken by Lieutenant Gass's men after an unopposed approach. Called upon to surrender, the enemy refused, whereupon the use of a flamethrower led to a change of mind and an officer and about ten men gave themselves up.

The whole operation had taken less than thirty minutes. The two platoons then secured the high ground to the north and east of the bunkers and began digging in. Lieutenant Gass's last bunker became a command post. Sometime afterward a telephone in the bunker started ringing, but as no one spoke German it was left unanswered. But the position was under observation from higher up the ridge, and enemy artillery fire was soon crashing down, causing numerous casualties.

The men of the two platoons had dug down only about a foot when they spotted a lone tank barely two hundred yards away. The tank came on and was within twenty yards of one of the sergeants when he engaged it with a bazooka. The round simply bounced off the tank turret, drawing the crew's attention to him. Two of the company's machine gunners then fired on the tank to keep it buttoned up while Lieutenant Schaefer called for artillery support, but both American machine guns were eliminated, and it was only when smoke began blinding the tank crew that they withdrew back up the hill to Das Lee Woods, where enemy tanks and infantry had been seen earlier and checked with artillery fire. At 1400 friendly artillery fire provided cover for the evacuation of the wounded as the survivors continued to dig in.

By noon that day, February 8, all the units in Sinz found themselves greatly reduced in strength. Not only were the casualties in dead and wounded considerable, but also the constant artillery and mortar fire falling on the village was leading to cases of combat exhaustion. F Company was brought deeper into the village and used to plug gaps in G Company's defenses, but the crews of the tank destroyers that had been ordered forward by Brigadier General Cheadle found themselves helpless in the circumstances, being outgunned and outranged. Only the field artillery was capable of providing effective defensive fire as the 88-mms and tanks on the high ground near Das Lee Woods blasted away at the new defenders of Sinz and Unterste Büsch.[3]

THE SECOND BATTLE OF BANNHOLZ WOODS

The enemy occupation of Bannholz Woods posed a direct threat to the American occupation of Sinz, so Lieutenant Colonel Dohs planned an immediate assault. Four teams of twenty-five men each, drawn from the 3rd Platoons of E and G Companies and the commandos, were to leave Sinz shortly after midnight on February 8 to penetrate the woods, where they were to destroy any tanks they might come across and to dig in before the arrival of other elements of the 2nd/301st later in the day. Once these teams were established, they were to send back guides to lead in some supporting tank destroyers so that they could be concealed before daybreak. These were fast but lightly armored M18 Hellcats, armed with 75-mm guns, from B Company of Lt. Col. James W. Bidwell's combat-experienced 704th Tank Destroyer Battalion, which had been with the 94th Infantry Division since January 7. Lieutenant Reynolds would command the E Company men; Lieutenants William S. Sollenberger and Christiansen, the G Company men; and Sgt. Harry J. Poynter, the commandos.

However, none of the teams could muster the required strength, and the men were already exhausted from the previous fighting. It was 0200 before they could move off, and it took another hour and a half for them to reach Bannholz Woods, by which time Sergeant Poynter's commandos were down to ten in all. The teams deployed with the commandos on the left, Lieutenant Reynolds's team in the center, and Lieutenant Sollenberger's on the right, while Lieutenant Christiansen took his team through to the northern part of the woods.

As they were digging in, the commandos were suddenly illuminated by a German flare, but by keeping still they escaped detection. Enemy soldiers could be heard shouting to one another deeper in the woods. The guides went back for the tank destroyers, which were deployed with one destroyer on the edge of the woods facing northwest and the other one echeloned about fifty yards farther back, deeper in the woods.

Enemy artillery and rockets began to fall in the area before dawn, while rifle and machine-gun fire heard in the woods indicated the presence of German infantry. A small patrol sent by Sergeant Poynter to contact Lieutenant Reynolds's team bumped into some of the enemy and was forced to return. Then the commandos' radio began to fail with the coming of daylight, only occasionally functioning sufficiently to either send or receive, but Reynolds managed to summon the support of two Hellcats from the 1st Platoon, B Company, of the 704th Tank Destroyer Battalion.

A mortar shell hit the rearmost Hellcat, jamming the turret and wounding one of the crew. Two of the crew then took their wounded comrade back to Sinz, while the others joined the crew of the undamaged tank destroyer. Soon after, three German tanks were seen moving slowly south between Adenholz and Geisbusch Woods. Artillery fire was called for, but none came.

Sergeant Poynter tried to repair his vital radio set and was working on it when a sudden burst of submachine-gun fire destroyed it between his legs. The fire had come from a German in the abandoned Hellcat behind him. Just then the NCO in charge of the other Hellcat shouted that German tanks were moving south to encircle the American position. The remaining Hellcat then drove off with five of the commandos clinging to its sides, spraying the undergrowth with its .50-caliber machine gun, and returned safely to Sinz. Deciding that his position was now hopeless, Sergeant Poynter withdrew with his remaining four men some nine hundred yards back to the Remich-Sinz highway. On the right, Lieutenant Sollenberger's team had no problem moving into the designated position and dug in on the eastern edge of the woods.

The two Hellcats that were supposed to support Lieutenant Christiansen's team just to the north of Sollenberger's did not arrive until after daybreak. They came across three German tanks in the woods that they were told had been knocked out. The leading Hellcat was abreast of two Panthers when it was fired upon by a panzerfaust, which only scored the turret. However, it was then fired on by a Panther, which was knocked out with the first shot of armor-piercing shell. As the Hellcats moved on, they were shot at and destroyed by the Panthers coming to life behind them, but the crews managed to get away and walk back to Sinz.

The tanks could then be heard crashing around in the woods. Christiansen reported to Battalion by radio that a tank was firing into his foxholes and that his position was untenable. Artillery fire was brought to bear, driving off the enemy tank, but it soon returned with a companion. Again Christiansen reported his position untenable and was instructed to sideslip to avoid the tanks and remain in the northern part of the woods.

In the late morning these two Panthers advanced methodically, reducing the American positions before them by spraying the undergrowth with machine guns and blasting the men out of their foxholes with their 75-mm guns. A few men got away. One soldier with a bazooka was cut down before he could fire it. Lieutenant Sollenberger's runner was killed and the platoon radio he was carrying was destroyed. Sergeant Babcock was wounded in the legs and side by splinters from an 88-mm shell, but managed to get away. The 3rd Squad at the southern end of the 2nd Platoon's position was cut down to a man.

When Lieutenant Reynolds's team from E Company entered Bannholz

Woods, nothing but many dead Germans was found. The two Hellcats allocated to the team's support arrived without incident and took up position. After daylight, patrols were sent out to look for any hidden German armor. Firing could be heard from the direction of Lieutenant Christiansen's position to the north, and from the south. Just before 0900 some German infantry approached the team's right flank in what appeared to be platoon column formation. Lieutenant Reynolds and SSgt. Robert G. Lehman ordered their men to open fire. The Germans began to outflank the position, so a withdrawal was ordered. The Hellcats were abandoned and the men made their way back to Sinz.

Back at the battalion command post, Lieutenant Reynolds heard that Lieutenant Christiansen and his team were still in the woods and offered to go to their rescue. But then he overheard Christiansen's final radio message—"The tanks are moving down the line, with infantry, firing into each foxhole"—and realized that it was too late to do anything.

This counterattack on February 9 by the 4th Panzer Company and its supporting panzergrenadiers of the 11th Panzer Division had been highly successful, taking twenty prisoners and destroying five tank destroyers. The division was about to be withdrawn for reallocation to the German First Army after repeated complaints from Lieutenant General von Wietersheim that his valuable division was being bled to death in terrain that was unsuitable for tanks. However, elements of Panzer Regiment 15 would remain for another forty-eight hours to provide a strong counterattack force should there be an American breakthrough. Advance parties from the 256th Volksgrenadier Division, which was due to arrive that night and take over the sector between Sinz and the Moselle from the 11th Panzer and 416th Infantry Divisions, had already arrived in the Saar-Moselle Triangle.

For Lieutenant Colonel Dohs's 2nd/301st and B Company of the 704th Tank Destroyer Battalion the attack had been an unmitigated disaster. The infantry and supporting artillery were utterly exhausted. The 356th Field Artillery Battalion alone had fired seven thousand rounds of 105-mm ammunition in support of the operations in the last three days.[4]

THE THIRD BATTLE OF BANNHOLZ WOODS

On the afternoon of February 9 the decision was made to replace Lieutenant Colonel Dohs's exhausted 2nd/301st with Lieutenant Colonel Martin's

2nd/376th for an attack to be launched the next day. General Malony believed that one more push would result in a complete breach of the Orscholz Switch and would provide an opportunity to roll it up from the rear.

The attack plan was to make a frontal assault with Captain Whitman's F Company and Captain Heath's G Company, with the heavy machine-gun platoons of Capt. Robert Q. Smith's H Company attached, as well as additional bazooka teams from the regimental antitank company. Once the attack was well under way, Lieutenant Colonel McNulty's 3rd/301st would seize Adenholz Woods to cover the west flank. Captains Blakely and William C. Jones of the 919th Field Artillery Battalion were assigned as forward observers.

A reconnaissance party from F Company set off shortly after nightfall on February 9 for Unterste Büsch Woods, but an enemy artillery and mortar barrage, coupled with the darkness, effectively nullified the mission, and both Lt. Richard A. Hawley, the company executive officer, and Sgt. Otto H. Fikjs, the company communications sergeant, were wounded.

At about 0100 on February 10, the 2nd/376th dismounted from trucks in Nennig and marched off east along the Remich-Sinz highway as far as the southern edge of Unterste Büsch Woods. They then followed taped paths through the minefields to the line of departure.

Captain Heath's G Company advanced with Lt. Adolph A. Janulis's 2nd and TSgt. William Johnston's 3rd Platoons leading, and reached the southern edge of Bannholz Woods by dawn. They were met by small-arms fire but continued their advance into the woods with marching fire, overrunning the enemy positions they encountered. Sergeant Johnston was wounded and SSgt. Henry Johnson took over the 3rd Platoon. The troops then dug positions in the western part of the woods. At 0800 Lieutenant Janulis radioed Captain Heath to express his concern about his exposed left flank, so SSgt. William B. Malloy's 1st Platoon was ordered up to fill the gap. With full daylight, enemy tanks could be seen in Geisbusch Woods to the north, and machine-gun fire periodically raked the exposed southwest approaches to Bannholz Woods.

As Sergeant Malloy's men moved forward, they came under fire from the tanks in Geisbusch Woods, and machine-gun fire soon started hitting the ground around them. Malloy ordered his men to run for the trees, but only seventeen of his forty men made it to the woods. The survivors then deployed and dug in on the western edge of the woods, and by the time Captain Heath arrived at 1000 the men were well entrenched.

Captain Whitman's F Company left the line of departure a little after G Company because of a delay in sorting out the attached bazooka teams. The company moved with Lieutenant Weston's 2nd and Lieutenant Mason's 3rd Platoons in the lead. The progress of the 2nd Platoon was slowed down by the presence of heavy, tangled undergrowth, and they had to veer to the left. Because of this slight detour, they entered the woods in G Company's area, joining Sergeant Malloy's group.

Lieutenant Mason's platoon came under enemy machine-gun fire while still one hundred yards from the woods, and the men dashed forward for the cover of the trees. In this dash TSgt. Mariano Scopoli and two squads of the 3rd Platoon veered left of the others and immediately lost contact as they came under artillery and mortar fire, which also pinned down Lt. George B. Wilson's support platoon in the open and resulted in many casualties. Two Panthers concealed in the southeast corner of the woods then opened up with their 88-mm guns to bring tree bursts raining down on the scattered pockets of troops.

Lieutenant Mason and his bazooka teams set out to engage the enemy armor. Pfcs. Leonard L. Neff and Otis L. King, bazooka man and loader respectively, fired repeatedly at one of the Panthers, but caused no damage, although the Panther eventually began to withdraw. A mortar round then landed almost on top of them, mortally wounding Neff. King stayed with his dying comrade, firing round after round until Neff died. Lieutenant Mason kept the tanks buttoned down by firing his M1 at them until he was seriously wounded by a shell burst.

When the retreating tanks reached the corner of the woods, one of them turned around and engaged the 1st Platoon, which was still out in the open in front of the woods together with the heavy machine-gun platoon, the 60-mm mortar section, most of the company command group, and two litter teams. Casualties from the ensuing mortar and tank fire were severe.

Captain Blakely and his radio operator, Tech-4 Adolph Singer, arrived separately and set up their forward observation post for the 919th Field Artillery with G Company's 2nd and 3rd Platoon positions, from where they had good views to the north and west. Shortly after their arrival, two tanks were seen on the near edge of Geisbusch Woods. Artillery fire was directed on the tanks but did not appear to deter them, apart from keeping them buttoned up. When the bazooka teams attempted to engage the tanks at long range, the blast of the bazookas gave their positions away and the tanks immediately responded with heavy fire. It so happened that the enemy tanks had just been equipped with new bazooka skirts, and as these proved effective, the confidence of the tank crews grew in facing bazooka-armed infantry that day. Also, as long as the tanks kept moving, the constant artillery fire directed at them did not pose much of a problem.

Captain Whitman was already inside the woods with his radio operator and runner, and at about 0815 the three men found Technical Sergeant Scopoli and the two squads of Lieutenant Mason's 3rd Platoon. Whitman then ordered the troops to sweep north through the woods along the eastern edge, and as they moved off, the enemy artillery fire slackened. Once the men had gone, Captain Whitman took stock of the situation, which was confused to say the least. He was out of touch with Lieutenants Mason, Weston, and Wilson, and he did not know where his bazooka teams were. He reasoned that Weston had moved forward on the left of the company's sector, so he decided to go to the site he had previously determined for his command post. There he found Lt. Robert C. Pierce, the platoon commander of the heavy machine guns attached to his company. Whitman and Pierce moved on northward through the woods together, virtually parallel to Sergeant Scopoli's route on the right, and encountered Scopoli as they approached the northeastern corner of the woods. Sergeant Scopoli's men were busy digging in, having heard tanks in the vicinity, but Scopoli had seen nothing of Lieutenant Weston on his way.

Still convinced that the 2nd Platoon was farther to the north, Captain Whitman ordered the group forward again. He and Lieutenant Pierce then started back to G Company, which they reached at 1000, both having been wounded by mortar fire on the way. Locating Lieutenant Weston, Captain Whitman ordered him to take his 2nd Platoon to reinforce Sergeant Scopoli's group. Meanwhile, pushing north, Scopoli's group came to a traverse track about 150 yards short of the far end of the woods, where it was engaged by German infantry in well-prepared positions and armed with captured BARs and MIs. The Germans were too strong for their small group, and when a tank joined in, they withdrew in good order, encountering Lieutenant Weston and his platoon on the way back. Captain Whitman then had Weston's platoon deploy in what was really F Company's sector. There was still no news of either Lieutenant Mason or Lieutenant

Wilson, and the strength of G Company was down to about forty men, many of whom were wounded.

Lieutenant Colonel Martin now had no communication with his forward units, the only working radio being Captain Blakely's, which was needed for directing essential artillery support coming from the 248th, 390th, and 919th Battalions. The battalion communications officer, Lt. James C. McCullough Jr., tried five times to get communication line teams into the woods, but each time they were pinned down in the open and took casualties. The stream of wounded men returning from the woods was the only source of information available.

There were so many injured soldiers coming back that the battalion medical officer, Lt. Percy Heidelberger, took a jeep forward to Sinz and went forward on foot to within three hundred yards of the German tanks southeast of the woods waving his red cross–marked helmet to attract attention. A German tank commander came forward, who allowed Heidelberger to go ahead and treat the wounded as long as he agreed to treat both Germans and Americans. Heidelberger thus managed to save the lives of several men from both sides and was thanked by the German tank commander upon his return. However, his group of wounded then came under fire for a while from a Hellcat trying to get at the German tanks, but eventually they got through to Sinz without sustaining further casualties. (Lieutenant Heidelberger was later awarded the Silver Star with Oak Leaf Cluster.)

The basic problem the troops faced was the lack of armor to assist the infantry, since the Hellcats were not really up to the task, although they did try; they scored an occasional hit, and one German tank was damaged, although not put out of action. Then heavy rain, which created mud everywhere, made the situation more difficult for everyone. Captain Blakely estimated there were twelve tanks in front of his position. Two of them were hit by phosphorus shells and went off trailing smoke, but the rest appeared to be unaffected by the fire he called down on them.

With the enemy tanks sniping at individual soldiers with their 88-mm guns from barely twenty-five yards, and German infantry infiltrating their position from the east, at 1130 Captains Whitman and Heath sent a message via Captain Blakely's radio requesting smoke to cover their withdrawal. Their request was refused, however, and they were told that reinforcements were coming. As the situation continued to deteriorate, Lt.

Edward G. Litka, G Company weapons platoon leader, volunteered to go back and emphasize the seriousness of the situation, but he was wounded before he had gone very far and had to crawl back into the woods. He later managed to reach Unterste Büsch Woods. At 1530 Whitman radioed a second request to withdraw. His company was being engaged by at least ten tanks and was under accurate 120-mm mortar fire. Again his request was refused, and again he was told that reinforcements were on the way.

At 1615, having been wounded seven hours earlier and now hardly able to walk, Captain Whitman handed over the remaining men of his company to Captain Heath. Whitman was about to set off to meet E Company, who were supposed to be coming up to reinforce them, when Sgt. Manuel M. Delagoes arrived trailing a wire from Unterste Büsch, thus providing the day's first contact between Lieutenant Wilson's platoon and Captain Whitman. Sergeant Delagoes told Whitman how the platoon had got trapped in the open and suffered many casualties. Captain Whitman then telephoned Maj. John R. Dossenbach, the battalion executive officer, to brief him on the situation in Bannholz Woods and arranged to meet Captain Darrah on his way back. As Captain Whitman and Sergeant Scopoli hobbled back to Unterste Büsch Woods, they were overtaken by several soldiers running back. G Company's forward positions had been overrun by a German counterattack involving five tanks and a company of panzergrenadiers, and more enemy infantry could be seen preparing to attack.

Lieutenant Colonel Martin was with Captain Darrah's E Company advancing up the draw leading to Bannholz Woods when he met the battered and exhausted survivors of F and G Companies making their way back at 1655. The men all withdrew to Unterste Büsch Woods, where E and H Companies formed a new line north of the Remich-Sinz highway, while the remains of F and G Companies made their way back to Wies to reorganize. Lack of reliable communications had led to the decimation of the battalion. G Company was now down to 78 men out of the 124 who had entered Bannholz Woods that morning, and F Company had been reduced to 1 officer and 50 men.

At 1147 that day, February 10, I and K Companies of Lieutenant Colonel McNulty's 3rd/301st met with only light resistance as they advanced, as planned, to cover the 2nd/376th's left flank in their attack on Bannholz Woods. Capt. William C. Warren's K Company placed a roadblock across the road leading from Adenholz to Bannholz Woods and laid antitank mines, but they were too far away to be able to see clearly what was going on. When the 2nd/376th were eventually driven out that afternoon, the 3rd/301st were ordered back, but continued to occupy the northernmost tip of Adenholz Woods and the roadblock until the next morning.[5]

Meanwhile, Major General Franz's 256th Volksgrenadier Division took over the sector that had previously been occupied by the 11th Panzer Division on February 10, linking up with Grenadier Regiment 713 east of Sinz. However, one tank company of the 11th Panzer Division remained in support of its successors.[6]

On February 11 Colonel McClune's 376th Infantry took over the left of the division's line from the 301st Infantry, establishing its headquarters in Wies. Lieutenant Colonel Thurston's 3rd/376th relieved Lieutenant Colonel McNulty's battalion and had E and H Companies of the 2nd/376th attached, while Lieutenant Colonel Miner's 1st/376th relieved the 2nd/301st at Sinz. Major Stanion's 1st/302nd remained on the division's extreme left flank under command of the 376th.

According to Thurston, McNulty's battalion suffered several unnecessary casualties during their daytime handover when McNulty sent a convoy of trucks up to Nennig to collect his men, thereby attracting the attention of the enemy artillery. Thurston had expected this and sent his own men marching well dispersed from Besch. When he saw the convoy on the highway, he hastily had his battalion make a detour.

By February 12 all of Colonel Hagerty's 301st Infantry were recuperating and reorganizing in reserve at Veckring. In response to a request made to XX Corps two days earlier, the men of Lt. Col. Richard P. Sullivan's 5th Ranger Battalion were transferred from the 26th Infantry Division on the right flank to come under the command of the 302nd Infantry and take over a section of the line in a nonoffensive role so as to release the 1st/302nd and 3rd/302nd for operational purposes. Using aggressive patrolling, the 5th Rangers were able to give an impression of greater strength than they actually had, while the battalions they had relieved went into divisional and regimental reserve respectively, the 1st/302nd moving to the town of Apach.

While the 301st Infantry and the two battalions of the 302nd Infantry were out of the line, considerable attention was given to reviewing lessons learned in the previous fighting, particularly the need for better cooperation between the infantry and the tank destroyers. A Mark IV German tank that had been abandoned in Nennig was found by Maj. Samuel H. Hayes, the Assistant G-3 at Division Headquarters, to be still in working order and was used both as a training aid and for experimental purposes.[7]

General Malony was eager to resume the offensive as outlined in his Division Field Order Number 10. He assumed that since the latest fighting had taken place on his left flank, the Germans would have moved most of their resources to the same area, so now would be a good time to strike a blow on the right. As objectives he selected the group of bunkers and pillboxes east of Campholz Woods and west of the Perl-Saarburg highway. Major Maixner's 2nd/302nd was assigned the task for February 15.

Between February 9 and 14, activities in the Campholz Woods were confined to minor skirmishing that resulted from patrolling and holding the positions that had been taken previously. B Company of the 319th Engineers destroyed the bunkers taken west of the woods with explosives. The enemy continued to bring down accurate artillery and mortar fire, adding to the misery of life in the muddy woods, where antipersonnel mines still claimed the occasional victim.

In preparation for the attack, a sand table model was constructed at the battalion command post in Borg to enable the officers and NCOs involved to study the terrain in some detail, and the company commanders were even flown over the area in artillery-spotter aircraft. The main objectives were three pillboxes capped with steel machine-gun cupolas, numbered 151, 152, and 153, surrounded by several other bunkers for accommodating the German infantry who were manning the defenses and surrounding trenches. The whole area was dominated by the higher ground of the Münzingen Ridge to the north.

Major Maixner decided to use E and F Companies for the assault. Captain Kops's F Company was to thrust forward from the northeast corner of Campholz Woods to secure the high ground around Pillbox 151 and reduce Pillboxes 151 and 153 and three other nearby emplacements to the south. Two platoons of Lt. John D. Anderson's E Company were to thrust directly east to take Pillbox 152 along with four other emplacements to the south and east of it. They would be supported by Lt. Joseph F. Cody's heavy machine-gun platoon. E Company's remaining platoon, under Lt. Oliver K. Smith, was to strike northeast from Borg and seize Pillbox 94. The whole operation would be supported by the 301st Field Artillery and C Company, 81st Chemical Warfare Mortar Battalion. The 3rd/302nd would continue to hold Campholz Woods during the attack, and diversionary attacks would be mounted to the east by the 5th Rangers and to the west by the 376th Infantry. F Company was driven up to Borg at midnight on February 14, from where Captain Kops's men marched up to Campholz Woods and were in their forward assembly areas by 0300, followed in turn by E and H Companies.

The men of Lieutenant Alvarado's assault groups were crouching in the communication trenches marking their line of departure when an intense mortar and artillery concentration descended on the eastern part of the woods, prompting many of the newly arrived and untested replacements to take to their heels. A captured German artilleryman later revealed that the enemy fire plan called for six box concentrations on the northern part of the woods that were fired at the least suspicion of American activity.[8] This bombardment resulted in many casualties to F Company, and it was well into the afternoon before it could reorganize and mount its attack.

On the other hand, E Company got away just before dawn and the 3rd Platoon took Pillbox 152 completely by surprise. A phosphorous grenade thrown into the pillbox set fire to some ammunition, and the twenty-five occupants quickly surrendered. Lieutenant Butler's 1st Platoon seized its objectives with little trouble, and Lieutenant Smith's platoon was equally successful with Pillbox 94. By 0730, E Company had completed its mission and set up its command post in Pillbox 152. Lieutenant Lewies then provided one of his squads to assist Lieutenant Butler in the defense of the newly won positions. Unfortunately, neither the telephone line nor the radio E Company had brought with them would work, but the company commander, Lieutenant Anderson, and Lt. L. A. Meyer, the artillery observer from the 301st Field Artillery, brought fresh batteries with them through a gauntlet of enemy fire to reach Pillbox 152.

H Company took a pounding in the woods from the enemy fire, during which Lieutenant Cody displayed extraordinary courage in moving about among his men, encouraging them to hold their ground. (For these actions he later received the Silver Star.)

When Lieutenant Alvarado's assault group from F Company eventually got away, creeping along a series of communication trenches, they found the German defenders of Pillboxes 151 and 153 fully alerted to the situation after the fall of Pillbox 152. There was no cover, and a bazooka round fired at one of the cupolas simply ricocheted off. The expected tank destroyer support failed to materialize. The men had to dig in under enemy fire and wait for nightfall, when it was proposed that the attack should be renewed. Then at about 2000, enemy tanks were heard advancing toward them and they withdrew into the woods once more. Lt. Charles P. Davis was wounded during the withdrawal and became lost in the darkness. Later TSgt. Howard J. Morton of the 2nd Platoon went back with a medic, Tech-4 Oscar E. Summerford, found Davis, and brought him in.

The men of E Company also heard the tanks, which came right up to their positions, but a fire call from Lieutenant Meyer drove them away again. E Company's position had previously been held by the 2nd Company of the Germans' Grenadier Regiment 713, whose commander was now responsible for retaking it. At midnight on February 16, a short mortar and artillery barrage was followed by an attack from about one hundred German infantry supported by ten tanks and self-propelled guns, which approached from the east via a draw running parallel to the east of the highway.

Flares revealed enemy armor swarming all over the area, and Lieutenant Meyer had to call artillery fire down on the company position. Lieutenant Smith evacuated the bunker he was occupying east of the main position, but was ordered back in and complied. Pfc. Wayne N. Woolman took a panzerfaust and knocked out a tank between Pillboxes 152 and 10, but TSgt. Tommy Nettles and the men with him were forced to surrender when the barrel of an 88-mm gun was thrust into their bunker. Despite the 301st Field Artillery Battalion's efforts, the Germans recaptured one small pillbox and three bunkers from E Company.

The Germans attacked again at 0200, concentrating on Pillbox 152, but the fire put up by the defense held them in check and they were driven back with heavy losses. Lieutenant Anderson now had only eleven effectives left in Pillbox 152. He informed Battalion that he was evacuating his position, and they headed back to the woods carrying their five wounded. Once more the lack of armored support had brought failure and heavy casualties to the infantry.[9]

While this was going on, Lt. Joseph P. Castor III of G Company had been manning a listening post on the outskirts of Oberleuken to warn of any enemy attack coming from the direction of Kirf. He had been reporting enemy movements and directing the fire of the 301st Field Artillery, which had successfully destroyed several self-propelled guns and inflicted heavy casualties on the German infantry. During the early hours of that same morning SSgt. William R. Moon led a patrol from Lieutenant Castor's listening post to successfully demolish a troublesome 120-mm mortar position, taking advantage of the Germans' habit of leaving their mortars to take cover in shelter bunkers during artillery bombardments. On their way back the patrol encountered and took prisoner a three-man mine-laying detail.

The German attack posed a threat to Borg, and Major Maixner recalled F Company from the woods at 0400 to dig in east of the woods, just south of the German pillboxes. He also had some tank destroyers of the 704th Tank Destroyer Battalion and one of his own battalion's antitank guns brought up to safeguard the crossroads north of Borg.[10]

The previous afternoon the weather had started to clear, and by the morning of February 15 it was cold and bright. Four squadrons of P-47s from the XIXth Tactical Air Command dropped twenty-four tons of high-explosive and phosphorus bombs on Beuren, Das Lee Woods, Bannholz Woods, Kirf, and the woods to the east of Kreuzweiler before strafing Kreuzweiler, Dilmar, Orscholz, and Bannholz Woods, damaging two enemy tanks.[11]

6
The Division Unleashed

The lack of armored support for the 94th Infantry Division's operations was a problem recognized by Major General Walker at XX Corps. It was clear that the division had little chance of breaching the Orscholz Switch without armor. He appealed to General Patton, noting that the 10th Armored Division was resting and stocking up in his area, but General Eisenhower refused to release this reserve until the 94th Infantry Division had proved itself by breaching the Orscholz Switch. Consequently, Walker met General Malony at the 2nd/302nd's command post in Borg on February 15 to confer. He stressed the need for an early breakthrough and agreed that the successful execution of Malony's plan to take the Münzingen Ridge should be enough to convince Eisenhower that a breach had been achieved. However, there was only one tank company available. The remainder of the 778th Tank Battalion, whose B Company was already with the 94th, would not arrive before March 16. Malony asked Walker for permission to use the full weight of his division in the next attack, and Walker replied, "All right, shoot the works!"

Meanwhile, Major General Walker at XX Corps had been working on Field Order Number 16, his plan for clearing the Saar-Moselle Triangle. The plan included the use of Major General Morris's 10th Armored Division, which was now standing by in the Metz area. The division had been fully replenished after its experiences in the Battle of the Bulge and a later attachment to the Seventh Army, in which it had been involved in repelling a German counterattack. It now had two combat commands on call to assist the 94th Infantry Division from February 20.[1]

Walker's unleashing of the 94th Infantry Division resulted in Malony's Field Order Number 11, calling for a full-scale attack by all three regiments on February 19. Colonel Hagerty's 301st Infantry was to make the main assault on Münzingen Ridge from Sinz, Butzdorf, and Tettingen with the objectives of Münzingen and Faha. Colonel Johnson's 302nd Infantry was to attack from Campholz Woods with Orscholz as its main objective. Colonel McClune's 376th Infantry was to seize Bannholz Woods and then secure the division's left flank by supporting the attack on Münzingen Ridge and occupying Der Langen Woods at the northern end, while retaining one battalion of men on trucks as divisional reserve.

The artillery fire plan was carefully coordinated by Brigadier General Fortier and Brig. Gen. Julius E. Slack of XX Corps. The corps artillery would engage targets beyond an arbitrary line drawn five thousand yards from the existing front line. To obtain maximum surprise there would be no firing before H-hour. The corps artillery would begin with fifteen minutes of fire on German command posts so as to disrupt communications and control. The enemy artillery positions would be engaged for the next thirty minutes with a maximum volume of fire, after which neutralization of these positions would continue for a further hour. Then all known and suspected enemy lines of communication would be engaged for the next ten hours. In view of the narrowness of the battlefield, it was thought that interdiction on all focal points, such as crossroads and townships, might not only prevent any reinforcement, but might also cause abandonment of vehicles and heavy equipment in case of a retreat. The plan also allowed flexibility for engaging any targets of opportunity that arose.

The divisional artillery, including the cannon companies of the 301st and 302nd Infantry, would concentrate on the enemy defenses, command posts, and lines of communication within the five-thousand-yard belt of operations, firing at the maximum sustained rate for thirty minutes after H-hour, thereafter switching to neutralization and on-call requests. The 774th Tank Destroyer Battalion was also given a role in this fire plan.

Part of the fire plan was a bombing attack by nine squadrons of the U.S. Army Air Force, but because of low, broken clouds on the morning of February 19, their participation in the attack was postponed until the afternoon. All units were urged to carry out detailed reconnaissance. One patrol made it to the crest of Münzingen Ridge and was able to plot the enemy positions there, while another, under Sgt. Frederick J. Ramondini of the 301st's intel-

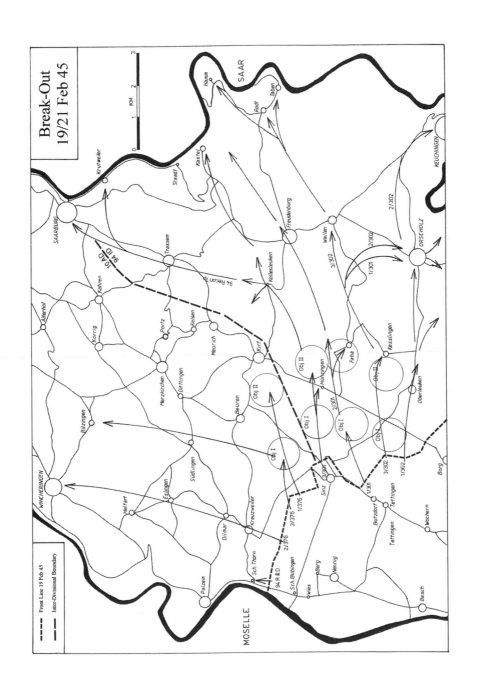

Break-Out
19/21 Feb 45

KM 0 1 2 3

SAAR

MOSELLE

Front Line 19 Feb 45
Inter-Divisional Boundary

WINCHERINGEN
Bilzingen
Palzem
Helfant
Esslingen
Südlingen
Dilmar
Kreuzweiler
Sch.Thorn
94 R.R.D.
Sch.Bübingen
Berg
Wies
Wenning
Besch
Wochern
Tettingen
Butzdorf
Tettingen
Borg
Sinz
Sinzer
Beuren
Obj I
Obj II
Obj I
Obj I
Obj II
Obj I
Obj II
1/376
2/376
3/376
2/301
3/301
1/301
3/302
1/302
2/302
1/302
3/302
1/301
2/302
Oberleuken
Faha
Hellendorf
Hübingen
Kesslingen
Weiten
Freudenburg
Kollesleuken
Kirf
Meurich
Kelsen
Portz
Oittingen
Merzkirchen
Körrig
Kahren
Altenhof
SAARBURG
10 AD
94 ID
94 Recon Tp.
Trassem
Staadt
Kastel
Krutweiler
Hamm
Rodt
Taben
ORSCHOLZ
KEUCHINGEN

ligence and reconnaissance platoon, actually got into Münzingen, where it found tanks concealed among the buildings. This patrol information was plotted on sand table models so that the troops could be thoroughly briefed beforehand. Meanwhile, the units stocked up with replacements of men and equipment.

On the evening of February 18 the entire division began moving up to its forward assembly areas as the artillery readied themselves to fire a devastating fifteen-thousand-round preparation.[2]

Lieutenant Colonel McNulty's 3rd/301st, which had Das Lee Woods as its primary objective, left Sinz at 0200 and began climbing the Münzingen Ridge with Captain Frierson's L Company leading. On the way up, L Company unexpectedly overran a German mortar position and was able to capture the team without attracting attention. The crest of the ridge formed the line of departure, where L Company deployed with Captain Devonald's K Company on its right. Das Lee Woods could be seen silhouetted against the skyline some six hundred yards away.

The beginning of the artillery preparation at 0400 was the signal to attack, and the two companies moved forward using marching fire into the darkness. L Company came across a minefield, but found a lane through it that had been cleared by the enemy tanks, and this allowed the company safe passage. K Company had to blast its way through the same minefield with Primacord. Only minimal enemy resistance was encountered. The troops cleared the woods and dug in on the eastern edge, having taken twenty-six prisoners. Then artillery, rocket, and mortar fire began to fall on their positions.

Major Hodge's 1st/301st, which was to storm the ridge south of Das Lee Woods, marched out of Butzdorf up the Sinz road and turned off of it just short of the village to go up a small draw with Captain Drenzek's C Company on the left and Lieutenant Cancilla's B Company on the right.

As C Company moved off at 0400 it immediately encountered mines and came under mortar fire. Lt. Walter M. Stempak's 1st Platoon suffered many casualties, including Stempak himself, so Captain Drenzek withdrew the company to detour around the minefield. The company then pushed forward rapidly to reach its objective before daylight. Drenzek then discovered that he had veered to the north, so he swung his company south, sweeping the top of the ridge to reach their assigned objective, and the company dug in. When Drenzek was wounded during the approach, Lt. Howard Johnson took over the command. There were some enemy trenches in front of the company position, so Lieutenant Johnson went ahead with Private First Class Dionne to investigate. He found the trenches occupied by troops who were determined to defend them, but Johnson called for mortar fire, which brought a rapid change of mind.

Lieutenant Cancilla's B Company moved off with the 1st Platoon on the left and Lt. Arthur A. Shocksnyder's 2nd Platoon on the right. The 2nd Platoon came under misplaced American mortar fire and suffered fifteen casualties in as many minutes. The men of the 2nd Platoon went on to encircle a German bunker, one of whose occupants was killed and the rest went toward the 1st Platoon to surrender, but ran into the same minefield that was beginning to create havoc. As SSgt. John R. Koellhopper later reported:

Suddenly a mine went off, killing the scout, and the platoon leader set two men to probing for the edge of the field. No sooner had they started than they were blown up. The explosions alerted the Krauts in a bunker not fifty yards away and their machine gun opened up at point-blank range. Men hit the ground setting off more mines as they landed. Legs and feet were blown away. Men began screaming. Others cried, "Medic! Medic!" The men were trapped. They couldn't move a hand or foot for fear of hitting a Schü-mine. The enemy was throwing mortars and 88s and that machine gun was adding to the hell. The lieutenant was badly wounded. One of the men who had lost both legs was crying, "Get me out of here. God! Oh God! Get me out of here!" The platoon sergeant [TSgt. Henry E. Crandall] was desperately trying to make a path through the minefield. Another man trying to move set off another mine. As this man looked down on what was left of his two feet he started crying like a baby—not screaming, but crying. He didn't seem to be in pain, the shock must have been too much just then. Another Yank lay there, his bottom half a hell of a shape. All he kept doing was begging his buddy to shoot him. "Shoot me. Please shoot me. Damn it, can't you see I'm no good any more?" Still another man who was badly wounded was begging his buddy for his overcoat. "I'm cold. Damn I'm cold! Give me your overcoat, won't you? Oh please . . . please give me your coat?"

"The bastards! The dirty bastards! Won't they ever stop?" cried another voice as more and more mortar shells came pouring in. The
machine gun firing from the bunker had stopped and the Krauts were
shouting something in German. One Yank could understand them.
They were hollering, "It hurts, doesn't it? It hurts!" The platoon sergeant had heroically blasted a path through the minefield and was
leading the platoon to the far edge of the field. More men were lost
by the time the platoon had cleared the field. Now they were able to
get at those bunkers. But, no! As the platoon moved up to the bunkers, the Krauts quit. The objective had been reached and there were
sixteen men left.

Captain Colgan's A Company, which was in reserve, had the task of
clearing the remaining pillboxes south of the Sinz-Orscholz highway and
maintaining contact with the 302nd Infantry on the right. The 1st Platoon
occupied positions on the ridge between Butzdorf and Campholz Woods,
while the rest of the company was organized into assault teams under Lt.
Robert H. Wolf. The assault teams moved east out of Butzdorf up a draw.
As they came out into the open, they were caught in a vicious crossfire from
two machine guns. SSgt. Ichiro Matsuzawa managed to crawl unnoticed
in the half-light to the nearest one and threw in a grenade and charged.
Two Germans were killed by his grenade, and the remaining three were
wounded. When they surrendered, Matsuzawa then advanced on the second position and secured its surrender. (He was awarded a Silver Star for
this exploit.)

The 2nd Platoon pushed on to clear the bunkers in its path with the aid
of the 3rd Platoon, encountering little resistance, and secured the ridge in
their assigned sector.[3]

Colonel Johnson's 302nd Infantry had its 2nd Battalion holding Campholz
Woods, its 1st Battalion in Perl, and the 3rd in Eft. In preparation for the
attack, Lieutenant Colonel Cloudt's 3rd Battalion moved up to the northeast corner of Campholz Woods, collecting flamethrowers, pole and satchel
charges, and other demolition material from stockpiles on the way. Major
Stanion's 1st Battalion followed suit, taking up position just south of the 3rd
Battalion. Major Maixner's 2nd Battalion then withdrew into divisional reserve at Eft. Lieutenant Colonel Sullivan had volunteered his 5th Ranger

Battalion to assist in the assault, so they were placed under command of the 302nd Infantry with the task of taking the village of Oberleuken.

As the assault companies moved off at 0400, the Germans deluged the area of advance with flares. Despite the American artillery preparation, enemy small-arms, machine-gun, and mortar fire checked the advance. The Germans continued to use flares until daylight so as to prevent any surprise movement. The 2nd Platoon of Captain Williams's I Company ran into a minefield and suffered several casualties. All attempts to rescue the wounded were driven back by machine-gun fire. However, just before dawn, TSgt. James E. Hudson managed to get his assault group through the minefield to storm and take the first bunker.

As soon as dawn broke, the tanks of B Company, 778th Tank Battalion, moved out from Tettingen on the Sinz road, turning right on the Sinz-Orscholz highway to climb steeply up to the crest of Münzingen Ridge. A tank toward the rear struck a mine, and another bogged down trying to overtake it, but the remaining tanks found some hard ground and followed through. These tanks turned south from the point where the Peace Monument now stands and came to the support of I Company along a track cleared by the 319th Engineers during the night.

The tankers were then briefed on the situation and began tackling the most troublesome pillboxes and bunkers with their 75-mm guns. This had the immediate effect of reducing the enemy machine-gun fire and visibility of their mortar observers. Sergeant Hudson's assault group now pushed on to a second pillbox and placed demolition charges against its apertures. Lieutenant Edwards, the company executive officer, who had assumed command of the company shortly after the beginning of the attack, left Pfc. Ernest L. Buffalini with five others to flush out this position while he led the rest of the company forward.

Pillbox 153 was the northernmost of the complex and the most important, for it incorporated a command post with underground telephone communications and excellent observation facilities. Lieutenant Edwards and TSgt. Edward Cardell used the cover of the tank fire support to get their assault groups forward to attack this position. Pfcs. Alvin Cohen and Joseph J. Truss worked their way up to the entrance of the pillbox, where Truss rigged a demolition charge that blew in the door. Cohen then fired his BAR into the doorway as Sergeant Cardell and Private Truss threw in fragmentation and phosphorous grenades. The occupants, including German artillery observer Leutnant (2nd Lieutenant) Beikert, who had just been ordering a defensive barrage, surrendered. The barrage then arrived, which drove the Americans and their prisoners back into the pillbox until it was over.

With the reduction of all the pillboxes and bunkers in their sector complete, the men of I Company set up a machine gun to cover their left flank. A German machine-gun position was then located in a ditch to the north. The I Company machine gun kept this German position neutralized all day until it was overrun by the 301st Infantry, which advanced from the north and took thirty-eight prisoners.

Lieutenant Devonald's K Company had an experience that was similar to that of I Company. They hit the same minefield and came under the same heavy fire, so that little progress was made until the tanks turned up. Some of the tanks mistook K Company for Germans and started firing at it until Pfc. Ernest E. Climes had the courage to stand up in full view of the enemy and identify himself as American. The tanks then assisted in the systematic reduction of the pillboxes and bunkers in K Company's sector. Teams led by Sgts. Roy G. Watson and Sgt. Clarence Raffesberger cleared the last two pillboxes, enabling the company to close up to the Perl-Saarburg highway.

Major Stanion's 1st Battalion to the south encountered similar difficulties. Capt. Jack P. Haggart was wounded at the beginning of the attack, leaving Lieutenant Norquist to take over A Company, but the arrival of the tanks enabled the battalion to continue its advance so that by 0900 A and B Companies had also reached the highway. The move had been so fast that some of the enemy positions had been bypassed unnoticed. For example, Pfcs. James Linerich and Tyrone Tywoneck of A Company discovered one bunker that yielded eleven prisoners when they realized it was occupied and attacked it. Sgt. James A. Graham of B Company found another occupied bunker and took five prisoners. American troops now occupied the whole of the Münzingen Ridge, the key and backbone to the Orscholz Switch, so they could make a valid claim to having breached the Siegfried Line.[4]

On the division's left flank, Colonel McClune's 376th Infantry was deployed with the 3rd Battalion some two hundred yards north of the Remich-Sinz highway halfway between Nennig and Sinz, and with the 1st Battalion facing Bannholz Woods, less the 3rd Platoon of C Company, which was left to guard Sinz. The remaining line to the Moselle was covered by the 94th Reconnaissance Troop.

During the night of February 18–19, the company commander of one of the German antitank companies mistakenly drove down the road from Kreuzweiler to just outside Sinz, where his vehicle struck an American mine and caught fire. The incident proved that Germans had not mined the road in their sector and that it therefore could be used by American armor in support of the attack on Bannholz Woods if necessary.

Lieutenant Colonel Miner's 1st Battalion moved off at H-hour, with A and B Companies leading on the left and right respectively. Because of the identified minefields, Captain Dadisman's A Company advanced on a fairly narrow front. When it reached its objective and started digging in, the company came under raking fire from 20-mm antiaircraft guns from Geisbusch Woods and artillery fire from the direction of Kreuzweiler. With daylight, groups of Germans who had been bypassed in the woods began to surrender.

Captain Bowden's B Company also reached its objective with little loss of time and then sent patrols back in daylight to ensure that the woods were clear of enemy soldiers. One patrol came across a disabled German tank being used by two artillery observers as an observation post. With their capture, shelling of the battalion positions was reduced considerably.

Lieutenant Cornelius's C Company left the line of departure at 0430 using marching fire to reach its objective on the northern edge of Bannholz Woods, where it came under intensive mortar fire. Pfc. Thomas H. Goggins spotted several of the 20-mm mortar positions firing from Geisbusch Woods, which the accompanying tank destroyers were then able to engage. By 0815 hours the Bannholz Woods were securely in American hands.

Lieutenant Colonel Thurston's 3rd Battalion advanced from the line of departure north of the highway in Unterste Büsch Woods with K Company, now under the temporary command of Lieutenant Daly, heading for Adenholz Woods, and Captain Brightman's L Company for Geisbusch Woods. A narrow path had been cleared through a known minefield about four hundred yards ahead on K Company's route during the previous night, but when the troops started passing through in single file, they were met by heavy machine-gun fire. When the men scattered, they inadvertently set off the mines and incurred heavy casualties. After the fire lifted, Lieutenant Daly organized the evacuation of the wounded and pulled back his company to reorganize. Although wounded himself, Daly continued to lead his company until late afternoon.

Lieutenant Colonel Thurston then added I Company's 1st Platoon to K Company and ordered them to avoid the minefield by following L Company's route. Although Captain Brightman's L Company had been hit by the same barrage, they used marching fire as they pushed ahead running across the one thousand yards of open ground to reach Geisbusch Woods.

Lieutenant Daly's command attacked Adenholz Woods from the south and, supported by tanks, cleared the western half. Daly then passed the armor to Lt. Cecil G. Dansby of I Company to clear the remainder of the woods, which yielded his 1st Platoon some eighty prisoners. (Lieutenant Daly was later awarded a second Distinguished Service Cross for his performance that day, having been previously awarded one for his service in Brittany.)

With the exception of Oberleuken, where an electronically controlled minefield had proved the better of the 5th Ranger Battalion, all the division's objectives had been taken, but the day was not yet over.[5]

At 1000 all units were notified by Division that the attack would be resumed at 1230 to take the final objectives listed in Field Order Number 11. A fifteen-minute artillery preparation commencing at 1215 would be the signal for the attack. This artillery preparation was still in progress when at 1223 General Walker telephoned Colonel Bergquist at the 94th Infantry Division headquarters to inform him that the 10th Armored Division "ought to be on the way in two hours."[6]

The 1st Battalion of Colonel Hagerty's 301st Infantry had suffered heavily in the initial attack, so he ordered the 2nd Battalion to pass through the 1st Battalion and take up the advance on Faha. Lieutenant Colonel Dohs promptly moved his command post out of Wochern up to Münzingen Ridge.

Meanwhile, Lieutenant Colonel McNulty's 3rd Battalion prepared to attack the hamlet of Münzingen from the ridge. At H-hour four Shermans and three Hellcats raced out of the cover of Das Lee Woods and down the hillside, crossed the Perl-Saarburg highway north of Münzingen, and climbed the slopes of their objective, a hill referred to as Height 387. Captain Frierson's L Company did its best to keep up with the armor,

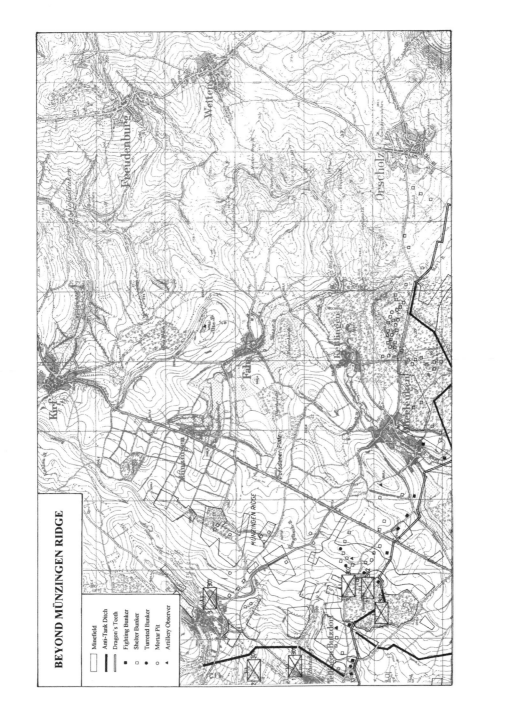

BEYOND MÜNZINGEN RIDGE

Minefield
Anti-Tank Ditch
Dragon's Teeth
Fighting Bunker
Shelter Bunker
Turreted Bunker
Mortar Pit
Artillery Observer

eliminating several enemy groups who were trying to engage the armor with panzerfausts. Simultaneously, Lieutenant Devonald's K Company swept across the highway south of Münzingen, wheeled right, and moved north to join the armor on Height 387. Captain Donovan's I Company then had the task of reducing the hamlet. A penetration was achieved in the southeast corner, leading to a ferocious battle in which the German tanks that had been previously reported in the hamlet joined in. I Company kept up the pressure as they worked from the south, reducing one building after another, while the rest of the battalion on Height 387 prevented any breakout. One German tank tried to shoot its way out but was checked by the Hellcats from hull-down positions on the hill and destroyed. By 1620 Münzingen was safely in American hands.

K and L Companies on Height 387 could hear Germans in Das Brüch Woods east of them, so TSgt. Elmer H. Kinateder's 3rd Platoon of L Company was sent to investigate. They returned shortly with thirty prisoners who had been about to launch a counterattack.

The two assault companies of Lieutenant Colonel Dohs's 2nd/301st formed up on the reverse slope of Münzingen Ridge and then swept across through the 1st Battalion at H-hour and down across about twenty-five hundred yards of open ground to reach the little village of Faha. Artillery fire fell on them as they advanced, but the troops kept going, reached their objective, and began fighting for its possession. By 1630 more than half the village had been taken and its conquest assured, so G Company was sent off to seize Height 406, the Alterberg, that dominated the village from the north. By 1830 the village had been taken, and G Company linked up with the 3rd Battalion to the northeast.[7]

On Height 406 was a German artillery observation post, which had been manned since January 29 by a small team under Staff Sergeant Schaewen of the 4th Battalion, Artillery Regiment 416. Schaewen's logbook was discovered several years later, and his entry for this day read:

Suddenly at 0400 hours an abrupt heavy barrage of salvoes fell on Oberleuken, the line of bunkers and the northern corner of the Das Lee copse. It was as if the maws of hell had opened. Half an hour later the artillery hammered Kirf. At 0555 hours phosphor shells fell on Kirf and Freudenburg. At the same time the artillery fire jumped over

the rear area with a barrage on Trassem. Towards 0630 hours individual flares rose over the waterworks area, the Münzingen and Faha
parish water tower in the Das Lee copse. There were several bursts of
machine-gun fire in the direction of Borg[,] and rifle fire from the
direction of Das Lee copse could be heard. Shortly after daybreak, at
about 0815 hours, the first smoke shells landed with a thump right on
the observation post.

0830–0930 hours, seven tanks in the direction of Potsdamer Platz
with 20–25 men.[8] 1030 hours, sounds of combat from direction of
Potsdamer Platz-Oberleuken. 1215 hours, tanks in the waterworks
area. 1222 hours, heavy barrage on Münzingen, 200 shots. 1227 hours,
barrage on the Alterberg. 1248 hours, infantry attacking between Das
Lee copse and waterworks, among them a lot of men with raised
arms. 1300 hours, tanks breaking through to the Kirf road. 1315 hours,
enemy in company strength on Münzingen-Faha road.[9]

Colonel Johnson's 302nd Infantry had to modify their plans as a result of
the 5th Ranger Battalion's failed attack earlier in the day. The 1st Battalion,
which had originally been given the mission of taking Kesslingen, was
switched to taking Oberleuken, and the 3rd Battalion was assigned to
Kesslingen in its place.

To reach Oberleuken, Major Stanion's 1st Battalion had first to take
Height 388, which overlooked the village from the west and was well
fortified. A and B Companies crossed the Perl-Saarburg highway with
some tanks of the 778th Tank Battalion and moved rapidly up Height 388,
taking pillboxes and bunkers in quick succession. Enemy artillery and mortar fire fell on the hill, but mainly on the rear elements, with the assault
companies suffering few casualties. The bald hilltop offered no cover to the
heavy machine-gun fire coming from the pillboxes around Oberleuken, so
it was decided to withdraw to the reverse slope, leaving only a few observers
on the crest.

Meanwhile, Lieutenant Robinson's C Company had moved out of Borg
with the intention of attacking Kesslingen in accordance with the original
plan, and it was not until he arrived at Height 388 that Robinson learned
about the change of plan. The platoon of tanks that were to accompany his
company were already in position on the northern foot of the hill, ready to
attack Kesslingen, so Pfc. Bernard Piotrzkowski was sent forward to inform

the tankers of the change. By banging with his rifle butt on the turret of the first tank, the lieutenant was able to attract the attention of its crew and get the message passed by radio to the others. The tanks then changed position and started firing at the pillboxes that were defending Oberleuken.

C Company then advanced over the hill as the 302nd's cannon company and the 301st Field Artillery Battalion bombarded the village. Pfc. Edward C. Burnshaw, a member of a forward observation team, continued directing the artillery fire despite being badly wounded by an exploding mine. (For his devotion to duty while in intense pain he was later awarded the Distinguished Service Cross.)

The fire was lifted as the infantry approached, and SSgt. Frederick R. Darby led the infantrymen in, firing a light machine gun from the hip. Once the infantry had gained a foothold, they were followed in by two tanks to provide close support, while the remainder of the platoon provided covering fire. By 1630 the village had been cleared and 110 prisoners and seven 120-mm mortars had been taken.

Lieutenant Colonel Cloudt's 3rd Battalion, with I and K Companies in the lead, stormed forward some two thousand yards to Height 376, the Kesslinger Berg, northwest of Kesslingen, and took it quickly, despite coming under artillery and mortar fire on the way. Fire was also directed at the accompanying tanks from Oberhardt Woods, north of the hill. The tanks returned fire, and four BAR men from Captain Williams's I Company—Pfcs. Alvin Cohen, James M. Bender, and Kyle Thompson, and Pvt. Edward Mayfield—were sent to check out the woods, which they did by encircling from the north. To their surprise, the only enemy they encountered were two women manning an antitank gun.

The men of Lieutenant Travers's L Company were then brought forward from reserve to Height 376 to complete the battalion mission by taking the village. An artillery preparation was arranged, and Lt. Charles C. Misner's 2nd Platoon charged down the hill under cover of fire from the tanks. The platoon met fierce resistance. TSgt. Francis E. Kelly, the platoon sergeant, was badly wounded in the neck from an exploding mine, but refused to be evacuated. Lieutenant Misner went back alone to guide the tanks in, then rejoined his platoon to display some inspiring leadership, while Sergeant Kelly directed the tank fire at the worst points of resistance. The fierce struggle for the town continued until 1730, after which Misner and Kelly supervised the evacuation of the numerous wounded. (Lieutenant Misner was later awarded a Distinguished Service Cross for this action, and Sergeant Kelly received a Silver Star.)

At nightfall Captain Woods's B Company moved down from Height 388 into the Unter den Eichen Woods between Kesslingen and Oberleuken to link the new locations of the 302nd Infantry's 1st and 3rd Battalions. T5g. Robert Hoots and Pfc. William B. McElwee were sent forward to man a machine-gun post at the junction of the Kesslingen road with the Remich-Orscholz highway and found a German machine-gun team already occupying the site. They captured the German team and also its relief who arrived the next morning to take over.[10]

Behind the 301st and 302nd Infantry, the 319th Engineer Combat Battalion had had a busy day blowing up German installations and clearing the roads of mines, as well as bridging the antitank ditches on the Perl-Saarburg highway and Borg-Oberleuken road.[11]

Colonel McClune's 376th Infantry, on the left flank, also helped increase the size of the breach in the Orscholz Switch that afternoon. At 1100 Lieutenant Colonel Miner was recalled to Sinz to be given final instructions on the taking of Der Langen Woods northeast of Sinz and Height 398, the Ehringer Berg, beyond it.

Regiment allocated A Company, 708th Tank Destroyer Battalion, to support the 1st/376th with six Hellcats, and the 3rd Platoon of C Company, which had been detached to guard Sinz that morning, was returned to the battalion. E Company of the 2nd Battalion was ordered to replace the 1st Battalion in Bannholz Woods.

Lieutenant Colonel Miner had all the heavy machine guns of D Company deployed on the northeastern edge of Bannholz Woods to assist with fire support for the assault by A and B Companies. It was 1300 before they could move off under their own covering fire, with Captain Bowden's B Company on the left and Captain Dadisman's A Company on the right, while the 81st Chemical Warfare Mortar Battalion provided a smoke screen to block enemy observation from the north between Moscholz Woods and the Münzingen Ridge. The troops advanced in squad columns until they reached within two hundred yards of their objectives. They then formed skirmish lines as the fire cover lifted.

B Company came under a very heavy artillery and mortar concentration as they approached Der Langen Woods. The 1st Platoon was pinned down for almost an hour by enfilade fire coming from 20-mm guns in Moscholz Woods, but the remainder of the company reached Der Langen Woods. SSgts. Charles H. Nichols and Robert E. Burnett led their squads through a series of communication trenches that encircled the woods, eliminating the Germans they encountered.

The Hellcats then moved forward to close up with the infantry, but three of them were knocked out in quick succession by an 88-mm gun concealed in Moscholz Woods. The remaining Hellcats then continued to Der Langen Woods by a less exposed route, only to have the leading vehicle knocked out by an 88-mm gun concealed in the southeast corner, which in turn was attacked and captured by the infantry. Staff Sergeant Brewster of the 919th Field Artillery then called for a concentration on the enemy guns in Moscholz Woods. In the end, it took several concentrations to subdue the enemy artillery here.

A Company discovered a whole network of trenches south of Der Langen Woods. Private First Class Kamins came across a German soldier crying in one of these trenches. When called upon to surrender, the German pointed silently to a nearby position, and Kamins was able to take another fifteen prisoners. By 1400 the whole of the area was securely in American hands. That evening the battalion was informed that reserve troops would take over as soon as the 10th Armored Division passed through the next morning.[12]

The day's operations had yielded seven square miles of dominating ground, with the capture of 5 pillboxes, 23 bunkers, and 827 prisoners, and the destruction of 4 enemy tanks. The way was now open for the 10th Armored Division to enter the fray, and all through the night of February 19–20 the vehicles of that division moved forward into the 94th Infantry Division's rear areas.[13]

General of Infantry Walther Hahn's LXXXII Corps had both the 416th Infantry and the 256th Volksgrenadier Divisions engaged. The American artillery fire had prevented the redeployment of reserves earlier in the day, and by day's end there were no troops available to mount counterattacks to regain any of the lost ground. Serious consideration was given to withdrawing into the main Westwall defenses across the Saar while it was still possible to move the artillery and heavy equipment, but Army Group G would not accept this. Instead they ordered the standard counterattack to regain lost ground for such a situation and the release of those surrounded bunker crews who were still in touch on the fortress underground network. Consequently, two companies of infantry were alerted and some self-propelled guns were ordered forward from their harbor area near Saarburg. The fortress artillery batteries sited near Mettlach were ordered to provide support.

The attack at daybreak achieved surprise and contact was made with some of the surrounded bunkers, but American artillery supremacy soon brought an end to this enterprise.[14]

7
Clearing the Triangle

At 1800 hours on February 19 the men of Colonel McClune's 376th Infantry were transferred lock, stock, and barrel to Major General Morris's 10th Armored Division, together with one company of the 81st Chemical Warfare Mortar Battalion, to form Task Force 376. The reason for this transfer was that the structure of an American armored division at that time did not provide sufficient infantry to allow it to operate satisfactorily in an area like the Saar-Moselle Triangle with its many towns and villages. However, as we shall see, the result was that the brunt of the infantry work during the next phase of operations would fall to the 376th in order to preserve the integral armored infantry battalions for future operations.

The 10th Armored Division consisted basically of three tank battalions, three armored infantry battalions, and three field artillery battalions that were split between three combat commands—A, B, and R—commanded by Brig. Gen. Edwin W. Piburn, Col. William L. Roberts, and Col. Wade C. Gatchell respectively. These combat commands were then normally divided into two combat teams, all of which remained highly flexible in composition to meet varying operational demands.[1]

The 376th had a temporary attachment of Capt. Scott T. Ashton's 94th Reconnaissance Troop and the Division Headquarters defense platoon, the latter having volunteered to get some action as a change from guard duties. General Walker tasked the remainder of the 94th Infantry Division with clearing the eastern part of the Triangle between the Leuk Branch and the Saar River. The 10th Armored Division's mission was to attack the northeast and make every effort to seize intact the bridges at Wiltingen and Kanzem and establish a bridgehead to protect them. These bridges would give access to Trier, Patton's main objective, but the 10th Armored Division's initial objectives were given as, first, the high ground between Wincheringen on the Moselle and Saarburg and, second, the northern tip of the Triangle.

On the left flank the action started with an attack on Schloss Thorn and the huddle of houses around it by Lt. Frank A. Penn's Headquarters defense platoon. Supported by two light and two medium tanks, the troops delivered a five-minute artillery preparation. The attack was launched at 0700 on February 20 and immediately came under heavy mortar and artillery fire. Densely positioned antipersonnel minefields protected the troops' approaches, and one of the tanks was disabled by an antitank mine. Its crew dismounted and joined in as infantry, but the tank commander and a corporal were killed by enemy fire. Leaving one tank to secure the valley road, the other two tanks provided close support for the attacking infantry.[2]

A German view of the attack is provided by Ernest Henkel, then serving with Regiment 481 of the 256th Volksgrenadier Division, who was in the castle as a forward observer for a mortar platoon equipped with 80-mm mortars:

I woke at dawn on the 20th February to unusual sounds. I went through the small stairwell up to the big corner room, from where one had the best view of the gully and the road leading up from the Moselle. I leaned out of the window with a stick grenade. I caught my breath. The little road was buzzing with activity. American infantry, with the occasional Jeep, were making their way up.

I hurried back to the cellar. A corporal from a section of infantry occupying a cellar outside our yard burst in from the inner courtyard, took an assault rifle and left the cellar again by the outside steps. I told them in the cellar what was happening and slipped back up again.

In the castle courtyard, seen quite close from the landing, an American tank drove in with a man on the back behind a heavy machine gun or quick-firing cannon. He was not being heroic, just damn stupid. Only the fact that I had left my rifle in the cellar saved his life. So back to the cellar, grab my rifle and back up again, but the tank had gone. Even today, after several post-war visits to the castle, I still cannot understand how he got in and then vanished again. He could not have come in through the arched gateway, as it was too narrow. But through the gateway I could see a Sherman tank with its gun pointing toward us.

I turned round again, crossed the corridor and went down the narrow steps, stopping at the intermediate landing. Through the arrow-slit I had a good view of the road and the hilly ground beyond. American infantry were coming through a narrow gap in this hilly ground and jumping down on to the roadway. That was what we had heard the night before. Sheltered by the hills, the Americans had dug a communications trench parallel to the Moselle riverbank road and made the last cutting during the night. The first steep difference in height had to be covered with a two-meter jump down, the remaining four or six meters by sliding down as best as one could. Strangely enough, the GIs were not even looking at the castle where their enemy was. They saw their problem as being the first jump.

Without hesitation, I set my sights at 100 meters and took aim at the first one. He looked down, jumped, and I squeezed the trigger. Hit as he jumped, he bent his knees and slid down on his stomach down to the roadway, where he lay still on his stomach. I reloaded and already the next candidate was preparing to jump. He was a small, fat chap. I squeezed the trigger and he slid down on top of his comrade. A third man had already appeared. The game was repeated, he jumped and I fired.

Now some medical orderlies appeared. At the same time a Jeep drove up the road and an officer in the front passenger seat started giving instructions with many gestures. From the white stripe on his helmet I could easily see that he was a lieutenant. After my shot he slumped forward and slid down. Because of the medical orderlies that attended to him straight away, I held my fire. Apart from this, I could hear the crunch of footsteps from outside. If the Americans were already there and one of them threw a hand grenade through the arrow-slit, that would be my lot. Despite these thoughts, I still tried to bring a machine gun into position, but the slit was too narrow. I could not set up the bipod properly, nor could I lean forward into it enough to take the recoil. My attempt failed miserably. The recoil ripped into my right shoulder and the machine gun fell clattering to the ground. Now I had had enough. I went down into the cellar, where the lads looked at me questioningly. I gave a brief account and came to the conclusion: "We are sitting like rats in a trap!"

The artillery forward observer told me that he had ordered fire on our own position. I do not know whether we as forward observers for the mortars had given a similar order with Very Lights [signal rockets fired from a special pistol]. It is unlikely, for the firing position must have been experiencing the same as ourselves. Schloss Thorn was being raked by our own weapons, and there was also heavy fire on the American infantry advancing on Kreuzweiler.

After a short discussion we came to the decision to give ourselves up, otherwise we would be smoked out. One of us would have to go outside. Nobody wanted to be the one to go, but the lads picked on me as apparently I had once casually said something about speaking a little English. I opened the cellar door and climbed over the corpse of the corporal that had collected an assault rifle from us. He had been shot in the head by a sniper from the other side of the Moselle. The damaged screen that had sheltered us from view from the other side of the Moselle had fallen down, and we had not found it necessary to put it up again last night. No one had felt responsible, and this poor devil died because of it.

My main problem was now the sniper across the way, for as I climbed the steps he would have me in his sights. Would the same thing happen to me as to the poor devil on the cellar steps? I knew from my own experience how great the urge is to squeeze the trigger when one has one's enemy in one's sights. I raised my hands as high as they would go, climbed the first step and shouted out aloud: "American soldiers, we surrender!"[3]

Once the castle and the surrounding buildings had been taken, yielding twenty-five prisoners, the 1st Platoon of Captain Ashton's 94th Reconnaissance Troop secured the area, but then at 2200 the castle was bombarded by 120-mm mortars, wounding fifteen men of the platoon. This composite force was supposed to revert to its parent division when the armor passed through, but the tanks had top priority on the roads for their move forward, so it took until the following day for the change to occur.[4]

Farther to the right, Lieutenant Colonel Martin's 2nd/376th advanced on Kreuzweiler, as described by Capt. Frederic D. Standish III of F Company:

> The Line of Departure was the edge of a deep draw to the south of the village, just east of the Thorn-Sinz road. With Companies F and G leading, the attack left the Line of Departure at 0600 and led across an open field toward the woods immediately south of the village. Following an artillery barrage on the edge of the woods, which lit up the field with a cold light in white flashes, the foot troops advanced at a slow run, protected on both flanks of the narrow attacking column by heavy machine guns of Company H. Just inside the edge of the woods, the men who were new to combat, some 120 in all in the two advance companies, momentarily froze. The plan of attack called for a marching fire operation to carve a swathe through the woods, and probably the intense bedlam of noise caused the men fear. However, this was but a momentary reaction, and again the columns swept forward, literally tearing the trees and undergrowth to shreds by a continual hail of fire.
>
> It was impossible during the advance to give orders or signal, or do anything but shoot and run forward. Almost before anyone knew it, the far edge of the woods was reached, and then it became apparent that it would be quite a task to actually find the village of Kreuzweiler. Fog and smoke had obliterated any trace of civilization. But Captain [Arthur] Dodson and myself agreed that the column had swung too far to the right in order to get a straight shot at the village. As soon as the fog and smoke cleared, the companies entered the village and cleared it, but even before the last houses had been searched, a task force of the 10th Armored Division rolled through the town. Tanks, half-tracks, two-and-a-halfs and even jeeps. Strangely enough, while snipers were still shooting down the streets, there appeared the armored division commander in his jeep, followed by the corps commander in his, followed by another general in his. Surely now the Siegfried Line had been cracked, and the whole XX Corps could pour through.[5]

Lieutenant Colonel Martin's 2nd/376th attacked Kreuzweiler at 0805, and by 1000 half the village had been cleared and ninety-six prisoners taken, every building having to be fought for, so platoons were passed one through the other to keep up the pressure on the Germans. At about 1300 a counterattacking force of four tanks and about one hundred infantry was seen moving south from the village of Dilmar on the road into Kreuzweiler. When it reached a road junction at the halfway point that had already been registered by the 919th Field Artillery, it was stopped cold by a devastating barrage.

Combat Command R started passing through Kreuzweiler at 1335, a blown bridge on the riverside road having caused this detour from the riverside route. The tanks passed through the still enemy-occupied parts of the village with their guns blazing and moved on through Dilmar. Kreuzweiler was completely cleared within the next half hour, with a total bag of one hundred prisoners. The battalion then had to clear the woods in the area.

Farther east Lieutenant Colonel Thurston's 3rd Battalion moved northward and eastward in the wake of the 10th Armored, meeting with no opposition as formidable as that they had encountered during the early days of the attack on the Switch. By 1100 the battalion had reached Bilzingen, where they were ordered to wait. They used the time to regroup and then moved on again at 1700 to Mannebach, where the 376th Infantry's command post, moving ahead on wheels, was already established.

The 10th Armored Division's plan of attack deployed Combat Command R on the left, A on the right, and B in reserve. Once Schloss Thorn and Kreuzweiler were taken, Combat Command R had a clear run to Wincheringen, which was already in American hands after an assault by the XII Corps' 2nd Cavalry Group across the Moselle that morning.

Combat Command A was split into Task Force Chamberlain advancing on the left and Task Force Richardson on the right. Task Force Chamberlain was deployed between Merschweiler and Eft by 0100, and the team commanders were then given their orders for the attack. This task force was to advance via Tettingen and Sinz to seize the high ground between Bilzingen and Körrig in the first phase, and then along the Fischönsdorf-Fellerick axis to seize the high ground near Tawern at the northern tip of the Triangle. Teams Shaddeau, O'Grady, and Holehouse were to move up to the line of departure in that order. Team Holehouse, which contained most of the infantry, would remain initially as reserve in Sinz.

The columns moved off at 0600, but were then delayed by a traffic jam resulting from having to trace an unmapped American minefield that had taken out the leading tank as it approached the line of departure. There was also uncertainty about the location of the 376th Infantry's front line.

The line of departure was eventually crossed at 0855 by Team Shaddeau. Team O'Grady had been ordered to wait in Sinz, where it could oversee Team Shaddeau's progress cross-country and so avoid the enemy minefields and numerous antitank positions. Team Shaddeau flushed twenty Germans out of their foxholes in Moscholz Woods on the left and thirty-five more from the Waldtresch Woods northeast of the village of Beuren, where an artillery position with five 75-mm guns and three half-tracks was destroyed. Occasional enemy small-arms, artillery, and mortar fire was encountered, but Team Shaddeau was able to make good progress and reached the high ground dominating the village of Dittlingen by 1400 without much difficulty, although they had lost four tanks.

Team O'Grady then took over the lead with Team Holehouse following to mop up the ground that had already been cleared by the tanks and to prepare the road for their supply trains. Contact was established with the 2nd Cavalry Group from across the Moselle near Söst. Further progress was slowed down by enemy artillery fire, numerous craters, roadblocks, and the hilly ground, but by 1700 Teams O'Grady and Shaddeau had reached their day's objective—the high ground near Tawern. However, there appears to have been a lack of urgency at this point, for the orders to go on and seize the vital bridges across the Saar at Kanzem and Wiltingen were not issued until 1220 the next day, with the inevitable result that the enemy was able to blow the bridges as late as the early hours of February 22.

Meanwhile, Team Holehouse had cleared Dittlingen in a two-hour fight that yielded forty-five prisoners. The team then went on to clear Merz-kirchen village and took an additional thirty prisoners. The supply trains, attached tank destroyers, and supporting field artillery battalions closed in on Dittlingen by early evening.

The men of Task Force Richardson, taking the Perl-Saarburg highway, made contact with the enemy just before reaching the village of Kirf, where they ran into a minefield. The engineers cleared a passage for the tanks, but shortly afterward the column was hit by fire from assault guns and machine guns coming from the approaches to the village. This resistance was quickly overcome and the tanks moved into the village.

Team Billet was then ordered cross-country left of Kirf to attack the next village, Meurich, from the west. But they ran into antitank fire and were held up for thirty minutes until the mortars of Headquarters Company were able to silence the enemy positions. Meurich then fell without further resistance.

The remainder of Task Force Richardson then turned north off the highway for the village of Kelsen, where the command post of Regiment 456 of the 256th Volksgrenadier Division was overrun and some ninety prisoners taken.[6]

Lieutenant Colonel Dohs's 2nd/301st set off for Freudenburg at 0715, crossing the Leuk Branch, whose bridges had been blown, so the supporting tanks and tank destroyers had to wait until the engineers finished constructing a bridge. There was a steep climb up to the town from the branch. Resistance was slight and a battery of Russian 76.2-mm guns was surprised and captured, but only after enemy gunners had destroyed the guns.

Captain Sinclair's F Company fought its way into the southwest corner of the town shortly before noon and encountered strong resistance. Captain Stockstadt's E Company joined in, but progress was slow until Lieutenant Christiansen's G Company was committed from reserve in the mid-afternoon, and the town was then secured by nightfall.

Lieutenant Colonel McNulty's 3rd/301st did not start off toward Kollesleuken until 0800, moving out in column of companies with Captain Frierson's L Company leading. Part of this unit lost their direction in Das Brüch Woods and emerged in the 2nd Battalion's sector. Advised of this circumstance, the troops went back into the woods and came across their supporting tanks, which they mounted and then moved due east down the open ridge toward the Leuk Branch. However, as they emerged on the crest overlooking Kollesleuken, they came under fire from the north and the advance came to a halt. They pulled back to reorganize when they realized that the fire was coming from German units that had been forced out of Kirf by Combat Command A's advance. The tanks and infantry then deployed to engage the enemy in the valley below, forcing them back into the woods north of the Kirf-Kollesleuken road.

The 1st Platoon of L Company set off to outflank the German column, but were held in check by a German machine gun when they got close to the strip of woodland on the nearside of the stream separating the main woods from the road. The 2nd and 3rd Platoons then provided covering fire, which failed to relieve the pressure on the 1st Platoon. Communications with Battalion were out, so the tanks and heavy machine guns that were with the company lined up along the crest and were fired in lieu of artillery, enabling L Company's 2nd and 3rd Platoons, together with Lieutenant Devonald's K Company, to charge down the hill and across the stream into the woods beyond. K Company cleared the woods, while L Company turned east into Kollesleuken, where there was some bitter fighting before the village was secured at 1500.

Captain Donovan's I Company then occupied Kollesleuken with the task of maintaining contact with Combat Command A in Kirf. The remainder of the battalion then moved on across the Leuk Branch. The bridge across the stream had been burned, but the tanks and tank destroyers were able to use a ford. The men of Company L's 2nd Platoon were then detailed as tank escorts, swiftly overtaking their comrades on foot as the track vehicles drove straight up the Eiderberg overlooking the northern tip of Freudenburg. Four pillboxes on the southern edge of this hill quickly surrendered.[7]

Lieutenant Colonel Cloudt's 3rd/302nd moved off at 0700 on February 20, heading for the village of Weiten with I Company on the left, L Company on the right, and K Company in reserve. Halfway to their objective, the assault companies came under fire from two heavy machine guns on Height 366 in front of them. Pfc. Peter Maculawicz and two other men outflanked the enemy from the right and charged the nearest gun, taking the crew prisoner. The second enemy machine gun then succumbed to the combined fire coming from the assault companies.

As the battalion continued across the hill and down the far side, they saw that the bridge across the Leuk Branch below was still intact. As they got nearer, a lone German soldier was seen racing through the woods for the bridge and was pinned down by rifle fire, while the leading elements of Lieutenant Devonald's K Company made a dash for the bridge, which the Germans had fully prepared for demolition. The demolition wires were cut and all the troops crossed on dry foot, except for those of Captain Williams's I Company, on the left, who had to wade the stream.

The battalion then waited in the woods west of Weiten for their armored support. A Battery of the 465th Antiaircraft Artillery Battalion was the first to arrive and used its quadruple .50-caliber machine guns to rake the village. The tanks drove straight for the village, but were engaged by a German antitank gun as they emerged into the open. Lt. Carmen L. Ramirez of L Company took the 2nd Platoon to outflank the gun, which was knocked out by Pfcs. Raymond H. Laabs and William F. Eggers.

The tanks moved forward once more, firing at the buildings at the western end of the village, then at 1415 I and L Companies attacked both sides of the Faha road. After the leading platoons had reached the center of the village, SSgt. James E. Capps led the 4th Platoon and Company Headquarters to mop up behind the assault. In one house they found the command post of Grenadier Regiment 713 with several German staff officers, who told them that the attack had been totally unexpected. Several armored vehicles and some antitank weapons were discovered intact under camouflage netting. It seemed that the disruption of German communications had been complete. The village was secured by nightfall.

Major Stanion's 1st/302nd moved off from its overnight positions near Oberleuken on the morning of February 20 and began the lengthy process of clearing the Unter den Eichen Woods on the way to Orscholz. They reduced six enemy-held pillboxes that day.[8]

Task Force Gaddis was formed from Major Maixner's 2nd/302nd and Lieutenant Colonel Miller's 1st/301st under Lt. Col. John W. Gaddis, the executive officer of the 302nd Infantry, for the purpose of taking the large village of Orscholz at the eastern end of the Switch. The task force assembled in Kesslingen on the night of February 19 and set off the following morning with the 2nd/302nd following some four hundred yards behind the 3rd/302nd as it advanced on Weiten.

Gaddis had selected a position in the woods five hundred yards northwest of Orscholz for his forward assembly area. The advance was led by G Company, followed in turn by E and F Companies, with the 1st/301st four hundred yards farther back. The lead scout, Pfc. Robert S. Karlix, took the initiative as they approached the assembly area at 1150, capturing nineteen prisoners with three horse-drawn carts. The plan was to attack south using the Weiten road as the boundary between the 1st/301st on the right and the 2nd/302nd on the left. The 301st Field Artillery provided artillery support for the operation, having observers with both battalions. H Company's mortars were also in the forward assembly area, as were a platoon each of light and medium tanks. These tanks had problems crossing the Leuk Branch, so the attack was postponed until they were in position.

Meanwhile, a patrol led by Sgt. Simond J. Sendric was sent off toward Weiten to check whether the area behind the task force was clear of the enemy and to establish contact with the 3rd/302nd. While this was happening, Captain Butler's E Company, which had been designated as battalion reserve, dug in to foil any enemy attempt at a counterattack.

With the armor finally in place, the attack was launched at 1400, too late to arrange an artillery preparation, so the tanks provided covering fire. Sgt. Joseph A. Romanowski's heavy machine-gun section backed Captain Kops's F Company on the far left as it advanced and came under fire from enemy machine guns in Orscholz. F Company then charged straight in. Captain Griffin's G Company negotiated some minefields north of the village and began clearing their section of the village without too much difficulty. Once in the village, which had been shattered by bombing and previous bombardments, Pfc. James Heard of H Company set up his heavy machine gun to cover the main street and prevent any enemy crossing. One of his crew was hit by sniper fire, but the sniper threw down his rifle and surrendered as other infantrymen closed in on him. By 1800 the battalion had completed clearing their part of the village. The battalion command post then moved into the village and began planning operations to clear the area to the south the next day.

The 1st/301st, whose B and C Companies had been seriously depleted in the attack on Münzingen Ridge the day before, used Capt. Charles B. Colgan's A Company for the assault, with the others mopping up behind. The battalion experienced little difficulty taking their part of the village house by house.[9]

February 20 had been an extremely successful day for the 10th Armored and 94th Infantry Divisions, and General Walker at XX Corps was quite pleased. That same morning he presented General Malony with the Bronze Star for the 94th's success of the previous day.

Final clearance of the Triangle was now obviously in sight, a matter of hours perhaps. That afternoon all German troops that were not needed for the fighting west of the Saar were ordered to withdraw to the east bank of the river. The defense of the Saar-Moselle Triangle had cost the Germans

1,024 soldiers killed, 1,592 wounded, and 2,390 prisoners. The German artillery had lost nineteen guns to air attack and artillery fire, and a further sixteen pieces had been overrun and captured intact.

The 94th U.S. Infantry Division had lost just over 1,000 soldiers. According to the regimental history, during these first three days of its attachment to the 10th Armored Division, the 376th Infantry sustained 176 battle and 34 nonbattle casualties.[10]

At 0900 on February 21, Lieutenant Colonel Martin's 2nd/376th and Lieutenant Colonel Thurston's 3rd/376th began a massive sweep of the western part of the Triangle from just north of Kreuzweiler, each battalion with three companies abreast. They met with virtually no resistance and came across evidence of the formidable force of the American artillery and bombing attacks on German artillery positions. The only mishap occurred when G Company emerged from the northern edge of Loschenkopf Woods and was fired on by elements of the 10th Armored Division. Captain Dodson then went forward with an improvised white flag and identified himself.

At 1800 the 2nd/376th assembled at Wincheringen, where they were told to proceed to Mannebach immediately. The 3rd/376th reached Bilzingen a half hour later and was given the same instructions, while the 1st/376th, which had been motorized and placed in regimental reserve before the attack of February 19, was also ordered forward to Mannebach.[11]

With the 301st Infantry, Lieutenant Colonel Dohs's 2nd Battalion continued their advance from Freudenburg in the morning, encountering no resistance, and by 1100 the men of Captain Sinclair's F Company were looking down on the Saar River. Similarly, Lieutenant Colonel McNulty's 3rd Battalion pushed on to reach the village of Kastel on the heights overlooking the Saar. Although the battalion encountered some resistance, the village was secured by 1025.

Lieutenant Colonel Cloudt's 3rd/302nd pushed on due east out of Weiten to take the villages of Taben, Rodt, and Hamm by the middle of the afternoon, while Major Stanion's 1st/302nd completed clearing the highway and woods up to Orscholz from Oberleuken.

Major Hodges's 1st/301st remained in Orscholz all day, while B Company's 2nd Platoon was sent to investigate the pillboxes south of the village, most of which were unoccupied. 1st Sgt. William M. Kelley, one of the survivors of the disastrous first attack on Orscholz, volunteered to accompany the patrol, as it would be passing through the area where the company had been isolated. He found several items of clothing bearing serial numbers he recognized, and he also came across the graves of some of the men whom the Germans had buried south of the village.

Major Maixner's 2nd/302nd's E and G Companies also searched the area south of the village in their respective sector. A roadblock at the southern end of the village had to be blown to allow the accompanying armor to pass through. At the first bunker they came to they saw a German soldier sitting at the entrance calmly reading a newspaper. He told them that nearly all the German soldiers had fled during the night, and he was one of only two prisoners taken by the American soldiers. As Lieutenant Butler of E Company led his men to the last bunker near Nohn, contact was established with the 5th Ranger Battalion covering that flank.

That evening Lieutenant Hunter of F Company's 1st Platoon took a combat patrol, augmented by one light and two medium tanks and a mortar squad, to check out the village of Keuchlingen, which lies at the bottom of the Saar valley opposite the town of Mettlach. They made a thorough search of the village, which took them twelve hours, and were then relieved by elements of the 5th Ranger Battalion.[12]

With the clearance of the Triangle almost complete, General Patton called on General Walker at the 10th Armored Division's command post on February 21 to check on progress. Satisfied with the situation, Patton turned to Walker and said: "Johnnie, cross the Saar and take Trier."[13]

8

Crossing the Saar

General Walker returned to XX Corps headquarters and had Field Order Number 17 drawn up, implementing Patton's orders for the 10th Armored Division. Walker also extended the order for crossing the Saar to the 94th Infantry, ordering them to cross between Saarburg and Hamm on the night of February 21–22, with the aim of establishing a bridgehead and being "prepared to continue the advance to the northeast on Corps order." In doing so, the men of the 94th were to maintain contact with both the 10th Armored on the left and the 3rd Cavalry on the right. Meanwhile, the other division under command, the 26th Infantry, and the 3rd Cavalry Group, to which the 5th Ranger Battalion was attached, were to maintain their defensive positions.

Patton's desire to take Trier, the ancient Roman city that was now the German communications center and the main gateway to the Rhine at Koblenz along the winding path of the Moselle, was tactically sound, and the 10th Armored Division was the instrument that could secure it for him. After their decisive defeat in the Triangle, the Germans might well be caught unprepared by this immediate follow-up. However, Patton was expecting the exhausted and depleted 94th Infantry Division, whose troops had no experience of river crossings, to negotiate a swollen, icy river that was in full flood from the melting snow and rains of the past two months. Further, he was sending the troops straight into the main Westwall defenses on the dominating east bank without adequate reconnaissance or intelligence of what to expect. The whole operation was nothing but a reckless gamble.

Bearing in mind that these decisions and orders were made on February 21, it remains puzzling that more emphasis was not given to rushing the bridges across the Saar at Kanzem and Wiltingen, which were still standing and would have provided the armor more direct access to Trier. But as previously mentioned, Task Force Chamberlain, which had reached the vicinity of Tawern by the evening of February 20, did not move against these bridges until the following day. This may have been because of delays in refueling or a lack of belief that the bridges would still be standing. However, as the troops approached Wiltingen, they found that the route was blocked by a substantial minefield, and just as a way through had been cleared, the Germans blew the bridge, followed shortly after by another explosion at Kanzem.

Spirits rose among the troops as the 94th Infantry Division closed up to the Saar River during the afternoon of February 21, 1945. The final drive through the Saar-Moselle Triangle had been spectacular as the enemy withdrew over the Saar, blowing the few bridges, and the corps commander himself had indicated that the troops could now expect to enjoy a well-earned rest once they had completed this task and set up outposts along the river.[1]

As Major Harold F. Howard, S-3 of the 301st Infantry, later recorded: "The 301st Infantry continued the advance to the Saar River line on 21 February. The enemy was cleared from the zone and the towns of Kastel and Staadt were taken. The companies however were by this time down to an average strength of 120 men, and the men were extremely tired from the hard going."[2]

Capt. John S. Young, S-2 (staff officer for intelligence) of the 302nd Infantry, recorded: "On the morning of the 21st orders were received to push on to the river and secure the towns of Taben and Hamm. The 3d Battalion, under command of Lieutenant-Colonel Otto B. Cloudt, mounted the infantry on tanks and tank destroyers and rode right down into the towns of Taben and Hamm. The enemy at this time was thoroughly disorganized and rapid progress was made against relatively no opposition. The 2d Battalion also mounted up on tanks, tank destroyers and other available vehicles and moved into Keuchlingen. The entire river line was in our hands by the evening of 21 February."[3]

The 94th Division's first intimation of this development came at 1400 that afternoon when one of its liaison officers at the XX Corps command post, Lt. Harold J. Donkers, called Division Headquarters in Freuden-burg, saying, "Back here they're talking about a river crossing, and if it's made, we'll be making it!" Although the idea of an immediate crossing hardly seemed credible, the divisional commander had the commanders of the 301st and 302nd Infantry Regiments and the 319th Engineer Combat Battalion alerted so that preliminary preparations could start immedi-ately. Time available for reconnaissance and planning was negligible, and it seemed highly improbable that the necessary equipment and supplies for such an operation could be found and delivered at such short notice. The divisional artillery commander, Brigadier General Fortier, ordered an aerial reconnaissance along the Saar River from Merzig to Trier by one of the Tiger Cub spotter aircraft available to him, while the regimental com-manders sent out patrols to investigate the west bank of the river for pos-sible crossing sites and likely observation posts.

Intelligence could provide very little information on enemy dispositions on the far side of the Saar, but it was assumed that the Germans would still be confused and disorganized from the events of the previous three days. Nevertheless, the main defenses of the Siegfried Line would be encoun-tered, providing the enemy with good observation and clear fields of fire from well-constructed pillboxes and bunkers, all protected by mines and wire, linked by good underground communications, and backed by well-sited artillery positions. Unfortunately, nothing was known of these posi-tions, as the corps' 7th Field Artillery Observation Battalion was too far from the river to obtain accurate plots on the German battery positions.[4]

XX Corps Field Order Number 11 was delivered to Division Head-quarters by Lieutenant Donkers at 1804: "The XX Corps attacks 22 Febru-ary to exploit their breakthrough, seize Trier, and expand the bridgehead to the line Pfalzel to Hamm and will be prepared to continue the attack to the northeast or north on Army Order . . . The 10th Armored Division (attached 376th Combat Team) attacks to the northeast to seize Trier . . . The 94th Infantry Division attacks across the Saar between Saarburg and Hamm on the night of the 21st–22d of February to establish the line Geizenburg south to the river bend at Hamm, and will be prepared to con-tinue the attack to the northeast on Corps order."[5]

This order also named certain units to be attached to the division for this operation: the 778th Tank Battalion (less Company C); the 704th Tank Destroyer Battalion (less Company C); the 465th Antiaircraft Artillery

Battalion; the 774th Tank Destroyer Battalion; and Company C of the 81st Chemical Warfare Mortar Battalion. Backed by the 1139th Engineer Combat Group, direct support would also be provided by the 135th Engineer Combat Battalion, whose A Company was tasked with building a treadway bridge, B Company to road maintenance, and C Company to assist the division's own 319th Engineers at the crossing sites.

The division's remaining 301st, 356th, and 390th Field Artillery Battalions had to be assigned new positions from the map, as there was no time to carry out a proper reconnaissance. However, the XX Corps Artillery assigned its 5th Field Artillery Group of several battalions to reinforce the 94th Division Artillery with its 105- to 155-mm guns, and also allocated general support (to be shared with the 3rd Cavalry) by the heavier 195th Field Artillery Group, with howitzers of up to 240-mm caliber.

As General Morris had the 376th Combat Team of the 94th Infantry under command, he proposed conserving his armored infantry for the assault on Trier and using the 376th for the river crossing. Thus the entire river crossing operation would be conducted by elements of the 94th Infantry Division. Morris ordered the tank destroyers of Combat Command B to provide heavy covering fire for the river crossing and to be ready to pass through the bridgehead as soon as a bridge had been constructed. Combat Command A was also ordered to provide covering fire for the crossing, and Combat Command R was to remain in reserve. Meanwhile, Lt. Col. Cornelius A. Lichirie's 90th Cavalry Reconnaissance Squadron was to provide a counter-reconnaissance screen, maintain patrols, and liaison with friendly forces along the line between Saarburg and Mertert on the Moselle.[6]

An appreciation made at Fort Knox in 1949 on the 10th Armored Division's operations in the Triangle reads:

> The western approaches to the Saar River gave commanding observation to the enemy located on the high ridges which formed the eastern bank. At almost all points this dominating terrain was reinforced by the fortifications of the Siegfried Line. Like the Switch Line at the base of the Triangle, the concrete pillboxes were positioned to insure [sic] mutual support and to cover the likely avenues of approach to the western bank. The Germans had carefully considered these natural avenues before constructing their defensive instal-

lations. Where the river and the ridge together were not considered to be of sufficient strength additional concrete defensive works had been added. Ockfen was an example, for there the defenses were approximately three kilometers in depth, forming a formidable obstacle to any attempted crossings.

However, in the vicinity of Taben and Serrig, where the eastern banks of the Saar River formed an almost perpendicular cliff, the Germans believed additional field fortifications unnecessary. The river was from 120 to 150 feet wide in the vicinity of both crossing sites. The steep eastern banks made fording impossible. German pillboxes were able to cover the river by direct small arms and machine gun fire, and observed artillery fire. Along the western bank the terrain was open with some scattered wooded areas which did not provide sufficient concealment to prevent enemy observation. In addition, there was considerable marshy ground which would confine all vehicular movement to the roads.

The 10th Armored and 94th Divisions had little time for detailed planning of the attack or for reconnaissance of the terrain surrounding the crossing sites, as had been the case in the initial penetration and breakthrough.

A study of the situation confronting the 10th Armored Division at Ockfen will set the picture of its proposed crossing. The German defenses at this point were manned by three fortress battalions in addition to the remains of the two divisions[,] which had been badly battered in the Triangle but had been able to make their way back across the Saar in small groups. There were also many hastily improvised formations of service and supporting troops, along with the Saarburg Volkssturm. Although they were not first-class troops, their primary mission—sitting in pillboxes and keeping machine guns trained on the river—did not require highly trained personnel. It was apparent that speed would be the essential element of the proposed crossing in order to deny the Germans time to man and possibly to reinforce the already well-fortified Saar River line.[7]

Detailed plans had now to be formulated and coordinated, crossing sites selected, infantry and artillery units deployed into new positions, and additional engineers and river-crossing equipment obtained and brought to the crossing sites. Food, ammunition, and fuel was to be moved forward from supply dumps, which in some instances had been left forty and more miles to the rear by the rapid advance of the past three days.

During the afternoon of February 21, General Walker called Major General Malony, exclaiming that this was the "opportunity of a lifetime" for the 94th Infantry, the corps, and the Third Army. He telephoned again that evening to warn Malony that he could expect a visit from General Patton the following afternoon. Again he stressed that this was the "opportunity of a lifetime," but he must have had some misgivings about the feasibility of the project, for he added that if the division proved unable to accomplish the task, he was "not going to blame you, because you carried out the most wonderful masterpiece, and the Boss (Patton) appreciated it, and I do too." As the 94th was being sent in blind to tackle the main defenses of the Siegfried Line in this sector, some apprehension on Walker's part was fully justified.

By 2000 the plans had been made and approved, and a division field order was issued barely eight hours before the crossing was due to begin at 0400 next day. The 301st Infantry's orders were to establish a bridgehead from Serrig northward to a point opposite Krutweiler (just south of Saarburg), continue the advance, and gain the 94th Infantry Division's initial objective, a chain of hills some six thousand yards east of Serrig, while maintaining contact with the 10th Armored Division on the left and the 302nd Infantry on the right. Similarly, the men of the 302nd were to secure a bridgehead from Serrig southward to the river bend at Hamm, push eastward, and also seize part of the chain of hills east of Serrig. They were to protect the 301st's southern flank and maintain contact with the 5th Ranger Battalion farther south on the west bank of the Saar.

Having established a suitable bridgehead across the Saar, the division's next task would be to advance eastward along the Beurig-Irsch-Zerf road. The only roads leading down to possible crossing sites on the division's front were at Saarburg, Krutweiler, Staadt, and Hamm, but the first two locations had yet to be cleared of the enemy and it was already dark.

Reconnaissance of the Staadt and Hamm sites was made by the infantry and engineers. The engineers found a suitable site at Staadt next to a disused ferry directly opposite the east-bank village of Serrig. They also looked for a possible ford, but without success. Hamm was on a flat peninsula that was completely overlooked by enemy positions on the high ground surrounding the sharp bend. The area was found to be too exposed and had no road leading up to the river, so the 302nd Infantry's suggestion of using the site of a blown bridge below the village of Taben farther south was checked by the engineers and approved. This too was dominated by enemy-held high ground, but the site was in such a deep defile that it was sheltered from defilade artillery fire. Military police reconnaissance of the routes leading to the two chosen sites at Staadt and Taben confirmed suitability for two-way traffic. The selection of these crossing sites thus made the large east-bank village of Serrig a primary objective for these two infantry regiments.

The 319th Engineer Combat Battalion had only twelve assault boats on hand, so another fifty were requisitioned from the 1139th Engineer Combat Group, which had only sixty assault boats and five motorboats left at its disposal, as most of the Third Army's crossing equipment had been sent off to support the First and Ninth Armies farther north during the Battle of the Bulge. XX Corps also allocated the 135th Combat Engineer Battalion in support of the 94th Infantry Division.

The convoy conveying the boats failed to arrive by 2230, so the operations officer of the 319th Engineers in Freudenburg, Maj. Albert F. Hoffman, set off to look for it. He found the convoy two miles to the south, where the drivers had pulled off the road to settle down for the night. Upon arrival at Freudenburg the convoy was then split to enable each crossing site to receive thirty-one boats each. The Staadt allotment was further delayed by a supply column having mistakenly taken the turn out of Freudenburg to Kastel, where its individual vehicles had to make three-point turns to get back, only to have the assault boat convoy arrive and try to force its way through as this traffic mishap was going on. One of the assault boat trailers ditched and overturned in this confusion and was abandoned. Consequently, the boats did not arrive at the launching sites until between 0400 and 0500. A proper traffic control system using eight military police checkpoints and priority allocations was not established by Division until later in the day.

A similar incident occurred with the 376th Infantry's boats. The 10th Armored's engineer, Lt. Col. Wadsworth P. Clapp, set off for Tawern to rendezvous with the pontoon bridge–carrying convoy that was bringing the necessary boats and bridging equipment allocated to them by the 1139th

Engineer Group. However, Clapp returned with only three trucks still following him, the remainder having got lost on the way.[8]

General Patton arrived at XX Corps late the next morning, February 22, with his usual train of war correspondents and photographers in attendance, expecting to go on to a grandstand view of the operation. However, General Walker informed Patton that because of the missing convoy, the 10th Armored would be unable to cross until the next day. Patton immediately flew into a violent rage, demanding that the attack go ahead regardless. He drove on to the 10th Armored Division's command post in Ayl, where he vented his rage quite openly, as Pvt. Russell Bryant, a replacement with B Company, reported:

> February 22 we were milling around Ayl, when General Patton pulled up in a Jeep with the rest of his entourage. He's talking with his various commanders about crossing the Saar River. Some 20 or 30 of us enlisted men were close enough to hear their discussion. Some of his direct subordinates were cautioning him against a direct assault across the river.
>
> I heard him say loud enough for all to hear: "I don't care if it takes a bushel basket full of dog tags, we're crossing the river right here!"
>
> There was a gasp from all us enlisted men. If Patton heard it, he ignored it.[9]

Patton's attitude toward casualties no doubt reflected the fact that his Third Army had already lost 47,000 men since leaving Normandy, with 2,190 killed in the fighting for Metz alone. His feelings about the Siegfried Line defenses were aptly summarized by historian Charles Whiting in relation to the earlier attacks across the Sauer River to the north:

> After inspecting a captured bunker (it had been taken through the back door), he pontificated that it showed "the utter futility of fixed defenses . . . In war the only sure defense is offense[,] and the efficiency of offense depends on the warlike souls of those conducting it."
>
> It was evident that Patton had learned nothing from the last half year of frontal attacks on the Siegfried Line. He adhered to the

theory of attack, attack and attack again, which was already outdated by the time of the Civil War nearly a century earlier, and which had caused so many young American lives to be needlessly thrown away.[10]

Another account of the scene at Ayl comes from T. Jerome French of B Company, who was then a private: "By noon the boats had not come, the Germans had not seen us because we all got inside and stayed there. The latest was that we would wait for night before venturing outside. Then a high-ranking officer came on the scene and started throwing a tantrum, ordering an immediate crossing as soon as the boats came. . . . The big-shot got in his Jeep and went away."[11] Patton, with the extra-large stars on his helmet, would have been mortified at not being recognized for who he was!

Patton later told Walker at Headquarters XX Corps that "Morris had let his train get lost, and therefore was not across at Saarburg, and that, at a late hour in the afternoon when I met him, he was being held up by small arms fire from the far side of the river." He then told Walker: "You should have seen that it was in place. So should I. We have all three fallen down on the job." By the time Patton left, he was blustering: "General Morris will lead his division across the river in the first boat, or, if necessary, swim." This irrational display of temper, typical of Patton, demonstrates how he chose to ignore the reality of the situation.[12]

THE AYL CROSSING—FEBRUARY 22

The 376th had been assembling at Mannebach during the afternoon of February 21 when late in the day Colonel McClune, the regimental commander, received orders from the 10th Armored Division calling for an assault crossing of the Saar at 0400 next morning. He summoned an immediate conference of his various subordinate commanders to discuss the issue. By the time the conference was over, it was already dark. None of the 376th Infantry had yet seen the river or the bunker-studded hills to the east, for the 10th's armored infantry were still engaged in clearing the area west of the Saar from which the crossing would have to be made, and a study of the map proved far from encouraging.

The selected crossing site was outside the village of Ayl on a tilted plain about a mile long and 1,200 feet wide that gave an easy approach to the water's edge. Across the river, the village of Ockfen extended along a narrow valley that was flanked on the left by a steep, vine-covered hill. Capping the hill was the Irminer Wald, rising some 740 feet above the Saar River. On the right, the gentler slope of another, unnamed hill rose about 340 feet, while behind this hill and the village rose the even higher regimental objective of the Scharfenberg Ridge, some 900 feet above the river and about 2,200 yards east of Ockfen.

Colonel McClune decided to employ two battalions abreast for the operation. The 3rd Battalion would cross directly east of Ayl to seize the steep ridge north of Ockfen, while the 1st Battalion would cross one thousand yards upstream to take the high ground south of the village. Once these dominant pieces of terrain were secure, the 2nd Battalion would cross at the northern site and take Ockfen. With the entire regiment across and its initial objectives seized, the two flank battalions were to push east to the final objective. With these three pieces of high ground in American hands, the armor would have a secure bridgehead through the Siegfried Line's defenses. It was hoped that the Saar could then be bridged and the tank columns driven eastward, deep into the enemy rear.

McClune's meeting with his commanders to make these plans ended at about 2100, leaving only seven hours in which to prepare. The regimental field kitchens arrived in Mannebach after dark, but orders came for the troops to march off to Ayl before most of them could be fed. The men's only chance of the first hot meals in days, and for days to come, had to be abandoned. They smashed their stolen plates on the cobbles as they marched off in disgust.

Colonel McClune then decided to examine the crossing site himself, dark though it was. To his surprise, his jeep encountered German troops when entering Ayl, and he was lucky to escape. When he reported this incident to the 10th Armored Division headquarters, he was assured that the armored infantry were about to take the village.[13]

It was midnight before the leading elements of the 1st Battalion entered Ayl, prepared for any eventuality, but soon they encountered the armored infantrymen who had taken the village only a little while before. The 3rd Battalion followed them in, while the 2nd Battalion camped outside in the woods behind the village. No assault boats had yet arrived, so Colonel McClune again consulted the 10th Armored Division and was assured that the boats were on the way and would arrive in time for the crossing.

Lieutenant Colonel Thurston and his 3rd Battalion waited about a half mile or so to the northeast of Ayl. He later reported that an occasional round clattered down on Ayl and that there was an occasional burst of German machine-gun fire in the distance, but generally all was quiet for nearly six hours. At about 1300 the regimental command post was set up in Ayl, and about an hour later the 10th Armored Division also set up its command post in the village only a few doors away.

Then, in the middle of the afternoon, a smoke-generator company drove through Thurston's assembly area and started setting up its equipment a half mile from the riverbank and in full view of the enemy, who made no attempt to intervene. It took almost thirty minutes to set up the equipment, but the company then dispersed without having generated any smoke, much to Thurston's annoyance. After another thirty minutes passed, the convoy with the assault boats arrived, the engineers onloaded them with a lot of noise, and the trucks left. At last the Germans responded with an artillery concentration that smashed every one of the boats and wrecked the smoke-generating equipment.

Then, as a result of General Patton's visit to the command post of the 10th Armored Division that afternoon, at 1625 the 1st and 3rd Battalions received orders to "cross at once," although they were still without boats. The battalions began moving forward along the narrow road leading to the Saar while it was still daylight. Fortunately, the German artillery failed to intervene, but enemy snipers who were concealed in the small cemetery at the junction of the Ayl and Konz-Saarburg roads opened fire, killing Captain Brightman, the commander of L Company, and wounding Lt. James Cornelius, the officer commanding C Company, who had to be replaced by the sole remaining officer in the company, Lieutenant Chalkley.[14]

When the 10th Armored Division headquarters had been told of the destruction of the assault boats, Colonel McClune was asked to estimate the earliest possible time at which he could resume crossing, to which he had replied, "One hour after I receive sufficient boats." More craft were promised. At 2130 the second shipment of assault boats began to arrive at Ayl, and the crossing was then scheduled for 2300. The boat convoy slipped through the village and east to the junction with the road paralleling the river. There the boats were divided, with each of the assault battalions receiving half of the shipment, about a dozen each.

Acting on his own initiative, Lieutenant Colonel Thurston took his 3rd

Battalion along the road leading north until it reached the small stream running into the Saar northeast of Ayl, half a mile farther downstream than had been planned. All the while the men moved under the strictest silence so as not to attract enemy attention. The boats were carried to the river-bank, where the men who were to man them waited anxiously for the order to launch. On the order, the heavily laden men climbed cautiously into the fragile craft and paddled furiously into the fast-moving stream. For the most part they were inexperienced in handling assault craft, and it took considerable time to negotiate the swiftly flowing river.

The 3rd Battalion's crossing went smoothly, and the incredibly loud sounds of the protective barrage being laid by the tank destroyers for the 1st Battalion farther upstream appeared to have effectively distracted the enemy opposite the 3rd, for it encountered no opposition. The assault squads of Lt. William R. Jacques's I Company pushed forward rapidly in what amounted to a mass infiltration to reach the battalion's primary objective, the top of the hill capped by the Irminer Wald.[15]

Sgt. Robert K. Adair, one of this company's squad leaders, later recorded his experience:

By then it was about 5:00 p.m. I got a little to eat and tried to get some sleep before 11:00 p.m., when we were supposed to start out. But I was so scared that I couldn't sleep much. I kept wondering how we could possibly make it against what seemed to be excessive odds.

Then 11:00 and we were off. Busy getting everybody together, checking that everyone knew what he was to do, I no longer had any time to worry. We joined the engineers with the boats in a concealed position perhaps two hundred yards from shore. There was to be a squad—I had eight in my squad at that time—in each boat, each man with a paddle, plus two engineers. The engineers were to steer the boats across and the two of them then take the boats back for another load.

About 11:30 we grabbed the heavy twenty-foot-long plywood boats, dragged them down to the water, and started across the two hundred feet of water to the other side. We paddled hard, quartering against the spring-time current, and I would guess that it took us less than five minutes to cross but we felt very much exposed. . . . But nobody shot at us.

We got out of the boats on the far shore with no difficulty. There were Schü mines spread on the bank, but we could see them fairly well and were careful not to step on them, and there was also some barbed wire. Cutting the wire, we crossed the railroad tracks that ran along the east bank of the river and started up the steep hill with the three Second Platoon squads abreast and leading the company. Again I was much too busy seeing that everyone was there, spread out properly and keeping roughly in line, to worry much. Still nothing happened. It turned out that the only "pillbox" in my squad's zone of responsibility was not a pillbox but an unoccupied old stone tower. There were a few startled Germans in one position to our left who promptly surrendered to the First Squad. After about thirty minutes of climbing the steep, brush covered hill, we were at the top, and no one had even shot at us.

I collected and reformed my squad at the top and started down a path flanked on both sides by artillery carts and guns. But no Germans. Then we heard some noise and a man came out of the woods carrying what turned out to be a large can of stew. He was astonished to see us and surrendered with no difficulty. We waited for the men who were to eat the stew, but they had left their supper as well as the guns.[16]

It hardly seemed possible, but the 3rd Battalion had achieved complete surprise, and in an amazingly short time I Company was on top of the sheer rise of the Irminer Wald, some 740 feet above the river. 1st Lt. Cecil G. Dansby's 1st Platoon, bringing up the rear of I Company, came under spasmodic fire from some bypassed bunkers on the northern slopes, and K and L Companies similarly encountered resistance from these bunkers as they followed behind, but all got through without difficulty.[17]

The engineers had laid out their assault boats for the 1st Battalion along the sandy beach at the water's edge and they were ready for launching. Lieutenant Colonel Miner had elected C Company to lead the assault under Lieutenant Chalkley, all of his platoon commanders now being NCOs. He was given a heavy machine-gun section from D Company and two rifle squads from B Company to augment his numbers. As previously mentioned, covering fire was provided by a tank destroyer battalion from the 10th Armored Division, using a lot of tracers.

Just as C Company closed up to the riverbank, Colonel McClune was badly wounded by shrapnel in both thighs as he went forward to check the progress of the operation, and was wounded again in the chest before he could be evacuated. The executive officer, Lt. Col. Raynor E. Anderson, then assumed command of the 376th Infantry Regiment.[18]

Bob Trefzger, then assistant squad leader of the 3rd Squad of the 3rd Platoon, C Company, reports:

> Leaving Ayl under cover of darkness, we proceeded to the west edge of the Saar River. The plywood assault boats were there along the shoreline, having been trucked into position, also under cover of darkness. Each boat was supposed to carry twelve men: ten infantrymen with their equipment and two combat engineers. The engineers' job was to guide the boats across the river and then bring them back to the friendly side for another load of infantrymen.
>
> We were quickly assigned to our boats; the combat engineers told us that there was a paddle for each man (they were very similar to canoe paddles) and that we were to paddle as though our lives depended on it. Good idea!
>
> Shortly before H-Hour an incredibly spectacular covering barrage of vivid pink tracer shells and bullets started up from the west side of the valley, passing well over our heads. The shells were larger, single tracers from some sort of cannon. The machine gun tracers were in long chains, probably from .50-caliber machine guns. We had no idea who were [*sic*] providing this very welcome barrage, but we were very impressed and very grateful. The noise of the "friendly fire" was indescribable!
>
> At H-Hour, on the tracer-illuminated shore of the river, we had little problem launching and climbing into our boat. Paddling quickly across the river, we could see and feel the swiftness of the current. No enemy fire was visible, either muzzle flashes or machine gun tracers, and we were very thankful for the continuing covering barrage of pink tracers. The swift current and unfamiliarity with paddling an assault boat made it seem as though the Saar was very wide.
>
> Our boat stopped several feet from the east shore when it ran into submerged barbed wire entanglements. The ten heavily loaded infantrymen struggled into the bow so as to get out of the boat where the water was shallower, about knee deep. As we tried to disentangle

ourselves from the submerged wire, the friendly covering barrage of pink tracers stopped. Almost instantly, while I was still in the water, an enemy machine gun began firing pale yellowish tracers from a large concrete fortification just downstream from our landing. The machine gun fire came from an aperture 12 to 15 feet above river level, so it was no immediate threat to us. We were frustrated, however, as there was nothing we could do to stop it.

Once on shore we struggled up a very steep bank next to the vertical south edge of the concrete fortification. At the top of the bank, to our amazement, we came upon a wide, double set of railroad tracks. The night was very dark and very quiet except for enemy machine guns firing across the river from the concrete fortifications. Even in the dark, it soon became obvious that there was no hill to assault where we were and no other C Company GIs in sight. Where did they all go?[19]

Marshall Miller, a squad leader in B Company's 3rd Platoon, reports:

At 2300 the attack commenced. The Saar River is only about 100 feet wide at Ayl. Since it was winter, the river was swift and icy. The Germans poured mortar and machine-gun fire from pillboxes and trenches in the hills on the east bank. The engineers lit smoke pots to try to hide our movements. They dragged the boats to the river's edge. We waited behind a stone fence about 100 yards uphill from the water. Every ten men were counted and, when given a signal, ran to the river in single file. It was complete confusion. Smoke was everywhere, shells were coming in, but were not very accurate. Ten of us scrambled into a boat, and with two engineers, pushed off. We were told to grab a wooden paddle from the bottom of the boat and start paddling.

We had never practiced a river crossing. We paddled furiously, but we were not coordinated. The swift current caught the boat and turned us around and we sped stern first northward towards Trier. We were unable to turn the boat around, nor could we paddle towards the enemy's east bank. Approximately a mile down river we crashed into the supports of a demolished wooden bridge. Two or three other boats were wedged into the timbers when we struck them. It was very dark and cloudy. The moon occasionally broke through the clouds.

This was our good fortune. The Germans could not see us. We were about 30 feet from their side of the river. I could hear the noise of the battle back at the crossing site. It was quiet at the bridge.

Another boat struck our wedged flotilla. The soldiers were starting to panic. Some started to talk, a few were moaning. It was so dark that I could not recognize anyone, nor tell from what units they were, or even if there was an officer among the 40 to 50 soldiers mired in the mass of boats. I admonished everyone to keep completely quiet and, if the moon broke through the clouds, to remain motionless. We were "sitting ducks" if the Germans saw us.

One fellow decided he would swim back to our side of the river and jumped in. I doubt if he made it since the river was cold and the current fast, and with all of his gear he could not possibly swim. It was about four in the morning and I realized in 60 to 90 minutes it would be light enough for the Germans to spot us. If that happened we would all be killed.

I persuaded the soldiers in the last boat that became wedged to use their oars and push against the pilings and our boat to free themselves. Pushing with great effort, they broke free and were back out into the current. My boat was next, and we managed to clear the bridge and were able to row back to our side of the Saar before it became light. It had to be a horrible night. At some time during the preceding six hours I had been hit in the right hand by a small fragment and a medic removed it with a knife. I had received my "million dollar" wound and a Purple Heart. Another piece of shrapnel also pierced my pants and was stopped by a silver metal cigarette case I had liberated from a German soldier.[20]

It is not known how many assault boats were lost as a result of the swift current and the soldiers' total lack of training in their use, nor is it known how many of the 1st Battalion's boats made a successful crossing, probably six or seven.

Pvt. Jerry French of B Company stated: "Some B Company men crossed the river in the first wave. There were more boats than C Company needed. I distinctly remember when I jumped out of the boat into the water, because the boat was hung up on barbed wire, the boat engineer said, 'I hope my luck holds next trip!' All the firing was over our heads from the machine guns on the friendly side! We could see the tracers come from behind and hit the railroad track up the hill from us."[21]

When the tank destroyers lifted their covering fire, the first wave of men found that cloud cover was making it quite dark. Each boatload of men had to struggle up the steep, often slippery slope between the river's edge and the railroad tracks. They could not see the concrete pillboxes along and above the tracks, nor could the Germans inside these defenses see them. No machine-gun fire came from along or across the tracks; only the machine guns in the pillboxes situated along the water's edge were firing across the river.

Pvt. George Jaeger of D Company reported: "I still remember that climb up the hill to the crest where we stumbled on a trench about five feet deep and about half a mile long where we set up our heavy 30-caliber machine guns at each end to wait for a counterattack that never came."[22]

At least two of the first-wave boats successfully crossed the river but landed too far downstream. The men did not realize that they had landed on the side of the twenty- to thirty-foot railroad embankment running across the mouth of the Okfen valley, and when they reached the tracks, they found there was no hill beyond to assault as they had expected.

Lieutenant Chalkley was in the first boat to land too far downstream. For some inexplicable reason this group headed north along the tracks in the opposite direction from the hill south of Ockfen that they were supposed to capture. They continued until they came to where the railroad went through a cutting at the foot of the Irminer Wald Ridge. They then started climbing the steep slope above them, but were checked a third of the way up by machine-gun fire and a shower of grenades. Lieutenant Chalkley was wounded, and the company communications sergeant was killed. The survivors then dropped back to a German communication trench that followed the contours.

Bob Trefzger's boatload landed a few minutes after the lead boat. He later gave this description of events:

Our leader took our ten-man group north along the tracks; I was bringing up the rear, somewhat slowed by the BAR and the heavy belt of ammunition. About 100 yards from where we came to the railroad tracks, I noticed an open doorway on the west side, probably the back door of a concrete fortification. As I was at the back end of our group,

I decided it would be a good idea (and safe too) to toss a grenade through the doorway, just in case enemy Soldaten were hiding there. The grenade explosion itself was not remarkable. However, it started a spectacular fire, probably burning ammunition and supplies in a storage room.

As we continued north along the tracks we could discern, even in the dark, that the slope along the east side of the tracks was getting higher and steeper, as though we were approaching the south side of a hill. There had been no nearby shooting at all while we progressed along the tracks.

When we had climbed up the side of the valley a ways, we caught up with some other Company C GIs in a communication trench parallel to the hill slope contours. They told us that there were enemy Soldaten up the slope from us and that they had been machine-gunning and throwing grenades down the slope. They also told us that Sergeant [Orville] Strong, the Company C communications sergeant[,] had been killed by a grenade and that Lieutenant Chalkley, our CO and our last officer, had been wounded.

As we were not interested in making a suicide charge up the steep slope in the dark, into the teeth of enemy machine gunners and Soldaten throwing and rolling grenades, we set up a defensive perimeter and waited for daylight.[23]

TSgt. Tom D. Huthnance, who was later to receive a battlefield commission, reported: "Meanwhile the Second Platoon, losing contact with the Third, had dug in in a vineyard with part of the First. One squad of the First Platoon, under Staff Sergeant Harold Price, was engaging a pillbox by the railroad tracks, which ran next to the river. This box was made to look like a shack. It had a mortar on the top, and the embrasures through which the mortar fired were very rusty and screeched every time they opened. It was well defended and Sergeant Price's squad was unable to crack it. It eventually fell to A Company."[24]

THE STAADT CROSSING—FEBRUARY 22

On the intimation of the impending crossing, Major Harold F. Howard, S-3 of the 301st Infantry, reported:

At 1900 the regiment received its orders: "94 Division attack across Saar between Saarburg and Naha the night of 21–22 February. 301 Infantry crosses river at 220100 and will hold bridgehead with a force of not less than a battalion. Prepare to continue advance to northeast on Division order. . . . "

Colonel Hagerty replied at 1917, 21 February: "Reconnaissance troops not able to enter Krutweiler. Battalion unable to get down to river to prepare for crossing there; only other possible crossing site within this sector at ferry between Staadt and Serrig; high cliffs one side or other of river at other points make ferrying impossible."

The reconnaissance platoon from I Company had selected the crossing site at Staadt. There were high hills on each side of the river at this point, and the enemy from its side possessed observation of the crossing. The above message makes it clear that no other crossing place was available in the 301st Infantry zone, and it proved to be hazardous and costly to the units that crossed.[25]

Because Lieutenant Colonel McNulty's 3rd/301st were the first troops to arrive at Kastel above Staadt, they became the natural choice to lead the assault crossing, and the battalion's I and K Companies were chosen to cross abreast in the first wave. As the boats arrived at the crossing site, they were unloaded and carried to the water's edge. All seemed ready for the crossing, but it was discovered that the two previously briefed companies had deployed in reverse order in the fog and darkness. Furthermore, the loss of the trailer load in Kastel had resulted in a shortage of assault craft. Lieutenant Colonel McNulty therefore decided to have the battalion cross in column of companies instead, with I Company leading.

The noise of the leading company moving the boats down the last few yards to the water's edge alerted the enemy, for the fog in the valley bottom acted as a sound conductor, and machine-gun fire began to whip across the river. The men took cover and it took some time to get them going again when the fire lifted. Boats were then rushed to the water's edge and the assault troops piled into them.

As they pulled away into the turbulent river, in which they had to contend with a seven-mile-an-hour current, the American artillery let go with their prearranged fire plan. The mortars of H and M Companies in Kastel added the weight of their support, and the battalion's heavy machine guns

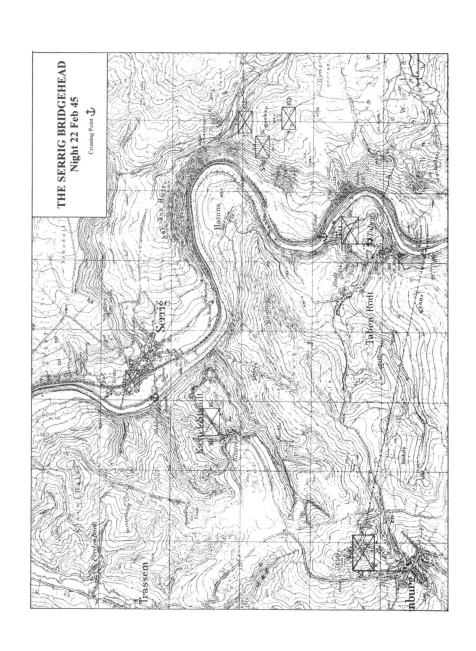

THE SERRIG BRIDGEHEAD
Night 22 Feb 45

Crossing Point

along the road paralleling the river also opened fire. Even though the men were firing blindly into the heavy fog, they hoped to keep the enemy down while the boats of the assault wave battled their way across the swollen stream.

By 0750, after many difficulties, Captain Donovan's I Company was across. The swift current and the inexperience of most of the troops in handling assault craft resulted in the company being irregularly scattered along a wide frontage of the far bank. Many of the boats encountered low wire entanglements at the water's edge, and the main barbed-wire obstacles were found to be too close to the river to permit the safe use of the bangalore torpedoes and Primacord ropes with which the engineers were equipped, so the wire had to be cut by hand. While this work was in progress, the area was raked by fire from enemy bunkers along the riverfront. Fortunately, the dense fog limited the enemy's observation to only a few feet.

Near Serrig some men of I Company became isolated and pinned down in an antitank ditch. Pfc. Robert L. Chapman jumped out of the ditch and charged the nearest pillbox with his BAR. He then worked his way around to the rear of the pillbox, where he captured a prisoner and persuaded him to talk his comrades into surrendering. Chapman's squad joined him in the pillbox, but were forced to return to the antitank ditch when the Germans made a counterattack. Chapman, who was covering their withdrawal with his BAR, was knocked down by a concussion grenade that threw him into the ditch, where he was wounded in the shoulder. Nevertheless, he regained his feet and killed the enemy soldiers who were threatening his squad. (For this action he was later awarded the Distinguished Service Cross.)

Meanwhile, the engineers manning the assault craft had started back to the west bank of the river for the second wave. Several of the undermanned craft were swept downstream and had to be dragged back by the engineers. One boat ended up on the east bank, where one of the crew was killed and the other had to hide for three days before being rescued when the area was finally cleared. Of the sixteen boats that had made the first crossing, only six returned, and only one of those had sufficient paddles, since many of the inexperienced troops had taken their paddles ashore with them. A detail was sent back to salvage the boats and paddles on the upturned trailer in Kastel, and an urgent request was dispatched for outboard-motor boats to speed up the crossing operations. At 0825 word was received that the motors were on their way.

There were no more attempts to make the crossing in waves. Instead, the three companies were being fed in as fast as possible under the enemy fire, which grew increasingly more accurate even though the enemy could not see the crossing site through the fog. Some snipers who the previous day had been bypassed in the rugged terrain on the American side of the river began harassing the steep road leading down from Kastel to Staadt, so a patrol was sent to clear them out. By 0930 German artillery and mortar fire began landing on Staadt, which added to the confusion.

The fog dispelled as the sun's rays fell into the valley, thus improving the enemy's ability to observe the American troops. To counteract this increased vulnerability, B Company of the 81st Chemical Warfare Mortar Battalion dropped white phosphorous shells across the river to screen the vision of the German gunners and observation posts. Smoke pots were also brought forward and ignited.

Enemy mortar and artillery fire, which at first had been sporadic, began to increase in tempo and some of the few remaining assault boats were hit, the shortage of craft making it impossible to send Captain Warren's K Company over in a single wave. At 1140 an artillery concentration sank two of the boats and punctured several more. When the outboard motors arrived at about noon, only one of the original boats was left undamaged.

The storm boats and their 22-horsepower motors were quickly unloaded, but as the motors were unpacked, it was discovered that they were new and had never been serviced. The noise produced as the engineers began to service the engines only drew additional and more accurate enemy fire, resulting in two of the storm boats and three of the operators being hit, so the servicing was then conducted in the basements of nearby buildings, where the outboards were tested in barrels of water. Since there were no replacements available for the wounded boat operators, it became necessary to draft inexperienced men to take over their jobs. While these activities were going on, more assault boats arrived. Although the Germans could not see the crossing site through the fog, they continued to spray the general area with incessant machine-gun fire.

At 1415 the remainder of K Company crossed, together with the battalion commander and his command team, which included an artillery liaison officer, Capt. Donald Aschermann, cannon company observer Lt. Rodney A. Goodling, and Capt. Emanuel P. Snyder of M Company. Captain Donovan was waiting to receive them on the east bank and lead them into Serrig.

Most of K Company was concentrated in the immediate area and constituted a large enough force to start pushing into the village. But before the advance could begin, it was necessary to eliminate the enemy machine guns firing down the streets and between the buildings. Lieutenant Colonel McNulty decided they would have to dispense with smoke-screening the crossing in order to locate them. When the air finally cleared, the infantrymen had their first good look at the main Siegfried Line defenses facing them.

However, as the smoke lifted, the Germans also gained an unobstructed view of the crossing site, and their artillery and automatic weapons began to accurately engage the boats along the river's edge. A radio jeep parked on the road in Staadt was riddled by a ten-minute machine-gun burst, and a 20-mm gun on the high ground behind Serrig blasted away at the hotel in Kastel that was being used as a command post and general assembly area, making it suicidal for the occupants to step out of doors. Attempts were then made to move forward a tank destroyer to engage these enemy weapons, but each time a motor started up the Germans threw over a terrific artillery concentration. It became obvious that any further attempt at crossing the river before nightfall would be unsuccessful. Activity at the river was therefore halted, and when darkness settled on the valley, the terrible intensity of the enemy fire began to ease off. But even after nightfall, the slightest noise in the vicinity of the crossing site brought instant and accurate reaction from the German artillery.[26]

Between dawn and the late afternoon of February 22 the Germans supplemented the local defense Volkssturm battalions in this part of the Westwall with those remnants of the 256th Volksgrenadier Division who had managed to cross the Saar at Kanzem and Wiltingen before the last bridges were blown. To meet the American threat, General Hahn's LXXXII Corps' southern boundary was altered northward to coincide roughly with the eastern end of the Orscholz Switch, thereby releasing one regiment of the 416th Infantry Division for redeployment. He also still had a panzergrenadier battalion of the 11th Panzer Division under command.[27]

Across the river, I and K Companies proceeded with the task of clearing the northern portion of Serrig. Captain Frierson's L Company managed to cross early in the evening with only minor casualties, but as the moon rose the advancing companies encountered a steady volume of small-arms fire. They made a request for smoke, and as it was not known exactly how far the 1st Battalion had penetrated the village, the chemical warfare mortar company decided to place their white phosphorous rounds between the railway tracks on the far bank and the river, thus providing smoke without endangering either of the attacking forces.

Tech-5 Michael Petri of K Company, who spoke reasonable German, found a local inhabitant who claimed to know the location of all the pill-boxes in the vicinity. Using a field telephone in one of the captured pill-boxes, Petri managed to persuade the occupants of another pillbox to sur-render. However, when he approached the pillbox in question, he was fired on and retaliated with a bazooka round, which killed the German machine gunner and resulted in the surrender of the other occupants. Repeating this method, Petri and his squad cleared eleven pillboxes and took 247 prisoners, an action that gained Petri a Silver Star.

For Lieutenant Colonel McNulty's 3rd Battalion the day had been one of close, hard fighting. By late in the afternoon ammunition had run so low that it became necessary to collect rounds from the wounded. Three radio operators in I Company had been hit, but miraculously their radio escaped unharmed. Throughout the day the 94th Reconnaissance Troop was em-ployed clearing Saarburg and the surrounding area of any remaining Ger-man troops.[28]

THE TABEN CROSSING—FEBRUARY 22

The commander of the 1st Battalion, 302nd Infantry, Major Stanion, later recorded:

> At 212200 the 1st Battalion was ordered to make a crossing of the Saar River at 220400 February. The battalion was ordered to make the crossing at any point they desired, and to secure the southern part of the town of Serrig and the high ground to the east. From the G-2 information the battalion gathered that there was a possibility of underwater mines on the other shore of the river and also there was a

destroyed bridge as shown on the map. It was decided by the Battalion Commander and company commanders of the 1st Battalion that they would cross at a point just below this wrecked bridge. The Battalion Commander, accompanied by the company commanders of his battalion[,] made a hasty reconnaissance of the situation at 212400, while his executive officer was bringing the troops from Oberleuken to Taben in trucks.[29]

C Company, which had been designated to lead the crossing, arrived in Taben first. At this time there was little enemy fire falling on the village, but the engineers reported that the corps boats had not yet arrived. Eventually at about 0500, one hour after the designated time of crossing, the corps boats arrived in Taben. The leading engineer vehicle was quickly unloaded, and six assault boats, each of which weighed one thousand pounds, were transported down the steep, twisting road to the river, manhandled by the infantrymen who were to make the assault crossing. In the river valley the fog was as thick as milk. Chemical smoke could not have provided better concealment, but sound traveled extremely well in the damp air. After an hour and five minutes of backbreaking work, the first boat reached the water's edge, leaving the men who had sweated and strained to get it into position utterly exhausted.

The time consumed in this process led Lieutenant Colonel Ellis, the commanding officer of the 319th Engineers, to order the drivers of the unloaded boat trucks to cut their motors and coast down the hill to a point about three hundred yards from the riverbank. The remaining boats were soon in place at the crossing site. At the water's edge, the troops discovered it was impossible to see the far bank through the fog. From recent thaws, the river was swollen and turbulent, and the rush of the stream tended to cover the little noise made by the men of Lieutenant Robinson's C Company as they prepared to cross. They were crossing blind into enemy-held territory. The maps showed a road and railroad following the line of the river on the far side below cliffs, with a steep hillside towering about a thousand feet above.

The first boat, under SSgt. John F. Smith, set off in the strong current at 0650 and reached the opposite bank without incident. There the squad encountered a twelve-foot retaining wall at the water's edge, but a breach in the wall and a ladder that the Germans had left in place enabled them to scramble up to the road, where they surprised two Germans standing outside a bunker and took them prisoner. Seven more prisoners were taken from this same bunker without a struggle.

By this time, most of the 2nd Platoon had arrived, and a search began of the area to the left of the landing site. Fifty yards from the first bunker, a German soldier was spotted walking around a second fortification. He was shot and the leading squad pushed farther north. Soon afterward the platoon came under sniper fire, which checked them until they were able to outflank the opposition and push on downstream, where they encountered a third bunker and took its occupants prisoner. They then decided to return to the crossing site, and on their way back they rounded up the four snipers they had previously bypassed.

Back at the crossing, Sergeant Smith reported to Major Stanion, who then instructed him to move south and eliminate any enemy to the right of the slender bridgehead. Eighteen more prisoners were captured from another bunker 250 yards upriver, and a German-speaking NCO took one of the prisoners with him to assist in clearing the other fortifications in the vicinity, which resulted in the capture of another forty-seven Germans. Several more bunkers were located and searched as well. The rest of the battalion followed across in short order, and the only mishap in the operation occurred when one of the assault boats capsized and four men were drowned.

In accordance with the battalion plan, after the crossing point was secured, C Company, augmented by the heavy machine guns of D Company, which was led by TSgt. James Cousineau, climbed up the steep, eleven-hundred-odd feet to the summit of the Höckerberg, which came to be known as Hocker Hill. Captain Woodburn's A Company and Captain Wancio's B Company followed. As A and B Companies rested from their exhausting climb, Lieutenant Robinson sent a patrol to reconnoiter the path that led from west of the summit of Hocker Hill above the Auf der Hütte cliffs down to the road into Serrig. The patrol proceeded only a short distance before returning to report that they had seen no Germans.

A and B Companies moved off for Serrig at about noon. The 1st Platoon of C Company was then ordered to cross over Hocker Hill and outflank the enemy positions that were occupying the high ground above the path. This maneuver proved successful, for the enemy withdrew as the troops advanced, and on its way the platoon seized three unmanned artillery pieces of small caliber. At the point where the path followed by A and B Companies joined the converging road into Serrig, the Germans had built a bunker in the semblance of a small brick house. To the left of the bunker, the terrain fell away sharply to the river far below, while to the right, the ground rose still higher. A Company, in the lead and marching in single file, passed this point unopposed, but as B Company reached the junction, enemy bunkers to the east opened fire. B Company managed to filter through, but the arrival of the attached platoon from C Company brought more enemy fire. Lieutenant Robinson reacted by sending Lieutenant Richards with a squad from the 3rd Platoon up the hill to silence some snipers, while Technical Sergeant Cousineau was detailed by radio to take the 1st Platoon to outflank the enemy positions over Hocker Hill.

When A Company spotted a group of about one hundred Germans some nine hundred yards ahead in the valley below, the artillery liaison officer who was with them, Captain Bruhl, called down artillery fire as the company's machine guns opened up. Practically all of the enemy troops were either killed or wounded in the ensuing carnage. The advance on Serrig was then continued without interruption until the troops came under fire from a small orchard outside the town. The company employed marching fire as they overran this position, in which they found twenty-seven dead Germans.

On the left, Captain Wancio's B Company, which had been augmented by the 2nd Platoon of C Company, was having trouble with some bunkers near the railroad tracks. After capturing three of these fortifications, further advance was stalled by heavy machine-gun fire until the Germans were outflanked. The advance continued and more bunkers were taken, some troops being left behind to garrison these positions. The troops had entered the village at 1900, having been led through a series of minefields by two liberated Russian slave laborers, while to the right A Company had also arrived in Serrig. Although the 3rd/301st was known to be in the northern portion of the village, no contact was made that night. Meanwhile, C Company, less the aforementioned platoon, occupied a position for the night on the high ground due east of the town and north of the Auf der Hütte cliffs. Just after dark the 3rd Platoon of this company had to repulse a violent enemy counterattack.[30]

The uncertainty of the situation on the ground led Lieutenant Colonel Brimmer, the artillery operations officer back at Division, to establish a "No Fire Line" east of Serrig for the night.[31] The rest of the night passed quietly, but with the coming of dawn there was another German assault, which was driven back only after an hour of hard fighting. With their supply route cut, the next day the 1st/302nd, in the southern part of Serrig, radioed a request for medical supplies, blood plasma, food, and radio batteries, which were dropped by the division's Cub aircraft.

With the Taben crossing secure, General Walker of XX Corps decided to disrupt the enemy's main line of communication by establishing a road-block on the Saarburg-Zerf highway. He therefore arranged for the replacement of the 5th Ranger Battalion covering the 94th Infantry Division's right flank on the west bank of the Saar and had them move into Taben, from where they could cross the river and strike off through the wooded hills to a suitable location for the roadblock. As this roadblock would obviously come under considerable pressure, General Walker planned to relieve the rangers by an armored thrust out of the bridgehead.[32]

Shortly before noon Lt. Col. Richard P. Sullivan, commanding the 5th Rangers, received instructions to report to Colonel Bergquist, from whom he learned of his infiltration mission but could obtain little information. At that time he had two of his six companies in Orscholz, two in Weiten, and two already in Taben. He ordered his battalion to assemble in Taben while he proceeded with a small escort to climb Hocker Hill to confer with Lieutenant Colonel Gaddis, the 302nd's executive officer, and discovered that the 302nd Infantry was having difficulty holding its bridgehead. He then sent back for his battalion, which lost six men killed and eighteen wounded of Capt. Charles E. Parker's A Company from enemy fire while passing though the 302nd's lines.

Enemy artillery fire on Taben had increased in intensity and some machine-gun fire was being received from the cliffs across the river. However, it was still little more than harassing fire, which continued throughout the afternoon. With Captain Smith's L Company leading, Lieutenant Colonel Cloudt's 3rd/302nd began its crossing soon after 1300. The boat carrying the mortar section of K Company capsized and all its equipment was lost, but by 2200 all elements of the battalion had crossed the river and started the long haul to the top of Hocker Hill, where the three rifle companies set up a perimeter defense. Only Captain Hurst's M Company remained in Taben to support the other companies if necessary.

That night there was considerable confusion on Hocker Hill as the 3rd

Battalion tried to set up a perimeter defense without allowing sufficient time for a proper reconnaissance. A soldier behind a light machine gun of L Company killed several Germans who had not realized that the Americans had taken over the hill.

Meanwhile, Major Maixner's 2nd/302nd in Keuchlingen had been alerted to follow the 3rd/302nd across at Taben. Once over the river, it would be their task to clear the river road leading into Serrig and the cliffs paralleling it, which were harboring many snipers.[33]

Lt. Col. Albrecht Roeschen, who was later captured in Trier, described events that day from the German side.

> The defenses were far from completely occupied when the 301st and 302d Infantry struck across the Saar. The river and hills were blanketed under a thick morning fog, which hung on the river until nearly 1000. Artillery and mortar concentrations thundered down on Serrig, the noise echoing around the hills many times magnified by the fog. Men in the pillboxes seemed so isolated, unable to see anything or know what was going on. Then the men in Serrig could hear the splashing of paddles and voices out on the river and the splutter of an outboard engine. Nervously they opened up, firing wildly at the sounds, hoping they could hit what they couldn't see. At Taben the first indication of the American attack were [sic] men banging on the doors of the pillboxes and the sight of a long file of men struggling up the hill and across the plateau west of Hocker Hill. No one could have expected that the Americans would attack across this steep country, but they did. By afternoon the Germans in Serrig who had lost some houses west of the railroad tracks to the attack of the 3rd Battalion, 301st Infantry, were dazed by the sight of Americans attacking down the hill from the east, from their rear. The 1st Battalion, 302d, swept down into Serrig, seizing part of the town before dark slowed down operations. At Ayl the defenders were amazed at mid-afternoon to see the 376th Infantry advance across the open meadows toward the river and push their boats out into the water in the very face of artillery and mortar fire adjusted from the hilltops and machine gun fire from the pillboxes along the base of the hill. If there was any doubt about the American intention to cross the river, it was

dissipated by dark. They were coming across in force. The main crossing sites seemed to be at Serrig, Taben and Ayl. At Serrig the 94th Division had a foothold, but the crossing site was dominated by the observation on the hills around the town. The Ayl crossing had been repulsed, but the crossing at Taben, deep down in the river gorge, couldn't be reached by flat-trajectory weapons. The best that could be done was to try to interdict and harass the road leading to the crossing.[34]

Maj. Gen. Harry J. Malony, Commanding General of the 94th Infantry Division, and his aide, Capt. John C. Gehrig.

An infantryman of the 1st Battalion, 376th Infantry, dashes through the orchard outside Tettingen. Heavy fire was falling on this area as the picture was taken.

Schloss Berg.

Casualties in men and materiel were frequent on Nennig's fire-swept
streets.

Nennig was littered with dead Germans.

Wearing improvised snowsuits, a patrol moves into the woods in the Wochern-Tettingen area.

Well dispersed, a relief party moves into the woods west of Tettingen.

TSgt. Arnold A. Petry and some of his men after being rescued from the orchard between Nennig and Tettingen.

Dragon's teeth and blown pillbox north of Borg.

Carefully treading a path cleared by the engineers, a relief party moves toward the northern edge of Campholz Woods.

A 94th Division Weasel crosses a tank ditch near Sinz.

"Sinz" . . . even the name was ominous.

Before making a fast dash to the rear, medics strap a casualty to the litter
rack of their jeep.

A knocked-out German Mark IV tank with part of its bazooka skirt still in place.

Saarburg on the Saar River.

As enemy shells burst near them, men of the 376th Infantry cross open ground as they prepare to move into the bridgehead.

Cases of K rations destined for the 3rd Battalion, 376th Infantry, are lashed to packboards by members of a carrying party.

Treadway bridge at Taben. The center pontoon, which has been
hit and deflated, was repaired shortly after this picture was taken.

Camouflaged pillbox in the vicinity of Serrig.

Stinking compost piles and fresh German cadavers line the muddy streets of Irsch.

Throughout the fighting east of the Saar River, prisoners of war were used extensively as litter bearers as they moved to the rear.

A German Mark V tank knocked out east of Irsch.

For gallantry in action, Lt. Perry Heidelberger Jr., receives the Silver Star Medal with Oak Leaf Cluster from the division commander.

Lampaden after the attack of the 6th SS Mountain Division.

SS prisoners being collected in the courtyard of a château north of Lampaden.

9
Establishing the Bridgehead

THE AYL BRIDGEHEAD—FEBRUARY 23

The men of Lieutenant Colonel Martin's 2nd/376th, charged with the taking of Ockfen, followed the 3rd Battalion across at the northern crossing site and were met by some harassing machine-gun fire and a few rounds of artillery, which exacted some casualties in Company E while still on the west bank, but by 0400 all the troops were across. From the riverbank the battalion had first to move down the railroad tracks to opposite Ockfen, descending to move up to the village. The whole area was now covered in dense early morning fog. Lieutenant Maness's F Company, in the lead, waited two hours for Captain Standish's F Company to arrive with the heavy machine-gun platoons of Capt. Robert Q. Smith's H Company, then led the advance on the village, while Captain Dodson's G Company, in reserve, moved partway up the vine-covered slope of the 3rd Battalion's hill to get above the smoke level and cover the left flank.

The heavy machine-gun platoons took the wrong route and were lost for a while until they found their way back to the railroad underpass. The attacking companies captured a few surprised Germans before daybreak, and then cautiously advanced across some four hundred yards of flat marshland leading to the village that was flanked by the steep hills on either side. The leading platoon of E Company and the first two platoons of F Company had just checked the first five houses when at 0945 sixteen enemy tanks supported by infantry began counterattacking from the other end of the village. The murk was so dense that the bazooka men could not pick out the tanks firing at the American-occupied buildings at point-blank range, and the troops were obliged to withdraw in haste up the slopes of the adjacent vineyard.[1]

Describing their efforts to take Ockfen, Captain Smith reported:

We were expecting the engineers to start building a bridge at any time to bring the armor across, and apparently the chemical boys were too. All night and day they kept laying in heavy smoke screens. And every time the smoke would roll across the Saar and up the valley around Ockfen. It kept us blinded all day and we cursed it plenty. But one time we were glad it was there. It saved us many casualties. I was up on the high bluff to the left of Ockfen overlooking the river when E and F Companies pulled back out of the town. I had just placed a heavy machine gun section above the dense cloud of smoke so they could fire on any movement in the far end of town. Imagine my surprise when I started down to see the whole battalion swarming up the side of this steep—and I do mean steep—hill. Later in his report over the radio, Colonel Martin really hit the nail on the head when asked if his battalion was in any danger. "Nothing," he said, "but mountain goats or scared infantrymen could ever climb this hill, and my whole damned battalion is up here."

The Germans very obligingly had built some excellent trenches on this hill, and we reorganized the battalion there without the loss of a man under cover of the same dense smoke. For a couple of hours the Colonel and I took turns adjusting artillery and cannon fire on targets that were very clearly visible from our roost on top of the world. Finally, about 1300, Colonel Martin said: "Well, Smith, I guess they'll want us to take that town, so I guess we'd better do it." Then he gave me a quick outline of his plan and sent me to contact Captain Standish while he went to orient Lieutenant Maness, commanding Company E.

The time of the attack was to be 1415. Well, at 1350 I was still frantically trying to find Standish . . . Finally I went back to tell Colonel Martin he'd have to delay the attack until I could find him. Imagine my chagrin when I found that the colonel himself had seen both company commanders and had arranged for a heavy artillery preparation while I was still lost in the smoke. But that TOT [time-on-target] fire the colonel had called for!

Never in my life have I seen anything so exciting or as pretty as that! Imagine if you can the first rounds of eight artillery battalions plus our Cannon Company all exploding at exactly the same second on an objective the size of a very small town. It looked as if the town just blew up. And it was wonderful the way E and F Companies crawled in under the barrage and were right there at the first houses when it lifted. They stormed into town, running, shouting and shooting, taking one house after another, just as if it had been rehearsed. Inside of an hour they had cleared the town, put up a defense with heavy machine guns all round it, and Lieutenant Murphy had his Mine Platoon with about ten German prisoner "volunteers" putting in a minefield to prevent another tank counterattack.[2]

By 1630 Ockfen was safely in American hands, although the bunkers around it were still enemy occupied. The eight-battalion barrage described by Captain Smith above had been intended as a ten-minute action, but after half that time had elapsed it became necessary to issue a cease-fire order, for the shelling had begun to affect the troops of the 2nd Battalion five hundred yards away.

Clearing the village proved a simple matter, for the artillerymen had done their work well. Ockfen was a shambles and several of the ruined buildings had started to burn. Of the enemy soldiers who remained alive, most were too shocked and dazed to have any fight left in them. The enemy tanks that had survived the bombardment could be heard withdrawing up the valley to the east. The mine platoon of the regiment's antitank company followed the infantry into Ockfen and laid mines along the eastern approaches to the village. Heavy fire continued to come from pillboxes southeast of Ockfen, and enemy snipers also remained troublesome. That evening the battalion command post received a direct hit that wounded three of the battalion's staff officers.

Captain Heath's G Company then took the castle-like Ockfener Domäne halfway up the hill above the village. Having witnessed the bombardment of Ockfen, the German defenders surrendered readily, and the company continued up to the top of the Irminer Wald Ridge to take up position alongside the 3rd Battalion. G Company was so depleted that its foxholes were sometimes up to one hundred yards apart. Food was scarce and cap-

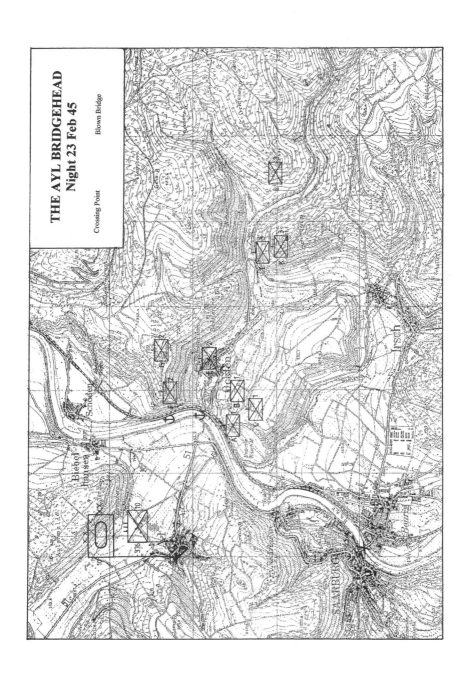

THE AYL BRIDGEHEAD
Night 23 Feb 45

Crossing Point   Blown Bridge

tured German rations were put to good use. There were no blankets and the nights were still extremely cold.[3]

Lieutenant Colonel Thurston's 3rd Battalion's three rifle companies, with the heavy supporting weapons of M Company, spent the day digging in on top of the Irminer Wald Ridge. Although they expected at any moment to come under enemy shellfire, they remained undisturbed by the enemy. Several bunkers were found unoccupied but well stocked with food and ammunition.

That afternoon the men had a grandstand view of the 2nd Battalion's fighting in Ockfen below them and were able to contribute some machine-gun and even artillery fire to the fray, as Sergeant Adair describes in his account:

> As the sun rose on a clear day, Ockfen[,] six hundred feet below our hill to the south, was covered by a ground fog with only the church steeple occasionally emerging into our view.
>
> As the fog dissipated we could see the town clearly. A few men fired their rifles at the town but there were few reasonable targets. Several enterprising (to my mind, fool hardy) men found some ammunition for one of the German field pieces and bore-sighting the gun, actually fired one or two rounds at the town. They were more successful than I feared—they probably harmed no Germans but they didn't blow themselves up.
>
> Then the town exploded. It seems that all the artillery that could be mustered by the combat team (I heard that there were eight battalions) fired TOT (time-on-target) at Ockfen. That is they timed the flight of the shells so all of the shells—perhaps a hundred—landed on the small town at the same instant. They did this a number of times and left the defendants so in shock that the Second Battalion was able to move into the town with little opposition.[4]

Then the battalion received orders to move on and take the Scharfenberg Ridge, the main regimental objective. The men set off at 1600 in single file with K Company leading and by dusk had reached the foot of the Backsteinfels Ridge, where a dirt road connected Ockfen with the hinterland. At that moment a column of troops approached, chattering noisily, that could only be German. Thurston had two BAR teams mount an immediate ambush that resulted in every one of the enemy being killed, wounded, or captured. More than thirty Germans were killed and were buried by the Americans the next day.

Capt. Ralph T. Brown's K Company troops were then sent up the Scharfenberg Ridge to establish an all-around defense about half a mile from the road. The men of K Company were to form the point of a triangle, with the other two companies closer to the road. As L Company's troops were arriving, the rear of the column was hit by artillery fire, wounding several men, including Lieutenant Foster, who had been in command for only one day. Appreciating that the enemy fire was concentrating on the road, Thurston had his men move uphill and so avoided further casualties.[5]

It is not known how many assault boats returned to the west bank to bring over the 1st Battalion's B Company. At least four boats, including Marshall Miller's, had lost control and drifted downstream from the first wave. The second wave came under enemy fire, and some failed to make the crossing.[6]

TSgt. Ralph Reichley, the platoon sergeant of the 2nd Platoon, B Company, was in this second wave:

> There was much confusion, which resulted in several casualties, including engineers. There were no boats available and there was a lot of firing from across the river. I laid [*sic*] down behind an engineer that I assumed to be dead and a few other men jumped into a low area that offered some protection. Finally we found a boat and six or seven of us crossed the river on February 23rd. Two or three soldiers were hit in the arm or shoulder. I never knew their names, as they were replacements from the day before. As I remember, the current was very swift. Once out of the boat, we had to climb over barbed wire and then cross a railroad.

This group noted that the machine-gun fire along and across the tracks was sporadic, as the bunker occupants could not see them and were firing blindly. They were thus able to cross the tracks between bursts but did not climb the 1st Battalion's objective hill until after dawn.

Pvt. Russell Bryant, who was also in Sergeant Reichley's platoon, reported that his eight-man squad came under machine-gun and 20-mm armor-piercing shellfire as their boat crossed. Two men were killed and Bryant was wounded. The boat drifted downstream until it came up against the destroyed bridge, where the squad leader ordered the men out. Bryant was pinned down by the fatally wounded men and was unable to get out, but the boat drifted across to the west bank, where he was able to get assistance.[7]

With the departure of the second wave, a third of B Company and all of A Company remained on the west bank without boats and were taking heavy casualties from the mortar and artillery fire falling in the area, as the only cover available was some water-filled ditches alongside the road. Unable to cross here, Lieutenant Colonel Miner then ordered the remainder of his battalion to head for the 3rd Battalion's crossing point, which they reached at 0500. The fog was thick here, and they were able to use flashlights to guide in the assault boats to pick them up. By dawn most of the 376th's troops were successfully across the river. Once Captain Dadisman's A Company and the remainder of B Company had completed the crossing, they moved south along the railroad tracks to rejoin the battalion.

Bob Trefzger, then sergeant and assistant squad leader of C Company, recounted:

> As dawn approached, it turned out to be very foggy. Before long our battalion commanding officer, Lieutenant Colonel Miner, arrived to confer with the acting company commander, Technical Sergeant Huthnance, the platoon sergeant of our First Platoon. They were just up the hill from us, looking at a map and what could be seen of the terrain in the dense fog (very little). After a short while, they determined that we were on the wrong hill! If we had turned right (south) when we got on the tracks, we would have found the hill we were supposed to assault.
>
> So we went down the hill to the tracks and moved south along the tracks to a point a few hundred yards beyond where we landed and joined up with the others from C Company.

The 1st Battalion quickly reorganized and at 0730 began its ascent of the hill slopes south of Ockfen with B Company on the left, C Company on the right, and A Company in reserve along and near the railroad tracks. As it was still very foggy and the bunker occupants could not see the advancing troops, there was little to no opposition, and the top of the steep part of the slope was reached quickly. The advancing men came to the long north-south communication trench that had been occupied by the D Company heavy machine-gun section since midnight. Continuing on about another five hundred yards, they then came under heavy machine-gun fire raking through the fog, forcing them to either dig in or withdraw to the shelter of the communication trench. The fog soon dispersed to reveal four huge, mutually supporting bunkers some four hundred yards away across their front. Clearing them would require the close support of heavy flat-trajectory gunfire, but there was no armor yet across the river. Unable to attack, the 1st Battalion used the existing communication trench system to establish a strong defense against possible counterattack. This stalemate on the 1st Battalion's hill obliged a change in plan, and it was now ordered to change direction and strike south along the river toward Beurig.

Although the 376th had secured Ockfen, the Irminer Wald Ridge north of it, the northern part of the Scharfenberg Ridge beyond it, and most of the hill to the south, the Germans still had observation of the Ayl bridge site from a large number of bypassed bunkers along the river's edge, the railroad track, and on the steep slopes above on either flank, particularly from south of the village of Schoden. Once the early morning fog and any smoke had cleared, the Germans maintained an almost continuous rain of machine-gun fire that punctured pontoons and riddled the bridging equipment as fast as the engineers could haul it to the river. German artillery also helped to render the area untenable. Every attempt by the engineers to erect a bridge met with failure and heavy casualties. The situation was such that on the next day the 10th Armored Division was constrained to detail an armored infantry company to attack toward Schoden. With much difficulty a ferry was maintained in operation and was used to transport a small number of vehicles across the river. For the most part, though, supplies were sent over by assault boats and moved on to the companies by carrying parties.[8]

THE STAADT BRIDGEHEAD—FEBRUARY 23

It had taken all day and most of the night to get Lieutenant Colonel McNulty's 3rd/301st across the Saar and penetrate part of the main Siegfried Line. But by 0400 on February 23 the riverfront had been cleared,

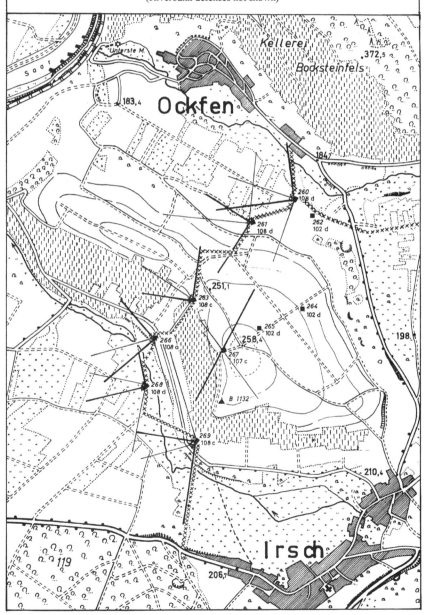

German Fortress Engineers' Design
for the Ockfen-Irsch Defenses

(Riverbank defenses not shown)

nineteen houses on the outskirts of Serrig taken, and the battalion was pushing south. Contact was soon established with the 1st Battalion of the 302nd Infantry, and joint plans were made for clearing the village, which was accomplished by 1820 despite constant harassment by enemy artillery and mortar fire. The battalions then adopted defensive positions for the night.

The situation at the Staadt crossing point failed to improve on the second day of operations. Enemy small-arms fire had ceased during the previous night, but artillery fire increased in intensity throughout the day until it became more deadly than the direct fire had been. There was a heavy demand on counter-battery fire. During the course of the day, liaison aircraft spotted more and more enemy batteries. Of particular menace were the highly mobile enemy rocket batteries.[9]

That morning Captain Ashton's 94th Reconnaissance Troop was ordered to clear Krutweiler and the west bank of the Saar north of Staadt of any enemy troops. To assist him in his task he was allocated B Company of the 778th Tank Battalion and a platoon from the 81st Chemical Warfare Mortar Battalion. After a preparation by the 4.2-inch mortars, two of his platoons attacked at 1600 and, despite the antipersonnel minefield encountered and heavy fire coming from across the river, took Krutweiler within forty-five minutes.[10]

C Company of the 319th Engineers replaced A Company and stretched a rope across the river to facilitate ferrying. However, the rope came apart as the first boatload of men attempted to haul their craft across, and the backbreaking job of paddling had to be resumed. In a determined effort to get the 2nd Battalion across before daylight, Colonel Hagerty, the commander of the 301st Infantry, decided to revert to the use of the storm boats and accept the resulting casualties. Motorboats moved the first two platoons of G Company to the far shore before the Germans were able to react, but soon mortar and artillery fire was pouring into the area on what seemed a far greater scale than ever before. Throughout the latter hours of darkness and the early morning, the 2nd Battalion and the engineers took heavy losses.

Shortly after daybreak crossing operations had all but reached a standstill, and Lieutenant Colonel Dohs came forward personally to take charge. As the boats were about to push into the stream again, a tremendous concentration hit the launching site, again inflicting heavy casualties. Many of the infantry and engineers lay wounded, dead, and dying, including Dohs

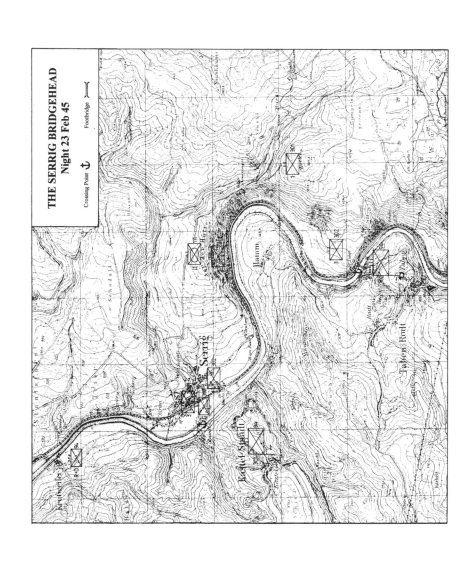

THE SERRIG BRIDGEHEAD
Night 23 Feb 45

Crossing Point ⚓   Footbridge ⊐⊏

and some of his staff, as well as Captain Sinclair of F Company, who was mortally wounded. Not one of the boats escaped the weight of the murderous barrage, and more assault craft were needed before there could be any continuation of the operation. Undoubtedly one of the greatest problems for the engineers during this period was the inadequate number of assault boats. The enemy was shooting them up almost as soon as they arrived. More than two hundred craft were used during the entire operation, but only twenty-seven of them remained in operation once the infantry had successfully crossed the river.

By the time the replacement battalion commander, Maj. George W. Brumley (formerly the regimental operations officer) arrived in Staadt at 1100, a limited number of additional assault boats had been obtained. Fifty minutes later, the next boat was sent across loaded with medical supplies, blankets, and radio batteries, all of which were urgently needed by the 3rd Battalion on the far side. This craft having made the round trip safely, it was decided to try to get the remainder of the 2nd Battalion across, but Division cancelled the move just before it could be implemented. The battalion was now to move back to Freudenburg, where it would become divisional reserve. As the 2nd Battalion withdrew back up the hill to Kastel, it was shelled by the German artillery, but to little effect.

By nightfall fire on the abandoned crossing site had practically ceased, so it was decided to keep a motor ferry in operation for the resupply of the 3rd Battalion, which so far had received only the one boatload of medical items and some ammunition that had been dropped by liaison planes. Neither food nor drink was a major problem, as the German civilians in their hasty withdrawal had left ample provisions behind and the bunkers captured were also found to contain stocks of food. In addition, Schloss Saarfels outside Serrig, which had been captured by I Company, was found to contain thousands of bottles of wine, much to the delight of the conquerors.

By 1930 all the wounded on the far side of the river had been evacuated, and supplies were moving over in a steady stream. Shortly thereafter attempts were made to string a telephone wire across the river. This line held, and for the first time in forty-eight hours there was telephone communication between the 3rd Battalion and Regiment. The battalion aid station, the battalion antitank platoon, and the regimental antitank company stood by to cross at this site during the night of February 23, for the Germans were now paying little heed to the Staadt area. Meanwhile, during the day Major Hodges's 1st Battalion had been moved up by truck from Orscholz to Trassem and was standing by waiting for its turn to cross the river.[11]

THE TABEN BRIDGEHEAD—FEBRUARY 23

At 0200 Lieutenant Colonel Sullivan's 5th Ranger Battalion moved out from the 302nd Infantry's lines on Hocker Hill on a compass bearing for their objective on the Irsch-Zerf highway. The battalion moved in two columns with fifty yards between companies. In the first echelon were Capt. Jack A. Snyder's C Company in the left-hand column and Capt. George R. Miller's D Company on the right.

Almost immediately 1st Lt. James E. Greene Jr.'s E Company and Capt. Bernard M. Pepper's B Company in the second echelon were hit by an artillery barrage and small-arms fire. The forward artillery observation party attached to the battalion was knocked out, and B Company suffered several casualties. This barrage had temporarily split the battalion, and it took half an hour for them to reorganize. Somehow Lt. Louis J. Gambosi's 2nd Platoon of B Company remained separated from the rest and were left behind when the battalion moved on. Later in the day radio contact was established, and the men were told to report to the Serrig beachhead.

The battalion continued to come under fire as they advanced in the dark, their presence being betrayed by the rattling of the antitank mines that the men were carrying, but nothing could be done about the situation, as the mines were needed at their objective. The battalion then came across a large group of Germans, whom they quickly captured. At daybreak the troops found a suitable location for a rest and an opportunity to reconnoiter the next stage of the route. They then continued in a box formation, keeping as far as possible to wooded areas and using artillery-spotting rounds to maintain direction. Three pillboxes were encountered and yielded another thirty prisoners.

Shortly afterward the battalion was attacked by about fifty Germans, who had mistakenly taken them for only a patrol and attacked across open ground at their own cost. This brought the number of prisoners up to nearly one hundred, so B Company, which had meanwhile taken some casualties and was now down to only sixteen men, was detailed to guard them.

All day the battalion kept on encountering German troops, so it became necessary to change course from time to time to avoid betraying their objective. At one point a German ambulance and doctor were captured, the doctor exclaiming: "this is 4,000 yards behind the lines—no, no—you can't be here!" The doctor then attended the wounded of both sides as the number of prisoners increased.[12]

Major Stanion, who was commanding the 1st/302nd at Serrig, later recorded: "All the day of the 23d the battalion remained in the same position and began to receive intense small arms fire from the hill at 179085. The battalion supply route had been severed by the enemy by this time and the river road was being used. Even this was dangerous as snipers were active in the high ground overlooking the road and the river. The battalion requested blood plasma, food and radio batteries, which were dropped in the A and B Company sectors by Cub planes. The battalion aid station was still in Taben. This request was successfully fulfilled."[13]

By 0655 the men of Major Maixner's 2nd/302nd were completely across the Saar. Movement had begun shortly after midnight and was harassed only by occasional artillery fire that caused little damage. As elements of Captain Butler's E Company reached the far side of the river and scaled the retaining wall, they ran into a twelve-man German patrol that had slipped through the beachhead defenses in the darkness. The enemy soldiers seemed as completely surprised as the Americans they encountered, and a small firefight developed that resulted in a speedy surrender by the Germans. A thorough search of the area was then made and the perimeter was strengthened. Crossing operations were resumed, and the remainder of the battalion was brought across without further interruption.

In order to accomplish the battalion's task of clearing the river road, it would also be necessary to eliminate those enemy forces emplaced in the rugged cliffs above it. The decision was made to scale these heights and move the battalion along a path running across the face of the Auf der Hütte cliffs, while a strong patrol moved along the river road abreast of the remainder of the battalion above. This patrol started downstream toward Serrig, checking the numerous bunkers embedded beneath the railroad tracks that paralleled the river road at a slightly higher level. Most were empty and the patrol advanced as far as the south side of the hairpin bend opposite Hamm, where late in the afternoon they met a party from their 1st Battalion, which had worked its way upstream from Serrig. The road was now clear of enemy soldiers, and the only obstacle to the passage of wheeled vehicles was a huge crater on the Hamm bend.

Meanwhile, the rest of the battalion had moved up Hocker Hill and along a path beyond it that led just below the top of the Auf der Hütte Ridge to the vineyards that terraced the cliff opposite Hamm. Suddenly, Captain Kops's F Company, which was leading the battalion, was hit by a hail of machine-gun fire, which forced the advance elements to fall back to better cover. Several attempts were made to renew the advance, but these were stopped cold.

The battalion had been caught in an impossible position by the 2nd Battalion of Panzergrenadier Regiment 111, which had been detached from its parent 11th Panzer Division and was entrenched high in the cliff of Auf der Hütte on the north side of the hairpin turn. On the left of the path the terrain fell away almost vertically some four hundred feet to the river, while on the right the almost vertical cliff rose to terminate in an overhanging ledge. The terrain was completely exposed and there was no room for maneuver. Attempts to push forward along the rock wall on the right of the path were stalled by volleys of grenades that the Germans dropped from above. A wire-mesh fence along the left of the path provided the enemy above with a perfect backboard for bouncing grenades under the overhanging ledge. Fortunately, the Germans seemed to possess only concussion grenades. Potato-mashers (German grenades) employed in the same way would have made the position completely untenable.

The enemy on the heights soon realized that the rest of the battalion was stretched out along the path behind F Company, and as there was no overhanging ledge topping the cliff above the other companies, the Germans started using their mortars. Enemy shells bursting up and down the path tightened the trap even further as the troops frantically tried to dig in among the rocks. A heavy machine gun was set up on a small ledge to the left of the path, and the gunner sprayed the cliff on the far side of the hairpin bend in an effort to neutralize some of the fire being directed against the battalion. Time and again enemy mortar barrages were thrown over the hill in an effort to knock out this weapon, but without success. The battalion remained unable to advance, and even the coming of darkness did not improve matters. Unknown to the Americans, German troops had been pouring into this area for the past twenty-four hours, for it was appreciated that while the Ayl and Staadt crossing sites could be contained by artillery fire, the key to containing the awkward Taben site was control of the Auf der Hütte cliffs in order to prevent access to Serrig from Hocker Hill and to dominate the riverside road below.[14]

Because of the difficulties his regiment had experienced from the very outset at Staadt and the comparative ease with which the 302nd Infantry was crossing the Saar at Taben, Colonel Johnson suggested to Division that his 1st Battalion, which had yet to cross, be attached to the 302nd Infantry, an idea that was approved.

Although enemy fire in the vicinity of the 302nd's crossing increased with the coming of daylight, most of the artillery fire was directed against Taben itself and against a point on the riverbank several hundred yards from where the crossing was being made. The heights of Hocker Hill provided protection from enfilade fire for the actual crossing site.[15]

Major Hodges, commanding the 1st/301st, reported to the 302nd Infantry's command post in Taben and was instructed to cross the Saar as soon as possible. It was estimated that it would take at least six hours to move the battalion to Taben and complete the crossing, during which time the situation on the far bank could have changed, so up-to-date orders would best be given upon arrival on that bank.

The 1st/301st was brought forward from Trassem by trucks. After unloading in the village, one of the companies failed to contact their guide and set off down the main road to the crossing, only to come under enemy machine-gun fire from the high ground above Saarhausen. An ambulance and an engineer truck coming up the hill also came under machine-gun fire, and the truck driver was wounded, as was Lieutenant Wolf by shellfire. The company then pulled back into Taben, from where it proceeded down to the river over the path used by the rest of the battalion.

At the bridging site, Major Hoffman of the 319th Engineers and his men were assembling a footbridge, so Major Hodges offered the assistance of B Company in manhandling the boats to support it. The bridge was completed at 1730 and the battalion crossed to the east bank. They were then ordered to relieve the 3rd/302nd on Hocker Hill after dark that night.[16]

Captain Smith, then commanding L Company of the 3rd/302nd, later recorded: "At 1800 on the night of 23 February, the 1st Battalion of the 301st Infantry relieved the battalion and it moved back down the hill to prepare to move up behind the 2d Battalion of the 302d Infantry. As the 2d Battalion was held up and could not advance, the order was changed and the 3d Battalion moved up into the area of Serrig just before dawn using the river road as its route of approach. No fire was received during this move and about one hour later anyone that tried to come up the same route was pinned down."[17]

THE AYL BRIDGEHEAD—FEBRUARY 24

The men of Lieutenant Colonel Thurston's 3rd/376th were still digging in on the side of the Scharfenberg Ridge during the night when orders were radioed from Regiment to send a company back to secure their crossing place. Both the 3rd and 2nd Battalions had used the same crossing point, but Regiment had made no effort to secure it until German troops had begun filtering back. Despite the fact that other units were much closer, the acting regimental commander insisted on compliance. Consequently, Lt. Jesse W. Hodges's L Company had to make a trek of more than three miles back across the hills to the river in complete darkness. The trip was conducted cautiously, but the company encountered no enemy either on the way or at the crossing site.

The remainder of the battalion had to endure a night of harassing artillery fire and the occasional seemingly random rifle shot. Sentries were posted at the roadside with instruction to capture anyone going past, whether soldiers or civilians, a move that yielded a number of surprised prisoners, and a prisoner-of-war cage had to be improvised in a small ravine. Lieutenant Daly was killed in an unfortunate incident when he gave chase in an encounter with a German soldier who hid in a foxhole and shot Daly in the back as he went past.

Daylight revealed that the battalion position was enclosed on three sides by about a dozen well-sited bunkers and pillboxes, all fully manned, but the battalion had no suitable equipment to take them. The 350 men remaining were out of range of their own mortars, and their artillery observer seemed unable to persuade his unit to provide support.

The battalion was now extremely short of food and ammunition, al-

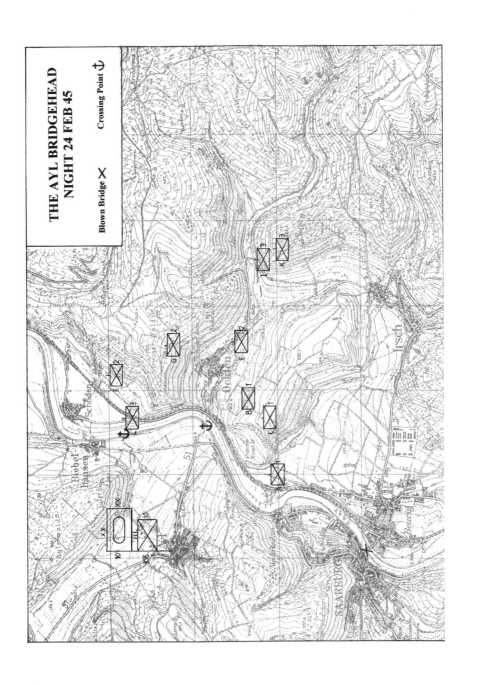

THE AYL BRIDGEHEAD
NIGHT 24 FEB 45

Blown Bridge ✕   Crossing Point ⚓

though there was plenty of water available from the stream that flowed past the company positions. Appeals for supplies from Regiment eventually resulted in men from M Company, the battalion Headquarters Company, and other available personnel being formed into two porter teams. One of the teams would load up one-man packboards with the required supplies, then dash to the boats and paddle furiously across the river under accurate machine-gun fire. They then had to carry their loads up the Irminer Wald hill, from where the second team would take the loads to the battalion on the Scharfenberg Ridge.

On the first night, the Germans spotted the unpainted ration boxes gleaming in the darkness and fired at the team with automatic weapons, forcing the men to take cover and camouflage their loads. That night a party of stretcher bearers arrived with their equipment and some food and ammunition. The prisoners and walking wounded were then detailed in parties of eight per stretcher for the journey back, because the route was so difficult to negotiate. The men were fired on from time to time, causing some confusion, but managed to get through. For some unaccountable reason, Lieutenant Colonel Anderson then forbade the further use of German prisoners for carrying wounded. At one stage the Germans infiltrated a machine gun and sniper team between the K and I Company positions, threatening to isolate them from each other until Captain Brown of K Company tracked down the enemy team and eliminated it with a well-aimed rifle grenade.[18]

A Company of Lieutenant Colonel Miner's 1st/376th started working their way upstream along the banks of the Saar and destroying the bunkers they encountered, while B and C Companies safeguarded the end of the hill that they had taken the previous day. There were bunkers all along Captain Dadisman's A Company's route, and many more were seen on the higher ground to the east, their machine guns being fired incessantly whether or not the gunners could see anything. Nevertheless, A Company, backed by flamethrower teams, took eight bunkers and about one hundred prisoners that day, but the task proved to be such that Lieutenant Colonel Miner ordered Captain Bowden's B Company to assist A Company the next day.[19]

Lieutenant Colonel Martin's 2nd/376th's Company E remained in occupation of Ockfen, while that afternoon Captain Standish's Company F was ordered to move up the vineyard and continue due north through the Irminer Wald to take the high ground above Schoden. Although they followed the order, the company was unable to cross the open ground beyond because of the number of German bunkers on the slopes. At 2100 Captain Standish was ordered to tackle the bunkers near the riverbank that were responsible for holding up the bridging operations, and he detailed two platoons for this task. By midnight, after some on-the-spot training of the new men in the use of satchel and beehive charges, Captain Standish himself led the detail.[20]

Early on February 24, in order to speed up the operation to take Trier, General Morris was ordered by General Walker at XX Corps to send his armor over the Taben bridge, which was still under construction and not completed until 1350 hours that day. General Patton had been fighting a rearguard action against the return of the 10th Armored Division to General Eisenhower's reserve, and on February 23 had only managed to obtain a grudging forty-eight-hour extension, so there was no time to waste. Morris then decided to put his armored infantry across the Saar at Ayl to reinforce the 376th Infantry under the overall command of Brigadier General Piburn. The new command structure would become effective at 0850. The armored infantry battalions were to assemble at Ayl and be prepared to cross beginning at 1500, leaving their vehicles behind to await the construction of a bridge. The men were provided with sufficient food and ammunition to sustain them without need of resupply for two days.

At 1600 Lt. Col. Jack J. Richardson's 20th Armored Infantry Battalion began crossing the Saar under cover of a smoke screen and under continuous machine-gun and artillery fire. The battalion's task was to pass through the 376th Regiment and advance along the main road to Irsch, which meant passing through the 1st Battalion's area. While the 20th Armored Infantry were still crossing, they received an order to seize Irsch.[21]

THE STAADT BRIDGEHEAD—FEBRUARY 24

Ferrying operations progressed satisfactorily throughout the night of February 23–24, but shortly after daylight enemy artillery again began to shell the crossing site. A direct hit was made on a raft that was ferrying a jeep, a 57-mm gun, and a Weasel across the river, but the raft was brought back to shore before it sank, and the gun and vehicles landed. A second raft was then constructed, and as this craft made its initial trip across the river, another artillery concentration crashed down on the ferry site. Soon afterward the men noticed movement on the cliff above the Staadt, and the crew of a .50-caliber machine gun was ordered to rake the cliff at periodic intervals. Several hours later three Germans, who had been manning a radio, surrendered. They admitted that they had been in a concealed position on the cliffs directing artillery fire for the past three days.

The previous evening a platoon of Lieutenant Devonald's K Company had occupied some outbuildings of Schloss Saarfels that turned out to be the actual vinery. Early in the morning, movement was detected near a large opening in the hillside nearby and identified as that of German soldiers. Believing this to be the rear entrance to a bunker, the platoon crawled along a ditch to a sandpit opposite the entrance and launched a surprise attack that yielded the capture of three officers and fifty-four enlisted men of the artillery fire-direction center for the Serrig area.

At 1100, at the suggestion of Colonel Hagerty, Division Headquarters announced a temporary transfer of battalions between regiments to rationalize the unusual situation that had arisen. Thus Colonel Hagerty's 301st Infantry took on the 1st and 3rd Battalions of the 302nd to add to its own 3rd Battalion and the two platoons of G Company who had already crossed to Serrig, and Colonel Johnson's 302nd Infantry took on the 1st and 2nd Battalions of the 301st to add to its own 2nd Battalion.[22] Colonel Hagerty arrived at Staadt at about midday and was ferried across to take over command of all the troops in the Serrig area, including those who had meanwhile arrived from Taben. He set up his command post in the village.[23]

Of these new attachments, Major Stanion, commanding the 1st/302nd, reported: "The battalion was ordered to take over Serrig and to patrol along the river road and keep it open. Besides this they were to maintain contact between the 301st and 302d Infantry Regiments, which meant patrolling between points 193084 and 191096. Two different times the battalion attacked downhill to take out the pillbox at 193084, but without success. The terrain was definitely against an attack of this nature. Many casualties were received here."[24]

And Captain Smith, commanding L Company of the 3rd/302nd, reported:

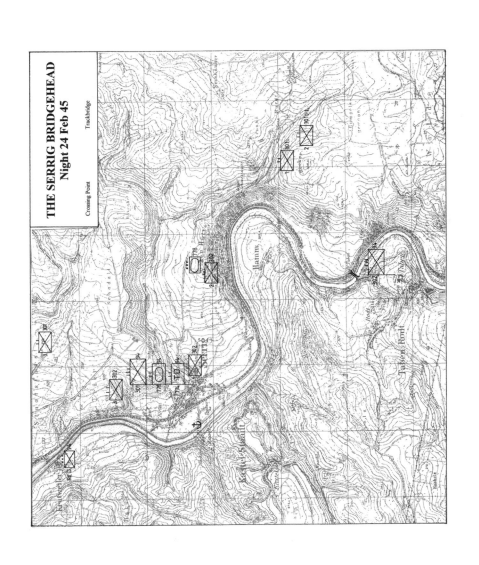

THE SERRIG BRIDGEHEAD
Night 24 Feb 45

Crossing Point

Trackbridge

Upon arriving at Serrig at about 0800, the battalion came under control of the 301st Infantry Regiment. It was here also that M Company and Battalion Headquarters Company rejoined the battalion. The order was then received to take the three pillboxes in conjunction with the 3d Battalion of the 301st Infantry. These boxes were located at the following points: No. 1 at 170110, No. 2 at 172103, No. 3 at 182103. The battalion plan was for I Company to take pillbox No. 1, and L and K Companies to take Nos. 2 and 3. It was after dark before the attack got under way on these boxes, and K Company ran into trouble. I Company had a comparatively easy job with its, however.

On 25 February, after much reconnaissance, L Company took No. 3 in ten minutes. This proved to be very dominating terrain for the regiment.[25]

The situation Captain Smith described arose out of a decision to clear the high ground immediately to the north of Serrig. Captain Frierson's L Company, which had the two stray platoons from G Company attached, advanced on the west flank. Lieutenant Christiansen's G Company platoons were checked by the numerous bunkers encountered along the riverbank, but L Company was able to outflank these positions and sent a group to attack the first bunker from the rear, which was duly taken. The advance was continuing to a second bunker when enemy fire suddenly came from behind, mortally wounding Lieutenant H. Glass. The enemy had meanwhile reoccupied the first bunker, which then had to be recaptured and a guard left on it.

The 3rd/302nd continued to make progress all day, with most problems being experienced with the dense fortifications along the riverbank, and by late afternoon the high ground north of Serrig had been secured and the battalion command post established in Schloss Saarstein about one thousand yards north of the village. While the men of the 3rd/302nd were thus engaged, those of the 3rd/301st were ordered to press forward another one thousand yards to the line of the stream opposite Krutweiler. This was done with I and K Companies sweeping the woods on either side of the road and a roadblock established where the road crossed the stream.

The armored column arrived in Serrig from Taben at 1800 to be met by Major General Malony. The 3rd/301st then pushed out to the high ground northeast of the village, clearing the ridge in its area with little difficulty until the troops came to the last bunker, whose automatic weapons were sited for grazing fire where the top of the ridge was perfectly flat. After several attempts had been repulsed, a tank was brought up in support, and the position was reduced just before dusk.

A platoon of four tanks was detailed to accompany SSgt. James A. Graham of B Company, 1st/302nd, to occupy a position on the reverse slope of the Auf der Hütte cliffs overnight in the hope that this maneuver would compel the German troops pinning down the 2nd/302nd to withdraw, as indeed turned out to be the case.[26]

THE TABEN BRIDGEHEAD—FEBRUARY 24

The 5th Ranger Battalion continued their advance throughout the night of February 23–24, alternatively marching and resting. At each halt patrols were sent out to check the area and the route ahead. Several bunkers and other fortifications were encountered, and the number of prisoners continued to grow.

Shortly before dawn the battalion closed to their objective. The men of F Company were sent forward to reconnoiter and captured some fortified houses, from which another thirty prisoners were extracted. Lieutenant Colonel Sullivan then began organizing his roadblock. B Company came under fire as they entered the position, and an enemy attack was expected at any moment. E Company laid mines on the road and then adopted covering positions, while the rest of the battalion formed an outward-facing protective screen. Soon afterward a self-propelled gun came down the road, but its crew jumped out and ran away before the rangers could engage it. The E Company bazooka team failed to destroy the gun, so it was doused with gasoline and set on fire. Later, Capt. Charles E. Parker's A Company was attacked while changing position, and it took two hours of fire from the remainder of the battalion to get the situation under control.

Anxious to provide an early relief for the 5th Rangers, General Walker at XX Corps ordered General Malony to push his infantry north from Serrig to secure Beurig and General Morris to send his armor down to cross the new bridge at Taben, which was to be ready by 1600. Together elements of both divisions would then secure Beurig, from where the armored infantry would escort the armor up the main road through Irsch to the 5th Rangers' roadblock.[27]

Major Brumley's depleted 2nd/301st, which had been withdrawn from the Staadt crossing and designated divisional reserve on the previous afternoon, began moving to the Taben crossing point at 0300 on February 24, crossing at 0400. On their way to the crossing site several men of this battalion, including Captain Stockstad of E Company, passed out from sheer exhaustion and had to be evacuated.

The remnants of F and G Companies, numbering only seventy men in all, had been formed into a combined company under Capt. Otto P. Steinen and were followed by Lt. Edmund G. Reuter's E Company, now down to about fifty effectives. The battalion was sent straight up Hocker Hill to take position to the right of Major Hodges's 1st/301st. As the lead platoon under SSgt. Carl W. Hager reached some open ground on the hilltop, the twelve men came under enemy machine-gun fire and Sergeant Hager was concussed from a grenade, so Sgt. James C. Hullender took over. Captain Steinen decided his company was too weak to tackle what appeared to be a major strongpoint and ordered a withdrawal. Then Lt. Kenneth E. Kearns tried to tackle an 88-mm gun position, but was driven back by machine-gun fire. Support from the 356th Field Artillery was called for, and the enemy position was inundated.

Meanwhile, Lieutenant Reuter, who had no maps, was bringing up E Company on the battalion right when he encountered a patrol from battalion Headquarters Company led by SSgt. John H. Kinnan and came under sniper fire. Soon after, they came across another German strongpoint and reported its presence back to Major Brumley. E Company was down to only thirty-eight effectives, so Major Brumley ordered the twenty-two-strong antitank platoon to reinforce them as riflemen, with SSgt. George F. Fell taking charge of the reinforcements. Lt. Robert E. Trinkline called for another artillery concentration, and the company went into the attack at 1430, taking the position and capturing twenty-five dazed Germans.[28]

As previously mentioned, when the men of Lieutenant Colonel Cloudt's relieved 3rd/302nd reached the foot of Hocker Hill early in the morning, they were sent off north along the riverside road to clear the route to Serrig. They encountered no difficulties, even though they had to pass beneath the still trapped 2nd/302nd on the Auf der Hütte cliffs, and reached Serrig at 1130.[29]

Up to this point, XX Corps had been able to supply the division with only one M2 treadway bridge and barely enough floats to span the river. The original plan was to put this first vehicular bridge at Staadt, but because of the amount of enemy fire directed against this location, General Malony ordered its construction at Taben instead. His infantry urgently needed the armor that had been allocated to him for this operation. This task was carried out by the 135th Combat Engineers assisted by A Company of the 319th, starting at 0230 on February 24 and not completed until 1350 that same day. The length of time needed was due to construction difficulties offered by the nature of the site and some enemy interference. The Germans continued to harass Taben with mortar and artillery fire from what appeared to be Height 471, but the bridge itself was in defilade from the artillery until the enemy moved their guns to give enfilade fire up the river.

The Broadway trucks could move to the crossing only one at a time and had to run a two-hundred-yard gauntlet of long-range German machine-gun fire to reach the river. Many of these vehicles arrived at the banks of the Saar peppered with holes, but fortunately none of the drivers was hit during the operation and not a single vehicle stalled to block the narrow road. The engineers then had to breach the twelve-foot retaining wall along the east riverbank with explosives and do a great deal of work on the approach to the far bank. This was begun by hand and finished off by an angledozer as soon as the bridge was completed. An armored Caterpillar was then sent ahead along the river road to fill the huge crater on the Hamm bend.

The weight of the first tank that crossed the bridge caused one of the inshore pontoons to puncture on some sharp rocks on the riverbed, necessitating repair, and the western approach had to be heightened before the remainder of the 778th Tank Battalion's column crossed. With the passage of the tanks, enemy artillery fire increased, continuing into the night. The pontoons were punctured several times, but fortunately the bridge received no direct hits. The engineers who were maintaining the structure repaired the damaged floats immediately, and there was no interruption to the flow of traffic.[30]

1st Lt. Bertil T. Anderson and Sgt. Clifford G. Bailey of the military police later recorded this joint statement:

> At 241600 armor of the 778th Tank Battalion and 774th Tank-Destroyer Battalion crossed the bridge. Shortly thereafter orders came to move across the river a group of 300 POWs that had been collected at Serrig. It was feared by Division that they might be liberated by a counterattack that was developing. The POWs were taken to a ferry site near Hamm, where an engineer captain had the winch of a 2 1/2 ton truck hooked up to the ferry. About 49 POWs were ferried across before the current capsized the raft. By shouting his orders across the river, Major John Schaub, 94th Military Police Platoon commanding officer, had his men march the POWs down the road along the east bank of the Saar and across the bridge at Taben. This road at the time was under sniper fire. Trucks could not be brought into Taben due to artillery fire. However, they were marched through the town and on to where the trucks were parked.[31]

Immediately upon completion of the treadway bridge at Taben, plans were made for a similar construction at Staadt, since another M2 bridge had become available and there was little enemy fire then falling in that area.[32]

10
Developing the Bridgehead

THE AYL BRIDGEHEAD—FEBRUARY 25

On February 25 Lieutenant Colonel Anderson, commanding the 376th Infantry Regiment, received orders to launch an attack to the south in order to link up with the 3rd/301st near Beurig. This would connect the two bridgeheads and clear the area of German fire, thus enabling the construction of a bridge connecting Saarburg and Beurig. This task fell to the 1st/376th, which was covering the southern flank. Lt. Col. James O'Hara's 54th Armored Infantry Battalion crossed the Saar during the night and rested up in Ockfen until dawn, when it assisted in clearing the bunkers along the riverbank leading south to Beurig.[1]

During the early hours of the twenty-fifth, Captain Standish and his men of F Company, 2nd/376th, tried to get close to the bunkers that were interfering with the bridging operations, but were unable to do so because of the heavy interlocking crossfire. Artillery assistance was requested and received in the form of white phosphorus and "time-on-target" barrages. Tank destroyers then assisted from across the river, using direct fire through the gaps in the artificial smoke, which was more effective than the efforts of the artillery.

The 61st Armored Infantry, commanded by Lt. Col. Miles L. Standish, crossed the river during the morning. That afternoon its B Company and two additional platoons were attached to the 2nd/376th to assist in its task at Schoden. The armored infantry company worked north along the river and, after some heavy fighting, forced its way into the southern edge of the objective, while on the right the F Company group followed the railroad tracks through a more heavily fortified area. As they advanced, their right flank was exposed to the fire of a series of enemy bunkers on the high ground to the east; progress was slow and the first bunkers were taken only after some bitter fighting. By early afternoon the objectives had been taken, but B Company then found itself isolated in Schoden.

At about dusk a column of Germans coming down the railroad tracks from the north was taken to be prisoners of war, being moved to the rear by the 61st Armored Infantry. This column was almost on top of the F Company troops deployed around the sole remaining bunker that the engineers had not destroyed, and in which about half the party was resting, before the men realized that the Germans were armed. Fighting developed at close quarters, and the numerically superior enemy surrounded the bunker, preventing all attempts to escape.

The remainder of Captain Standish's F Company, which had been enjoying a short rest in Ockfen, had been heavily hit by enemy artillery the previous night, and when they got word that their fellow troops were under heavy attack, they set off to the rescue. The relief party succeeded in breaking through the German perimeter and fought its way up a communication trench to the American-held bunker, but found itself trapped against a blank wall and unable to communicate with the occupants. Enemy soldiers eventually placed a large demolition charge in one of the box's embrasures, and at 0145 hours there was a terrific explosion. Finally, at 0300 the relief party was obliged to withdraw after having been outflanked.[2]

SSgt. Glenn Luckridge of F Company later reported:

The Krauts were resorting to endless means to get in the box. Every time we would yell to our trapped comrades (who apparently did not know we were there) we would get a prolonged burst from the machine guns. We were so near and yet so far from them. We had no way to get at them, as showing our heads above the trench would have been certain death.

At about midnight the Krauts fired a bazooka round at the box in an effort to get our men out, after which they taunted them. We had no grenades as we had not been able to replenish our supply. And, not knowing the true conditions before us, we were afraid to try anything desperate for fear of hurting our own men. Time crept by slowly, a minute seemed an hour, and our nerves were nearly cracked from being in such a helpless position . . . We just sat and prayed.

Finally at two in the morning there was a terrific explosion in front of the box. It didn't take much deduction to figure they had blown a hole in the box, and now our men had little choice. After about ten minutes we went through the most agonizing sensation in the world, hearing our buddies surrender. They had no choice. When we heard them go our hearts all sank. We had done our best but failed at our objective.[3]

While attempting to observe these operations, both Lieutenant Colonel Martin and Major Dossenbach, the battalion commander and executive officer respectively, were injured and had to be evacuated. Later in the day Captain Standish was found wandering around in a dazed condition and also had to be evacuated, as he was suffering from exhaustion.[4]

Meanwhile, E Company was under heavy attack in Ockfen, and Lieutenant Colonel Thurston's 3rd Battalion remained isolated on the hills beyond.

The remaining troops of the 1st/376th's A Company were assembled, leaving the rest of the battalion stretched to breaking point along its extended front. Captain Dadisman's A Company then attacked south along the riverbank, but was met by a hail of machine-gun fire from American positions west of the Saar. When the machine gunners realized their mistake and lifted their fire, the company continued down the hill toward the enemy-held bunkers in the valley as two platoons of tank destroyers on the west bank provided their fire support. To add to the difficulty of the situation, the Germans manning the bunkers under attack called for mortar fire. However, by nightfall the company had reached the point where the Ockfen-Beurig road crossed the railway tracks, so they dug in.

During the afternoon they were joined by Captain Bowden's B Company, while Capt. Frank Malinski's C Company, which had sustained the most casualties in the assault crossing, continued to safeguard the hill behind them. As they advanced, they came under constant harassing fire from bunkers farther inland. In spite of the onset of darkness, which made locating enemy positions extremely difficult, the platoon commanders of B Company skillfully directed the supporting 90-mm and 150-mm artillery fire on to their targets.[5]

The supply situation for Lieutenant Colonel Thurston's 3rd/376th on the Scharfenberg Ridge was now getting desperate. But circumstances improved somewhat when a hay wain drawn by two oxen came along the road and was found to be full of hams, and while that was being appropriated, another came along loaded with large carboys of local wine.

Meanwhile, Thurston's pleas for help, which had failed to extract a response from Regiment, had filtered through to the parent 94th Division, and with General Malony's approval, artillery liaison planes were pressed into service for vertical resupply. The Piper Cubs made trip after trip, dropping food, ammunition, radio batteries, and medical supplies, not all of which fell into the battalion lines. As the planes swooped low over the American positions, the Germans would send up a hail of lead from every available weapon, causing the Cubs to duck and weave. On one occasion two Messerschmitt Me-109s jumped the aerial column, and only the maneuverability and slow airspeed of the tiny planes saved them from the fast German fighters. While most of the twenty Piper Cubs that participated in these operations had scars to prove the accuracy of the enemy's fire, not a single plane was lost.[6]

According to Lieutenant Colonel Thurston, part of an armored infantry battalion arrived at 2200, armed only with light weapons. Ignoring Thurston's advice and without making any reconnaissance, the lieutenant colonel who was commanding led his men uphill toward the interlocking line of pillboxes that Thurston did not have the equipment to attack and had therefore kept picketed to prevent an enemy counterattack in a mutually acceptable "live and let live" arrangement. About midnight he and his men heard sustained bursts of machine-gun fire, and sometime afterward the armored infantrymen returned carrying their wounded. Apparently their colonel had led them directly into the attack in column of threes. He had been one of those killed, and his second in command had ordered a retreat, leaving Thurston's men to bury the dead the next day.[7]

The Fort Knox research report into "The 10th Armored Division in the Saar-Moselle Triangle" describes other events that were going on at the time:

Task Force Richardson was continually held up by pillboxes to the south. These pillboxes were located south of Ockfen in a staggered formation. There were eleven in all, of which ten were marked on the infantry's 1:25,000 maps. Teams were organized before setting out to clear the pillboxes. A detailed plan was devised which called for co-ordinated assaults on each pillbox. This, in turn, required a well-defined plan of attack. It was decided that Task Force Richardson would clear the pillboxes southeast of Ockfen, while Task Force O'Hara would move east, initially following the path which had been taken by Task Force Standish in its move to Scharfenberg Hill. Task Force O'Hara would then turn south and, fighting abreast of Task Force Riley, clear the pillboxes in its zone along the road leading to Irsch. The attack was to begin at dusk.

The clear-cut plan of attack called for the dismounted infantry to reduce each fortification methodically. Two machine gun sections would set up in partial defilade on the flanks of the pillboxes, and by firing on the embrasures would force the occupants to close them. Bazooka teams would then move forward and blow off the ports. Following that, the engineer teams would crawl up and place their satchel charges. In the meantime, the artillery on the west side of the Saar would be on call to place fire on the remaining pillboxes in order to keep them occupied. An almost identical situation had been re-hearsed by the infantry while they were training in the Metz area, and this proved extremely helpful.

The 54th Armored Infantry Battalion was assigned the following missions: The first two pillboxes were to be taken by A Company, the next four by C Company, and the last two again by A Company. At approximately 1830 A Company moved out toward the first two pill-boxes. Very little resistance was offered after artillery and machine gun fire had been placed on the boxes. C Company then passed through A Company and moved on to take the next two pillboxes, supported by machine-gun and artillery fire. The Germans put up a dogged resistance and fired flares to light up the area for spotting targets. Friendly artillery fire was increased on the pillboxes and two tank-destroyers, which had been ferried across the river during the day, fired direct fire on the fortifications. This was sufficient to force the Germans to surrender.

However, the next two pillboxes assigned to C Company were far more difficult to reduce. As the assault team moved up, the Germans brought additional machine guns onto the slope to the east and opened fire to deny the approach. In spite of this increased automatic fire, the assault teams reached the pillboxes and placed their satchel charges. But even after the charges were detonated, the Germans continued fighting. It was necessary for the company to withdraw so that friendly fire and tank-destroyer fire could be placed on the boxes. After two hours of this fire the Germans surrendered.

The tank-destroyers then further assisted A Company in the reduction of the remaining pillboxes, which, fortunately, quickly surrendered.

This operation had taken most of the night and resulted in 20 enemy killed and 54 prisoners of war taken. C Company only suffered four casualties. It had definitely been proved that pillboxes do not form insurmountable obstacles to armored infantry if the attacks have been carefully planned and carried out with speed and teamwork.[8]

As we shall see, the armored infantry battalions were to link up with Task Force Riley in Irsch that evening.

That night the commander of the 376th Infantry, Lieutenant Colonel Anderson, sent a situation report to General Malony, commanding the 94th Division, in the hope that Malony might be able to extend some help, even though the 376th was still attached to, and under command of, the 10th Armored Division. The telexed message read:

Our lines are so extended that we cannot prevent enemy infiltration. Enemy occupied pillboxes still exist inside our bridgehead. All troops have been committed since the first day of the operation. I have no reserve. One company of armored infantry has been attached temporarily.

Except for two platoons of tank-destroyers on the friendly side of the river, we have no support of heavy direct fire weapons. It is expected that these two platoons will be withdrawn tomorrow.

Until 1900 this date, all evacuation and supply has been hand-carried. One Weasel and seven Jeeps may be able to cross tonight. At present all ferry service is out of order. I expect that all heavy trucks, prime-movers, cannon and artillery weapons will have to cross the Saar at your bridgehead. If so, this will be a critical period for the infantry battalions, and they must be reinforced and supplied by another unit.

If we cross all vehicles here it will take two or three days and place the vehicles in an area getting observed artillery fire.

In our beachhead we have captured about sixty percent of the pillboxes, one 88-mm gun, one battery of mountain artillery, and 452 prisoners. Estimated killed 300.

Since 21 February I have lost 14 officers and 161 enlisted men. I am understrength 47 officers and 506 enlisted men.

I recommend that this combat command be passed through, if the 94th Division is to continue the attack to the north.

If the 94th Division is to protect the Saarburg crossing, I recommend that this combat team be reinforced to hold its present position. Such reinforcement should include tank destroyers and infantry.[9]

THE SERRIG BRIDGEHEAD—FEBRUARY 25

At 1030 hours on February 25, XX Corps informed Major General Malony that the 94th was to attack north from its bridgehead, while the 376th Infantry, which was still attached to the 10th Armored Division and had crossed the Saar at Ayl, was to attack south to link the two bridgeheads. Further, the 94th was to clear the road from the Taben site to Beurig and uncover the Saarburg-Beurig-Irsch road so that armor could be committed to the east. As the 10th Armored Division had been unable to put a bridge over the Saar at its crossing site, its tanks were to move south and cross on the 94th's bridges.[10]

Clearing the area north of Beurig and securing the lateral route from Saarburg to Irsch before the arrival of the armor in the bridgehead presented a major problem. Since the 3rd Battalions of the 301st and 302nd Infantry were in the best positions to make the sweep north, orders were speedily issued to them for a simultaneous thrust with Lieutenant Colonel McNulty's 3rd/301st on the left aiming at Beurig, and Lieutenant Colonel Cloudt's 3rd/302d on the right aiming for Irsch.

While waiting for dawn to advance, I Company took cover in some

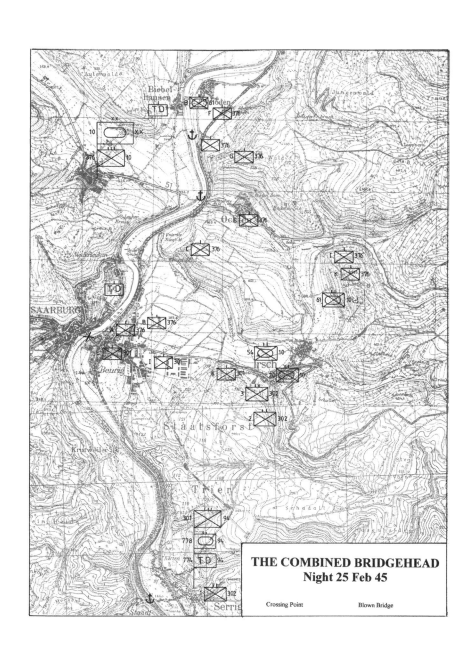

THE COMBINED BRIDGEHEAD
Night 25 Feb 45

Crossing Point   Blown Bridge

houses on the edge of the woods, but as the troops settled down to rest, they were inundated with an intense concentration of mortar bombs that forced them out again into the woods behind. It was later discovered that this concentration came from a belt-loaded, 50-mm fortress mortar installed in a pillbox that could put as many as twenty-seven bombs into the air before the first exploded.

In front of McNulty's 3rd/301st lay about fifteen hundred yards of dense woodland shown on the map as the Forêt de Trèves (Trier Forest), and beyond this was the fortified village of Beurig. The rifle companies swept through these woods, routing out snipers and reducing machine-gun nests until L Company was looking down into Beurig. The exhausted infantrymen had to tackle one pillbox after another without the support of the tank destroyers that were still on the other side of the river. The ground before them was wide open, studded with pillboxes and bunkers, wire entanglements and tank traps, communication trenches and minefields. On the right, facing the Beurig-Irsch road, was also a deserted German army barracks complex.[11]

Commenting on this episode, Major Howard, operations officer of the 301st Infantry, later wrote: "On 25 February, the 3d Battalion, 301st Infantry, advanced into Beurig after clearing six pillboxes of the enemy along the river line. The Germans were mainly talked out of their pillboxes during the advance, when a T/5 [Tech-5] from K Company and two German POWs approached each pillbox in turn and explained the situation to the men inside. One of the German POWs was killed during one approach, but over 100 of the pillbox occupants emerged waving white surrender flags."[12]

Meanwhile, on the right flank Lieutenant Devonald's K Company had reached the edge of the woods overlooking the narrow village of Irsch, and even farther east Cloudt's 3rd/302nd deployed on the high ground on the near side of the stream flowing north into Irsch. Here they rested until the arrival of the armor.

As the 3rd Battalions of the 301st and 302nd Infantry Regiments moved northward, a gap was created between the regiments, so the 2nd/302nd, which had spent the night on the hill east of Serrig, was tasked with forming an east-facing line along the stream running north into Irsch. At the same time, the right flank of this battalion was instructed to link up with the left flank of Major Hodges's 1st/301st on the near side of the Auf der

Hütte cliffs. At 1300, as a result of the foregoing deployments, another reshuffle took place within the 94th Infantry Division. Colonel Hagerty's 301st Infantry Regiment was made responsible for the area north of Serrig, with the 2nd/302nd, 3rd/301st, and 3rd/302nd Battalions under command, and moved its command post into Schloss Saarfels. Colonel Johnson's 302nd Infantry Regiment was made responsible for the area south of Serrig, with the 1st/301st, 1st/302nd, and 2nd/301st Battalions under command. In essence, the 301st Infantry exchanged the 1st/302nd for the 2nd/302nd after the previous day's reorganization.[13]

The Fort Knox report on the 10th Armored Division resumes:

Lieutenant Colonel Riley of CCB [Combat Command B], like Richardson, received orders to move his tanks and half-tracks to Freudenburg in order to cross on the Taben bridge. Although the bridge was under heavy artillery fire, the Task Force crossed with A Company, 21st Tank Battalion (reinforced with a light tank platoon of D Company) leading, followed by Headquarters Company and the empty half-tracks of the infantry.

Serrig by this time was in our hands, and it was here that Riley received orders from CCA [Combat Command A] to attack through the 94th Division bridgehead and push on to Irsch. There he would pick up the 61st Armored Infantry Battalion of Task Force Standish and move east to relieve the 5th Ranger Battalion, and seize the high ground west of Zerf.

While in Serrig, Riley met Lieutenant [Louis J.] Gambosi of the 5th Ranger Battalion, who had with him 24 men and two officers. These troops were loaded into the half-tracks following behind A Company. Riley, with his S-3, Captain R. V. Earkley, moved forward to the head of the column where the 94th Division was still engaged in heavy fighting against enemy small arms, mortars, and machine guns at the limits of the bridgehead near Beurig. In order not to become involved in this action, the armor was forced to take secondary roads, which were impassable except for medium tanks. The light tanks, therefore, were attached by cables to the M4 Sherman tanks and the column continued intact.

With the delay caused by this expedient, it was not until late in the afternoon of February 25th that the column closed upon the town of

Irsch from the west, with the 1st Platoon of A Company leading. Lieutenant Colonel Riley believed at that time that Task Force Standish had cleared the town with his 61st Armored Infantry Battalion. This proved a costly mistake since Task Force Standish was still fighting to reach Irsch from its Scharfenberg Hill position.

Lieutenant Hanover, commanding the 1st Platoon of A Company, moved into the center of the town. To his immediate front he observed a roadblock across a fork in the road. The two lead tanks fired at the block with 76-mm fire. They then bypassed the roadblock to the west and continued through the town.

However, they failed to observe that the roadblock was covered from either side by two German bazooka teams, one ground-mounted 88-mm gun, and a Panther tank. When the third tank in Lieutenant Hanover's column attempted to pass the roadblock, it was fired on by the 88-mm gun and set afire, blocking the road. The fourth tank was hit by the bazooka team on the right. The fifth tank was hit by the other bazooka team, but did not burst into flames. Meanwhile the Panther tank covering the roadblock opened up and hit two light tanks of the 2nd Platoon further back in the column.

Captain Eardley, commanding A Company, immediately contacted the men of the Ranger Battalion and organized them as an infantry team in order to clear the obstacle. The Rangers came forward and, upon arrival at the roadblock, they flushed the enemy crews into flight. The Rangers then proceeded on to contact the two tanks which had succeeded in getting past the roadblock. They reached the tanks, and formed a flank guard to prevent further bazooka fire from knocking them out while being escorted back to the main column.

At 2030 B Company of Task Force Riley (20th Armored Infantry Battalion) came into Irsch from the northwest. It immediately began clearing the town, taking 290 prisoners of war from the 416th Volksgrenadier Division [*sic;* the actual title was the 416th Infantry Division]. The action up to this time had cost five tanks and approximately five killed and 20 injured.

Captain Holehouse, commanding A Company, 20th Armored Infantry Battalion, arrived from Ockfen at 2240 and assisted in clearing the town, taking 250 prisoners of war. When a Panther tank to the south of the town opened up, the prisoners of war started to scatter.

One of Company A's half-tracks covered the prisoners of war, and when the fracas was over, 15 of them were dead. C Company, 20th Armored Infantry Battalion, arrived almost on the heels of Captain Holehouse.

The three armored infantry battalions of the 10th Armored Division had succeeded in reaching Irsch with the assistance of the 376th RCT [Regimental Combat Team].[14]

Elements of the 94th Infantry Division also assisted in clearing Irsch. Lieutenant Devonald's K Company of Maj. Gilbert N. O'Neil's 3rd/301st moved out from the cover of the woods to help take the village, and half the village had been cleared before the company was withdrawn to prepare for the battalion attack on Beurig the next morning. Task Force Riley had expected to meet their own armored infantrymen in Irsch, but they had yet to arrive, so the task force welcomed this assistance. K Company was replaced that evening by Lieutenant Colonel Cloudt's 3rd/302nd, who then assisted in clearing the rest of the village.

Instructions were received for the newly constituted "Temporary Team A," consisting of Task Force Riley and the armored infantry, to move on immediately to the relief of the 5th Ranger Battalion. However, as the team started off with two Rangers sitting on each of the tanks and the remainder in the half-tracks, a Panther tank blocked the road ahead and set the two leading Shermans on fire, followed by the half-tracks, which the Ranger occupants managed to evacuate just in time. The column had made the fatal error of moving out bumper to bumper within the narrow, twisting confines of the village, and were thus unable to maneuver to engage the Panther, which escaped unharmed. The column then pulled back into Irsch to sort themselves out with a radioed plea to Division that they could not move in darkness without infantry support, but were ordered to move on regardless.

Finally the Rangers were ordered forward to clear the way through the village, which involved clearing another three roadblocks and chasing the Panther off, only to find a fourth roadblock at the far end of the village covered by yet another Panther tank. The Rangers called for artillery support, but because of an ammunition shortage could get none, so they went ahead anyway and cleared the roadblock, capturing sixty prisoners. Fortunately, the second Panther declined to attack without infantry support.[15]

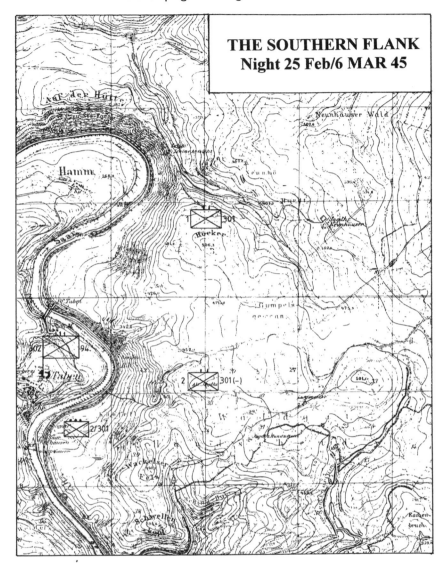

THE SOUTHERN FLANK
Night 25 Feb/6 MAR 45

The troops of Company A of the 319th Engineers were able to begin constructing a Class 40 pontoon bridge at Staadt at 0800, for the ground dominating the crossing point was now entirely in American hands, since the continuing expansion of the bridgehead had forced the withdrawal of the German batteries that had been shelling it. By 1515 the bridge was ready for traffic, and Combat Command A of the 10th Armored Division crossed immediately.[16]

HOCKER HILL—FEBRUARY 25

During the moonlit night of February 24–25, the men of Major Maixner's 2nd/302nd, who had been trapped and isolated on the Auf der Hütte cliff path since the afternoon of the twenty-third, made another attempt to proceed and found that they could do so, as most of the Germans had disappeared. The German withdrawal was presumed to have been caused by the deployment on the back of the hill of four tanks escorted by infantry coming up from Serrig. The battalion encountered only slight resistance before meeting up with troops from the 1st Battalion, to whose location it then proceeded. It was only then discovered that the 2nd Platoon of G Company, which had been covering the battalion's flank on the cliff track from a captured bunker, was missing. The platoon leader and platoon sergeant had both become casualties, and the men in the bunker remained unaware of the battalion's departure.

This isolated bunker was attacked by German troops during the night, forcing the Americans out. German troops also retook the bunker at the Y-shaped junction at the Serrig end of the footpath, thus cutting the path once more. Consequently, the 2nd Platoon was obliged to scramble down the cliffs to the river road to get to Serrig and rejoin the battalion. Just before dawn a twenty-man patrol from Captain Colgan's A Company, 1st/301st, recaptured the troublesome Y-junction bunker, killing seven Germans and capturing twenty-three. However, this was not the end of the matter, for just before dawn Lieutenant Cancilla's B Company of the 1st/301st on Hocker Hill was ordered to maintain contact between the battalion and the 2nd/302nd east of Serrig, some three thousand yards away. Cancilla took the same cliff path across the Auf der Hütte cliffs that Major Maixner's 2nd/302nd had taken before, and as Lt. Richard E. Eckstrom's lead platoon reached the unoccupied bunker at the far end, it came under enemy machine-gun fire. Blocked in by the sheer cliff and the enemy deployed across its front, the platoon took cover in the pillbox. The Germans then grenaded the bunker, resulting in several injuries and forcing the men out again. That afternoon Eckstrom and TSgt. Robert O'Hara led their platoons in a coordinated attack following a preparatory concentration organized by Lt. Paul Boland of the 301st Field Artillery. They gained their objective, but the enemy retaliated with mortar, machine-gun, and sniper fire. The platoons then received orders to return to Hocker Hill. That afternoon A Company was attacked on Hocker Hill by SS Panzergrenadier Battalion 506, which had just arrived in the area, but the company was able to successfully repel the enemy attack.

At one point in the afternoon the Y-fork bunker was attacked by a tank of the 778th Tank Battalion, whose crew no doubt believed it was occupied by Germans. After firing five rounds at point-blank range, the tanker crew placed a satchel charge against the door, planning to blow it open. A firing slit in the bunker then opened, and the two men of B Company and three gunners of the 301st Field Artillery who were inside told the tank crew in no uncertain terms what they thought of them. Fortunately, no one was hurt, but this incident serves to demonstrate both the strength of the German positions and the complexity of the situation.

Meanwhile, Major Maixner's 2nd/302nd had set off to the northeast and crossed the Serrig valley and were advancing through a wooded area on the tip of the next hill, when they suddenly came under attack from a large group of Germans just as American artillery began to fall on both groups. Lieutenant Colonel Cloudt's 3nd/302nd had seen the enemy attack forming in the woods and, mistaking their 2nd Battalion for the enemy, had called for artillery fire. However, this broke up the enemy attack, and as soon as the fire lifted, the 2nd Battalion continued up the ridge, crossed the road running along it, and deployed as ordered.[17]

XX Corps' orders to the 94th Infantry Division were interpreted as giving priority to the Taben bridge, so the key position of Hocker Hill had to be held "at all costs." With the 10th Armored Division having to pass along the 94th's main supply routes to reach the Taben bridge, strict traffic control was necessary. Consequently, a traffic control system was established using two-man military police posts at the vital points that were all connected by field telephone under the direction of Lt. Col. John D. F. Phillips, the divisional G-4 (staff officer for supply/logistics) at Freudenburg. Before a convoy was allowed to enter the controlled area net, it had to telephone ahead the number and type of vehicles. It was then given the exact time it could enter, and its progress had to be reported as it passed through. This allowed for convoys to be halted should an area ahead come under enemy artillery fire or be blocked by an accident.[18]

Company A of the 1st/301st came under attack from the newly arrived SS Panzergrenadier Battalion 506 during the afternoon of February 25. The company stood fast in the fierce engagement, but the Germans were able to advance their positions to within seventy-five yards of the Americans.[19]

Of the occupation of Hocker Hill, Maj. Harold F. Howard later reported:

> The 1st Battalion, 301st Infantry, still under control of 302d Infantry, was meantime on Hocker Hill, and when the 2d Battalion, 301st Infantry, had crossed at Taben and taken over the sector between Hocker Hill and the Division right flank on the river, the 1st Battalion was ordered to outpost a three-mile line, tying in with the 2d Battalion, 302nd Infantry, to the north. While proceeding northward, B Company struck heavy resistance to the northwest of Hocker Hill in the vicinity of a kind of crevice containing a pillbox. German SS troops were entrenched in this crevice and used the pillbox as a base for their defense. Company B upon attacking the crevice met fanatical resistance, since the SS troops thought their position of great tactical importance evidently, and were bent upon holding it. The pillbox during the fight changed hands several times, and every time the Americans succeeded in regaining it, blew it with demolition charges. Upon making contact with the 2d Battalion, 302nd Infantry, B Company was driven out by the counterattack of the SS troops, and late in the afternoon of 25 February B Company was withdrawn from that area and the battalion mission changed to defend Hocker Hill at all cost, and the enemy continued to hold the crevice. This defense of Hocker Hill by the 1st Battalion, 301st infantry, continued for several days.[20]

Major Brumley's 2nd/301st were also engaged. At 1800 Captain Steinen's company passed through Captain Stockstad's E Company to launch an attack on the Wackelser Fels hill to the south using marching fire, but were only partly successful. The top of the hill remained in the hands of enemy soldiers, who were able to bring down a considerable volume of fire from machine guns, artillery, and snipers on the attackers. The situation remained unpredictable here.[21]

THE AYL BRIDGEHEAD—FEBRUARY 26

On the morning of February 26 the first three tanks to arrive in the 376th Infantry's bridgehead appeared in the 2nd/376th's area. They had been ferried across on a raft made out of bridge sections that the engineers had been able to salvage. Lieutenant Colonel Martin then sent the 3rd Platoon of Captain Darrah's E Company with the tanks to extricate the forty-eight men of F Company who were still fighting for the pillboxes located south of Schoden, where they were virtually cut off.

Two of the tanks failed to reach the designated line of departure in time, so the seventeen remaining men of the 3rd Platoon moved off with just one tank in support. Their first objective was three mutually supporting pillboxes. The first one fell easily, but the second pillbox was surrendered only after the enemy soldiers inside poured a heavy volume of small-arms and mortar fire on the platoon. Inside this pillbox they found American helmets, M1s and other equipment, and a wounded soldier from F Company. All the rest had been either killed or captured. The men then attacked the third pillbox, during which the American tank became the target of every enemy weapon in the area. The tank commander was wounded and crawled out of his hatch, and the tank stopped firing. The platoon commander, 2nd Lt. Ernest N. Dryland, was mortally wounded and there were many other casualties. At this point Tech-5 Paul E. Ramsey dashed to the tank through a hail of fire and administered first aid to the tank commander, whom he then sent back along a communication trench. Ramsey then climbed up on the tank and literally took charge of the battle, directing the tank's guns and using the tank's radio to give a clear and concise report on the situation to the battalion command post. (Ramsey was awarded the Distinguished Service Cross for his outstanding initiative in this action.)[22] Eventually, what was left of F Company and the 3rd Platoon of E Company withdrew to Ockfen to await necessary reinforcement. B Company of the 61st Armored Infantry Battalion were still trapped in Schoden.

Lieutenant Colonel Miner's 1st/376th set off toward Beurig at 0500 and encountered only slight resistance. Unknown to the men of the battalion, the Germans had retreated during the night after the arrival of the American armored columns in Irsch coming from the Taben crossing point. The advance continued and the battalion pushed into the northern edge of Beurig, searching the village house by house. The battalion rounded up a few Germans, and at about noon they made contact with the 3rd Battalion, 301st Infantry, who had entered Beurig from the south.

The linking of the bridgeheads enabled a brief respite for the troops. Kitchen trucks were brought up, and the men were given their first hot meal in five days. Some lucky soldiers even received belated Christmas parcels from home. The 1st Battalion was then ordered to turn around and march back to Ockfen, where it was to pass through the 2nd Battalion and attack northward the next day.[23]

While Lieutenant Colonel Thurston's 3rd/376th on Scharfenberg Ridge was waiting to be passed through by the armored infantry, an enemy patrol approached Captain Brown's K Company's area. The men in the patrol were almost upon the company before they realized Germans were occupying the area. The American troops opened fire at point-blank range, killing or wounding all of the enemy party. Later the armored infantry arrived and pushed through the woods west of Height 426 on the southern tip of the Scharfenberg Ridge, thus releasing a good deal of pressure on the 3rd/376th. The situation improved further as the armored columns drove east through Irsch. For the first time in three days the battalion members had only one front with which to concern themselves. In any case, they were about to be relieved, as we shall see.[24]

THE SERRIG BRIDGEHEAD—FEBRUARY 26

At 1000 Lieutenant Colonel McNulty's 3rd/301st launched their attack on Beurig. The open ground surrounding the town bristled with enemy fortifications, and the companies moved forward slowly. Surprisingly, the first pillboxes were taken with a minimum of effort, and after this there was practically no resistance. The troops advanced cautiously through the silent, deserted village checking houses methodically. As previously mentioned, Lieutenant Colonel Miner's 1st/376th arrived from the north, thus finally filling the gap between the bridgeheads. By noon the village was firmly in American hands and the Serrig-Beurig-Irsch road had been swept for mines and readied for traffic.[25] With the clearing of Beurig, the 135th Engineer Combat Battalion began construction of a third pontoon bridge at Saarburg, which was completed by midnight.[26]

A reorganization took place in the 3rd/301st when Lieutenant Colonel McNulty was appointed regimental executive officer in place of Lieutenant Colonel Hardin, who had been wounded at Staadt on the twenty-second. Major O'Neil took over command, and his place as battalion executive officer was taken over by Captain Frierson, who in turn handed over his L Company to Lt. Samuel T. Minich.

Late in the afternoon XX Corps moved the boundary between the 94th Infantry and the 10th Armored Divisions farther north. This boundary change materially increased the 301st Infantry's area of responsibility on the left or northern flank of the division.[27]

Lieutenant Colonel Cloudt's 3rd/302nd was ordered to move to the Scharfenberg Ridge and Height 426 on the Ockfener Berg northeast of Irsch, where Lieutenant Colonel Thurston's 3rd/376th, on the northern tip, had been resisting a series of strong attacks for days. As Cloudt's battalion advanced that afternoon, they encountered a network of pillboxes and bunkers. Fortunately, these structures were mainly unoccupied, with what little resistance there was coming from an occasional sniper or machine gun. The troops continued up the steep wooded slope of Height 426 and then down the ridge, sweeping the enemy's feeble resistance before them. Thurston's 3rd/376th was encountered as expected, the positions on Height 426 and the Scharfenberg being taken over by Major O'Neil's 3rd/301st, while Cloudt's 3rd/302nd moved on to occupy the Irminer Wald hill.

Thurston's exhausted troops withdrew to Ockfen for a well-earned rest. With them went L Company, who with G Company of Major Dossenbach's 2nd/376th had endured constant bombardment on the Irminer Wald hill. One position alone had taken an all-night pounding that left half of its twenty-two defenders wounded. On another occasion a two-man team from the G Company machine-gun section trailed and captured a seven-man German patrol.

With Maixner's 2nd/302nd occupying the ridge south of Irsch, the dispositions of the 301st Infantry that night secured the bridgehead and main supply route that was about to open through Saarburg.

The 94th Infantry Division now held a bridgehead eleven thousand yards wide and five thousand yards deep. CCB of the 10th Armored had

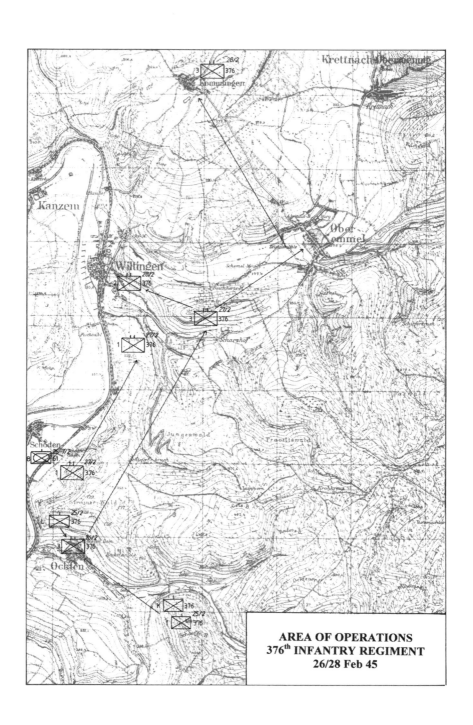

AREA OF OPERATIONS
376th INFANTRY REGIMENT
26/28 Feb 45

completed crossing at Taben by 0222 hours, and CCA of the same division began its crossing at noon over the new bridge at Serrig, the tanks taking the hill road east for Zerf, where they were to turn north for Trier.[28]

The newly constituted Temporary Team A of the 10th Armored Division had taken all night to reorganize in Irsch, and it was 0930 before the drive to relieve the 5th Ranger Battalion along Highway 407 resumed. B and C Companies of Lieutenant Colonel Richardson's 20th Armored Infantry Battalion had gone ahead on foot to clear the first one and a half miles. However, there was little opposition, and the tanks and infantry half-tracks moved on until an observation plane supporting them reported the presence of some antitank guns up ahead. The armored infantry were able to deal with the guns and captured sixty prisoners. The column then came under intermittent heavy artillery and mortar fire being brought down on the highway and either side of it, and the advance continued in fits and starts during the pauses in firing. It took three hours to reach the hamlet of Biedchen, about halfway to Zerf, where the column came under point-blank fire that was believed to be coming from a 75-mm gun aimed straight down the road from a point west of Zerf.

The tanks stayed on the road, but the infantry took cover in a parallel draw about one hundred yards from the highway. At this point contact was made with the 5th Rangers, and Lieutenant Gambosi's platoon split off to rejoin them. A request came back for the transport to remove their wounded, so five half-tracks were detailed off for the task. This was the third day that Lieutenant Colonel Sullivan's 5th Rangers had held their roadblock. Before being relieved, they had just ambushed a column of enemy soldiers, capturing 145 men and killing several others. Orders now arrived from the 94th Infantry Division attaching them to the 301st Infantry, whose troops had also been striving to reach them.

The artillery fire continued, but a thick fog arose, restricting visibility to about fifty yards, and the column was able to make better progress. Just west of Zerf, B Company moved off to the southeast to attack Oberzerf, which was taken at 1700 with little resistance. Lt. Melvin I. Mason's C Company moved northeast to take Niederzerf, only to spot six Panthers in the village, so they held back from attacking.

Meanwhile, the remainder of Temporary Team A assembled on the high ground overlooking the valley in which these villages lay. Included in the

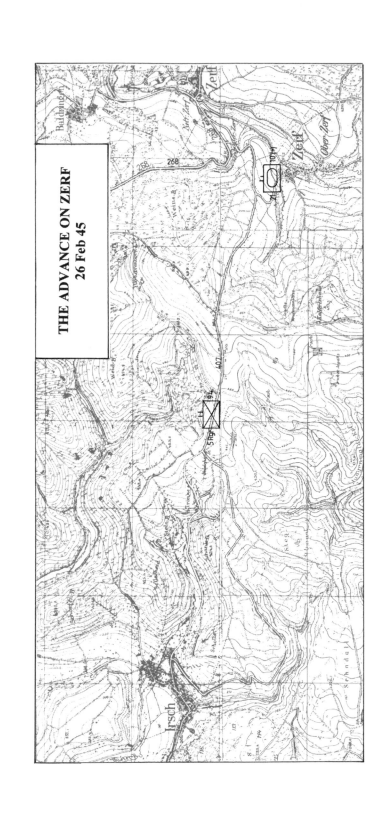

THE ADVANCE ON ZERF
26 Feb 45

assembly were the tanks of the 21st Tank Battalion, two platoons of B Company, 609th Tank Destroyer Battalion, and the half-tracks of the 54th Armored Infantry Battalion. Lieutenant Colonel Richardson organized these elements into three teams. One was to take the high ground on either side of Oberzerf, the second was to take Niederzerf and the high ground around it, and the third was to go into Zerf itself and secure the high ground east of it. The attack on Zerf was launched at 1800 but stalled on minefields in front of the village. While these were being cleared, a platoon of Hellcats moved to some commanding ground six hundred yards to the east of the village and shelled it with its 75-mm guns for ten minutes, after which some dismounted infantry moved in. A Panther was seen on the village outskirts, and bazooka teams fired at it, scoring a hit, but did not disable it. The tank withdrew and the village was secured by 0100. During the night Temporary Team A was disbanded, having captured more than one hundred prisoners during its brief existence, and its subordinate units reorganized themselves in readiness for pushing on without delay.[29]

HOCKER HILL—FEBRUARY 26

Enemy artillery fire continued to fall on Taben with clocklike precision and surprising accuracy, and the men soon realized that the best time to enter or leave the village was immediately after the German artillerymen had finished a concentration. All supplies for the battalions on Hocker Hill coming through the village had to be brought across the Saar River and then hauled up the steep cliff paths on backpacks by carrying parties formed from rear area personnel, who then brought the wounded back with them. German prisoners of war were also used as litter bearers in this sector.

There was little activity in the 301st Infantry's area, but Major Brumley's 2nd/301st sent a platoon to establish a roadblock in the hamlet of Saarhausen, which was upriver from the Taben crossing. On the way there Pfc. Melvin C. Magnuson, who was acting as platoon sergeant, saw a German soldier standing outside a pillbox. He first grenaded the position, then persuaded the occupants to surrender. An NCO among the prisoners volunteered to negotiate the surrender of a further six pillboxes, as a result of which the platoon took seventy prisoners in all. Once the platoon had set up its roadblock in Saarhausen, it was well fed for the next few days by a local housewife.[30]

11
Taking Trier

General Patton telephoned General Bradley about retaining the 10th Armored Division, saying that if he could keep it a bit longer, he was certain of taking Trier soon. Bradley, who knew that SHAEF would not intervene at this stage, gave him permission to keep the division.[1]

DIVISION FIELD ORDER NUMBER 14

On the morning of February 27 Brigadier General Collier, chief of staff to XX Corps, telephoned General Malony, who had previously commented that he needed mountain troops for the next area of operations, saying: "General, you have your wish for mountain troops! The German 2d Mountain Division is now in front of you."[2]

The Germans' Army Group G had allocated Maj. Gen. Hans Degan's 2nd Mountain Division, consisting of the Mountain Infantry (*Gebirgsjäger*) Regiments 136 and 137, and Mountain Artillery Regiment 11, Tank Hunting Battalion 55, Mountain Engineer Battalion 82, and divisional support units bearing the number 67, to LXXXII Corps. This division, originally stemming from the Austrian army, had been seriously depleted in the fighting in northern Finland before it was replenished in Denmark with men taken from rear-area units, most of them Austrian. The first elements of this division to arrive had already been engaged against the 5th Rangers.

General Malony's comment arose from new orders from XX Corps to increase the side of his bridgehead, as a result of which he issued Division Field Order Number 14 on February 27, nominating eleven hilltops west of the Ruwer River that were to be the next objectives for the 94th Infantry

Division. The division was thus to be deployed from south to north in the following order:

2nd/301st	Wäckseler Fels (Height 440)
	Saarhausen
1st/302nd	Hill 1 (Höckerberg) (Height 506)
	Hill 2 (Height 536)
5th Rangers	Hill 3 (Height 502)
3rd/301st	Hill 4 (Height 494)
	Hill 5 (Height 463)
	Hill 6 (Mühlenberg) (Height 468)
	Oberzerf, Zerf
2nd/302nd	Hill 7 (Height 472)
	Hill 8 (Height 468)
	Baldringen, Hentern, Kummlerhof, Schömerich
3rd/302nd	Hill 9 (Height 464)
	Hill 10 (Height 500)
	Hill 11 (midway between Niedersehr and Ollmuth)
	Paschel, Lampaden, Obersehr, Niedersehr, Ollmuth[3]

In order to reach their objectives, Major Maixner's 2nd/302nd and Lieutenant Colonel Cloudt's 3rd/302nd would have to cover a considerable distance through wooded territory that was still not cleared of the enemy.

Major McNulty's 3rd/301st left Ockfen that same morning and reached Irsch at about noon. Priority of traffic on Highway 407 was for the 10th Armored Division, so the infantrymen had to march in extended single file carrying all of their equipment up the long hill. By the time Lieutenant Devonald's leading K Company turned off the highway at a point opposite Hill 4, with its objective still some fifteen hundred yards away, the men were exhausted. K Company advanced in extended order and had gone about five hundred yards when a sharp command to halt was given. At the same time the distinctive cocking of a machine gun could be heard. Then someone fired a rifle and a firefight broke out, but Lt. Robert L. Vinue was certain that the order to halt had been given by an American, so he dashed forward shouting to hold fire. K Company had bumped into the 5th Rangers, totally unaware that the Rangers had already been there for four days and had needlessly lost three men killed and seven wounded.

Captain Warren learned from the Rangers that enemy troops were occupying his objective and that there was a line of manned pillboxes across his approach route, so he decided to wait until daylight to make a reconnaissance. Meanwhile, the remainder of the battalion had continued marching to Zerf. Patrols were then sent out to check Hills 5 and 6 to the east of the village. Hill 5, the southernmost, was found to be occupied by the enemy, but the other hill was clear and Captain Donovan's I Company went on to occupy it, while Lieutenant Minich's L Company settled down in Zerf to wait for daylight.[4]

Upon receipt of the new orders of February 27, Lieutenant Colonel Cloudt's 3rd/302nd prepared to move northeast against the Ockfener Berg, the high ground from which Lieutenant Colonel Thurston's 3rd/376th had been so heavily fired upon while occupying the northern tip of the Scharfenberg Ridge. Cloudt used as many antiaircraft, tank, and tank destroyer guns as he could muster to cover his attack at 1750. The crest of his objective was so battered by this onslaught that the enemy began surrendering when his battalion was still five hundred yards away.

While checking the ridge, Captain Smith's L Company came across four mutually supporting pillboxes and negotiated for their surrender. The senior German NCO in charge agreed to the capitulation, providing the Americans staged a mock battle to save his reputation, so the Americans duly fired their weapons into the air and the occupants of three of the pillboxes surrendered. The soldiers in the fourth pillbox refused to comply, so as it was now dark the attack was postponed to the morning.

Meanwhile, K Company had come across some large caves in the side of a hill that were crowded with civilians. The civilians were sent off to Irsch under guard and on the way were attacked by a nine-man German patrol. The American escort engaged the patrol, which then opted for surrender. By 1950 all the battalion's assigned objectives had been taken.[5]

Major Maixner also received orders for his 2nd/302nd to move on that afternoon, but because much of the ground in his area on the ridge south of Irsch was open and without protection, he decided to wait for the cover of darkness. The battalion moved off at 1915 and took the ridge across its

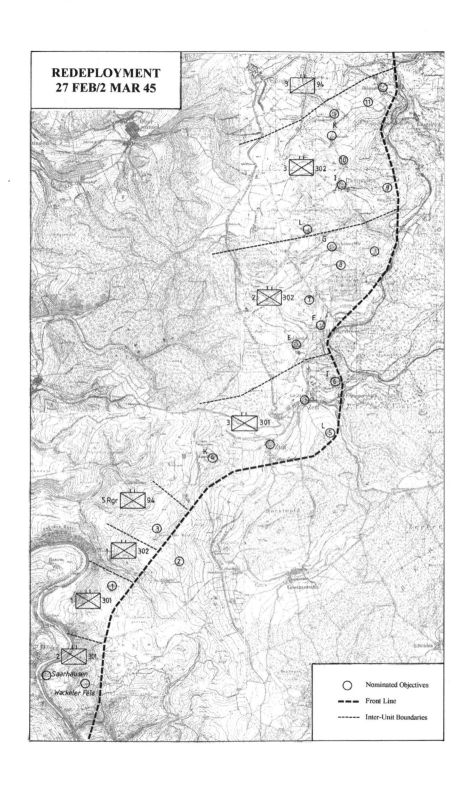

REDEPLOYMENT
27 FEB/2 MAR 45

Nominated Objectives
Front Line
Inter-Unit Boundaries

front without difficulty. Then, as the men of Captain Kops's F Company were crossing a bald hill, they came face-to-face with a group of Germans, who opened fire on the company with machine guns, raking the area. While under this fire, one of the men who could speak a little German managed to communicate with the enemy and gained the impression that they would be prepared to surrender. The word was passed to Captain Kops, a fluent German-speaker, who crawled forward and met the German captain, who also had been brought forward by his men. After much wrangling, the German captain eventually agreed to surrender, together with the pillboxes commanding the hill.[6]

Major Stanion's 1st/302nd also attacked on February 27. Supported by some light tanks, A and B Companies assaulted the high ground to their front and captured four pillboxes. While questioning some of the prisoners, a telephone in one of the pillboxes rang, so Lieutenant Baumgaertner answered it. A German artillery officer was asking if more fire was needed to repulse the Americans. Baumgaertner assured him that the action had involved only a small patrol and that the area was now quiet, thus acquiring three artillery-free hours.[7]

THE AYL BRIDGEHEAD—FEBRUARY 27

On February 27 Lieutenant Colonel Miner's 1st/376th, supported by the regimental cannon company, the 919th Field Artillery, and some tank destroyers on the Saar's west bank, attacked northward, passing through the 2nd Battalion's lines, which were held by Captain Standish's F Company on the riverbank and Captain Heath's G Company on the hill above.

Captain Dadisman's A Company was tasked with clearing the pillboxes south and southeast of Schoden, while Captain Bowden's B Company advanced toward the village along the riverbank. Enemy resistance increased with the advance, and A Company soon ran into difficulties. The pillboxes in their area were so well camouflaged that two patrols failed to locate them. Sgt. Leon D. Crutchfield of the 2nd Platoon resolved the problem by changing direction to approach the perimeter buildings in the village, which would undoubtedly be covered by fire from the hidden pillboxes. The ensuing mortar and machine-gun fire soon revealed their locations, which the American tank destroyers across the river then engaged with direct fire. One by one the pillboxes fell to the aggressive attacks of both companies, and by evening B Company of the 61st Armored Infantry Battalion had been relieved from the positions in which it had been isolated for two days. Forty-two pillboxes had been cleared, with about 250 Germans captured and 38 killed or wounded.[8]

That morning of February 27, Captain Smith's L Company of Lieutenant Colonel Cloudt's 3rd/302nd closed in on the one pillbox whose occupants had refused to surrender the previous evening; however, the German defenders had had a change of heart and gave up without a fight. The battalion then received some welcome replacements to share among the companies, but the effective strength was still so low that a platoon each from K Company was attached to I and L Companies to bring them up to reasonable size. The advance was resumed at 1605, and some manned pillboxes were encountered on the next hill. The troops of I Company used their attached K Company platoon to conduct a right flanking movement while they themselves made a frontal assault. By 1940 all the enemy positions had been taken.

The battalion reorganized before moving off on a compass bearing through the dense woods, aiming for a designated enemy strongpoint. The men had to negotiate a deep ravine in the dark before pushing on. No trace of the objective could be found, so the artillery was asked to drop a smoke shell on the objective's coordinates, which proved to be one thousand yards back on the route the battalion had already traversed. The bunkers were so well camouflaged that the scouts had walked right over them without detecting them.[9]

The 135th Engineers constructed another pontoon bridge that day at Niederleuken, between Ayl and Saarburg, which was ready by 1600.[10]

HOCKER HILL—FEBRUARY 27

The troublesome bunker on the Hamm bend of the ridge road was taken at last on February 27, when Lts. Arthur Shocksnyder and Richard Eckstrom led their 2nd and 3rd Platoons of B Company, 1st/301st, in a two-pronged attack that finally cleared the area of the enemy. Major Brumley's 2nd/301st launched another attack to clear the Wackseler Fels cliffs that day, but the enemy's perfect observation from the heights above and the depleted strength of Captain Steinen's company prevented an effective result, and the battalion was obliged to return to its original positions. During this action SSgt. Murry W. Forsyth of H Company was hit in the back and both legs by shellfire, but he continued manning his observation post and directing his company's 81-mm mortars until he was evacuated later that afternoon.

That night a patrol that included a recent German-speaking replacement, Pvt. David H. Troupe, was challenged by a sentry as they approached a German strongpoint. Troupe replied in German with: "Shut your mouth! What do you want to do, call the officers?" The patrol moved on without further incident.[11]

THE RUWER VALLEY—FEBRUARY 27

Early on the morning of February 27, leaving Task Force Richardson with the mission of holding Zerf and fending off any enemy counterattacks, the remainder of Combat Command A moved off north on Highway 268 for Trier. Task Force Chamberlain led with the infantry of Captain Eisberg's A Company, 20th Armored Infantry, in front and on the flanks of Teams O'Grady and Shaddeau. The nature of the terrain, with its steep, sometimes wooded slopes, obliged the vehicles to remain on the road. At 0200 the column came under direct fire from some woods on the left flank, starting a two-hour battle to clear the woods and prompting the column to postpone further movement until dawn. A Company set off again at 0545 and immediately ran into a self-propelled 88-mm assault gun and Panther tank lying in wait around a bend in the road. The infantry quickly dealt with this ambush and the column moved on. Progress remained slow, however. Four pillboxes were encountered, and then a heavily defended bunker at Steinbach, all of which had to be stormed and destroyed.

Eventually the column emerged from the wooded area on more suitable ground. The tanks of Team O'Grady deployed ahead of the infantry, who mounted their half-tracks, and swept across country, but soon they ran into a minefield beyond Steinbach that disabled two of the tanks as heavy enemy artillery and mortar fire began falling on the column, directed from a ridge five hundred yards to their front. The infantry dismounted and began working their way around the enemy from the left flank, using the ditches and roadside foliage for cover and concealment. Attempts to bring the column forward of the ridge were met with heavy direct fire. At 1500 Lt. Col. Thomas C. Chamberlain ordered the attached 3rd Platoon of A Company, 55th Armored Engineer Battalion, to clear the three-hundred-yard-deep minefield so as to enable his tanks to maneuver their way around. The task was not completed until 0115 the next morning.[12]

Meanwhile, Task Force O'Hara of Combat Command B had been following Task Force Chamberlain on Highway 407 from Irsch to Zerf and had come under the same gauntlet of shelling. As the column reached a sharp bend in the road west of Zerf, it was fired on by an 88-mm gun, and Lt. Col. James O'Hara was killed in his vehicle.

From here this task force continued along a parallel ridge road east of Highway 268 with orders to seize the village of Paschel and Height 508 and then go on to attack Trier. Team Devereauz dismounted short of Paschel at 1630 and took the village without opposition. Capt. John D. Devereauz then took his men on to attack Height 508, which they took after a short firefight with a battery of direct fire weapons. Here and along the road leading to the hill they rounded up 158 prisoners.[13]

The experience here was later described as follows: "The operation from Irsch around the hot corner at Zerf and on into Trier was worse than Bastogne. We lost more vehicles and men. The enemy was sitting on the hills where we couldn't find them or get at them with artillery. They had their artillery zeroed in on the roads. They would hold their fire until we were close[,] and sometimes they would allow the first column to bypass their position and then open up on the second column. The infantry in the half-tracks were vulnerable to the air-burst artillery. There was not enough infantry left at the end to flush out the hills and clear out the gun positions."[14]

That night Combat Command B ordered Maj. Warren B. Haskell, the executive officer of the 54th Armored Infantry, to assume command of the task force, which then took his name.[15]

THE IRSCH-ZERF HIGHWAY—FEBRUARY 27

Major O'Neil's 3rd/301st was now scattered over four thousand yards of frontage, and its rifle companies were focused on Hills 4, 5, and 6, but the area between was subject to enemy infiltration, which could only be countered by patrolling. The bend on Highway 407 above Zerf, where Lieutenant Colonel O'Hara had been killed, was now being dubbed "Dead Man's Corner," and the area was still covered by an 88-mm gun sniping at all who passed. The windshield of an escort vehicle to General Malony was lost to gunfire here.

Captain Warren's K Company had still to take Hill 4 south of the Irsch-Zerf highway. The company spent all morning reconnoitering for an attack against six well-manned pillboxes that blocked access to its objective. The attack was launched with the assistance of Lieutenant Colonel Sullivan's 5th Rangers at 1400 in the face of heavy fire, but the pillboxes were reduced one by one in an operation that took two hours before the company could deploy on Hill 4.

Back at Zerf, Lieutenant Minich's L Company attacked Hill 5 at dawn, taking the enemy completely by surprise in a brief action, and dug in on the hilltop. At 1515 the company was hit by a ten-minute artillery concentration, followed by a company-sized infantry attack backed by six tanks coming from the east. This attack by the Germans' 13th Company, 3rd Battalion, Mountain Infantry Regiment 137, succeeded in knocking out both the company machine guns and the supporting heavy machine guns of M Company. During the action, which continued throughout the night, the fifty-four men remaining in L Company were reinforced by troops filtered through from a battalion reserve in Zerf. After Lieutenant Minich was wounded, Lt. Robert H. Henley took over his command.

The volume of artillery and mortar fire on Zerf and its approach roads increased by the hour. German patrols were active, and there were frequent minor counterattacks. The company positions were gradually improved by laying barbed wire, trip wires, antitank mines, and booby traps, while numerous prearranged concentrations were plotted for the artillery and mortars.[16]

THE AYL BRIDGEHEAD—FEBRUARY 28

By February 28 the strength of Lieutenant Colonel Miner's 1st/376th was gravely depleted, and Captain Malinksi's C Company, who so far had been in reserve because of the number of casualties sustained in the river crossing on the night of February 22–23, now took over the lead and advanced northward along the ridge to the east of Schoden. Although they encountered some stubborn resistance, the company eventually gained the hill overlooking the village of Wiltingen. Captain Bowden's B Company, which had earlier finished clearing the Schoden area, took over from C Company at 1500 and began digging in on the forward slope of the hill about 1100 yards from Wiltingen.

That evening the battalion received orders for its final task in the bridgehead: to clear the four pillboxes that lay between the battalion's forward positions and Wiltingen. These pillboxes had to be taken immediately so that Major Dossenbach's 2nd/376th could pass through to attack the village the next day. The task was given to Captain Bowden's B Company and proved less difficult than expected:

> The chances for assaulting the pillboxes by daylight were fading rapidly, and finally disappeared altogether, for it soon became as dark as the inside of a hat. The tank-destroyers which were in position on the west bank of the Saar, waiting to support the assault[,] had already radioed that it was too dark to see their targets and were signing off. It looked like rifles and grenades against concrete and MG 42s.
>
> Knowing that the chances of taking the pillboxes by assault in time for the 2d Battalion jump-off were slim indeed, Captain [Edwin] Brehio, the Battalion S-2, suggested that a prisoner of war who had just been brought in by a patrol be made to lead a small patrol to the key pillbox and attempt to take it by trick. Staff Sergeant [Hans] Vogel of Prisoner of War Team 98 spoke German fluently and had done some splendid work along this line only a few days before in Beurig, accounting for over 60 prisoners. Major Zimmerman, the Battalion Executive Officer, agreed, and Captain Bowden said that he'd try anything once. Sergeant Vogel persuaded the prisoner to take an active part in the plot, much against his wishes, and finally everything was ready.

The trick worked. It so happened that all the Germans in the complex had assembled in the key pillbox for orders and were captured intact without a shot having been fired.

Company A's strength was now so low that some men of the weapons platoon had been drafted in as riflemen. When two of these men were captured by a German patrol, SSgt. W. T. Pillow slipped down a communication trench and overtook the patrol and ambushed it as the rest of his platoon covered him. Not only did he recover his two men, but he also convinced a whole German platoon to surrender. (Staff Sergeant Pillow was subsequently awarded a Silver Star.)[17]

Lieutenant Colonel Thurston's now rested 3rd/376th moved forward through Captain Heath's G Company's lines to align on the right of the 1st/376th overlooking the Wiltingen-Oberemmel road. Beyond this rose the vineyard-covered slopes of the Scharzberg Ridge, the battalion's objective, which was to be taken by nightfall. A platoon from Captain Brown's K Company, supported by a section of heavy machine guns, was detailed for the task. As this group neared the crest of their objective, they came under enemy fire. When the American soldiers returned fire, a German soldier carrying a load of flares exploded in a multicolored blaze of light. After a short exchange the position was taken and all the enemy soldiers were captured, except for one officer, who escaped down the reverse slope. Shortly afterward the position came under a heavy mortar barrage. It was impossible to dig in on the rocky crest, but the troops held their ground, suffering many casualties. Twice artillery observers were sent forward from the battalion to see if they could bring down fire to silence the enemy mortars, but in both cases the observers were injured before they could do so.

Lieutenant Colonel Thurston had the wounded evacuated by hay wagon to be cared for by Capt. John J. Ryan, who had just rejoined as battalion surgeon, fully recovered from the stress that had invalided him in January.[18]

THE IRSCH-ZERF HIGHWAY—FEBRUARY 28

After assisting the 3rd/301st in taking Hill 4, Lieutenant Colonel Sullivan's 5th Rangers went on to take Hill 3 at 1540 against considerable opposition. The Germans counterattacked at 1745 and were beaten back with heavy casualties and the loss of 150 prisoners.[19]

THE RUWER VALLEY—FEBRUARY 28

Major Maixner's 2nd/302nd also received replacements on February 28. At 1425 the battalion advanced rapidly with three rifle companies abreast, mopping up a few scattered snipers and some machine-gun nests to reach the top of a ridge. Captain Kops's F Company then went on to occupy Hill 7 unopposed, while Lieutenant Anderson's E Company moved into Baldringen, where they encountered the first strong resistance since Irsch.[20]

THE ADVANCE ON TRIER—FEBRUARY 28

With the route clear enough of mines for the tanks to continue, Lieutenant Colonel Chamberlain had now to take the village of Pellingen across the highway ahead. His plan was for Task Force Shaddeau to remain on the approach ridge to provide covering fire while Task Force O'Grady moved along another ridge some one thousand yards on the left to provide covering fire for an infantry attack on the village. The infantry moved off at 0500 and worked their way into the village under covering fire from the armor. The enemy pulled back out of the village to some high ground some 750 yards to the northwest, from where the infantry again routed them by 1015.

At 1030 new orders arrived, changing Task Force Chamberlain's mission to clearing the Konz suburb of Karthaus, where Highway 268 meets the Moselle River, and thus protecting the 10th Armored Division's drive on Trier. Task Force Norris, Combat Command A's reserve, passed through at 1500 and continued straight on for Trier.[21]

At 1100 on February 28 Task Force Haskell sent Team Kafkalas to attack the village of Obersehr, which was thought to be the beginning of a new switch line that the Germans were building to protect Trier. As the tanks inched up to this village from the southwest, the enemy engaged with a battery of 80-mm mortars and machine guns ensconced in the houses. Captain Kafkalas approached with his armored infantrymen from the high ground to the south and took the village under cover of an artillery barrage and direct fire from the tanks, capturing eighty Germans, who surrendered without much fight. However, the position then came under artillery and 105-mm mortar fire from the north and northeast.

Beyond Obersehr, Captain Kafkalas came across a minefield belt, which was covered by observed artillery and machine-gun fire and ran across the high ground north of Niedersehr fronting the villages of Pellingen and Ollmuth. Captain Kafkalas had his infantry deploy under cover, then took his engineer platoon to clear the road of mines, coming under heavy fire from machine guns and registered artillery tree-bursts. The infantrymen

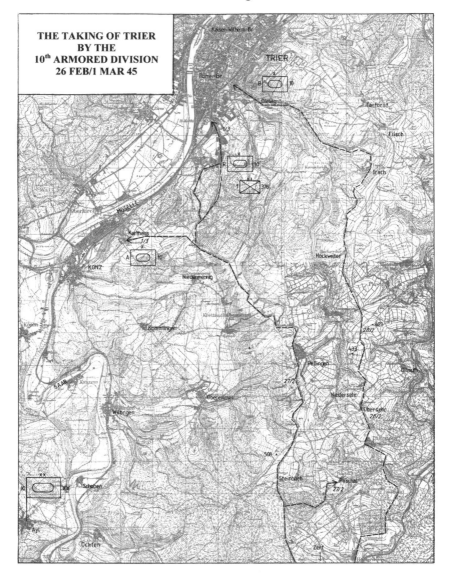

**THE TAKING OF TRIER
BY THE
10th ARMORED DIVISION
26 FEB/1 MAR 45**

succeeded in clearing the way, but Kafkalas, the engineer platoon leader, and 40 percent of his men were injured in the process, which took until late afternoon. Lieutenant Cook then took charge and led the infantry forward to establish a bridgehead beyond the minefield. He too was wounded.

Team Lang then passed through, leading the remainder of the task force.

Their route was under observed artillery fire coming from both sides of the road. Even though the men had insufficient infantry to cover the advance by deploying them on either side of the road and engaging these enemy positions, they decided to push on regardless, keeping a sharp eye open for indications of enemy artillery positions that could be engaged by their covering artillery.

Just south of Height 433 that evening, the head of the column came under heavy artillery fire from the east that knocked out one of the tanks and several half-tracks. However, the column carried on until it came opposite Height 427 at 2200, when it was decided to stop and bivouac for the night.[22]

Task Force Cherry of Combat Command R, who had crossed the Saar at Saarburg on the twenty-seventh, moved on during the night of February 28th–March 1st to clear the area east of the main advance as far as the line of the Ruwer River, which runs into the Moselle north of Trier.

Back at Zerf, Lieutenant Colonel Richardson's task force was relieved by Major Hodges's 1st/301st and was ordered to move on to Trier using the same valley road through Olewig that Task Force Haskell had used.[23]

THE AYL BRIDGEHEAD—MARCH 1

On March 1 the 1st and 3rd Battalions of the 376th Infantry were in a north-facing line from the point just north of Schoden where the Saar River resumed running due north. That evening Lieutenant Colonel Miner's 1st Battalion, less A Company, withdrew to Schoden, having been replaced by Major Dossenbach's 2nd Battalion coming out of reserve to attack Wiltingen, which was found to be clear of enemy. The 2nd Battalion advanced a further fifteen hundred yards before being checked by heavy machine-gun fire coming from bunkers.

Lieutenant Colonel Thurston's isolated 3rd/376th on the Scharzberg Ridge discovered the immediate area relatively free of enemy. Although the village of Wiltingen on the left lay outside the battalion boundary, it was decided to send Lieutenant Brown with a strong patrol to find out if there were any of the enemy there. German soldiers were indeed found in the village, and Brown and his men encountered stiffening resistance, so Lieutenant Colonel Thurston informed Regiment about the situation by radio, but was told to leave the matter to the 2nd Battalion, which was now temporarily under the command of Major Kelley since the wounding of Major Dossenbach.

The 3rd/376th then received orders to occupy Oberemmel, which was believed to be unoccupied. However, a reconnaissance patrol found the village occupied, and it took a two-hour battle with mortar and artillery support to secure it. The battalion then moved on in single file toward Kommlingen, having to pass through a pine forest and then a dense plantation of young trees in the falling light before settling down in company bivouacs for the night.[24]

THE RUWER VALLEY—MARCH 1

On the morning of March 1 Captain Kops's F Company of Major Maixner's 2nd/302nd moved down from Hill 7 into Hentern, the first village the troops encountered whose inhabitants had not been evacuated. The civilians were rounded up in the village school and placed under guard. SSgt. Paul Pflueger later related how he became involved with a childbirth situation but was called away before the actual birth, as the village was evacuated under shellfire and threat of a counterattack.

Captain Griffin's G Company, on the battalion's left flank, swung to the east as it emerged from the woods and then moved across open ground toward the villages of Paschel and Schömerich and Hill 8. Small groups of snipers set to delay the American advance were encountered and quickly dealt with. By 1300 Hill 8 was in American hands.[25]

Lieutenant Colonel Cloudt's 3rd/302nd set off at 1115, making a wide sweep to clear the woods with I and K Companies, while L Company remained in reserve. Little resistance was encountered, and the battalion soon came out into open ground and crossed Highway 268 eastward. By 1830 I Company had taken Lampaden and K Company was in Obersehr.[26]

THE IRSCH-ZERF HIGHWAY—MARCH 1

Major Stanion's seriously depleted 1st/302nd advanced on Hill 2 (Height 536), southeast of Serrig, on the morning of March 1 with A and C Companies, while B Company remained in a defensive position on the battalion's left flank. The line of advance was fully exposed to the enemy's view and fire, and within three hundred yards of the line of departure the assault companies came under a hail of rocket, artillery, mortar, and small-arms fire that inflicted such severe casualties that they were obliged to withdraw again that afternoon and dig in for the night. In one squad in A Company only one man out of seven had escaped death or injury, and some of C Company's squads were reduced to two men.

In conjunction with Major Stanion's attack, Major Hodges's 1st/301st sent A Company forward on Major Stanion's right with the intention of linking the line of the two battalions should the attack succeed. However, the men of A Company met the same fierce resistance and were also stopped. By the time they withdrew, the troops were down from seventy-five to twenty-eight riflemen, and only Lieutenant Rives and two of his men survived from the heavy machine-gun section of D Company that had been supporting them.[27]

HOCKER HILL—MARCH 1

That evening Major Brumley's 2nd/301st obtained an accurate bearing on some mortars that had been causing trouble. The supporting artillery were unable to oblige, as another target took priority, but the regiment's cannon company used its six 105-mm guns to silence the mortars and in doing so also hit the assembly area for a German counterattack that was in the process of forming up.[28]

THE ADVANCE ON TRIER—MARCH 1

Unknown to Task Force Haskell, their overnight bivouac position was barely one hundred yards from a German battery that had refrained from disclosing itself as the troops settled down for the night. The German troops were in defilade position on the reverse slope of the hill east of the bivouac and were unable to depress their guns sufficiently to be able to engage the vehicles. But at 0300 the enemy troops opened up firing air-bursts and caused some fifteen casualties. While the Americans were still trying to locate the source of fire, two enemy machine guns started firing down the road and infantry attacked from the east. The infantry attack was repelled with M1 fire, and two half-tracks engaged the enemy machine guns with their .50-caliber weapons, breaking up the enemy attack. However, the two remaining half-tracks that had been in the lead failed to change position and had apparently been spotted by the enemy, for as soon as it was light enough they were destroyed by 88-mm guns.

Major Haskell then organized a counterattack on the enemy battery, sending B Company of the 54th Armored Infantry circling around the right of Height 427, while two Hellcats maneuvered to attack from the south. The enemy guns were spotted as they continued firing to the west and were then engaged by the Hellcats. The enemy battery soon surrendered, yielding four 88-mm antitank guns, twelve automatic weapons, and about thirty prisoners.

Task Force Haskell had received orders during the night urging them to move on to Trier as soon as possible. The intention was to continue moving along the ridge road, sending out teams to secure the villages of Filsch and Tarforst on the east flank. Just as the column was moving out with Team Lang in the lead, they came under direct fire from the northwest. The enemy artillery could not be located but were presumed to be on the high ground just east of the city. Within five minutes these 105-mm guns had knocked out five half-tracks and an armored car. As soon as the fire eased up, the column moved off, and by early morning the lead tanks were in Filsch, which was surrendered after a short fight with an enemy rear guard.

Although the column was still under enemy artillery fire, B Company of the 54th Armored Infantry deployed and assaulted Tarforst, meeting little opposition on the ground. B Company went on to take five 88-mm guns and forty prisoners on the high ground east of the village at about 1630, but both Captain Devereaux and his executive officer, Lieutenant Gale, were wounded by artillery fire.

Task Force Haskell was now down to four tanks and five half-tracks, the infantry losses had been heavy, and they still had to take Trier. Major Haskell used his wiremen, extra men from the assault-gun platoon, and men from the Headquarters Company as infantry replacements and assigned them to Capt. Steve Lang along with the remaining troops of B and C Companies and the Headquarters Detachment.

Team Lang's tanks moved rapidly to seize the hill east of the city, where they found barracks filled with Allied prisoners of war and forced laborers. Little opposition was encountered, but then an unmanned roadblock stopped the team's progress on the edge of the city. The roadblock was dismantled by hand, rather than using explosives that would have alerted the defense, and by 0400 the men from Team Lang were inside the city.[29]

THE AYL BRIDGEHEAD—MARCH 2

Lieutenant Colonel Thurston's 3rd/376th advanced twenty-five hundred yards on March 2, taking Kommlingen without resistance and capturing two bunkers and forty prisoners. That evening the 3rd/376th was told it would be trucked to the town of Dudelange in southern Luxembourg the next morning for a week's rest and recuperation. Lieutenant Colonel Miner's 1st/376th also received a message that night, this one brought by an engineer officer of the 10th Armored Division, to the effect that trucks were due to arrive to transport the battalion to assist in the taking of Trier.[30]

THE ADVANCE ON TRIER—MARCH 1

At 0800 the tanks of Teams O'Grady and Shaddeau of Task Force Chamberlain deployed on the twin peaks overlooking Karthaus at the junction of the Saar and Moselle Rivers and subjected the area to an hour's bombardment. The infantry of Team Eisberg then went in and cleared the location. Task Force Chamberlain remained in place as security for the left flank in the attack on Trier, while Task Force Norris moved in on the city from near Niedermennig. Lt. Col. Ned T. Norris's troops penetrated Trier during the afternoon and halted in place.[31]

Late in the afternoon of March 1 Task Force Richardson moved out of Zerf. When they reached the crossroads at Lampaden, they stopped to await further orders from Combat Command B's command post, which was now located in Obersehr. Lieutenant Colonel Richardson was told that the rest of the 10th Armored Division would be attacking Trier that night and that his task was to seize the two bridges across the Moselle—intact, if possible. Jump-off time would be 2200.

The Task Force moved off on schedule with Team Billet leading, followed by Team Riley and the Headquarters Company. It was a clear, moonlit night with excellent visibility, so the vehicles made good progress. At the village of Irsch (not the Irsch near Saarburg) they came across a German roadblock covered by three 88-mm guns, whose crews were asleep in the village. The leading tank fired two 75-mm rounds at the roadblock, rousing the Germans, who promptly surrendered and were put to work clearing the road. The column then drove on through Olewig and into Trier, where it stopped for fifteen minutes at a railway crossing while a company of surprised German infantry and four antitank guns were rounded up without a shot being fired. One of the prisoners had been detailed to warn a demolition party on the far side of the bridge when the Americans appeared, but was caught before he could do so.

Although this bridge, the Römerbrücke (Roman Bridge), was closer than the northern bridge, the Kaiser-Wilhelm-Brücke, Lieutenant Colonel Richardson decided to go for the latter bridge first, sending Capt. "Bud" Omar M. Billet's team to take it with Lieutenant Riley's team in support.[32]

THE IRSCH-ZERF HIGHWAY—MARCH 2

Major Stanion's 1st/302nd made a second attempt to take Hill 2 (Height 536) at 0900 on March 2, making contact with Lieutenant Colonel Sullivan's 5th Rangers on the left at 0950. The assault went forward slowly against increasing resistance, but shortly after noon a foothold had been gained on the northern part of the hill. A patrol was then sent to the Rangers requesting tank support for the final conquest of the hill. At 1426 Major Stanion reported by radio to the 301st Infantry, to whom his battalion was attached, that he had 37 men on the northern part of the objective, which was all that remained of the 175 men of his B and C Companies and D Company detachment when they started off that day. He was still awaiting word from his patrol to the Rangers when the Germans counterattacked at 1818, driving his troops off the hill in a hail of rocket fire.

Company A of Major Hodges's 1st/301st had again moved forward on the right flank in support and was again driven back with the remains of Major Stanion's troops.[33]

THE RUWER VALLEY—MARCH 2

Lieutenant Colonel Cloudt's 3rd/302nd continued its advance on March 2, and by 0837 had occupied Hills 9, 10, and 11 in accordance with the 94th Infantry Division's mission. L Company was brought forward in reserve to Paschel.[34]

THE SECURING OF TRIER—MARCH 2

Major Dossenbach's 2nd/376th moved on into the town of Konz, where the Saar River flows into the Moselle, and began several days of mopping up in the area, which contained many bunkers—some manned, some not. The battalion's big prize was Bunker III. This was first attacked unsuccessfully by a platoon from F Company, and when 1st Lt. Percy Heidelberger of the 376th Medical Detachment led a party of litter bearers forward to recover the wounded, they too were fired on at first, but then the firing stopped and some Germans appeared at the bunker entrance obviously wanting to talk. Lieutenant Heidelberger spoke with them and persuaded them to surrender, taking prisoner a major, two captains, two lieutenants, and fifty-four men from this one bunker alone, which proved to be vast. It was three stories deep and equipped with heating, showers, and an automatic mortar firing six-round clips that could put twenty-four rounds into the air at a time.[35]

At 0200 on March 2 Captain Billet reported back to Lieutenant Colonel Richardson that the northern bridge had been blown, so he sent Lieutenant Riley to take the southern bridge. Riley followed the riverbank avenue to the southern bridge and reported by radio: "Have reached the bridge. Bridge intact. Am receiving small-arms fire." Lieutenant Colonel Richardson hastened to the bridge and directed its seizure on the spot. He found that Lieutenant Riley's team was still on the east bank returning small-arms fire and had done nothing about getting across to the far bank. Richardson ordered .50-caliber machine-gun fire directed from his tank on the western approaches and had a platoon of tanks and Lieutenant Fletcher's dismounted infantry platoon rush across, where they were just in time to stop a German demolition team of five soldiers and a drunken major from getting to the bridge with their detonating caps and an exploder. Richardson then had a detail of men cut the demolition wires on the bridge and established a small bridgehead on the west bank to guard the approaches. The drunken German major informed his captors that seventeen other German officers were holding a party some two hundred yards farther down the street, so these men were quickly rounded up without incident.

By 1000 Task Force Richardson had seized some eight hundred prisoners, astounded that the Americans had been able to take over the city without a fight. The command post was established in the city center as the men of Task Force Haskell, who had been working all night clearing the northern part of Trier, continued a house-to-house search, in which they were joined by Task Force Norris, while the rest of the 10th Armored Division converged on the city.[36]

The promised trucks arrived to transport the 1st/376th, and by 0200 the column was under way in total darkness with little idea of the route or destination. The column moved off with Lieutenant Colonel Miner, his staff, and his engineer guide in the lead, followed by A, B, C, D, and Headquarters Companies in that order, then Major Zimmerman, the executive officer, Chaplain Buchanan, some medics, then the kitchen, baggage, and ammunition trains. When they stopped for a break in Pellingen, however, they found that from Major Zimmerman onward, the tail of the convoy was missing.

Chaplain Buchanan gave an account of what happened to the missing element of Lieutenant Colonel Miner's 1st/376th:

> Here we were ten to twelve miles from Trier. The fighting elements of the convoy were off ahead somewhere following the engineer lieutenant. In our small group we had the radio section of the battalion headquarters, the Antitank Platoon with their 57-mm guns, the battalion medics, the battalion surgeon, executive officer, adjutant and chaplain. To be utterly frank, our firepower was rather negligible. Yet somehow we had to win through those hills and get to Trier, for they would be needing us.
>
> The situation was vague, but it was obvious and important that we find the main body of the battalion before dawn. We very much wished to avoid the embarrassment of having the bright light of morning catch us wandering about with the enemy in position on either side of our path. With our meager fire power and rather noticeable train of kitchen trucks, it might easily prove to be somewhat of a sad scramble.
>
> So, cautiously, but with an undercurrent of urgent desire to get somewhere, we rolled on towards Trier. The shell bursts on the horizon became more frequent. Now and then we came upon a burning vehicle which barred our way and had to be bypassed. Quickly we rolled on, racing with the breaking dawn. Here and there along the highway stood muted pillboxes. Everybody was alert now.
>
> Several miles up ahead tracers from 20-mm and 40-mm guns partially lighted the skyline in front of the city. Sometimes they seemed to be traveling in our direction, so that we had a tendency to watch them a bit closely and with some misgivings. But always they fell

below the horizon. Just then, as I looked to the left, I saw a group of tanks in position along a defile near the highway. Several of them were warming up.

For a moment the convoy moved more slowly. For that split second we all peered apprehensively into the darkness with one common thought—whose tanks—friendly or enemy? Fortunately for us they turned out to be "Shermans," so we rolled on. Later none of us was quite able to explain why we had not paused here and investigated the why and wherefore of the "Shermans" in the defile. We were still a bit anxious to get to Trier, so it seemed.

A few minutes later the rumble of howitzers and heavy guns became quite ominous. The flashes became very distinct. We were very definitely on the edge of the city now. We rolled past two huge pillboxes flanking the road, and then came to a sudden stop. To our right several civilians, seeing us, turned about and ran into their houses.

As several of us jumped from our vehicles, we saw a dark form running towards us, hands held high, and once again we heard that familiar greeting "Kamerad!" Our interpreter, Sergeant Hans Vogel, questioned the Boche and concluded we were in Trier.[37] The German was on his way to some other soldiers, supposedly in position to our rear. Our presence in his path had definitely overwhelmed him. He told us the Americans were fighting to gain entrance to the north edge of the city. We, it seemed, were near the southern edge.

It was quite clear that the gun batteries no more than 100 yards to our right front were German. They were firing with great rapidity across the city, giving their all to stem the tide of the insistent Americans. We were very close, and on a hill, slightly above their position. We could see the gun crews at work and hear them as they snapped off orders.

We had entered the wrong end of the city, and now found ourselves sitting on a slight grade to the rear of the enemy's artillery batteries. We had several .50-caliber machine guns and three 57s. Sergeant Andrew Brusgard suggested to the Major that we hurriedly set them on the high ground, send the kitchen train back, keeping just enough vehicles to make a getaway after we had given the howitzer and "ack-ack" [antiaircraft] batteries everything we had in the way of 50s and 57s.

It might have worked. However, it was quite light now and any moment they would detect this motley crew at their rear. We weren't at all sure of their strength or their disposition. The mess sergeants and kitchen personnel were not spoiling for such an uncertain fracas, and our fire and manpower being what it was, the Major resisted the temptation to have a try at it and ordered the convoy to run down towards the partial roadblock, execute a sharp left turn, and hit the road out of the city towards Pellingen.

This was done quite rapidly and with a definite smoothness, except for one kitchen driver who got stuck in the roadblock, and could not find his reverse in his excitement. As the two-and-a-halves roared up the hill away from the city, the Germans apparently became aware of our presence and started to take potshots. But we were headed away from a strange and what might have been a grim experience, and there was no stopping us. German civilians peeked furtively from behind curtains as we rolled by, slightly confused perhaps at this strange onslaught on their ancient city. But they were not to be confused for long. Just two miles down the highway we met the "Shermans" roaring up for their first assault on this side of the town. Their reconnaissance captain stopped us and asked where the devil we had been. We quickly told our story. Everybody laughed. Wishing him and his gang good shooting, we continued to the rear. It was a happy ending. We could laugh now and enjoy our luck. But it might have been rough had the Boche known they had unwanted and slightly confused visitors at their back door—and so early in the morning too![38]

It was not until the main convoy reached Hockweiler that Lieutenant Colonel Miner learned what was expected of his battalion. Task Force Richardson had seized the Roman Bridge across the Moselle in the center of the city, but was isolated and needed his support. The battalion was to follow the armor's route into Trier, mopping up as it went.

Lieutenant Colonel Miner led the way in a half-track with A Company as his assault force. They ran into resistance at a heavily fortified railroad bridge, where they were met by fire from machine guns and an 88-mm gun, which inflicted several casualties, killing Private First Class Redner, the company aid man. A Company's machine guns returned the fire, enabling Lt. Aaron L. Colvin's 1st Platoon to move laterally to the next bridge across the railroad cutting, which turned out to be equally well defended, so the platoon moved along until it could cross the tracks and outflank these positions. The 3rd Platoon then made a frontal assault on the first bridge and overran the enemy in time to prevent its being blown. From then on the battalion encountered no further serious problems and soon established contact with Task Force Richardson. C Company was then tasked with protecting the Roman Bridge, while the rest of the battalion assisted in mopping up the city.

Early the next day, March 3, elements of the 76th Infantry Division of XII Corps made contact with 10th Armored Division in Trier.[39]

The ease with which the 10th Armored Division had taken Trier can be explained by the fact that the 76th Infantry Division's move in from the west had prompted the 212th Volksgrenadier Division defending the city to advance to meet it. Thus the city was left in the hands of only two Volkssturm battalions, the city police, and the crews of several multipurpose 88-mm guns.

General Patton was delighted with the outcome, but failed to get the response he expected from his superiors. He then received two messages, one from XX Corps confirming the capture of the city with an intact bridge across the Moselle, and the other from SHAEF ordering him to bypass Trier, as it would take four divisions to capture it. Gleefully, he signaled SHAEF via the 12th Army Group: "Have taken Trier with two divisions. What do you want me to do? Give it back?"[40]

12
The Battle of Lampaden Ridge

With the fall of Trier, Lieutenant Colonel Anderson's 376th Infantry reverted to the command of the 94th Infantry Division on March 3 as the 10th Armored Division thrust northward along the Moselle valley toward the Rhine. During its attachment to the 10th Armored Division, the 376th Infantry had suffered the loss of 21 officers and 403 enlisted men, plus 173 nonbattle casualties. The 376th had also taken 1,483 prisoners and reduced 155 defended bunkers.

The 3rd Cavalry Group was now attached to the 94th and was made responsible for securing the northern flank in front of Trier between the villages of Tarforst and Frankenheim. Captain Ashton's 94th Reconnaissance Troop now patrolled the area south of Taben between the bridgehead and the 26th U.S. Infantry Division's sector on the other flank.

The return of the 376th Infantry brought promise of a welcome relief to the 94th, who were now fully stretched between Ollmuth and the Saar River at Saarhausen. Lieutenant Colonel Miner's 1st/376th now moved into Wiltingen, but the men of Major Dossenbach's 2nd/376th were still engaged in mopping up pillboxes in the Konz area, while Lieutenant Colonel Thurston's fortunate 3rd/376th were enjoying rest and recuperation in Luxembourg as divisional reserve.

German artillery fire continued to fall on the division, the principal targets being Lampaden, Zerf, the Taben bridge site, and Taben itself. The Germans were frantically reorganizing their units into emergency combat teams (*Kampfgruppen*) to meet the new situation, using all of their resources, including rear echelon troops and alarm companies raised from convalescents and troops who were on leave to bolster the surviving combatant elements of the 416th Infantry and 256th Volksgrenadier Divisions. Most of the 2nd Mountain Division had arrived and were being thrust straight into the line.[1]

THE IRSCH-ZERF HIGHWAY—MARCH 3

C Company of Major Stanion's 1st/302nd, now down to only seventy effectives, made a third desperate attempt on Hill 2 (Height 536) at 1000 on March 3. The company was met by intense fire that brought the assault to a standstill. Having gone forward to the company command post to check the situation for himself, Major Stanion sent his S-3, Capt. Robert L. Woodburn, to Colonel Hagerty to report the impossibility of achieving his mission with such depleted forces. Colonel Hagerty then changed the battalion's task to holding its ground and establishing contact with the units on its flanks. He also arranged for the relief of the 1st/302nd by elements of Lieutenant Colonel Thurston's 3rd/376th the next day.

Late that afternoon two German prisoners taken from the 13th (Cannon) Company, Mountain Infantry Regiment 137, claimed that their 3rd Battalion, supported by 20-mm, 75-mm, and 105-mm guns, would be attacking Hill 5 (Height 463) the next morning. Two other prisoners taken later in the day confirmed that the attack would take place at 0330.[2]

THE IRSCH-ZERF HIGHWAY—MARCH 4

The fifty-four men of Lieutenant Henley's L Company of Major O'Neil's 3rd/301st were dug in on the southern slope of Hill 5 (Height 463) east of Zerf in a crescent formation. There were another forty replacements waiting to join them in Zerf under the first sergeant, but the constant artillery and mortar fire falling on the company positions made it impracticable to bring them forward, except to replace individual casualties as they occurred. Both the heavy machine guns and one of the light machine guns had been knocked out during the night, and only one of the three 60-mm mortars was still serviceable.

The artillery fire on the hill increased at 0430 as the delayed German attack got under way. L Company managed to check the German infantry with the fire of M1s and BARs, but two self-propelled guns advanced right up to the American line. Pfc. Frank A. Franchino tried to engage them with his bazooka, but the weapon had been damaged and was useless. The self-propelled guns fired a couple of colored flares as a signal for two more guns to join them and then moved up the crest to engage the two Hellcats positioned there, which unfortunately had no night sights. Meanwhile, the German infantry closed in, forcing the 3rd Platoon back, so Lieutenant Henley went back to Zerf to collect the remainder of the replacements as a counterattack force.

2nd Lt. Sylvester Beyer of the 356th Field Artillery, Tech-4 Paul E. Neuman, and Sgt. Harry C. Gersbaugh were captured and taken down the hill for questioning. When they refused to divulge any military information, a German soldier opened fire with a Schmeisser submachine gun, killing Sergeant Neumann and wounding the other two. Pvt. Irving S. Clemens of the 1st Platoon happened to see this and opened fire, enabling Lieutenant Beyer to escape back to the American lines. Beyer then refused treatment until he had directed fire on the enemy troops. This effectively separated the German infantry from their armored support, forcing them to retire. (Lieutenant Beyer was subsequently awarded the Silver Star.)

Meanwhile, in Zerf Major O'Neil had sent for Lt. Leon P. Johnson and his platoon from G Company, 2nd/301st, who were in reserve at Bruchsmühle and had been made available to him. Johnson was preparing to send forward the remaining replacements when SSgt. Ralph O. Minnich arrived to report that the position on the hill had held and the enemy's self-propelled guns had been withdrawn. Major O'Neil then sent off the replacements on the double under Sergeant Kinateder, while ordering the artillery to hold its fire. Sergeant Urban met the replacements and reported that L Company was down to seventeen effectives. Lieutenant Johnson and his platoon reinforced the position later in the morning when he took over the command.[3]

At 0600 on March 4 Lieutenant Colonel Thurston's 3rd/376th was attached to Colonel Hagerty's 301st Infantry. What had been intended as a week's break to rest and refit at Dudelange in Luxembourg had been abruptly cancelled. At an officers' conference the day before, it had been decided that stripping down and repairing the battalion's vehicle should take first priority while the troops were resting, so thirty out of forty of the vehicles on the battalion strength had been handed in for the motor pool's attention. Next day, Lieutenant Decker, one of the regimental liaison officers, appeared and asked how long it would take to assemble the battalion, load up, and leave. Two hours was the answer, but the battalion would need replacement vehicles, or twenty-four hours if it had to reassemble its own.

This attachment to the 301st infantry was ostensibly to relieve the 1st/302nd and the 5th Rangers, who were now down to one hundred men and about to go into regimental reserve. However, as Thurston discovered to his horror, the real reason was that Major Brumley's 2nd/302nd, which was also attached to the 301st Infantry, had been routed on the southern flank, and the hole in the line had to be plugged. Apparently, while the 2nd/302nd had been conducting an advance as ordered, the leading platoon had encountered a more resolute enemy than usual and had broken and run in such a panic that the fear had spread to the remainder of the company and then to the battalion, the officers being unable to stop the rout. This matter had to be kept a dead secret within the division to prevent either General Walker or General Patton from hearing about it, so no disciplinary action could be taken, and the whole incident was to be squashed.[4]

NEW PLANS

Divisional Headquarters was now preparing for a general relief in the bridgehead as a result of XX Corps' intention to replace the 26th Infantry Division in the Saarlautern area with the 65th Infantry Division. The 26th could replace the 94th, who would then move into Luxembourg for some well-earned rest and replenishment. The move was to take place under cover of darkness on the nights of March 6, 7, and 8, and XX Corps was providing 270 trucks for the purpose. All unit signs were to be removed to ensure secrecy. But this was not to be.[5]

Big plans were also afoot on the German side. General Hahn's LXXXII Corps had just been assigned a formidable reinforcement in the shape of Maj. Gen. (*Obergruppenführer*) Karl Heinrich Brenner's 6th SS Mountain Division "Nord," a three-thousand-strong formation of fit, young, and experienced troops, consisting of the three-battalion SS Mountain Infantry

Regiment 11 "Reinhard Heydrich"; the 2nd Battalion, SS Mountain Infantry Regiment 12 "Michael Gaismair"; SS Reconnaissance Battalion 6; SS Tank Hunting Battalion 6; SS Mountain Artillery Regiment 6 with four battalions; SS Flak Battalion 6; and SS Engineer Battalion 6.

General Hahn now planned to counterattack with a view to severing the main American supply route to Trier on Highway 268 and recovering any German troops who were still holding out south of the city, using the special infiltration skills in which the 6th SS Mountain Division had been trained. General Hahn's plan involved a three-directional attack. The men of the 6th SS Mountain Division were to seize the highway between Zerf and Pellingen, those of the 2nd Mountain Division were to capture the Mühlenberg (Hill 6) and protect the southern flank, while the 256th Volksgrenadier Division troops were to seize the commanding heights around Gutweiler and be prepared to advance from there. The artillery units of all three divisions were brought under command of the corps artillery to ensure strong supporting fire.

This kind of attack against the weak and scattered units of the 94th was to give a chaotic picture to the command, but the American troops proved themselves superior to the supposedly crack troops sent against them, the battle being won by ordinary soldiers with the assistance of a superb artillery backing.[6]

THE GERMAN COUNTERATTACK—MARCH 6

On the pitch-black night of March 5 the SS mountain troops began moving forward to their assembly areas, crossing the Ruwer River at about midnight in showers of sleet and snow. No artillery preparation announced their arrival as at about 0015 hours on March 6 they began penetrating the forward lines of the 94th Infantry Division.[7]

On the extreme left flank the 3rd Cavalry were attacked by elements of the 256th Volksgrenadier Division. A group of about fifty men took Height 405, which was undefended, and then moved on to Gutweiler. The 3rd Cavalry then counterattacked with such force that the surviving Germans surrendered after suffering numerous casualties. Another German group occupied Height 427 before going on to try to take Korlingen to the northeast, but were repulsed.[8]

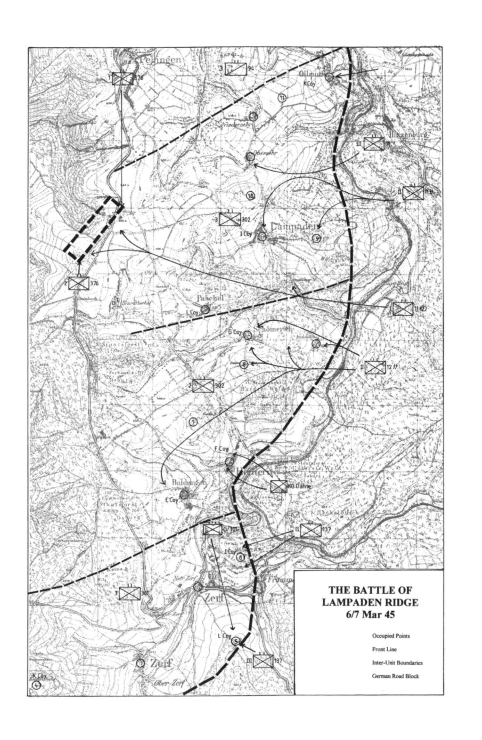

**THE BATTLE OF
LAMPADEN RIDGE
6/7 Mar 45**

Occupied Points

Front Line

Inter-Unit Boundaries

German Road Block

THE 3RD/302ND'S SECTOR—MARCH 6

Next in line, Lieutenant Colonel Cloudt's 3rd/302d, based in Lampaden village, were attacked by the 3rd and 2nd Battalions of SS Mountain Regiment 11, coming in from the northeast and east respectively. At 0200 hours the 3rd Battalion of SS Mountain Regiment 11 moved to surround Obersehr, which was occupied by K Company's 2nd Platoon under TSgt. William B. Grose, the 3rd Platoon of the regimental cannon company, and elements of B Company, 774th Tank Destroyer Battalion. Lt. Riggs Mahoney's 1st Platoon of K Company, in Ollmuth, on the battalion's left flank, was attacked at 0400 hours but beat off the enemy, and thereafter the situation there remained quiet apart from some intermittent shelling from across the Ruwer.[9]

Sgt. Max A. Ledesma left his foxhole in Obersehr at 0200 to visit the cemetery on the road to Lampaden, the contact point with Captain Donovan's I Company in that village. He saw several soldiers in the area, one of whom gave him the correct challenge, but then, noticing the shape of their helmets, he realized they were German and opened fire. Ledesma was severely wounded in the ensuing exchange, but started staggering and crawling back to Obersehr to raise the alarm.

Meanwhile, a sentry from the 1st Platoon, B Company, 774th Tank Destroyer Battalion, which was also in Obersehr, was approached by a German who in perfect English gave the correct response to the sentry's challenge and said he would be returning shortly with some other men. The German soldier duly returned with others, who surrounded the American sentry and took him prisoner. These German troops then began moving into the village. Sergeant Grose heard them coming and ordered his men to open fire. After a sharp exchange of fire, the enemy troops were driven back and began digging in around the village.

The Americans continued to engage any signs of movement until daybreak, with the Hellcats covering the street between the two rows of houses and Sergeant Grose's men covering the flanks. Grose asked his company commander in Niedersehr for flares, but Capt. Joseph Bugel had only three left. He promised to give notice of each firing by radio, and in this way Sergeant Grose's men were fully prepared for action each time they had the illumination to pick out their targets.

From in front of his position Sgt. Flaud E. Long heard groaning in the darkness followed by a few words of Spanish. Realizing it must be Ledesma, he dashed out of the house into the heavy fire and dragged the wounded man back into shelter. Sergeant Ledesma died of his wounds shortly afterward, still muttering something about the compromised password. (Sergeant Long was later awarded the Silver Star.)[10]

At one point the Germans sent forward an emissary to persuade the defense to surrender, but SSgt. William J. Murphy of the 774th Tank Destroyer Battalion replied: "See those tracks you made coming up here? Well, you fill them a hell of a lot faster going back!"[11]

At daybreak Lieutenant Colonel Cloudt in Lampaden ordered Lt. Anthony Czerboskas of L Company to send a platoon supported by three tanks to the relief of Obersehr. Lieutenant Ramirez's 3rd Platoon duly set off. One tank and a squad of infantry were to take the road around Height 500 to the west, while the remainder used the more direct north-south road between the two locations. For some reason, however, all three tanks accompanied the squad going around Height 500, where they came under heavy fire from the hill. One of the Sherman tanks was knocked out, so the rest withdrew. Lieutenant Ramirez set off again from Lampaden, this time coming under fire from machine guns and panzerfausts supported by high-velocity antitank fire coming from across the Ruwer.

During the advance a river fog kept alternatively falling and lifting to obscure and clear the line of sight. Three men in the 3rd Squad, on the left, including the leader, were hit almost immediately. Lieutenant Ramirez was then hit and TSgt. Albert I. Orr took over command. Partway up Height 500 the tank on the right stopped and pulled back a little, and the other tank did the same. Sergeant Orr then ordered up the reserve 2nd Squad between the two assault squads and fearlessly pushed home the attack, following the tanks up to the crest of the hill. SSgt. Daniel Pash, Sgt. Johan A. Regan, and the platoon medic, Tech-5 Harry E. Hebard, were killed. One of the tanks wiped out a machine-gun nest that was concealed in a pile of beets. The hill was taken, together with fifty SS prisoners.[12]

However, the tanks drew attention from across the river, as Pfc. Russel E. Wellman reported:

An 88 on the next hill commenced firing on our tanks. The men hugged the ground and prayed while the tank commander radioed for permission to withdraw to defilade. We had been glad to have the tanks, but now we were glad to see them go as they were drawing fire on us. From that time until the next night we just stayed there . . . wet, cold, no food and little water. Jerry [the Germans] threw concentrations of everything he had from mortars to rockets and 88s. We listened to the artillery around us and tried to figure out where the line ran. The next day they told us there were Germans all around us. Some of us found hard crackers and sardines on dead Germans. Hungry as we were they tasted good! On the second night a few men went into town for hot chow and the rest of us got K rations. The third day the platoon was relieved.[13]

Pfc. Paul L. Zaring of the cannon company's 3rd Platoon spent all morning fighting off German attacks in defense of both his platoon's guns and a seriously wounded comrade after the remainder of his companions had been penned up in a group of houses. Although he was under artillery and small-arms fire, Zaring kept the enemy at bay, killing eight of them, including an officer who got to within ten yards of him with a grenade. (Zaring was later awarded the Distinguished Service Cross for this action.)

In Niedersehr Captain Bugel had posted snipers drawn from his company headquarters to cover the eastern and southern approaches of the village with harassing fire should it be necessary, but the village was not attacked.[14]

At 0125 the leading elements of the 1st Battalion, SS Mountain Regiment 11, who were advancing up the draw leading to Lampaden from the Ruwer River, were challenged by the outposts of I Company at Lampadener Mühle. Sgt. Samuel Mallich, who was manning a light machine gun alongside the mill, fired a magazine at what he thought was a German patrol, then changed his firing position when he noticed that some of the enemy were infiltrating through. Appreciating that the enemy were in fairly large numbers, the outpost withdrew into the village, but two men were lost on the way. Pfc. James Bender first found his way to Schömerich and rejoined his company later that morning. Having set fire to the abandoned mill, the 1st Battalion, SS Mountain Regiment 11, continued up the draws between Lampaden and Paschel, heading for Dreikopf Hill off Highway 268. At this stage the troops in Lampaden could hear the Germans, but the dark night and the dense woods completely obscured them from view.

The main attack on Lampaden came from the north and the 2nd Battalion. The 3rd Platoon of Captain Williams's I Company, who were near the head of a draw on the left flank, were first struck when Pvt. Charles F. McCartney challenged a group of Germans who were approaching. As he received no reply, McCartney opened fire but was killed by a burst from an enemy machine gun. Fire from the remainder of the platoon held up the attack until SSgt. Sidney Schrager arrived with half a platoon to reinforce the position. Schrager was wounded on the way and was evacuated only with great difficulty under raking enemy fire. Then SSgt. Dominick J. Bondi brought forward a squad and a half to reinforce the center of the line and reached the top of the ridge under heavy machine-gun fire from Height 464 (Hill 9). (Sergeant Bondi later received a Silver Star for this action.)

The I Company outpost that had been forced back from Lampadener Mühle was reinforced by Captain Edwards, who ordered the men back to their old position, but the burning mill made movement beyond Lampaden impossible. Enemy movement had been discerned in the draw north of the village, and artillery fire was being directed on the draw both north and south of the village.[15]

At one point during the day Lieutenant Colonel Cloudt sent back to Irsch an ambulance and a two-and-a-half-ton truck loaded with twenty-five wounded Americans, including Lieutenant Ramirez, fourteen wounded Germans, and a six-man ammunition detail. These vehicles were stopped by enemy soldiers near Dreikopf Hill and were about to be allowed through when one of the German wounded complained of his treatment by the Americans, resulting in their detention in a nearby gun emplacement.

A wire party from the 356th Field Artillery Battalion was also stopped in this area when its jeep was hit by a panzerfaust. Sgt. Robert A. Klahn was killed, Tech-5 John R. Deller wounded, and Sgt. Woodrow J. Boyette captured. The two survivors were taken to join the other prisoners from Lampaden.[16]

Lieutenant Colonel Cloudt realized that he was cut off when the crew of a Hellcat positioned to the west of the village reported they had been overrun. This was confirmed when Lieutenant Najjar of the ammunition and pioneer platoon and his driver returned from a reconnaissance patrol with ten prisoners from the 2nd Battalion, SS Mountain Regiment 11, including a first lieutenant. Sgt. Eugene T. Hack of the intelligence section and Sgt. Robert A. Bawd of the intelligence and reconnaissance platoon also discovered that the German aim was to block the main supply route to Trier on Highway 268. Further confirmation came from three men of the 7th Field Artillery Observation Battalion who had been traveling in a three-and-a-quarter-ton truck traveling from Pellingen to Obersehr. West of Lampaden their truck had been hit by a panzerfaust and their lieutenant was seriously wounded. They had been captured but managed to escape under a hail of fire.

Lt. Robert O. Kimball assembled a force composed of cooks, drivers, mechanics, and tank destroyer men to clear the area behind the village. This force came under heavy fire from the road junction to the west of the village and took up a defensive position south of the road under SSgt. Bruno Felicelli.

Captain Smith's L Company then made another attempt to clear the road to Obersehr. Lt. John Travers of the 2nd Platoon sent Sgt. George H. Stockman's squad up Height 500 (Hill 10) with the tank that had not reached the crest in the earlier attack. The group climbed up the hill, but the tank was then driven back by panzerfausts and long-range antitank gunfire from the northeast. Sergeant Stockman's squad pressed on until contact was made with I Company's 3rd Platoon on the crest, but fire from the cemetery then killed Stockman and pinned down the rest of the squad. Two attempts to reach the 2nd Platoon from the crest failed, so Sgt. Philip D. Grant's squad, supported by a tank, was sent to clear the cemetery. However, as a result of furious automatic fire, panzerfausts, and artillery fire, this attack also failed.[17]

The relief of Obersehr was of considerable concern to Lieutenant Colonel Cloudt. He decided to send Sergeant Grant's squad and the 1st Squad of the 2nd Platoon under Lieutenant Czerboskas as tank-mounted infantry to crash into the village in a surprise attack. The squads moved up Height 500 and mounted a tank each, which then swept into the village, overran the enemy south of the village, and pushed on in to meet up with the defense. Together these forces then cleared the village. Using the tanks in similar fashion, Sergeants Grose and Long then stormed through the enemy positions on the far side of the village. In all some seventy prisoners were taken, more than one hundred enemy dead were counted, and twenty-six machine guns and forty-two panzerfausts were recovered from the battlefield. (Both Sergeants Grant and Long were later awarded the Silver Star.)

After relieving Obersehr, the two squads from L Company were allocated to Sergeant Orr's position on Height 500. The remnants of the 1st and 2nd Platoons, together with the battalion ammunition and pioneer platoon, took over the defense of the southern and eastern approaches to Lampaden, while L Company and Sergeant Felicelli's composite unit covered the rear of the village.

A German NCO appeared at Lampaden that afternoon with a sergeant from the 7th Field Artillery Observation Battalion who had been captured at Dreikopf Hill. The German NCO wanted to negotiate an exchange of prisoners, but Lieutenant Colonel Cloudt was reluctant to reveal the weakness of his position by releasing able-bodied SS men for wounded Americans. He procrastinated until dusk and then told the German NCO that he was not authorized to make such an exchange.[18]

Captain Edwards spent much of the day trying to round up his I Company, which had been badly split up in the fighting. Part of his 1st Platoon, who had been driven out of Lampadener Mühle before dawn, were now in the southeastern part of Lampaden. The rest of that platoon and a section of M Company's heavy machine guns were somewhere to the front. The 2nd Platoon, which had been in the center of the company line, had become isolated in the fighting, but some of the men had worked their way back to the village. Lt. John W. Bybee's 3rd Platoon was on the forward slope of the ridge north of the village and under machine-gun fire from both flanks, but Bybee himself had become cut off from his platoon while visiting the company command post, and all his attempts to rejoin his men were stopped by machine-gun fire, leaving TSgt. Leland B. McKee in charge. One of the platoon's light machine guns had been abandoned, and the other was isolated with a section of heavy machine guns east of the village on the 2nd Platoon's flank.

Sergeant Bondi led forward a squad and a half of men to reinforce the 2nd Platoon, but was held up by machine-gun fire until one of the tanks supporting the battalion intervened. Having maneuvered the line into some sort of order, it was then found necessary to withdraw to a new perimeter on the edge of the village. SSgt. John R. Routh and a BAR team were left behind in error on Hill 9 (Height 464) and were not traced until late in the afternoon.

Another problem was the German machine gun in the cemetery on the Lampaden-Obersehr road, whose gunner had already driven back three attempts to suppress it, and which continued to cut off I Company's 3rd Platoon and harass the line held by L Company and elements of the battalion Headquarters Company. Sergeant Orr on Height 500 was ordered to send an assault group to eliminate this position, which he achieved by sending SSgt. Cecil F. Durette with the 1st Squad working in from the northwest of the cemetery, while Sergeant Metz converged from the southwest with his tank. (Sergeant Orr later received a battlefield commission and a Distinguished Service Cross for his service that day.)

Meanwhile, since the telephone lines from his forward positions had gone dead, Lt. William J. Honan of M Company had been anxiously awaiting news from his machine-gun sections. Eventually he decided to go and investigate the situation, arming himself with a light machine gun. Sgt. Walter L. Cranford from I Company elected to join him, being concerned about the safety of some of his own men. On the southern edge of Height 464 they found Pfc. Wallace M. Gallant and three men manning the right gun of their section. Gallant and his men reported that they had been firing on various groups of the enemy all day. In order to conserve ammunition, Gallant had been using his M1 only against individual targets. They had even taken six prisoners, who had walked into their position while rolling up Gallant's telephone line (which would lead to an American position) and had been sent back under guard of two wounded men. One of the groups they had scattered had consisted of about twenty German officers. (Private Gallant was another recipient of the Distinguished Service Cross for action that day.)

The other machine-gun team on the left was also still operational, as was Pfc. Paul W. Chapman and his light machine-gun team, who were farther off. Lieutenant Honan ordered all three teams back into Lampaden and then stood up, openly firing his machine gun from the hip to cover their withdrawal. He and Sergeant Cranford continued their search for the second heavy machine-gun section, and whenever they encountered any of the enemy, Lieutenant Honan routed them with his machine gun as if it were a BAR. They were unsuccessful in their search, but in fact the second section, under SSgt. Brice P. Potthoff, were already working their way back with their guns by a circuitous route. They had had a busy day and had decided to return to the village at dusk for fear of being isolated and over-whelmed. (Lieutenant Hohan was later awarded the Distinguished Service Cross.)[19]

Lieutenant Bybee and Corporal Raley made a last attempt to reach I Company's 3rd Platoon on the ridge north of Lampaden before nightfall. They crossed the ridge but then ran into German machine-gun fire coming from what had been the platoon's foxholes. It seemed that the 3rd Platoon must have been wiped out or captured at some stage during the day. When Bybee reported this to Lieutenant Colonel Cloudt, he was ordered to form a composite platoon from the cooks and headquarters personnel of I and M Companies and commit it to the gap between the ammunition and pioneer platoon on the ridge and those elements of I Company on the western edge of the village. At the same time, Lieutenant Travers was ordered to form the mess and supply personnel of his L Company into a squad to guard the southern edge of the village. With the defenses thus reorganized, the 2nd/302nd settled down to await the inevitable night attack.

During the night, Pfc. Daniel W. Aman and Pvt. Harry R. Ellis of Sergeant Stockman's missing 3rd Platoon crawled over the ridge to safety. Both had been wounded and survived only by feigning death until nightfall. They believed all of their comrades were dead, for the SS troopers had first cut down the platoon with machine-gun fire and then shot Sgt. John Gedaminski, who was wounded but still alive.[20]

THE 2ND/302ND'S SECTOR—MARCH 6

In Major Maixner's 2nd/302nd's sector, the 2nd Battalion, SS Mountain Regiment 12, advanced on either side of Kummlerhof with Schömerich as their main objective. The right assault company began closing in on the 3rd Platoon of Captain Griffin's G Company at Kummlerhof, while the left assault company worked their way up through Hardter Wald Woods to Height 468 (Hill 8).

A four-man outpost under Sgt. Richard R. Wiles that had orders to pull back should the enemy approach was cut off before they could do so. Sergeant Wiles ordered his men to make a break for the F Company strongpoint in Hentern, but the artillery fire they were now coming under caused the men to freeze. Sergeant Wiles tried to get away on his own, only to be caught with the coming of daylight.

Communications between Captain Griffin in Schömerich and his 3rd Platoon in Kummlerhof were cut at 0130 just as Sgt. Vincent Sacco was reporting that his platoon was under small-arms and bazooka fire coming from all directions. Captain Griffin then asked Major Maixner for reinforcements, and Maixner ordered the 2nd Platoon of Captain Kops's F Company to move from its reserve position on Height 467 into Schömerich. Men were seen on the ridge four hundred yards east of the village at 0200, and when a patrol was sent to investigate, they were fired upon, leaving one man wounded. Bullets started ricocheting off the walls in Schömerich as G Company's 2nd Platoon started firing back into Hardter Wald Woods, which were now also under fire from the 356th Field Artillery.

Elements of F and G Companies were firing blindly into the darkness from Schömerich at any sounds of enemy movement. The Germans came right up to the barbed wire in front of G Company's 2nd Platoon on Hill 468 (Hill 8). Sgts. Domer V. Miller and John C. Finger opened fire at point-blank range with their heavy machine gun, expending three boxes of ammunition before they were overrun while reloading, but they killed the first German into their position. Sgt. Patrick J. Hassett, who was in charge of the other heavy machine gun, personally killed three enemy soldiers who were on the edge of his emplacement. When Technical Sergeant Ernst, who was commanding the position, reported the situation to Captain Griffin, he was ordered to pull back into the village. Sgt. Milton H. Stern and Pfc. Morgan H. Morgan yelled, "We're GIs! Let us in!" as they dashed to a house occupied by an antitank squad. The 2nd Platoon then helped bolster the defense in Schömerich. Meanwhile, Major Maixner had alerted both F Company in Hentern and E Company in Baldringen, as a result of which Sgt. Howard J. Morton's 2nd Platoon of F Company also moved into Schömerich, taking up positions on the northeastern edge of the village.

When the morning mist lifted, the Germans made a second attack on the village, but were stopped by the defensive fire. Captain Griffin, who was half blind from a head injury received at Sinz, was wounded in the head a second time, but continued to rally and direct his men. Pfc. Carl T. Swift of the 2nd Platoon, who had been given a squad of new men to lead, played a prominent role in checking the enemy attack with his squad's fire, and Staff Sergeant Stern and Pfc. Harvey J. Reynolds dropped hand grenades from a second-story window onto some Germans who had gotten close enough to set fire to a half-track. Long-range enemy artillery, rocket, and mortar fire crashed down on the village all morning, setting fire to several buildings. Some snipers penetrated the village, and the defense was also subject to attacks by panzerfausts.

Eventually the Germans succeeded in taking some buildings in the eastern and southeastern parts of Schömerich. One squad of G Company's 1st Platoon, a heavy machine-gun section, and a mortar section of H Company were overrun and captured. The Germans then donned the Americans' helmets and field jackets and even pressed some civilians into service as snipers for the fierce street fighting that ensued.

Sergeant Jacobson and Pfc. Francis A. Palet used a bazooka to eliminate the defenders of an enemy-held building, and Sergeant Ernst was wounded while attacking the building containing the mortar section prisoners. In the meantime, Pfc. Clifford R. McCumber raced from house to house distributing ammunition obtained from Lt. Robert E. Gobin's machine-gun platoon.[21]

Kampfgruppe Brockmann, a forty-man detachment under a German lieutenant of that name, had gone forward with the 2nd Battalion, SS Mountain Regiment 12, with the main task of linking the left flank of that battalion with Kampfgruppe Dahne farther south, and with the secondary task of disrupting communications and harassing artillery positions.

Meanwhile, Kampfgruppe Dahne began encircling Hentern and were met by a hail of fire from the 3rd Platoon of Captain Kops's F Company. This slowed down the attack but failed to prevent a small group of Germans from reaching the roadblock at the northern end of the village close to the company command post. As the German troops tried to remove the antitank mines in front of the roadblock, Captain Kops threw a grenade into them, detonating some of the mines and killing five of the enemy, but the explosion also blew in the side of a house, burying the man who had handed Kops the grenade. As the reserve team of Kampfgruppe Dahne circled around the rear of the village, Captain Kops ordered the 1st Platoon on Height 467 to come to his aid.

These efforts finished off Kampfgruppe Dahne and netted twenty-four prisoners. F Company then established radio contact with G Company's 3rd Platoon at Kummlerhof to find the latter still in control. E Company also reported having the situation under control in Baldringen and on Hill 7 (Height 472).

Part of Lieutenant Brockmann's force attacked Baldringen astride the road coming in from the west. Heavy fire from the village slowed down the attack, and the Germans then sent Sgt. Richard W. Finkbone, who had been wounded in the arm and captured on their way in, as an envoy with a view to surrendering to the Americans. The surrender was arranged, but as the prisoners were being marched back, a German artillery concentration caused a minor panic and some of the prisoners started to run. A few short bursts from Pfc. Michael A. Scioli's submachine gun quickly restored order. The remainder of the force surrendered shortly afterward, but another German artillery concentration eliminated all but Lieutenant Brockmann before this second group could be moved to cover.[22]

At 0800 Lt. Mark Hammer's C Company, 1st/302nd, followed by the five medium tanks of Lt. Norbert F. Krob's 1st Platoon, A Company, 778th Tank Battalion, left Irsch with orders to report to Major Maixner and relieve G Company at Schömerich. When they reached Highway 268 west of Baldringen, Lieutenant Hammer left TSgt. James A. Davis with his 2nd Platoon to take up positions in the woods at the road junction with orders to keep both roads open and capture any Germans in the immediate area. The company then moved on to the battalion command post located in a pillbox five hundred yards south of Steinbach. There Major Maixner briefed Lieutenant Hammer on the situation regarding G Company, who were bottled up in Schömerich, with their 3rd Platoon isolated at Kummlerhof, and their 2nd Platoon driven off Hill 8 (Height 468). His orders were for C Company to retake and hold the hill, while G Company would break out of Schömerich to assist in consolidating the battalion front.

C Company then moved to an assembly area in a small copse just short of the objective before assaulting the hill with TSgt. Leonard T. Paluszynski's 1st Platoon, a heavy machine-gun section under SSgt. Frank Schwemer, and four of the tanks, while TSgt. Marvin L. Kress's 3rd Platoon provided flank security. No artillery preparation was called for, but the attack met only light resistance. About ten Germans were killed and an equal number driven off. The company then reorganized on the hill with the heavy machine-gun sections securing the flanks. Radio contact was then established with Captain Griffin in Schömerich, who reported that he had insufficient strength with which to break out. His heavy machine guns and mortars had been captured, and he was now holding only four houses. He requested tank support.

As the tanks advanced toward Schömerich, the enemy troops began withdrawing, for they had expended all their panzerfausts in the house-to-house fighting. The village was soon cleared and most of the H Company prisoners were recovered. The tanks then returned to Hill 8 (Height 468) and Lieutenant Hammer joined Captain Griffin in the village. He arrived just as the remnants of the 2nd Battalion, SS Mountain Regiment 12, launched another attack with about fifty men and two assault guns firing from a ridge east of the village. This attack was met by a hail of fire from the riflemen of C, F, and G Companies; the heavy machine guns of D and H Companies; and a .50-caliber machine gun manned by the tank de-stroyer men. Lieutenant Krob moved his tanks to provide firing support. The first tank round sheared the barrel off one of the assault guns, and the other was hit by a shot from the Hellcat at the southern end of the village and withdrew in flames. This was enough for the German infantry, who also withdrew.

Lieutenant Hammer then received a message from his company command post on Hill 8 (Height 468) saying the company had already suffered eighteen casualties, including Sergeants Paluszynski and Schwemer, from the heavy shellfire falling on their position. The company commanders conferred and agreed that they barely had the strength to meet another hostile thrust. Lieutenant Hammer then radioed Major Maixner to report this situation and to suggest that he leave a small force on Hill 8 (Height 468) and reinforce Schömerich with the rest of his company, a plan with which Major Maixner agreed.

This proved a sound decision, for F Company in Hentern had received a radio message from G Company's 3rd Platoon in Kummlerhof saying they were under attack in their one remaining house by assault guns that were being fired through the windows. Practically all the men in the pla-toon had been wounded and their ammunition was exhausted.[23]

Late that afternoon Captain Wancio's B Company reached Steinbach on Highway 268 with their supporting tanks. The 3rd Platoon then deployed and moved across the open ground east of the road, followed by the tanks, while the 1st Platoon moved through the woods on the west side. Almost immediately intense automatic fire was received by the Americans from Height 507 to the north and against the 3rd Platoon from both sides of the highway. The tank on the extreme left was destroyed by a panzerfaust. Captain Wancio reported to Regiment that the roadblock appeared too strong for the company to tackle, so he was ordered to assume a defensive position north of Steinbach for the night.[24]

THE 3RD/301ST'S SECTOR—MARCH 6

At 0700 the 2nd Battalion of Mountain Regiment 137 attacked the positions of Captain Donovan's I Company, 3rd/301st, on the Mühlenberg (Hill 6) on the bend in the Ruwer River northeast of Zerf. Steadily advancing up the slope, the German troops assaulted and infiltrated the widely spaced positions of the 2nd and 3rd Platoons as they came to them, but Lt. James T. Flower, commanding the 2nd Platoon, managed to retain the right knoll by moving his men around to meet the threat.

Pfc. Bennett P. Katzen organized a small group and restored I Company's line. The company's machine guns and some mortar support held the enemy in check, but at 0930 an enemy artillery preparation heralded another attack on the hill, which was again successfully repulsed. Meanwhile, Captain Donovan organized the loan of Sergeant Kinateder's platoon from L Company to retake the left side of the hill.

Colonel Hagerty's 301st Infantry Regiment was relieved by the 328th Infantry of the 26th Infantry Division that night. The 301st Infantry moved back across the Saar and Moselle into Luxembourg together with the 301st Field Artillery Battalion, the 319th Field Engineer Battalion (less B Company), the 94th Reconnaissance Troop, B Battery of the 465th Antiaircraft Artillery Battalion, and miscellaneous service units. In total darkness the long columns wound their way over routes directed by the military police.[25]

REORGANIZATION

General Walker at XX Corps advised General Malony that the complete relief of the 94th Infantry Division would be delayed until Lieutenant Colonel Cloudt's position had been restored. Maj. Gen. Willard S. Paul, commanding the adjacent 26th Infantry Division, offered Malony the use of any of his nearby units. It was intended that the relief of the 94th by the 26th Infantry Division would take place on the nights of March 8 and 9.

As March 6 ended, the 94th Infantry Division was still holding its ground. Only the Lampadener Mühle outpost had been lost. However, the enemy penetration and roadblock on Highway 268 at Dreikopf Hill called for attention, and Lieutenant Colonel Anderson of the 376th Infantry, who were in reserve at Oberemmel, was ordered to deal with it. He sent forward Lieutenant Colonel Miner's 1st/376th.[26]

That evening the 1st/376th marched up to Pellingen with Lieutenant Colonel Miner going ahead in his jeep to reconnoiter. Lt. Joseph T. Koshoffer's A Company then marched south from Pellingen to make contact with the enemy at Dreikopf Hill, with Lt. William P. Springer's C Company following. Just north of Dreikopf Hill, A Company pulled in its flanking patrols and C Company deployed to cover the east flank. C Company also sent out patrols to try to make contact with the 3rd/302nd at Obersehr and Lampaden. Meanwhile, Lt. William G. Land's B Company moved down west of the highway to a small ridge across from Dreikopf Hill, and A Company moved forward opposite on the east side of the highway.

It was still dark when Lt. Carl A. Crouse led B Company's 1st Platoon south down a draw and took up a crescent-shaped position on the edge of the woods facing south to Height 507 and southeast to the highway. A patrol from TSgt. John F. Nagy's 3rd Platoon set off down the highway to contact the 302nd's B Company but ran into heavy fire, and C Company's patrols proved equally unsuccessful in contacting the 3rd/302nd. Another patrol, under Sgt. Herbert L. Monroe, was moving toward Lampaden but stopped at about 2200 when they heard a voice. It turned out to be a German soldier complaining about the bad weather and the water in his foxhole.

Lieutenant Colonel Miner decided to await daylight and the arrival of supporting armor before pursuing his mission further.[27]

LAMPADEN—MARCH 7

The expected German attack was launched in the early, cold, misty hours of March 7. At 0400 the battered remnants of SS Mountain Regiment 11, supported by assault guns, attacked Lampaden from the south and east after a blistering preparation by massed rocket, mortar, and artillery fire.

The American artillery blanketed the approach routes with fire. When the leading assault gun began firing on the first houses, TSgt. James T. Chapman engaged it with a 57-mm gun of the battalion's antitank platoon's 1st Squad, leading to a duel focused on each other's muzzle flashes. Lt. Charles H. Pausner Jr. concentrated the fire of his artillery on the eastern approaches to the village, while Capt. Benjamin F. Buffington at the command post called down the heavier shells of the 390th Field Artillery.

As dawn came and the mist began to thin, the whole area was a sea of fire. Private First Class Gallant now had his machine gun mounted on a manure heap, from which he continued to meet the enemy with burst after burst, while Sergeant Chapman's gun crew used up every round they had. Lieutenant Honan and Pfc. William T. Baxter each had a 60-mm mortar that they used single-handedly against the enemy, and Lt. Douglas L. Smith used an 81-mm mortar to drop a round on six SS men he spotted behind a haystack. Everyone in the village contributed to the curtain of fire.

The remains of SS Mountain Regiment 11 made their final desperate assault on Lampaden at 0900. Their assault guns pounded away, reducing several buildings to rubble and setting fire to the school before the regiment charged into the village. Lt. Charles M. Phillips had placed a Sherman with its 75-mm gun where the roads leading into the village from the east and southeast converged, positioning it so that it would form a roadblock if it were destroyed. The assault guns knocked this tank out with three rounds, but were unable to get past. Meanwhile, the enemy infantry had taken seven or eight buildings and were working their way toward the church in the middle of the village.

At this point Lieutenant Colonel Cloudt ordered his G-4, Lt. Warren C. Hubbard, to break out and explain to Regiment the seriousness of the position and to bring back some ammunition. Lieutenant Hubbard borrowed a half-track from the tank destroyers and set off with Pvt. Vernon D. Buskager as a volunteer driver along with four men from the battalion radio section. They came under machine-gun fire when they reached the top of the ridge near Height 500, but dashed past unscathed. At the next road junction they were struck by a panzerfaust, causing them to swerve off the road, so they continued cross-country until they reached the 1st/302nd's B Company near Steinbach.

The tide in Lampaden began to turn in favor of the defense as odd groups began clearing up with a vengeance. Private First Class Baxter encountered four Germans on his way to pick up more mortar ammunition. He killed one with his pistol and captured the other three. Sergeant Chapman had run out of 57-mm shells for his antitank gun, so he took a bazooka and started hunting the assault guns, knocking out four. Baxter then joined him with another bazooka and knocked out a fifth. Baxter then dashed into a burning building to help rescue two wounded comrades, and Sergeant Chapman organized an assault team to retake an enemy-occupied house. (Both were later awarded the Distinguished Service Cross.)

Meanwhile, Sergeant Kelly led a group of men who were clearing the buildings across the road from the church, while SSgt. George L. Brinkerhoff and Pfc. Louis A. Albert of the battalion S-3 section worked on the buildings east of the church. This attack cost the Germans thirty-five men killed and forty captured, plus five assault guns destroyed and two damaged.

Late that afternoon the Germans made another attempt at a prisoner exchange at Lampaden when Lieutenant Ramirez and a German sergeant appeared under a white flag. Again Lieutenant Colonel Cloudt refused; however, learning that there were now sixty-five American wounded held at Dreikopf Hill, he gave the Germans a supply of bandages, drugs, and blankets to take back. Although the German position remained under constant bombardment, fortunately the prisoner-of-war cage area had not been hit.[28]

DREIKOPF HILL—MARCH 7

During the night of March 6–7 the 356th Field Artillery Battalion continued to provide fire support for the 3rd and 2nd Battalions of the 302nd Infantry, despite the presence of German infantry on a ridge only fifteen hundred yards away. On the morning of March 7 the battalion also fired on the Dreikopf roadblock under direction of the forward artillery observer from the 919th Field Artillery Battalion with Lieutenant Colonel Miner's 1st/376th.[29]

Lieutenant Colonel Miner's 1st/376th launched their attack on the Dreikopf Hill position at daybreak, advancing south down Highway 268 with B Company's 2nd and 3rd Platoons on either side of the road, each supported by four Shermans. On the right Sergeant Nagy's 3rd Platoon moved slowly through the dense mist until it was struck by heavy machine-gun fire, the source of which the tankers could not see to retaliate. Then the German infantry closed in with panzerfausts, knocking out two of the tanks and damaging a third. The platoon, and its one remaining tank, was forced to withdraw to reorganize. The 2nd Platoon met a similar fate, losing two tanks to panzerfausts.

That night Lieutenant Colonel Miner was ordered to attack the German roadblock again the next morning, March 8. His new plan called for C Company to approach Height 507 from the west as A and B Companies attacked from the north. B Company of the 1st/302nd would prevent a breakout to the south.

Later in the morning, Maj. A. H. Middleton of the divisional artillery flew over Dreikopf Hill in a light liaison aircraft at less than five hundred feet. Returning for a second pass over the position, he was joined by an aircraft from the 195th Field Artillery Group, and both aircraft came under heavy fire. Major Middleton's aircraft received thirty-five hits and the observer in the second aircraft was killed, but both aircraft were able to return to base and land without crashing. Middleton estimated that Dreikopf Hill was being held by about four hundred enemy troops.

Lieutenant Land's B Company resumed their attack on Height 507 with the support of four Shermans that afternoon. The 2nd and 3rd Platoons were met by a tremendous volume of fire, and the Germans even used the turret of one of the damaged tanks to engage the Shermans. All four of the attacking American tanks were knocked out, and the infantrymen who reached the objective were too few in number to hold it. The attack had been beaten off even before the reserve platoon could be committed, and the survivors pulled back to their start position for the night.

The men of the 2nd/376th, which had been reorganized after their rout several days earlier, were brought up and their F Company placed under Lieutenant Colonel Miner's command, while G Company, followed by E Company, moved across country toward Obersehr, which they reached without encountering any opposition. At 1800, leaving E Company behind in Obersehr, G Company moved on to Lampaden, where they were to plug the gap in the 302nd Infantry's line in preparation for the divisional handover.

Lt. Harry W. McLaughlin's G Company took the road running west of Height 500 and found themselves under automatic fire before the tail of the column was even out of Obersehr. Lieutenant McLaughlin, who had been with the battalion for only nine days, was killed, along with three men of the 1st Platoon, and six were wounded. Lt. Marvin M. Kuers then took over the command and withdrew the company to Obersehr to reorganize, requesting a guide from Lampaden by radio. Pfc. Felix J. Grzyninski set off to report to G Company and led the company back over Height 500 without incident. Lieutenant Kuers then placed himself under the command of Lieutenant Colonel Cloudt, who ordered G Company to occupy the high ground north of the village, a move that was achieved soon after midnight.[30]

The situation for the 1st Battalion, SS Mountain Regiment 11, at the Dreikopf position was becoming critical by the evening of March 7. Despite having beaten back two strong attacks from the north, as well as some minor thrusts from the south and east, and from Height 507, the constant American artillery fire was wearing the German troops down. The battalion had been without food since the fifth, medical supplies were exhausted and casualties mounting, and ammunition was running out, for all supply routes were blocked by the Americans holding on to their villages. There was now imminent danger of being cut off.

Fortunately orders arrived that night for the evacuation of the position. All the captured American vehicles were immobilized, except the ambulance, and the walking wounded prepared for departure. Sergeant Boyette and several others feigned sickness and were left with the litter cases. Technician Fifth Grade Case and Private First Class Macon were allowed to stay behind to tend the wounded.

The Germans moved off at 0600 on March 8. The wounded numbered 73 in one column moving east and 143 in another column moving southeast. Sgt. Charles J. Mooney of Headquarters Company, 3rd/302nd, was one of the prisoners who accompanied them. He reported:

At about 0500 a Jerry woke all the non-wounded and told us to help carry the wounded. We filed out of our hole and went into the hole where the wounded were. We were told we would carry the wounded on stretchers about five kilometers to their aid station. We didn't like this and between Ferguson's glib tongue and my aches and pains we impressed the captain that we all had trenchfoot. So we got out of the carrying party. You no doubt found their wounded there.

Then this captain took his whole outfit, column of twos, and marched out at about 0600. He must have passed right between our lines. We passed between two towns in back of that outpost. A Jerry had a Schmeisser in each of our backs and demonstrated what he'd do if we yelled out. We could see GIs in Lampaden as we passed to the right of it. They took twelve of us non-wounded and left something like 49 wounded Americans. From then we just walked 301 miles to our final stop about 35 kilometers from Augsburg.[31]

At 0745 Sergeant Boyette saw two American riflemen coming over Height 495 toward the group of wounded Americans and Germans on Dreikopf Hill and shouted at them. They failed to recognize him and dropped to the ground to take up firing positions, but the two medics went forward waving a Red Cross flag and explained the situation. The artillery fire was then lifted. A two-and-a-half-ton truck immobilized by the Germans was quickly put into working order, and the wounded soldiers were loaded aboard it and the ambulance. The wounded men were then taken to the nearest aid station, which was in Lampaden. Lieutenant Colonel Cloudt then organized the evacuation of the wounded from Lampaden and Obersehr.

Tech-4 Joseph F. Gaynor reported: "There were many German wounded who insisted upon being carried out when a truck was backed up to evacuate them. They insisted they were unable to walk. So the medics, with a weary acceptance of the inevitable, carried them. The truck was well filled with Jerry casualties when it was bracketed with mortar fire. What followed came nearer to breaking our spirits than any of the thousand incidents of the previous 24 hours. Those poor, crippled, crying Jerries cleared the truck and found cover in faster time than it takes to tell about it . . . When the fire lifted, they walked to the truck."[32]

Lieutenant Colonel Miner's 1st/376th, along with F Company, 2nd/376th, attacked and then occupied Dreikopf Hill. B Company of the 1st/302nd patrolled the highway between Zerf and Pellingen and sent a reinforced platoon to secure Paschel.[33]

The following Unit Citation was prepared at divisional headquarters on October 5, 1945, but somehow went astray and was not made official until August 12, 1997:

Under the provision of Section IV, Circular 333, War Department, 22 December 1943, the following units are cited:

3d Battalion, 302d Infantry Regiment
3d Platoon, Antitank Company, 302d Infantry Regiment
3d Platoon, Cannon Company, 302d Infantry Regiment
1st Platoon, Company B, 774th Tank Destroyer Battalion
1st Platoon, Company B, 778th Tank Battalion

On 5 March 1945, after the assault crossing of the Saar River near Lampaden, a bridgehead five miles in depth was established. The German 82d Corps planned an all-out offensive to regain this vital ground, cut supply lines, and reestablish contact with troops believed to be occupying pillboxes south of Trier. On 6 March to 7 March 1945, these units, exhibiting unwavering fortitude and indomitable tenacity, successfully protected the division bridgehead in the face of over-whelming odds. Bearing the brunt of four fanatical assaults by the 11th SS Mountain Regiment (Reinhard Heydrich), supported by two assault-gun companies and two engineer companies which counter-attacked with relentless ferocity, they refused to give ground and, de-spite the savage onslaught, inflicted enormous losses on the enemy. When the sector was completely surrounded by an enemy envelop-ment and under continual shelling, although cut off from supplies and reinforcements, these gallant defenders remained in position and repelled all attacks by the numerically superior forces. Cooks, me-chanics and drivers abandoned their normal duties and fought tena-ciously as riflemen. Losses sustained were 116 officers and enlisted men killed, wounded and missing in action. The enemy lost over 500 killed, 170 captured and 7 assault guns destroyed. As a result of their tenacious stand and intrepid actions a severe enemy threat to the se-curity of the bridgehead was eliminated, thus permitting the marshal-ling of our forces on the east bank of the Saar, making possible the devastating drive to the Rhine River.[34]

13
The Race for the Rhine

The relief of the 94th Infantry Division by the 26th was about halfway complete when XX Corps intervened on March 8 with orders to stop. General Walker appeared at the joint divisional headquarters in Saarburg at 1245 the next day with fresh orders from General Patton calling for an all-out push to the Rhine. It was an undertaking in which the 94th would have to play a major part. With Trier secure, Patton was determined to get troops across the Rhine in what he saw as a race with Lt. Gen. Alexander M. Patch of the Seventh Army and Field Marshal Sir Bernard L. Montgomery, although troops of Lt. Gen. Courtney Hodges of the First Army had already seized the bridge at Remagen the day before and crossed over to the east bank.

After a considerable reshuffle of the troops on the ground, XX Corps was eventually lined up with the 94th Infantry Division on the left, Maj. Gen. Horace L. McBride's 80th in the center, and the 26th on the right. The XX Corps' plan of attack called for a push east to the Nahe River, where the corps would turn northeast up the river valley and head for Mainz-Kastel. On the left of the 94th Infantry, the 3rd Cavalry Group would cover the corps' northern flank. Right of the 94th Infantry, in a parallel move, the 80th Infantry would cover the advance's southern flank, while the 26th Infantry pushed south to roll up the Siegfried Line along the Saar River.[1] Within the 94th Infantry Division, the advance would be made with the 302nd Infantry on the left and the 301st on the right. These two regiments would pass through the 376th, who were holding the line and would then become the divisional reserve. The axis of both attacking regiments converged on Hermeskeil.

The attack was launched at 0300 on March 13 with a fifteen-minute preparation by thirty-one battalions of corps and divisional field artillery. The terrain was difficult, consisting of high, fir-covered hills with deep valleys and ravines, which the seriously depleted German units could defend only in isolated instances, and so often could easily be bypassed. The mopping up could be left for the reserve companies and battalions to do in daylight. By the third day the 302nd Infantry had moved to within three miles of Hermeskeil, and shortly after midnight General Walker ordered the 10th Armored Division to move off before daylight and pass through the 94th Infantry Division and head for the Nahe River, some twenty-five miles away.

When General Eisenhower visited Patton's headquarters in the late morning of March 16, Patton asked for more armor, and Eisenhower agreed to the release of the 12th Armored Division to augment XX Corps the next day. Hermeskeil, the 94th's primary objective, was taken that same morning. Now that the infantry had broken the crust of the German resistance in the hilly, densely wooded terrain of the Scharzwälder Hochwald, the 12th Armored Division pushed forward to take over the lead, heading eastward for the Kaiserslautern Gap, while farther south the 10th Armored Division headed for Kaiserslautern itself, taking the 301st Infantry along with it. The speed of the advance accelerated to a rapid pace, with the men of the 94th Infantry riding the tanks of the 10th and 12th Armored and any other vehicles at hand, getting off only to clear the points of opposition as they were encountered. The collapse of the German defense is demonstrated by the 94th's haul of prisoners on March 14, 15, and 16, which amounted to 344, 341, and more than 700 respectively. Thereafter the numbers of enemy soldiers who surrendered were between 3,000 and 3,500 a day.

The 301st Infantry was released by the 10th Armored on March 17, but because of a lack of transport they were stuck in Hermeskeil until March 19. After having cleared several areas of bypassed pockets of German troops, the regiment rejoined the 94th on March 22.

The sheer speed of the advance brought its own problems, including heavy congestion on the few roads. Every available vehicle was pressed into service to carry forward the infantry, thus creating a fuel crisis that was met by the quartermaster truck companies bringing fuel forward and returning

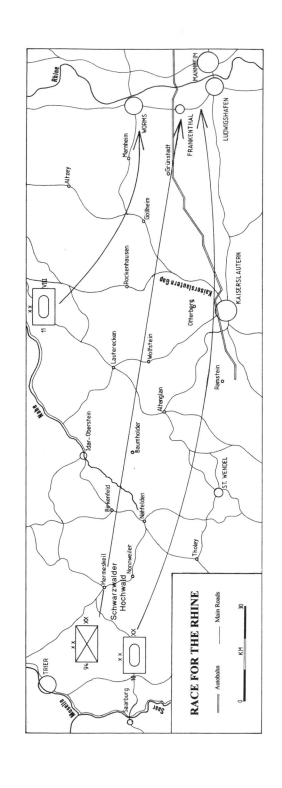

RACE FOR THE RHINE

——— Autobahn ——— Main Roads

0   KM   30

laden with prisoners. The artillery units found themselves without infantry protection and having to redeploy as often as four times a day. Fortunately there was little demand for their services, for the trucks of their ammunition trains were being used to carry infantry, having only the ammunition carried on their prime movers.

The remaining troops of General of Infantry Walther Hahn's LXXXII Corps were unable to check this advance, and as the Americans closed in on Kaiserslautern and the Kaiserslautern Gap, both General of Infantry Baptist Kniess's LXXXV Corps and SS Lt. Gen. (*Gruppenführer*) Max Simon's XIII SS Corps became in imminent danger of being cut off along the Saarbrücken front. The only possible line of retreat for these formations was through the dense Pfälzerwald (Pfalz Forest) farther to the south. The German First Army commander, General of Infantry Hermann Foertsch, ordered an immediate withdrawal. Everywhere the Germans were on the run, constantly harassed by the fighter-bombers of the XIIth Tactical Air Command, and obliged to move by both day and night as American forces converged on the area from the west and south. Authority for the German forces to withdraw across the Rhine did not arrive until March 23, but despite the chaotic circumstances and severe losses, they were still able to conduct a skillful withdrawal.

At a conference of his army commanders in Luxembourg City on March 19, General Bradley had told General Patton to take the Rhine on the run, which is exactly what Patton wanted. Patton had the necessary bridging equipment brought forward without delay, being desperate to cross before Field Marshal Montgomery's crossing scheduled for March 23. His aim was achieved when the 11th Infantry Regiment of the 5th Infantry Division crossed the Rhine at Nierstein and Oppenheim at about midnight on the twenty-second.

Elements of the 12th Armored Division approached the city of Ludwigshafen on March 20, expecting to be able to overrun it in the same way it had overrun the other towns and villages in its rapid advance from the Saar. But Ludwigshafen contained the main chemical plant of IG Farben Industries and was heavily protected by antiaircraft batteries of the 9th Flak Division, whose formidable 88-mm guns readily converted to the ground role. In addition, there were troops of several shattered divisions concentrated in the city with orders to defend it to the last man. Consequently, the taking of Ludwigshafen became the 94th Infantry Division's last major combat operation of the campaign. The battle involved the 301st and 376th Infantry Regiments with Combat Command A of the 12th Armored and took until the end of March 24 to complete.

During those last twelve days, March 12 to 24, the 94th Infantry Division had led XX Corps in an exhilarating advance of more than one hundred miles, taking more than two hundred towns and villages and capturing 13,434 German prisoners of war. General Patton acknowledged the contribution made by the division with a letter dated March 29, which read:

> My dear General Malony,
>
> Please accept for yourself and extend to your officers and men of your Command the sincere appreciation of all other members of the Third Army for the splendid work your Division has accomplished during its tour of duty with us.
>
> We appreciate what you have done, and we are sure that in your next assignment you will be equally successful.

At last the division had a chance of taking a short rest. The troops were trucked back to the German army training center at Baumholder, which they had captured a week earlier. Although equipment needed to be overhauled and all aspects of administration had to be attended to, the pressure was off and these tasks could be tackled at leisure. However, barely two days had passed before fresh orders arrived to move directly to the area of Krefeld for attachment to Maj. Gen. Ernest N. Harmon's XXII Corps of Gen. Leonard T. Gerow's Fifteenth Army.

While the majority of the division's men were moved in six railroad trainloads from Bouzonville, on the French border, to Willich, just five miles short of Krefeld, the motor transport was driven via Saarlautern to Thionville and then up through Luxembourg, across the littered battlefields of the Bulge and on via Liège and Aachen to Willich. Upon arrival in the Krefeld area, the 301st and 302nd deployed across the division's front along the Rhine, facing the Ruhr Pocket, while the 376th assumed an occupation role to their rear. On April 5 the troops were ordered to intensify patrolling activity along the division's front in order to relieve pressure on XVIII Airborne Corps, who were attacking the Ruhr Pocket from the north on the far side of the Rhine. Patrolling entailed having to traverse the wide distance across the Rhine to reach enemy-occupied territory, but as the Ruhr Pocket was gradually reduced by the encircling formations, this task eased off, and by April 16 the division soldiers found themselves switching from tactical to occupational duties.

On April 22 the division moved across the Rhine to take up occupational duties in the Düsseldorf area of the Ruhr District, which included the major industrial cities of Wuppertal and Leverkusen, setting up headquarters in the main offices of the Krupp Steel Works in Düsseldorf.

On May 7 news of the German capitulation reached the division, which held a victory parade in Düsseldorf on VE Day. General Malony issued the following proclamation:

WE HAVE SET A STANDARD

This is the day for which we trained and fought for two and a half years. What it has cost us, you only well know. That we have participated effectively in the days of combat which preceded this Day of Victory is a great satisfaction. We feel justly that we have pulled our share of the load.

Between February 19 and March 5 we breached the Siegfried Switch position and then, assisted by the 10th Armored Division, mopped up all resistance in the Saar-Moselle Triangle; successfully crossed the Saar River in the face of the main Siegfried Line; and established a Corps bridgehead after assisting in capturing Trier.

Between March 13 and March 24 we broke the enemy's lines east of the Saar and advanced to the Rhine; captured an untold booty in supplies and equipment; took over two hundred towns, including the key city of Ludwigshafen[;] and captured 14,434 prisoners of war.

This was the first evidence of the dissolution of the German Army west of the Rhine and came after seventy-four consecutive days of attack.

Until March 24 you have never been out of contact with the enemy more than five days since September 10.

This Division has never failed in a mission, nor has it ever permanently lost one inch of ground to the enemy; and whatever may be our next mission, we have set a standard which I ask each one of you to make it his personal business to meet.

Peace brought an opportunity for the men of the division to enjoy comfortable billets, and a rest area for them was opened in Aywaille, a resort in Belgium not far from Liège. Many of the men were able to obtain seven-day passes to visit England, and some even managed to get to the Riviera.

Then on June 10 the division moved again, this time to Czechoslovakia, where at noon on June 12 the division command post was opened at Susice, coming under General Patton's Third Army once more but still as part of XXII Corps. The division's new role was the maintenance of roadblocks along some forty miles of the Russian-American Control Zone separating the zones of occupation. This was later extended to include the area formerly occupied by the 26th Infantry Division to the south of the 94th's area and the Czech 1st Armored Corps' area to the north, and later on the 8th Armored Division's area even farther north. This increased the territory occupied by the division to a total of 3,600 square miles and the border control line to 190 miles.

Meanwhile, the strength of the division was being steadily reduced as men with high release points were transferred out before being returned to the United States for discharge. Replacements in the form of men with low release points did not make up the deficiencies, and the changes in personnel effectively saw the end of the 94th Infantry Division as such. Then, during the period January 29 to February 9, 1946, the division was officially inactivated at Camp Kilmer, New Jersey.

A report prepared by the division adjutant general on November 5, 1945, stated that in the 209 days of combat in which the division had been engaged, 1,087 officers and men had been killed in action; 45 had met non-battle deaths; 113 had been reported missing; 4,684 had been wounded or injured in action; and a further 5,028 had become casualties due to trench foot, frozen feet, and other causes. Since that date the number of deaths from all causes has been increased to 1,210.[2]

The division may have been inactivated, but its spirit lives on in the 94th Division Association, whose members still proudly cite their company and unit titles alongside their names.

Epilogue

The following is the text of an address given by the Rev. Charles H. Manning to the 94th Infantry Division Association at the 47th Annual Memorial Service held at Kansas City, Missouri, on August 31, 1996.

THE 94TH INFANTRY DIVISION

The Wind beneath the Wings of Victory

Few, if any, of us had any idea of the role that Almighty God had chosen for the 94th Infantry Division to play in World War II. The war was so big and so bad, and we were so small and naïve.

World War II was the only truly global war ever recorded in the history of mankind. God forbid there be another. Millions of people were—shot—hung—bombed—starved—gassed—frozen or drowned. It was a war in which the combatants found more ways to enslave—murder—annihilate and torture their victims than mankind has ever known. The world's first total war perfected the instruments of mass destruction and changed the nature of warfare—Dive Bombers—Stukas—Lightening Panzers—Spitfires—Thunderbolts—U-Boats—devastating B-29 Superfortresses and The Bomb that made the sun set twice in the land of the rising sun. Nazis turned humans into lampshades. Cities were vaporized. Europe became a continent levelled. North America, South America, Europe, Africa, Asia, and the Ocean Islands did not escape the role of "cause" and/or "effect" of the war. Air space was violated in both the Artic regions and the Antarctic regions alike. From [Monte] Cassino to the Coral Sea, heroes were willing to die for a cause greater than themselves. Ordinary human beings volunteered to drop behind enemy lines—attack unbeatable foes—present their bodies as a living sacrifice for suicide missions knowing that nine out of ten would never see another sunrise. Fifty million loved ones lost their lives in World War II—fifteen million were soldiers who, for one cause or another, offered up the supreme sacrifice of their lives; thirty-five million were made up of innocent men, women and children of all ages who were slaughtered for no good reason at all. Of the thirty-five million civilians slaughtered, twenty-nine million were Gentiles and six million were Jews. HOLOCAUST is not a big enough word to describe this global catastrophe in human history.

World War II was a world-wide conflagration, an evil fire that was burning out of control. Surrender was not an option. Annihilation of the satanic power in Berlin and Tokyo was the only solution left to end this ungodly slaughter of innocent lambs. The world had become a killing field. 911 calls in the form of prayer lit up the switchboard of heaven. A general alarm was sounded throughout the Allied World— one of the units dispatched to the scene in the heart of the conflagration was "Rescue 94," General Harry J. Malony, Chief.

The initial assignment sounded so very normal and logical. General Patton expressed it in this way when he wrote, "In order to use the 90th Division of the XX Corps to attack through the 26th Division and clean the Germans out of the pocket southeast of Bastogne, it was necessary (at least we were needed) to procure the service of the 94th Infantry Division. I proposed that when the 94th arrived, it would go to the XX Corps." In relationship to this gigantic, horrendous war, we were just another speck of sawdust on the sawmill floor. But keep your eyes on this little speck of sawdust on the sawmill floor. Listen up!

The God Who blesses America is capable of choosing to work through ideas that the world considers crazy and ridiculous. The God Who blesses America proves wrong those people that the world considers wise and great. The God Who blesses America is capable of using weak things to defeat the strong. The God Who blesses America is capable of doing things that make it impossible for a human being to explain away His miracles or to top His accomplishments. The God Who blesses America is capable of making a bunch of turkeys fly higher than eagles. Our memorial message starts here.

My mind goes back to New Year's Day, January 1, 1945. I was riding in the back of an open jeep in a nearly unbearable sleet and ice storm obeying orders which transferred the 94th Infantry Division from their defensive position in the Lorient-St. Nazaire sector to answer a 911 call for help to stop the German victories in the Battle of the Bulge. Unknown to any of us was the fact that either coincidence or divine providence had arranged a blind date for the 94th Infantry Division—a date with destiny!

On January 6, D-Day + 214, the 94th Infantry Division was assigned to General George S. Patton Jr.'s Third Army and General Walton H. Walker's XX Corps. On March 28, D-Day + 295, the 94th Infantry Division passed control of Ludwigshafen to the Seventh Army and was no longer assigned to General Walker's Third Army and no longer assigned to General Walker's XX Corps, but in that 81-day assignment, the 94th Infantry Division became the wind beneath the wings of victory west of the Rhine. Like a tide of the ocean, under control of an Almighty God Who chose to have them arrive at His own mysterious hour on His terms and by His grace, they took the initiative on January 6, 1945, and relinquished it on March 28, 1945. In 81 days military history had been made, in 81 days military tactics had been changed, and in 81 days World War II would never be the same. In General Patton's diary dated March 21, he wrote, "The operations in the Palatinate, namely the Rhine-Moselle Triangle[,] are practically completed and have been most successful, really a historic accomplishment. I really believe this operation is one of the outstanding operations in the history of war."

And you, soldiers of the 94th Infantry Division, were the wind beneath the wings of this victory in the Palatinate, otherwise known as the Rhine-Moselle Triangle.

Before the Third Army assignment, you were on the defensive at Lorient-St. Nazaire area of Brittany. You had 66,000 of Germany's finest trapped and out of business. After the Third Army assignment, you played the role of an occupation army. Just as no one knows a bird until he has seen it in flight—no one knows an infantry division until he has seen it in a fight. For 81 bone-chilling, foot-freezing, casualty-ridden, horrible days of combat at its worst, (1) you enabled Patton's Impossible Dream to become a reality; (2) you became the answer to a Jewish mother's prayers; (3) you proved those wrong who said it couldn't be done; (4) you proved that you loved America so much that you were willing to die for her if need be; (5) you proved that nothing is too hard for God; (6) and in the day-by-day fulfillment of your devoted efforts, you became the wind beneath the wings of victory in the Rhineland Campaign.

The weather was record-cold in the Saar-Moselle Triangle, but the vertical relationship of command was colder. Fighting a war that neither Washington nor SHAEF knew much about; in a stance of do or die; fighting what had been disguised and justified as live maneuvers; assigned to a mission impossible by a desperate General Patton who, because of fear of failure, acted as maniacal as a coach in a championship game, screamed at your imperfections; screamed about your frozen feet; screamed about your number of casualties; screamed about those who had no choice but to surrender. Not once did you hear a compliment from the lips of the general of all generals. Not once were you complimented when you had to go it alone to throw open the Siegfried Switch Line; not once were you complimented when you cleaned out the Saar-Moselle Triangle with only two days of help from the 10th Armored; not once were you complimented for your miraculous crossing of the Saar River; not once were you complimented for becoming king of Hocker Hill; not once were you complimented when you captured Trier, and by SHAEF's own admission, you did the work of four infantry divisions. Not once did the sunshine of success shine on the 94th Infantry Division while you were in the shadow of America's greatest general. Yet in spite of the trials and tribulations and in spite of the expectation to go beyond the limit of your endurance; and in spite of the deaths and wounds, somehow and in some way you were always satisfied to let the general shine, and to this day you say with pride, "I fought with Patton in World War II."

Everyone knows that General Patton was the one who received all the glory. History has ranked him among the world's greatest army commanders. American military analysts have named him the outstanding player, the star of the World War II war games[,] and placed him in the top spot in the Generals Hall of Fame. But hardly anyone knows the 94th Infantry Division was Patton's strength in the capture of the Saar-Moselle Triangle and the capture of Trier. Hardly anyone knows that you were the wind beneath his wings in his race to the Rhine.

(1) When I read that the 94th Infantry Division destroyed the Siegfried Switch Line and cleared the Saar-Moselle Triangle with only two days of help from the 10th Armored and that General Walter H. Walker received a citation from General Patton for the outstanding feat of war, I knew then that you were flying high because it was you, not General Walker, who accomplished this victory.

(2) When I read that the capture of Trier was the turning point of the war west of the Rhine and that the 94th Infantry Division and the 10th Armored Division had won this gold trophy, I knew that you were flying high.

(3) When Ed Alexander translated the German "All Points Bulletin" for me put out by Field Marshal Gerd von Runstedt, to stop the 94th Infantry Division at all cost or they would lose their defense west of the Rhine, I knew that you were flying high.

(4) When I read that Berlin Sally was broadcasting all over Europe and crying foul because of the success of "Roosevelt's Butchers" (the 94th Infantry Division), I knew that you were flying high.

(5) When I read that General Walker cited you for slicing and dicing through the remnants of eighteen German divisions on your way to being the first unit in the Third Army to reach the Rhine, I knew you were flying high.

(6) When I read that Reichsmarschall Hermann Goering said that the breakthrough of the 94th Infantry Division near Trier was one of the two great catastrophes to the German cause, I knew you were flying high. When I looked down the long hall of history and found no other single division had ever spearheaded two entire armies to a single destination, I knew you were flying high.

(7) When I read that Adolf Hitler found the 94th Infantry Division breakthrough the Siegfried Line near Trier totally and wholly incomprehensible, I knew you were flying high.

(8) When I saw a rescued Jewish prisoner of war hugging the leg of a G. I. with his whole body crying in total tears, I knew you were flying high.

Yes, I knew you were flying high, but I never knew just how high until I read some secret documents that I would like to share with you at this time.

[There followed nineteen recorded extracts from the 94th Infantry Division's telephone log covering conversations with XX Corps during the period January 18 to March 17, 1945. See appendix E.]

There is no doubt in my mind that you were the wind beneath General Patton's wings in the Rhineland Campaign, and there is no doubt in my mind that Almighty God was the wind beneath your wings in World War II.

When one looks down the long halls of history and explores the grand canyon of truth, one finds that beneath the wings of every high flyer is the wind of Almighty God: Abraham—Isaac—Jacob—Moses—David—Solomon—Peter—James—John—St. Augustine—St. Francis—Martin Luther—Peasants—Pilgrims—Patriots—Washington—Lincoln—Teddy Roosevelt—Wilson—Churchill—Franklin D. Roosevelt—they all knew that they became what they became and accomplished what they accomplished by the grace of Almighty God, they all knew that their Lord was the wind beneath their wings.

Upon realizing that the Third Army and its accomplishments had become the eighth wonder of the army world, General Patton wrote these words in his diary on March 23, 1945: "God be praised—I am very grateful to the Lord for the great blessings He has heaped on me and the Third Army, not only in the success which He has granted us, but in the weather which He is now providing."

(1) Doesn't it amaze you how that Almighty God took a speck of sawdust from the sawmill floor and blew it into the eye of the German War Machine resulting in a catastrophic event west of the Rhine? It should amaze you because you were the speck of sawdust on the sawmill floor.

(2) Doesn't it amaze you that Almighty God took one microscopic sperm and fertilized the egg of the Allied Cause and delivered a child named Victory? It should amaze you because you were that sperm.

(3) Doesn't it amaze you how that Almighty God took the stone that Patton rejected and used it for the chief cornerstone in his build-

ing of the great offensive west of the Rhine? It should amaze you because you were that stone.

(4) Doesn't it amaze you how Almighty God took a bunch of ordinary guys and caused them to become the wind beneath wings of victory in the Rhineland Campaign? It should amaze you because you were that bunch of ordinary guys.

The clock of time is wound once, but truth is eternal. Almighty God can bless one nation more than another and boldly make the statement, "Blessed is the nation whose God is the Lord." This statement should not amaze you because in January, February and March of 1945 you were that blessing to your nation. You were the wind beneath the Wings of Victory.

Appendix A
HQ 94th Infantry Division

HQ 94th INFANTRY DIVISION
Commanding General
Maj. Gen. Harry J. MALONY
ADC Capt. John C. GEHRING
ADC 1st Lt.

Asst. Div. Comd.	Div. Art Comd.
Brig. Gen. Harry	Brig. Gen. Louis J.
CHEADLE	FORTIER
ADC 1st Lt.	ADC 1st Lt.
ADC 2nd Lt.	ADC 2nd Lt.

Chief-of-Staff
Col. Earl C. BERGQUIST

General Staff

G-1 (Personnel)	G-2 (Intelligence)	G-3 (Operations)	G-4 (Logistics)
Lt. Col. William H.	Lt. Col. Robert	Lt. Col. Rollin B.	Lt. Col. John DF
PATTERSON	L. LOVE	DURBIN	PHILLIPS
	Asst. G-2	Asst. G-3	Asst. G-4
	Maj.	Capt. Samuel H.	Capt. John W.
		HAYS	SCHAUB (1)

Special Staff

Camp Comdt.	Surgeon	Engr.	Sig. Offr.
	Lt. Col.	Lt. Col. Noel H.	Lt. Col.
		ELLIS	
QM	Chaplain	Chem. Warfare Offr.	Ord. Offr.
Lt. Col. Paul G.	Lt. Col.	Lt. Col.	Lt. Col. Percival P.
KENDALL			WOOTERS

	Asst. Chaplain	A/CWO	
	Maj.	Maj.	
Finance Offr.	Judge Advocate	Special Service Offr.	Adjt. General
Lt. Col.	Lt. Col.	Maj.	Lt. Col.
A/FO	A/JA	A/SSO	A/AG
Capt.	Capt.	Capt.	Maj.
			Capt.
			1st Lt.
			1st Lt.

Military Police	94th Recce. Tp.	919th Air Sect.
Maj. John W. SCHAUB	Capt. Scott T. ASHTON	
1st Lt. Bertil T. ANDERSON		
301st Fd. Arty. Bn.	356th Fd. Arty. Bn.	390th Fd. Arty. Bn.
Lt. Col. Samuel L. MORROW	Lt. Col. Harold S. WHITELY	Lt. Col. Robert G. CRANDALL
919th Fd. Arty. Bn.	319th Med. Bn.	319th Engr. Bn.
Lt. Col. James M. CALVINESS	Lt. Col. Richard P. JOHNSON	Lt. Col. Keith BARNEY

Appendix B
301st Infantry Regiment

301st INFANTRY REGIMENT
Commanding Officer
Col. Roy N. HAGERTY
XO Lt. Col. Donald C. HARDIN (1)
G-3 Maj. George W. BRUMLEY (1)
G-3 Maj. Harold F. HOWARD (2)
Adjt. Capt.

1st Battalion	2nd Battalion	3rd Battalion
Lt. Col. George F. MILLER (1)	Lt. Col. Francis H. DOHS (1)	Lt. Col. William A. McNULTY (1)
Lt. Col. Donald C. HARDIN (2)	Maj. George W. BRUMLEY (2)	Maj. Gilbert N. O'NEIL (2)
Maj. Arthur W. HODGES (3)	XO Maj. William E. McBRIDE	XO Maj. Gilbert N. O'NEIL (1)
XO Maj. Arthur W. HODGES (1)	G-3 Capt. John FLANAGAN	XO Capt. FRIERSON (2)
XO Maj. William E. McBRIDE (2)		

A Coy	E Coy	I Coy
Capt. Charles B. COLGAN	Capt. Walter J. STOCKSTAD (1)	Capt. Charles W. DONOVAN
Lt. Robert H. WOLF	Lt. Edmund G. REUTER (2)	Lt. James T. FLOWER
Lt. Hamilton H. WALKER	Lt. John S. FISHER	

B Coy	F Coy	K Coy
Capt. Herman C. STRAUB (1)	Capt. Charles H. SINCLAIR (1)	Lt. David H. DEVONALD II (1)
Lt. Joseph E. CANCILLA (2)	Capt. Otto P. STEINEN (2)	Capt. William C. WARREN (2)

Capt. Harry C.
BOWDEN (3)
Lt. Richard E.
ECKSTROM
Capt. Arthur A.
SHOCKSNYDER

C Coy
Capt. Cleo B. SMITH (1)
Capt. DRENZEK (2)
Lt. Howard JOHNSON

Lt. Walter M. STEMPAK

G Coy

Lt. Richard H. MYERS
Lt. William S.
SOLLENBERGER
Lt. Arthur A.
CHRISTIANSEN
Lt. Leon P. JOHNSON

L Coy
Capt. FRIERSON (1)
Lt. Samuel T. MINICH (2)
Lt. Glenn H. GRASS

Lt. John R. FRABONI

Lt. HENLEY

D Coy
Capt. Gilbert S.
WOODRILL
Lt. Robert W.
JONSCHER

H Coy

Lt. Walter J. MULHALL
Jr.
Lt. SCHOFIELD
Lt. Dale REYNOLDS

Steinen Coy (F + G)
Capt. Otto P. STEINEN
Lt. Kenneth E. KEARNS

M Coy
Capt. Edmund P.
SNYDER

A/Tk Coy
Lt. James E. PRIOR

Appendix C
302nd Infantry Regiment

302nd INFANTRY REGIMENT
Commanding Officer
Col. Earle A. JOHNSON
XO Lt. Col. John W. GADDIS
LO Capt. Eugene B. WALSH
Chaplain Harrison

HQ Coy
Capt. James S. YOUNG
Lt. Joseph E. GLOVER
Lt. Joseph F CONCANNON

1st Battalion	2nd Battalion	3rd Battalion
Lt. Col. Silas W. HOSEA (1)	Lt. Col. Frank P. NORMAN (1)	Lt. Col. Otto B. CLOUDT Jr.
Maj. Warren F. STANION (2)	XO Maj. Harold V. MAIXNER (2)	XO Maj. Earl L. MYERS
Lt. Joseph F. CONCANNON	S-3 Capt. John FLANNIGAN	S-2 Lt. Harold C. NELSON
	XO Maj. Burgess G. HODGES	S-3 Capt. James E. COOK
		G-4 Lt. Warren C. HUBBARD

A Coy	E Coy	I Coy
Capt. Robert L. WOODBURN (1)	Capt. James W. BUTLER (1)	Capt. Allan R. WILLIAMS (1)
Capt. Jack P. HAGGART (2)	Lt. John D. ANDERSON (2)	Lt./Capt. Robert A. EDWARDS (2)
Lt. Samuel G. NORQUIST (3)	Lt. Harry J. LEWIES	Lt. William P. DOHERTY
Lt. Carl J. BAUMGAERTNER (2)	Lt. Oliver K. SMITH	Lt. John W. BYBEE

B Coy
Capt. Altus L.WOODS
Jr. (1)
Lt./Capt. Theo WANCIO

Lt. Edwin R. BLOOM

C Coy
Capt. Norbert C.
MAREK (1)
Lt. Mark HAMMER (2)
Lt. Carl D. RICHARDS
Lt. ROBINSON

D Coy
Lt. RIVES

F Coy
Capt. Herman KOPS Jr.

XO Lt. Maurice S.
DODGE
Lt. Joe D. ALVERADO
Lt. Herman W.
SIDEBOTTOM
Lt. Charles A. HUNTER
Lt. Charles P. DAVIS

G Coy
Capt. James W. GRIFFIN

XO Lt. Peter R. KELLY

H Coy
Capt. Orville M.
OWINGS
Lt. Robert E. GOBIN

Cannon Coy
Lt. Joseph K. HARDEN
Lt. Charles H. PAUSNER
Jr.

K Coy
Capt. William C.
WARREN (1)
Capt. Joseph BUGEL (2)

Lt. Carl W. SEEBY
Lt. Henry J. FINK

L Coy
Capt. John L. SMITH

Lt. Walter F. PIER
Lt. John R. TRAVERS
Lt. Anthony
CERBOSKAS

M Coy
Capt. Francis M. HURST

Lt. Douglas I. SMITH
Lt. William J. RAMIREZ

Appendix D
376th Infantry Regiment

376th INFANTRY REGIMENT
Commanding Officer
Col. Harold C. McCLUNE (1)
Lt. Col. Raynor E. ANDERSON (2)
XO Lt. Col. Raynor E. ANDERSON
Adjt. Capt. Fred BUCKEY
G-3 Maj. KELLEY
G-4 Maj. REDFERN
RLO 1/Lt. Jess L. LONG
MO Lt. Percy HEIDELBERGER

1st Battalion	2nd Battalion	3rd Battalion
Lt. Col. Russell C. MINER	Lt. Col. Olivius C. MARTIN (1)	Lt. Col. Benjamin E. THURSTON
XO Maj. ZIMMERMAN	Maj. John R. DOSSENBACH (2)	XO Maj. Sam ROPER
	Maj. KELLEY (3)	
G-3 Capt. Edwin BREHIO		Sigs. Offr. Lt. Joseph K. WILLIAMS
	XO Maj. John R. DOSSENBACH	Tpt. Offr. Lt. Frank MITTLE
		G-2 Lt. MALLARD
		G-3 Capt. DiROSA
		Chaplain Capt. STEINMEIER
A Coy	E Coy	I Coy
Capt. Carl J. SHETLER (1)	Capt. Simon D. DARRAH (1)	Capt. WATKINS (1)
Capt. Chester B. DADISMAN (2)	Lt. Arthur DODSON (2)	Lt. William R. JACQUES (2)
Lt./Capt. David F. STAFFORD (3)	Lt. MANESS (3)	Lt./Capt. Robert A. EDWARDS (3)
Lt. William P. SPRINGER (4)	Capt. STANDISH (4)	Lt. William M. GOLDENSWEIG

Lt. Erwin R. FLYNN
Lt. Tom HODGES
Lt. Richard L.
CREIGHTON
Lt. George L.
DUMVILLE

Lt. Gus E. WILKINS
Lt. Bernard F. SIMURO
Lt. Ernest N. DRYLAND

Lt. Raunal V. BURGMAY
Lt. Pablo ARENAZ
Lt. Raymond G. FOX

Lt. Dale E. BOWYER
Lt. Cecil G. DANSBY

B Coy
Capt. Edwin F.
DUCKWORTH (1)
Lt. James W.
CORNELIUS (2)
Capt. Henry C.
BOWDEN (3)
Lt. William G. LAND (4)
Lt. William BENDURE
Lt. George DESMARIS
Lt. Carl A. CROUSE

F Coy
Capt. George P.
WHITMAN (1)
Capt. Frederic D.
STANDISH III (2)
Capt. SCHUMACHER (3)

Lt. MANESS (4)
XO Lt. Robert HAWLEY
Lt. Thomas A. DALY
Lt. Wilfred WILSON
Lt. Gordon WESTON
Lt. Stanley MASON

K Coy
Capt. Julian M. WAY (1)

Lt. Thomas A. DALY (2)

Lt. FOSTER (3)

Capt. Ralph T. BROWN (4)
Lt. Dwight M. MORSE
Lt. KING

C Coy
Capt. William A.
BRIGHTMAN (1)
Lt. Ben R. CHALKLEY (2)

Capt. Frank MALINSKI (3)
Lt. PETERS

G Coy
Capt. John D. HEATH (1)

Lt. Harry W.
McLAUGHLIN (2)
XO Lt. Louis IACUESSA
Lt. Tom FAIRCHILD
Lt. JANULIS
Lt. Edward G. LITKA

L Coy
Lt. Jesse W. HODGES (1)

Lt. Anthony
DiLORENZO (2)
XO Lt. FOSTER
Lt. Joseph KLUTSCH
2nd Lt. Dale E. BOWER

D Coy
Lt. George L.
DUMVILLE
Lt. Claude W. BAKER

H Coy
Capt. Robert Q. SMITH

Lt. Robert C. PIERCE

M Coy
Capt. SIMCOX

Lt. WILLINGHAM
(A/Tk Pl)

Regimental Units

Mine Pl
Lt. MURPHY

A/Tk Pl
Lt. James E. PRIOR

A & P Pl
Lt. McMANUS

Appendix E
Selected Telephone
Conversations between
HQ XX Corps and
HQ 94th Infantry Division

1120 HRS, 18 JAN 45

Maj. Gen. Walton H. Walker: Just had a call a little while ago from "Georgie" [Patton]. He said, "I understand you are in full retreat." He was kidding, of course. You are going hard, aren't you?

Maj. Gen. Harry J. Malony: Hell, yes!

Walker: Has Snyder finally got there yet?

Malony: He is sitting beside me.

Walker: Told you about the 8th Armored? I don't think they will do a hell of a lot of good. Might be a psychological advantage.

Malony: They [the Germans] are still swinging away at me.

Walker: That's all right. As long as they do that, it's OK because it is drawing something away from [Bastogne]. He's going right ahead. Even if we weren't able to accomplish anything we can draw their fire and attention.

Malony: We have a hell of a lot of attention, I can assure you.

Walker: You don't like the reports that came in about two regiments?

Malony: I am now treating it as though it were two battalions.

Walker: However, I am sitting a hell of a way from there. It is easy for me to take a kind of smug attitude. Those people, "That ——— up there ought to see it."

Malony: That is what they say about me. Every time I go up there, they ask me for something. I am reshuffling a bit, and I am using one of those battalions that was thumbed down by you to back up a little area. The situation is not clear now.

Walker: All right, Harry. I just thought I would call you.

Malony: You tell Georgie he touched me on the raw. We aren't going any place.

Walker: Of course. He doesn't expect that. He got the report about the two regiments. I told him we weren't bothered. We got plenty to back up any attack, even if they bust through. I would like very much to be able as soon as we can to take a breathing spell to take that entire thing up too. It would be your job, but with some additional assistance—not assistance, but attachments from somewhere else.

Malony: We will need it. We can't do it by ourselves.

Walker: At least a combat command [armor].

Malony: Can you scrape me any more tank-destroyers?

Walker: I'm afraid not, not at the present moment.

2045 HRS, 18 JAN 45

Walker: This was a series of battalion, not-over-battalion fights. However, I authorize you to go on and as this fight was going on to reinforce.

Malony: You see, I now have a bridgehead through the line. I am trying to hang on to it. I don't know whether you would like it, with your other stuff you have got, or not. I can't go far.

Walker: I don't want you to go far, but I think you can hold on probably. We have the same thing at Saarlautern.

Malony: It is right in the middle of the damn line.

Walker: We have to go on what army wants to do. This thing as originally started was to peck off a little at a time; wherever we can improve or possess, hold on to it. On the other hand, if we have something where we have a weakness, we better improve it by pulling back. I would prefer that if you have got anything, to button up and hold it. However, at some times we will get out and see we have gotten something, but if it is, for instance, down so low[,] it will be sensible to pull down, in which case you use your own judgment to do that. I will have to have authority to go deeper in this thing from higher headquarters, and I don't think even Patton can give it. This is an aggressive offensive we are on.

Malony: Damn aggressive. Of course, I have got that bridgehead that I don't want to give up, and yet I would like to exploit it, and yet I can't without pushing, of course.

Walker: What do you think is in front of you?

Malony: I have got the 11th Panzer. I am quite certain it is there. We have had in the neighborhood of 20–25 tanks committed against us.

Walker: You think you have had that many?

Malony: We had an actual count of 18 at one time. Of those we have pretty well destroyed 9 and 5 half-tracks.

Walker: Well, your original plan, Harry, looked to me like it was damn good. You had another plan you were going to use later on after you had this one. If we can go on with that, that is the way to do it.

Malony: I got an opportunity for a little different plan, and I want to get pressure off that hell of a hot corner [Nenning, Berg, Wies]. What I was thinking of was exploiting what I gained, but I would have to push a damn sight harder and farther.

Walker: You are getting a combat command on the way up there now.

Malony: I have got that all right. If I use that, it means a considerable jump. What I am trying to find out now is, are you in shape to have us jump?

Walker: I would say no. You mean to take in that whole damn Triangle. I would say no, Harry. I have got to go on and make it local attacks until I can get clearance, and I will see tomorrow what I can do and maybe we can get some kind of clearance. I think perhaps we can take that thing.

Malony: These damn German tanks have been wandering all around the place, so it is true there is maneuver for battalions.

Walker: Maybe you can get our tanks through there.

Malony: I think I can. In fact, I am about to use a company for a local thing to take pressure off the hot corner.

Walker: All right, Harry. I will probably be up to see you in the morning.

Malony: I think I would like that a lot. When will you come?

Walker: I will see if the Boss [Patton] wants me. I have to talk to him, bring it to him.

Malony: I think I understand now.

Walker: If we get a clearance, we could throw a hole loose in there. We were given a defensive mission, and we are trying to keep them from getting us off balance. We have been pecking at them all the way along the line. I know how you feel.

Malony: You know that only half my show is dislocated. The other is right where it was. I would like to sock it like hell, and I can't do it with the limitations imposed on me with the forces I have.

Walker: You are now employing practically a regiment.

Malony: Yes, I am.

Walker: As a matter of fact, the original instruction was one battalion. So we have increased our bid three times, but I don't blame you. I think you did exactly right and I authorized you to do it, but I have to go higher to get someone to support me with authority if I go any deeper. I will see what I can do. These restrictions come from SHAEF. Even General Patton can't handle that. It's all coming from higher headquarters and past him.

Malony: I wish you would take a damn good look at the situation and see what you can utilize. I feel we have exploited what we have already and are over the hill.

Walker: I will see what I can do and will try to get to see you tomorrow.

Malony: All right. Thank you very much.

1215 HRS, 8 FEB 45

Walker: Harry, if you still had Johnny Devine's outfit [Maj. Gen. John M. Devine's General Officer Commanding 8th Armored Division), would you be able to use it up there?

Malony: Yes.

Walker: Could you get it broken out?

Malony: It depends upon the action going on right now. Assuming that we are going to stick to it, the answer is yes.

Walker: Did you get the counterattack?

Malony: Yes, by both infantry and tanks. The pillboxes are now surrounded by tanks and infantry. Our men are trying to hit them, but no hits so far.

Walker: How about your artillery?

Malony: They are working now.

Walker: Well, I have nothing to go on, but I want to know if you can use it before I go ahead. I am going up after lunch and ask for it, tell him that I can use it.

Malony: Good luck to you.

0955 HRS, 13 FEB 45

Walker: Are you going out of business up there?

Malony: No.

Walker: What's the matter?

Malony: I am cooking up another one.

Walker: There hasn't been anything happening in about three days now.

Malony: We pulled in a bunch of prisoners yesterday.

Walker: Everyone came across the line and surrendered. Don't take credit for that!

Malony: It was as a result of our operations for the preceding day.

Walker: Day before that you were relieving. That was a relief, being made properly, but you got a new outfit in there now. It seems to me you are losing time. This other new outfit is pretty badly bloodied up. With the 11th either going out, or already out, the other outfit in there is being tied to pieces. Now is a damn good time to smack them. You got the 376th in there. It seems to me you should go forward with the least possible delay.

Malony: I have got another scheme cooking here, and it is under way now. One battalion of that outfit you named was pretty badly torn up.

Walker: Don't halt too damn long, that's the point!

Malony: We are not stopping. We are moving along, but it takes time to brief this new outfit. In the meantime I am getting an old one together.

Walker: You've got the Rangers holding about half your front, and the rest of the people are not doing anything!

Malony: That is the outfit I am getting ready.

Walker: Take just as little time to get set as you can and hit these people while they are a little off balance.

Malony: I got a scheme that I think is going to cook, and as I said, it will take about three days to get briefed.

Walker: You mean you don't want to do a damn thing for three days!

Malony: We are going to do something, but it requires a bit of rehabilitation on the part of the outfit that came out.

Walker: I know that. The outfit that came out, there is no question on that. It should be in reserve, and your new replacements go into it, just like you did with the one before that you got now, but that has nothing to do with the present outfit you got in. I don't want you to go off half-cocked, but I don't want too much of a delay.

Malony: I will pull it as soon as I can properly prepare it.

Walker: All right, don't lose any more time than you can help it!

2205 HRS, 15 FEB 45

Malony: I would like to ask you for the attachment of the 778th Battalion that is down there working with the 26th and whose liaison officer has been here.

Walker: I don't know just exactly what you are talking about.

Malony: You gave me a change in objective today and I want to use it in the general effort. It is the 778th.

Walker: You mean the tank outfit?

Malony: Yes, the heavy rollers.

Walker: All right, shoot the works, Harry.

Malony: Have you time for me to tell you a little information? I will have to use [Col. Roy N.] Hagerty again. He has just been out three days. His is the 301st. Actually, I have been splitting replacements between him and [Col. Harold C.] McClune; they are about equally down. I am shy of about 600 men. Particularly, I am shy of platoon leaders, about 90 of them. My proportion of new men is about 70 percent. I want you to know our status.

Walker: I do, and I know that your outfit is shot pretty badly.

Malony: Well, I just wanted you to know.

Walker: I do know, Harry, I watch it and check on it all the time. I can tell you right now that we will forget this question of being—I am searching for a word—from now on we are fighting, and I don't think there is any point of being a little slow in getting forward. I want, well, from now on, let's shoot!

Malony: I am trying to do this for you just as hard as God will let me. I just wanted to let you know the situation.

Walker: From now on there is no question about defense. From now on we will go forward, there will only be attacks.

Malony: I have had casualties, about 4,000 now, and my battle casualties are about 2,200. As to the time, I have some reinforcements that are due in tomorrow morning, about 175 of them, and I will have to use them.

Walker: Not immediately, are you?

Malony: I will have to.

Walker: Why?

Malony: Because I am so damn short of riflemen.

Walker: What are your plans for tomorrow?

Malony: We are continuing the action. That will go on until we get into the bigger action. From now on everything will be engaged. I mean everything. As a matter of fact, I had a counterattack last night. Four tanks and unknown infantry. The report so far, which has not been confirmed, is that we got two of the tanks.

Walker: I got some reports tonight that the Rangers got almost to Oberleuken.

Malony: I don't think they have even crossed the roads yet.

Walker: I got the report from you that they had been across the road and through those woods all up there.

Malony: We have been through the woods before, but they have not been across any road unless I don't know about it.

Walker: You should know about it. I got the report from some of your people that the Rangers had gone forward[,] and I wondered why the whole outfit can't go forward. I don't know, I got that somewhere here tonight and it just looked to me like everything should go forward if they could.

Malony: All right. I have told you everything I started out to tell you. I wanted you to know the state of the division.

Walker: All right, I know that. Just keep on pushing. There is nobody on the other side of you that is half as good as you are.

Malony: I think that is true. The only thing is that I am not getting better with these new men; I am just getting worse. I don't want to ruin the new men.

Walker: I know, but now shoot just as fast as you can, and in the next few days I will talk to Georgie and see what we can do about putting you somewhere else.

Malony: I figure we could do this within the next two or three days.

Walker: Now! Not within the next two or three days! Are you going to do it tomorrow?

Malony: I can't put it on tomorrow for the reason I have not got Hagerty ready to go. I think it will be the day after tomorrow.

Walker: Are you continuing tonight and tomorrow what you have been doing?

Malony: Yes, we are, and with a full lay-out, but this big show can't go quite that fast.

Walker: But tonight and tomorrow you are continuing?

Malony: Oh, yes. The action is going on right now and will continue. The action is going on and with no let up. I am doing my goddamndest, I assure you.

Walker: I know that, Harry, and—well, I want you to know that I know it. I am as mean as hell, I know that, but—well, I want you to know I love you and I know you'll do your damndest.

Malony: You can count on me for that. You know me and you know I've been in this game too long for anything else.

Walker: Sometimes I am as nasty as hell and I start shoving things around, but it's because I want to get out there and get these things done. You've done wonderfully well and I want you to know that. Every once in a while I get damned mad, but I want you to know you have done damned well.

Malony: I want my troops to hear something like that.

Walker: I know and I'm going to write them a damned good letter, but I want them to get out there and do something so I can write about it.

Malony: It will help, because now they think they're only getting a kick in the ribs.

Walker: I know, but go ahead and do your damndest!

Malony: I will push this off just as soon as I can with any degree of decency.

0915 HRS, 16 FEB

Brig. Gen. William A. Collier: How are things going this morning?

Malony: Not worth a damn.

Collier: You weren't able to hold on to that place?

Malony: We got kicked out during the night.

Collier: Going back in the morning?

Malony: We don't want to go back in there now. That is the strongest point in the Siegfried Line and is heavily garrisoned now. I would rather make no more of these piecemeal attacks.

Collier: The general was hoping you would be able to slap them right back out of there again.

Malony: Well, I know, but as you know, that is the strongest section they [have] got, and I think it is too localized, so that it brings every one of their defenses to bear on every effort we might make there right now;

and the forces I've got to use are not sufficient now, that is, to carry out my general plan. I would rather make that as part of a big show.

Collier: That will come off very shortly, will it?

Maloney: Just as fast as we can get our troops set.

Collier: The general wanted me to call you up and see what you are doing.

Malony: I will tell you, Collier. I have been estimating that this morning very carefully. I think we would have a better chance of doing a push to make it all at once. That was the heaviest counterattack we have had in a helluva long time. I had about 8 tanks in it; we knocked out 5, which are still there in the field. I presume they are knocked out, but there are still 5 there.

Collier: The general wanted me to find out. He said to call you up and see what you intended to do about that; whether you were going back. All right, I will tell him. He is not here right now.

1818 HRS 16 FEB 45

Walker: I understand you wanted to get me today; I am sorry I was not around.

Malony: Yes, I wanted to discuss this plan with you.

Walker: Have you got another one?

Malony: I have got the big show.

Walker: By changing what you planned to do?

Malony: No, the plan is essentially the same, but it uses the whole works. I want to set this, but I don't want to tell you the time over the phone.

Walker: No, I don't want you to. Is it a reasonable time?

Malony: I think so, but I want to set it right.

Walker: That's it; there's no use having it unless it is set right. I don't want that; there's nothing to this business of going off half-cocked. On the other hand, I don't want people to look for excuses for delay.

Malony: I hope that's not what I am doing.

Walker: That's one thing I do have trouble [with]. I'm not pointing the finger of scorn at you, but it is the same thing all the way along. But goddamn it, it's that "just another day, just another day" all the time, and the big boys want to know why in the goddamned hell we're not doing something.

Malony: I know that, and I think I am doing it correctly.

Walker: All right, Harry, I'll take the rap on not doing anything in order that you might make the proper plans and get properly set.

Malony: Here's another thing that bothers me. We knocked off a lot of those Hun tanks today. They got stuck in the mud and couldn't get away.

Walker: How have you actually got them? Have you burned them?

Malony: We burned 6. Of 8 we worked over, I think 2 were self-propelled guns. We burned 6 but the other two must have been out of gas. We couldn't burn them.

Walker: But your artillery hit them and you battered them badly?

Malony: Yes, but the thing that bothers me is the terrain.

Walker: Bill [Maj. Gen. William H. H. Morris Jr., General Officer Commanding 10th Armored Division] told me about that in his conversation with you today. I guess you'll have to wait for that other stuff.

Malony: With this weather, I think a few more days will do it. I want to take advantage of what mobility there is.

Walker: I'm going up to see the Boss in the morning, and I'll talk to him and then I'll be down to see you in the afternoon. The other people are making good progress in the north and they are going to descend on us like a whirlpool if we don't clean this up.

Malony: I think it is possible, if you have the stuff you say you have.

Walker: I'll be down tomorrow afternoon, but don't wait there for me. If you are going out, just let some guide know where you'll be and they can take me to you.

1900, 19 FEB 45

Walker: Hello, Harry, how are you coming?

Malony: All right, thank you.

Walker: You did a fine job today, fellow.

Malony: Thank you very much.

Walker: Tomorrow I hope to end this thing.

Malony: Good.

Walker: And I believe we can do it. Have you got any indications at all of a strong counterattack?

Malony: Not yet.

Walker: I have been expecting it all day. Really not a strong one, but at least something. You have not had any sign of one, have you?

Malony: No, nothing that you could call a counterattack.

Walker: Bill Morris has come in now and taken over part of the zone, has he?

Malony: Yes, he has.

Walker: Those people of yours will revert to you when they pass through you.

Malony: Except for an RCT [Regimental-sized Combined Arms Team]. Here's something that bothers me. I got an order on that TD [tank destroyer] stuff, of which we have only a battalion, less a company, and I need it a damn sight worse than he does.

Walker: You mean that belongs to the RCT?

Malony: Yes, all attachments according to the order put out by your 3 go with the RCT, and that is going to take the very little I have away from me. I have one tank company and a company of TDs.

Walker: You want the tanks and TDs?

Malony: I sure do.

Walker: All right, Harry, take them.

Malony: Good, I have some very heavy objectives.

Walker: That is a big job you have ahead of you. It is not a bad job, except for the terrain. I don't think the enemy is going to give you much trouble. I think that you can go down to Orscholz from the north and clear that out. As a matter of fact, I think they are going to fold. You are behind them, aren't you?

Malony: Not right there.

Walker: Aren't you across the road? Have they got a road running west of the ravine in the stream line that breaks the triangle in two?

Malony: They can get by?

Walker: Anyway, I think their position is damn precarious, and I know damn well they are not going to give you much trouble as far as fighting is concerned. Harry, let me impress you. Steel your heart and force your people forward to get this goddamned thing finished. Then they can belly up against the Saar and spend the rest of the spring in a very pleasant position. I will tell you, I will get hold of Bill Morris as soon as I can and tell him about the tanks and TDs. That is all I am going to take away from them. The artillery I want to be with them. When we speak of a balanced RCT, we forgot about these little things. Bill said, "Am I going to have the artillery?" I said, "Yes, you are going to have the RCT intact." That meant to them I meant it, and I didn't mean exactly that. He doesn't need them and you do. I will get in touch with him and tell him they will revert at the time the other people revert. If I have any trouble getting him, you might call him and tell him I authorized you to say that to him.

Malony: I think he is holding a meeting now above with that RCT.

Walker: Good luck to you, Harry. It has been a fine show, and it has been just unusually good.

Malony: I think the division performed damn well all the way around.

Walker: That's fine, and I congratulate you and I will congratulate them. I will tell them so officially just as soon as I can get a breath.

Malony: That's fine. They will appreciate it.

1940 HRS, 21 FEB 45

Walker: What is the situation? Are they up against the stream?

Malony: Yes.

Walker: What I wanted to say to you was we got an opportunity of a lifetime here. I realize that I am kind of falling back on you. I am still pushing, but I talked to the Boss, and this next little initial business is very important and, as I said, it is an opportunity of an entire lifetime for you and for us and the entire army. So give it the works!

Malony: All right. I need some stuff from you, and I haven't got it yet.

Walker: I know what you mean. We will do our best to get it to you as quickly as we can.

Malony: I've got to have it!

Walker: All right, Harry, I understand.

2055 HRS, 21 FEB 45

Walker: George is coming into the area tomorrow. I am going to meet him where they are putting a bridge in, 1:15. I don't know where he is going or anything else. You might have a guide over there to take us wherever he wants to go but, Christ, keep going!

Malony: That is all we have been doing since I can remember.

Walker: Good for you! Goddamn you, you are a nice Irishman!

Malony: There isn't any use of my shedding any tears, but this is goddamn sudden.

Walker: I know it, but it is worth it, almost like Cumberland. Harry, it is an opportunity of a lifetime. If it don't work, I am not going to blame you, because you carried out the most wonderful masterpiece, and the Boss appreciates it, and I do too. Now if we can get going a little further, it will be that much better.

Malony: We will need a helluva lot of luck.

Walker: We have had luck. We always had luck. That is Johnny Walker luck. That is known throughout the army. I wouldn't be a corps commander if I didn't have it. I think it is going through. Whether or not it goes, it is a masterpiece so far, and just go on and SPEED and POWER! Goddamn, push them! As long as you got one man left, tell them, goddamn it, this means busting the whole damn line west of the Rhine! I believe it does, and I believe the Boss thinks that[,] and that is why the Boss changed and made me do something. I promised you would spend spring on this side of the Saar, didn't I? On the other side of the Saar now!

Malony: I think, on the other side of the Styx!

Walker: All right, Harry, go on. Goddamn it, you are a big Irishman!

Malony: I expect to get shot by 3 regimental commanders.

Walker: The hell with them! Tell them that the battalion commanders will shoot them! I think, Harry, it is going through. I don't think there is any doubt of it; otherwise I wouldn't agree to it, and I have agreed to it because, goddamn it, those sons of bitches are battered to hell. You did it and you battered them, and I think you can go right on through.

Malony: For God's sake, get that 3 of yours to give us the stuff we need.

Walker: We are doing our damndest. We are doing this on a shoestring. I will tell you what George told me. He said, "Johnny, you have done a wonderful job." The way he said it, he means you and the other fellow, but he said "and you done it without a goddamn bit of cooperation or support from anybody." That is pretty good coming from that fellow. That is what he said. You can tell your people that; that means something.

Malony: I've got to have something; I can't walk!

Walker: All right. We will do our damndest and when the time comes we will quit and we will throw up our hands! Go forward with everything you've got, and speed and power, and don't let anybody quit! That is all, don't let anybody quit on it!

Malony: If I can just get my rollers, I will like it like hell!

Walker: I know what you need and I am doing everything I can to give you everything I can get.

Malony: I am going to see Bill and see if I can't make a dicker.

Walker: He has first priority. All right, Harry, I am betting on you. Go to it! Goddamn it, you've got an opportunity in your hands to be one of two people that are going to win the war!

Malony: You've got a damn poor bet, Johnny, in my opinion.

Walker: I don't think so. I am betting on my luck. I have had such wonderful people doing the work for me that I am just betting on my luck.

Malony: At the moment, I don't feel so good.

Walker: Yesterday you were just wonderful; today you're down, but tomorrow you'll be right on top of the world. You are just another Irishman!

Malony: There is something in that.

Walker: Fine work, Harry! You've done a goddamn fine job. If you never did anything else in your life, you can still throw your shoulders back and say, "We took the Saar Triangle." I will see you tomorrow.

Malony: By the way, old Bill never lost a feather.

Walker: Yes, they have had a few people mashed up a little, but Christ in the foothills, he had one of the prettiest propositions I have ever seen. It looked like the trip we had across France, and you did it; there is no question about that. I am going to tell you about it later.

Malony: There is just one thing about this Siegfried Line. . . .

Walker: I don't think there is anything in it.

Malony: I hope to God, you're right!

Walker: If there's anything in it, you can't do what I want you to do—but, goddamn it, do your best!

Malony: You can count on that!

2105 HRS, 23 FEB 45

Collier: I want to tell just what the corps commander has in mind for this operation. I will have to talk pretty plain to you; nothing personal in this. The general is pretty goddamn disappointed in the day's operation. The entire corps and army effort is about to be jeopardized. There is not a goddamn thing out there in that line there except what small stuff there is. He wants you to bypass the small stuff and leave it, and get to your objective. He says that he wants the objective obtained if the Div Commander has to go out and lead it himself in person. If not, he will come up and lead it in person!

Col. Earl C. Bergquist: Is that all, sir?

Collier: We have got varying reports back here about how precarious your people are. You have got to be supplied by air; you have got to get this and that. The general wants you to select the place where you can get that bridge and get the heavy stuff over it.

Bergquist: That is exactly what we are doing. We're not in a precarious position. We are using every means we have at our hand.

Collier: Your supply people are yelling that you got to be supplied by air [3rd/376th]. That is poppycock. If we had to do that from Normandy, we never would have crossed the Seine River.

Bergquist: That shows they are trying every means. That is not holding up the operation at all.

Collier: Those boys doing that support job [the Rangers], they got away with it, didn't they?

Bergquist: Yes, sir.

Collier: What time do you estimate they will be at that place?

Bergquist: I don't think they will be at that place until midnight.

Collier: About midnight you ought to be on that place.

Bergquist: From experience, and I have been out there myself, I know you can't walk over that ground in that time.

Collier: We won't split hairs on an hour or so, but I think by midnight they ought to be pretty well up there.

Bergquist: I hope they are, and I think they will be.

Collier: You getting anything in the way of heavy stuff?

Bergquist: We are getting heavy artillery fire on the bridge site.

Collier: Why don't you move the bridge site?

Bergquist: That is exactly what we have been trying to do. It let up, and we have ordered the bridge in, regardless of fire.

Collier: We built bridges and had them shot from underneath us, and put them in again.

Bergquist: That is exactly what we are doing.

Collier: We would never have gotten across the last big river if we had waited.

Bergquist: We are not waiting at all.

Collier: Get your heavy stuff over and get them out to that line!

Bergquist: That is what we are doing!

Collier: As I said, I have been directed to give you this message and it came right from the top. My boss is prepared to come up there and take command in person.

Bergquist: I will impart that to my boss.

2055 HRS, 17 MAR 45

Malony: Your corps artillery liaison officer has brought in a XII Corps no-fire line, and I expect to reach it some time tomorrow with any luck. It ought to be lifted, because it will stop me sometime tomorrow, I think, and also Red Allen's outfit [12th Armored Division].

Walker: All right, Harry, I will take care of that right away. How are you coming?

Malony: Going swell right now.

Walker: Goddamn, I sure like to hear those words. You can wear your flag from now on. Trench foot and frostbite—goddamn, you have gone like a house on fire!

Malony: What did you expect? Hell's bells, if you don't do something about it, I won't be able to talk to you any more!

Walker: I will be at your old home [Freudenburg] tomorrow. We are moving up there tomorrow morning.

Malony: Come up and see us.

Walker: Harry, you are doing wonderful work! I will kiss you when I see you! I will see you maybe tomorrow; maybe the day after tomorrow. Keep going, fellow, goddamn it!

Notes

CHAPTER 1

1. Lt. Lawrence G. Byrnes, *History of the 94th Infantry Division in World War II* [hereafter referred to as *History*], 81–83; Nathan N. Prefer, *Patton's Ghost Corps*, 24.

2. Shelby L. Stanton, *Order of Battle: U.S. Army World War II*, Chart 2.

3. Byrnes, *History*, 1–8; Prefer, *Patton's Ghost Corps*, 19–23.

4. Byrnes, *History*, 53–55.

5. It was long believed by the men of the 66th that they had been saved from the more arduous conditions at the Battle of the Bulge because of this disaster, but the 94th had been advised of the handover on December 21. Maj. Gen. Hermann F. Kramer, the commanding general of the 66th, and his advance party of several officers visited the 94th headquarters in Brittany to plan the relief before the disaster took place. Byrnes also inaccurately attributes the handover to the disaster. (From a letter by Bob Trefzger [C376] in the spring 1997 edition of *The 94 Attack*, the division association magazine.)

6. Byrnes, *History*, 71.

7. Ibid., 1–76; George Forty, *The U.S. Army Handbook 1939–1945*, 65–67; Prefer, *Patton's Ghost Corps*, 18–23.

8. Prefer, *Patton's Ghost Corps*, 37.

9. Ibid., 13–14, 17, 19.

10. Dieter-Robert Bettinger, Hans-Josef Hansen, and Daniel Lois, *Der Westwall von Kleve bis Basel: Auf den Spuren deutscher Geschichte*, 18.

11. Neil Short, *Hitler's Siegfried Line*, 7–42, 112–14; see also Jorg Fuhrmeister, *Der Westwall: Geschichte und Gegenwart*, Dieter Bettinger and Martin Büren, *Der Westwall: Die Geschichte der deutschen Westbefestigung im Dritten Reich*, and Bettinger, Hansen, and Lois, *Der Westwall von Kleve bis Basel*.

12. *Merzig-Waderner Geschichtshefte* 1/2000: 31.

13. Prefer, *Patton's Ghost Corps,* 29.

14. In *Patton's Ghost Corps* Prefer gives November 20 as the date of the first attack (29–35), but Lester M. Nichols in *IMPACT—The Battle Story of the 10th Armored Division,* 40, gives November 21.

15. Prefer, *Patton's Ghost Corps,* 34.

16. Ibid., 30–35.

17. Ibid., 29.

CHAPTER 2

1. Byrnes, *History,* 84; Prefer, *Patton's Ghost Corps,* 37.

2. Robert K. Adair, *Letters Home from the Second Platoon, I Company, 376th Infantry, WW II, Europe,* 112–13.

3. Prefer, *Patton's Ghost Corps,* 28–29.

4. Byrnes, *History,* 86; Charles B. MacDonald, *The Last Offensive (The European Theater of Operations, United States Army in World War II),* 118; Prefer, *Patton's Ghost Corps,* 37–41; *Merzig-Waderner Geschichtshefte* 1/2000: 38.

5. Byrnes, *History,* 84; MacDonald, *Last Offensive,* 117; Prefer, *Patton's Ghost Corps,* 28.

6. Byrnes, *History,* 88–89; Prefer, *Patton's Ghost Corps,* 39.

7. Byrnes, *History,* 87; Prefer, *Patton's Ghost Corps,* 38.

8. Byrnes, *History,* 91–92; Prefer, *Patton's Ghost Corps,* 41.

9. Byrnes, *History,* 93–94; MacDonald, *Last Offensive,* 118–19; Prefer, *Patton's Ghost Corps,* 41–42.

10. George F. Nafziger, *The German Order of Battle,* Vol. 2, *Infantry in World War II,* 87.

11. Anton J. Donnhauser and Werner Drews, *Der Weg der 11. Panzer-Division, 1939–1945,* 174–75.

12. Byrnes, *History,* 97–98.

13. Robert Trefzger's letters to the author.

14. Byrnes, *History,* 98.

15. Ibid., 99–102; Prefer, *Patton's Ghost Corps,* 43–46; Lt. Col. Benjamin E. Thurston, *Ugly Duckling: 3rd Battalion, 376th Infantry Regiment, WW II, Europe,* 172–78.

16. Byrnes, *History,* 103–04; Prefer, *Patton's Ghost Corps,* 46; Thurston, *Ugly Duckling,* 186–87.

17. Byrnes, *History,* 104; Prefer, *Patton's Ghost Corps,* 47.

18. Byrnes, *History,* 104–05, 117; Prefer, *Patton's Ghost Corps,* 47.

19. Byrnes, *History,* 105; Prefer, *Patton's Ghost Corps,* 46.

20. Byrnes, *History,* 108; Prefer, *Patton's Ghost Corps,* 47.

21. Nafziger, *German Order of Battle,* 246; Prefer, *Patton's Ghost Corps,* 48, 127; Thurston, *Ugly Duckling,* 179.

22. Byrnes, *History*, 107–09; Prefer, *Patton's Ghost Corps*, 47–48.

23. Byrnes, *History*, 109–11; Prefer, *Patton's Ghost Corps*, 48.

24. Lt. Col. George P. Whitman, *Memoirs of a Rifle Company Commander in Patton's Third U.S. Army*, 29–31. In his account, Whitman says that Lieutenant Hawley lost his way guiding F Company *to* Perl, but this does not tie in with the company being able to attack from Wochern at 0700 the next morning, so it must have been *from* Perl, as I have written.

25. Allen Howenstine, quoted in Robin Neillands, *The Conquest of the Reich: D-Day to VE-Day, A Soldier's History*, 76–77.

26. Byrnes, *History*, 111; Prefer, *Patton's Ghost Corps*, 48.

27. A satchel charge is a prepackaged explosive in a carrying bag.

28. Byrnes, *History*, 117, 119.

29. Ibid., 119.

30. Ibid., 117–19; Prefer, *Patton's Ghost Corps*, 51–52.

31. Byrnes, *History*, 120; Prefer, *Patton's Ghost Corps*, 50.

32. Pfc. Richard J. Kamins, quoted in Byrnes, *History*, 124–25.

33. Ibid., 127.

34. Byrnes, *History*, 121–25; Prefer, *Patton's Ghost Corps*, 52–55.

35. Byrnes, *History*, 125–30; Prefer, *Patton's Ghost Corps*, 55–56.

36. Byrnes, *History*, 511.

37. Ibid., 113; Thurston, *Ugly Duckling*, 187–88.

38. Byrnes, *History*, 111–13: Prefer, *Patton's Ghost Corps*, 50–51.

39. Byrnes, *History*, 113–15; Thurston, *Ugly Duckling*, 193.

40. Adair, *Letters Home*, 113.

41. Byrnes, *History*, 116; Thurston, *Ugly Duckling*, 188.

42. Donnhauser and Drews, *Der Weg der 11*, 175. The original text refers to Schloss Thorn, presumably in error, for Schloss Thorn remained in German hands until February 20.

43. Prefer, *Patton's Ghost Corps*, 56.

44. Byrnes, *History*, 130–31; Prefer, *Patton's Ghost Corps*, 60–61.

CHAPTER 3

1. Byrnes, *History*, 132–38; A. Cleveland Harrison, *Unsung Valor: A GI's Story of World War II*, 198–210; Charles B. MacDonald, *The Last Offensive (The European Theater of Operations, United States Army in World War II)*, 121–23; Prefer, *Patton's Ghost Corps*, 61–62, 76.

2. Byrnes, *History*, 139–44; Prefer, *Patton's Ghost Corps*, 69–71; Thurston, *Ugly Duckling*, 197–98.

3. Byrnes, *History*, 144; Prefer, *Patton's Ghost Corps*, 71.

4. Prefer, *Patton's Ghost Corps*, 71–72.

5. Byrnes, *History*, 146–47.

6. Ibid., 147–48, 505; Prefer, *Patton's Ghost Corps*, 76–77 (citation from Byrnes).

7. Byrnes, *History*, 148; Prefer, *Patton's Ghost Corps*, 77.

CHAPTER 4

1. Byrnes, *History*, 149–58; Prefer, *Patton's Ghost Corps*, 74–78.

2. Byrnes, *History*, 153–54.

3. Donnhauser and Drews, *Der Weg der 11. Panzer-Division*, 175; *Merzig-Waderner Geschichtshefte 1/2000:* 55.

4. Byrnes, *History*, 154–58; Prefer, *Patton's Ghost Corps*, 78.

5. Byrnes, *History*, 158; MacDonald, *Last Offensive*, 123–24.

6. Prefer, *Patton's Ghost Corps*, 82–83.

7. Byrnes, *History*, 159.

8. Ibid., 159–63; MacDonald, *Last Offensive*, 124–25; Prefer, *Patton's Ghost Corps*, 83–84; Thurston, *Ugly Duckling*, 205–15.

9. Byrnes, *History*, pp. 163–64.

10. Byrnes, *History*, 164–67; Prefer, *Patton's Ghost Corps*, 85–86.

11. Byrnes, *History*, 167–69; Prefer, *Patton's Ghost Corps*, 86.

12. Byrnes, *History*, 169–70; MacDonald, *Last Offensive*, 123–25; Prefer, *Patton's Ghost Corps*, 86–87.

13. Byrnes, *History*, 170–76; MacDonald, *Last Offensive*, 125; Prefer, *Patton's Ghost Corps*, 87–88.

14. Byrnes, *History*, 177; Prefer, *Patton's Ghost Corps*, 89.

15. Prefer, *Patton's Ghost Corps*, 93.

16. Prefer, *Patton's Ghost Corps*, 92–94.

17. Byrnes, *History*, 177, 184; Gen. George S. Patton, *War as I Knew It,* 222; Prefer, *Patton's Ghost Corps*, 89.

18. Beehive charges are hollow charges for blowing holes through steel or concrete.

19. A bangalore torpedo is a long, tubular explosive used to clear paths through barbed wire and minefields.

20. Byrnes, *History*, 179–82; Prefer, *Patton's Ghost Corps*, 97.

21. Byrnes, *History*, 185–95; MacDonald, *Last Offensive*, 125; Prefer, *Patton's Ghost Corps*, 98–101.

CHAPTER 5

1. Byrnes, *History*, 196–204; MacDonald, *Last Offensive*, 126; Prefer, *Patton's Ghost Corps*, 123–24.

2. Byrnes, *History*, 204–11; Prefer, *Patton's Ghost Corps*, 104–06.

3. Byrnes, *History*, 211–13; Prefer, *Patton's Ghost Corps*, 106–07.

4. Byrnes, *History*, 214–18; Prefer, *Patton's Ghost Corps*, 107–11.

5. Byrnes, *History*, 218–28; Prefer, *Patton's Ghost Corps*, 114–18.

6. Prefer, *Patton's Ghost Corps,* 111.

7. Byrnes, *History,* 229–31; Prefer, *Patton's Ghost Corps,* 112, 118.

8. The term "box concentration" refers to a bombardment of a specified area.

9. Byrnes, *History,* 231–36.

10. Ibid., 236–37.

11. Ibid., 237–38.

CHAPTER 6

1. Byrnes, *History,* 239; MacDonald, *Last Offensive,* 126–27; Prefer, *Patton's Ghost Corps,* 119–21.

2. Byrnes, *History,* 239–42; Prefer, *Patton's Ghost Corps,* 121–22.

3. Byrnes, *History,* 244–47; Prefer, *Patton's Ghost Corps,* 125–26.

4. Byrnes, *History,* 246–51; MacDonald, *Last Offensive,* 127; Prefer, *Patton's Ghost Corps,* 126.

5. Byrnes, *History,* 251–53; Prefer, *Patton's Ghost Corps,* 127; Thurston, *Ugly Duckling,* 245–47.

6. Byrnes, *History,* 254; Prefer, *Patton's Ghost Corps,* 126.

7. Byrnes, *History,* 254–56; Prefer, *Patton's Ghost Corps,* 129.

8. It is noted that the timings given by Staff Sergeant Schaewen do not quite tally with the foregoing account. "Potsdamer Platz" was the name given to the Remich-Orscholz/Perl-Saarburg highway crossroads as a result of the defenses in that area having been constructed by Berliners, and is now so marked on current maps.

9. *Merzig-Waderner Geschichtshefte* 1/2000: 68, 72.

10. Byrnes, *History,* 256–61; Prefer, *Patton's Ghost Corps,* 129–30.

11. Byrnes, *History,* 259.

12. Ibid., 261–62.

13. Ibid., 262–63; Prefer, *Patton's Ghost Corps,* 131.

14. Prefer, *Patton's Ghost Corps,* 130.

CHAPTER 7

1. Byrnes, *History,* 265; Forty, *U.S. Army Handbook,* 67–74; Prefer, *Patton's Ghost Corps,* 121.

2. Byrnes, *History,* 265, 274, 276–77; Prefer, *Patton's Ghost Corps,* 132–33.

3. Ernest Henkel, article in *Kameraden* magazine, serials 522 and 523.

4. Byrnes, *History,* 277.

5. *History of the 376th Infantry Regiment Between the Years 1921–1945* (Regimental Historical Committee, Information and Education Office), 132.

6. Byrnes, *History,* 274–77; MacDonald, *Last Offensive,* 128; Prefer, *Patton's Ghost Corps,* 133–34, 137.

7. Byrnes, *History,* 266–68; Prefer, *Patton's Ghost Corps,* 135.

8. Byrnes, *History*, 268–70; Prefer, *Patton's Ghost Corps*, 135–36.

9. Byrnes, *History*, 270–73; Prefer, *Patton's Ghost Corps*, 136–37.

10. Byrnes, *History*, 280; MacDonald, *Last Offensive*, 128–29; Prefer, *Patton's Ghost Corps*, 134–35, 137.

11. Byrnes, *History*, 277–78; Prefer, *Patton's Ghost Corps*, 137.

12. Byrnes, *History*, 270–74.

13. Prefer, *Patton's Ghost Corps*, 137.

CHAPTER 8

1. Byrnes, *History*, 283; MacDonald, *Last Offensive*, 129; Prefer, *Patton's Ghost Corps*, 138–41, 149.

2. *The 94th Infantry Division: The Saar-Moselle Triangle.* Pike Military Research, Ref: 24067/203, 1999 [hereafter referred to as "Pike Military Research"].

3. Ibid.

4. Byrnes, *History*, 283–86; Prefer, *Patton's Ghost Corps*, 138, 143.

5. Byrnes, *History*, 283.

6. *The 10th U.S. Armored Division in the Saar-Moselle Triangle.* A research report prepared by Committee 15, Officers Advanced Course, The Armored School, 1948–1949, Fort Knox, Kentucky, May 1949 [hereafter referred to as "Fort Knox Report"], 73–74.

7. Fort Knox Report, 71–73.

8. Byrnes, *History*, 283–87; Col. Charles R. Codman, *Drive*, 260; Prefer, *Patton's Ghost Corps*, 141–44.

9. Prefer, *Patton's Ghost Corps*, 141–42; quotation in correspondence from Bob Trefzger (C376); Thurston, *Ugly Duckling*, 255.

10. Charles Whiting, *The West Wall: The Battle for Hitler's Siegfried Line*, 135.

11. Extract from a letter from T. Jerome French (B346) to the author.

12. Prefer, *Patton's Ghost Corps*, 142; Thurston, *Ugly Duckling*, 257–59.

13. Byrnes, *History*, 340–41; Prefer, *Patton's Ghost Corps*, 150.

14. Thurston, *Ugly Duckling*, 257–60.

15. Byrnes, *History*, 342–43; MacDonald, *Last Offensive*, 130; Thurston, *Ugly Duckling*, 263–64.

16. Adair, *Letters Home*, 158–59.

17. *History of the 376th Infantry Regiment*, 147.

18. Trefzger research; *History of the 376th Infantry Regiment*, 143.

19. Trefzger research.

20. Marshall Miller, *My Nine Lives*, 7–8.

21. Trefzger research (letter from T. Jerome French to Trefzger dated February 28, 1997).

22. Trefzger research.

23. Ibid.

24. Byrnes, *History,* 344. (Most of the Byrnes account of the 376th bridgehead proved highly inaccurate.)

25. Pike Military Research.

26. Byrnes, *History,* 284–85, 293–98.

27. MacDonald, *Last Offensive,* 130.

28. Byrnes, *History,* 298–99.

29. Pike Military Research.

30. Byrnes, *History,* 287–91; Prefer, *Patton's Ghost Corps,* 144–45.

31. Byrnes, *History,* 291.

32. MacDonald, *Last Offensive,* 131.

33. Byrnes, *History,* 291–93; Prefer, *Patton's Ghost Corps,* 153–54.

34. Byrnes, *History,* 300.

CHAPTER 9

1. Byrnes, *History,* 344–45; MacDonald, *Last Offensive,* 130–31; Prefer, *Patton's Ghost Corps,* 152–53.

2. *History of the 376th Infantry Regiment,* 149–50.

3. Byrnes, *History,* 348, 350.

4. Adair, *Letters Home,* 160; Thurston, *Ugly Duckling,* 270.

5. Byrnes, *History,* 348, Thurston, *Ugly Duckling,* 270–71.

6. Prefer, *Patton's Ghost Corps,* 153; Trefzger research.

7. Trefzger research.

8. Byrnes, *History,* 348–49.

9. Ibid., 299, 308.

10. Ibid., 307–08; Prefer, *Patton's Ghost Corps,* 147.

11. Byrnes, *History,* 303–06; Prefer, *Patton's Ghost Corps,* 160–61.

12. Byrnes, *History,* 307; Prefer, *Patton's Ghost Corps,* 156–58.

13. Pike Military Research.

14. Byrnes, *History,* 310–12. Byrnes describes the 2nd/302nd's predicament as being on a road, but it was in fact a narrow footpath running across the face of a precipitous cliff.

15. Byrnes, *History,* 306.

16. Ibid., 306–07.

17. Pike Military Research.

18. Thurston, *Ugly Duckling,* 271–77.

19. Byrnes, *History,* 348–50; Prefer, *Patton's Ghost Corps,* 162.

20. *History of the 376th Infantry Regiment,* 151.

21. Byrnes, *History,* 318; MacDonald, *Last Offensive,* 131–32; Prefer, *Patton's Ghost Corps,* 171.

22. Byrnes, *History,* 305–06, 312; Prefer, *Patton's Ghost Corps,* 161.

23. Byrnes, *History,* 312.

24. Pike Military Research.

25. Ibid.

26. Byrnes, *History*, 314–16; MacDonald, *Last Offensive*, 129–30; Prefer, *Patton's Ghost Corps*, 161.

27. Prefer, *Patton's Ghost Corps*, 158–59.

28. Byrnes, *History*, 309–11; Prefer, *Patton's Ghost Corps*, 160.

29. Byrnes, *History*, 311–12.

30. Ibid., 313–14; Prefer, *Patton's Ghost Corps*, 161.

31. Pike Military Research.

32. Byrnes, *History*, 317.

CHAPTER 10

1. Fort Knox Report, 86; Byrnes, *History*, 355.

2. Byrnes, *History*, 350–51; Prefer, *Patton's Ghost Corps*, 163.

3. *History of the 376th Infantry Regiment*, 152.

4. Byrnes, *History*, 353.

5. Ibid., 355.

6. Ibid., 350, Prefer, *Patton's Ghost Corps*, 162–63.

7. Thurston, *Ugly Duckling*, 278–82. Although Thurston refrains from mentioning names, this appears to have been Lieutenant Colonel Standish's 61st Armored Infantry, of which the 10th Armored Division's history comments only: "Standish was able to break through but found himself isolated on Scharfenberg Hill." Despite Thurston's scathing comments, Standish had already been awarded the Silver Star with one Oak Leaf Cluster, the Bronze Star Medal with one Oak Leaf Cluster, and the Purple Heart with one Oak Leaf Cluster.

8. Fort Knox Report, 86–89.

9. Byrnes, *History*, 354; Prefer, *Patton's Ghost Corps*, 163.

10. Byrnes, *History*, 318.

11. Ibid., 319–20.

12. Pike Military Research.

13. Byrnes, *History*, 320–22.

14. Fort Knox Report, 89–92.

15. Prefer, *Patton's Ghost Corps*, 170; MacDonald, *Last Offensive*, 132.

16. Byrnes, *History*, 318.

17. Ibid., 317–21.

18. Ibid., 318.

19. Ibid., 323, Prefer, *Patton's Ghost Corps*, 161.

20. Pike Military Research.

21. Byrnes, *History*, 323.

22. Ibid., 354; Prefer, *Patton's Ghost Corps*, 163–64.

23. Byrnes, *History*, 355.

24. Thurston, *Ugly Duckling*, 283.

25. Byrnes, *History,* 323.
26. MacDonald, *Last Offensive,* 132.
27. Byrnes, *History,* 324.
28. Ibid., 325–26.
29. Fort Knox Report, 94–95.
30. Byrnes, *History,* 326–27.

CHAPTER 11

1. MacDonald, *Last Offensive,* 132; Patton, *War as I Knew It,* 235; Prefer, *Patton's Ghost Corps,* 184.
2. Fort Knox Report, 84; George F. Nafziger, *The German Order of Battle,* vol. 2, *Infantry in World War II,* 466–67; Prefer, *Patton's Ghost Corps,* 182–83.
3. Byrnes, *History,* 328; Prefer, *Patton's Ghost Corps,* 181.
4. Byrnes, *History,* 328–29; Prefer, *Patton's Ghost Corps,* 181.
5. Byrnes, *History,* 329–30; Prefer, *Patton's Ghost Corps,* 181–82.
6. Byrnes, *History,* 329–30.
7. Ibid., 330–31.
8. Prefer, *Patton's Ghost Corps,* 164.
9. Byrnes, *History,* 332–33.
10. MacDonald, *Last Offensive,* 132.
11. Byrnes, *History,* 331.
12. Prefer, *Patton's Ghost Corps,* 178.
13. Ibid., 179–80.
14. Ibid., 180.
15. Ibid., 184.
16. Byrnes, *History,* 331–32.
17. Ibid., 358–59; *History of the 376th Infantry Regiment,* 156.
18. Byrnes, *History,* 359; Thurston, *Ugly Duckling,* 283–87.
19. Byrnes, *History,* 336.
20. Ibid., 333.
21. Fort Knox Report, 96–97; MacDonald, *Last Offensive,* 133.
22. Fort Knox Report, 97–100; Prefer, *Patton's Ghost Corps,* 184.
23. Prefer, *Patton's Ghost Corps,* 184–85.
24. Byrnes, *History,* 360; Thurston, *Ugly Duckling,* 287–90.
25. Byrnes, *History,* 333.
26. Ibid., 337.
27. Ibid., 336–37.
28. Ibid., 337.
29. Fort Knox Report, 100–02; Prefer, *Patton's Ghost Corps,* 184–85.
30. Byrnes, *History,* 362; Thurston, *Ugly Duckling,* 290–92.
31. Fort Knox Report, 103.
32. Ibid., 104; MacDonald, *Last Offensive,* 133; Prefer, *Patton's Ghost Corps,* 185–86.

33. Byrnes, *History*, 337–39.

34. Ibid., 337.

35. Ibid., 361–62.

36. Fort Knox Report, 104–06; Prefer, *Patton's Ghost Corps*, 186–87.

37. "Boche" is a French derogative expression for the Germans taken from World War I.

38. Byrnes, *History*, 362–63; *History of the 376th Infantry Regiment*, 161–63.

39. Prefer, *Patton's Ghost Corps*, 188; *History of the 376th Infantry Regiment*, 163–64.

40. Prefer, *Patton's Ghost Corps*, 187.

CHAPTER 12

1. Byrnes, *History*, 365, 367; Prefer, *Patton's Ghost Corps*, 188.

2. Byrnes, *History*, 339, 365.

3. Ibid., 366–67, 377–78; Prefer, *Patton's Ghost Corps*, 188, 190.

4. Byrnes, *History*, 367; Thurston, *Ugly Duckling*, 244–45.

5. Byrnes, *History*, 368.

6. Ibid., 368–69; George F. Nafziger, *The German Order of Battle*, vol. 3, *Waffen SS and Others Unite in World War II*, 80–81; Prefer, *Patton's Ghost Corps*, 190–91.

7. Byrnes, *History*, 369.

8. Ibid., 374; Prefer, *Patton's Ghost Corps*, 193.

9. Byrnes, *History*, 371–72; Prefer, *Patton's Ghost Corps*, 192.

10. Byrnes, *History*, 370–72.

11. Ibid., 377.

12. Ibid., 374–75; Prefer, *Patton's Ghost Corps*, 193.

13. Byrnes, *History*, 375, 377.

14. Ibid., 374, 379–80; Prefer, *Patton's Ghost Corps*, 194.

15. Byrnes, *History*, 369–72.

16. Ibid., 380; MacDonald, *Last Offensive*, 242.

17. Byrnes, *History*, 378–79; Prefer, *Patton's Ghost Corps*, 194.

18. Byrnes, *History*, 382, 384; Prefer, *Patton's Ghost Corps*, 195.

19. Byrnes, *History*, 383–85; Prefer, *Patton's Ghost Corps*, 195.

20. Byrnes, *History*, 386; Prefer, *Patton's Ghost Corps*, 197.

21. Byrnes, *History*, 369–70, 372–73, 378; Prefer, *Patton's Ghost Corps*, 192.

22. Byrnes, *History*, 369, 373–74; Prefer, *Patton's Ghost Corps*, 192–93.

23. Byrnes, *History*, 381–83.

24. Ibid., 384.

25. Ibid., 374, 377, 389.

26. Ibid., 388.

27. Ibid., 390–95; Prefer, *Patton's Ghost Corps*, 193, 199.

28. *History of the 376th Infantry Regiment*, 165.

29. Byrnes, *History*, 388–89.

30. Ibid., 391, 393–94.

31. Ibid., 395, 397.
32. Ibid., 397–98.
33. Ibid., 398.
34. Prefer, *Patton's Ghost Corps*, 224.

CHAPTER 13

1. Byrnes, *History*, 400–01; MacDonald, *Last Offensive*, 244; Prefer, *Patton's Ghost Corps*, 200.
2. Byrnes, *History*, 402–08; MacDonald, *Last Offensive*, 245–51; Prefer, *Patton's Ghost Corps*, 200–04.

Bibliography

Adair, Robert K. *Letters Home from the Second Platoon, I Company, 376th Infantry, WW II, Europe.* Private publication, 1995.

Bettinger, Dieter, and Martin Büren. *Der Westwall: Die Geschichte der Deutschen Westbefestigung im Dritten Reich.* Osnabrück, Germany: Biblio Verlag, 1990.

Bettinger, Dieter-Robert, Hans-Josef Hansen, and Daniel Lois, *Der Westwall von Kleve bis Basel: Auf den Spuren deutscher Geschichte.* Wölfersheim-Berstadt, Germany: Podzun-Pallas Verlag, 2002.

Blumenson, Martin, ed. *The Patton Papers, 1940–1945.* Boston: Houghton Mifflin, 1957.

Byrnes, Laurence G., ed. *History of the 94th Infantry Division in World War II.* Nashville, TN: Battery Press, 1948.

Christoffel, Edgar. *Der Endkampf zwischen Mosel, Saar und Ruwer 1944/45.* Trier: Volksfreund, 1985.

———. *Krieg am Westwall 1944/45: Das Grenzland im Westen zwischen Aachen und Saarbrücken in den letzten Kriegsmonaten.* Trier: Verlag der Akademischen Buchhandlung Interbook, 1989.

Codman, Charles R. *Drive.* Boston: Little, Brown, 1957.

D'Este, Carlo. *Patton: A Genius for War.* London: HarperCollins, 1995.

Donnhauser, Anton J., and Werner Drews. *Der Weg der 11. Panzer-Division 1939–1945.* Wunstorf: Traditionsgemeinschaft 11. Panzer-(Gespenster-) Division, 1982.

Ellis, L. F., with G. R. G. Allen, A. E. Warhurst, and Sir James Robb. *Victory in the West,* Vol. II, *The Defeat of Germany.* London: Her Majesty's Stationery Office, 1968.

Foley, William A., Jr. *Visions from a Foxhole: A Rifleman in Patton's Ghost Corps.* New York: Ballantine Books, 2003.

Forty, George. *U.S. Army Handbook, 1939–1945.* Gloucestershire: Sutton, 2003.

French, T. Jerome. Letter to author, 2005.

Fuhrmeister, Jorg. *Der Westwall: Geschichte und Gegenwart.* Stuttgart, Germany: Motorbuch Verlag, 2003.

Fussell, Paul. *The Boys' Crusade: The American Infantry in Northwestern Europe, 1944–1945.* London: Weidenfeld & Nicolson, 2004.

Gross, Manfred. *Der Westwall zwischen Niederrehein und Schnee-Eifel.* Cologne: Rheinland-Verlag, 1982.

Hansen, Hans-Josef. *Auf der Spuren des Westwalls.* Aachen: Helios Verlag, 1998.

Harrison, A. Cleveland. *Unsung Valor: A GI's Story of World War II.* Jackson: University Press of Mississippi, 2003.

Henkel, Ernest. Article in *Kameraden* magazine, serials 522 and 523.

History of the 376th Infantry Regiment Between the Years 1921–1945. Wuppertal: Regimental Historical Committee, Information and Education Office, 1945.

MacDonald, Charles B. *The Last Offensive (The European Theater of Operations, United States Army in World War II).* Washington, DC: Office of the Chief of Military History, United States Army, 1973.

Merzig-Waderner Geschichtshefte, Heft 1/2000.

Molt, Albert. *Der deutsche Festungsbau von der Memel zum Atlantik: Festungspioniere, Ingenieurkorps, Pioniertruppe, 1900–1945.* Friedberg: Podzun-Pallas, 1993.

Myers, Charles F. *Combat Badge.* Private publication, 2002.

Nafziger, George F. *The German Order of Battle,* Vol. 1. *Panzers and Artillery in World War II.* London: Greenhill Books, 1999.

———. *The German Order of Battle,* Vol. 2. *Infantry in World War II.* London: Greenhill Books, 2000.

———. *The German Order of Battle,* Vol. 3. *Waffen SS and Others Unite in World War II.* London: Aurum Press, 2001.

Neillands, Robin. *The Conquest of the Reich: D-Day to VE-Day, A Soldier's History.* London: Weidenfeld & Nicolson, 1995.

Nichols, Lester M. *IMPACT: The Battle Story of the 10th Armored Division.* Nashville: Battery Press, 2000.

Patton, George S. *War as I Knew It.* Boston: Houghton Mifflin, 1947.

Prefer, Nathan N. *Patton's Ghost Corps: Cracking the Siegfried Line.* Novato, CA: Presidio, 2000.

Schramm, Percy E. *Kriegestagebuch des Oberkommandos der Wehrmacht,* Vol. 4. Bonn: Bernard & Graefe Verlag, [1965].

Seck, Doris. *Unternehmen Westwall.* Saarbrücken: Buchverlag, 1981.

Short, Neil. *Hitler's Siegfried Line.* Stroud, UK: Sutton, 2002.

Stanton, Shelby L. *Order of Battle: U.S. Army World War II.* Novato, CA: Presidio, 1984.

The XX Corps: Its History and Service in World War II. Halstead, KS: W.E.B.S. 1984.

Thömmes, Matthias. *"Die Amis kommen!": Die Eroberung des Saar-Hunsrück-Raumes durch die Amerikaner 1944/45.* Aachen: Helios, 2001.

Thornton, Herman. Letters to author, 2005.

Thurston, Benjamin E. *Ugly Duckling: 3rd Battalion, 376th Infantry Regiment, WW II, Europe.* Self-published, 1997.

Trefzger, Robert. Letter published in *The 94 Attack* (spring 1997).

——. Letters to author, 2005.

——. Miscellaneous research supplied to author, 2003–2005.

Whiting, Charles. *The West Wall: The Battle for Hitler's Siegfried Line,* September 1944–March 1945. Staplehurst: Spellmount, 1999.

Whitman, George Philip. *Memoirs of a Rifle Company Commander in Patton's Third U.S. Army.* West Topsham, VT: Gibby Press, 1993.

OTHER DOCUMENTARY SOURCES

The 10th U.S. Armored Division in the Saar-Moselle Triangle. A research report prepared by Committee 15, Officers Advanced Course, The Armored School, 1948–1949, Fort Knox, Kentucky, May 1949.

The 94th Infantry Division: The Saar-Moselle Triangle. Pike Military Research, Ref. 24067/203, 1999.

Index

Aachen, 6, 294
Ackerman, Sgt. (C376), 79
Adair, Sgt. Robert K. (I376), 14–15, 47–49, 158–59, 194
Adenholz Woods, 94, 98, 104, 107, 111–12, 125–26
Alba, Sgt. Michael (F376), 35
Albert, Pfc. Louis A. (L302), 285
Albrecht, Maj. (Arty Regt 416), 15
Alterberg (Hill 406), 128–29
Alverado, Lt. Joe D. (F302), 59, 100, 114
Aman, Pfc. Daniel W. (L302), 277
Anderson, 1st Lt. Bertil T. (94 MP), 216
Anderson, Lt. John D. (E302), 113–15, 251
Anderson, Lt. Col. Raynor E. (376), 160, 208, 217, 221, 264, 283
Apach, 112
Ardennes, 5, 13
Arenaz, Lt. Pablo (I376), 46
Army Maneuver Area, 2
Army Specialized Training Program, 2, 52
Aschermann, Capt. Donald (Arty), 169
Ashton, Capt. Scott T. (94 Recce Tp), 134, 137, 199, 264
Asmussen, Tech-3 John (B302), 89
Atchinson, Pfc. Mark D. (E302), 82
Atencio, Pfc. Ernest (F301), 98
Auf der Hütte cliffs, 172–73, 203–5, 213, 215, 225, 230
Augsburg, 288
Austrian army, 240

Ayl, 154–58, 160–61, 175–76, 197, 205, 209, 217, 223, 233, 245
Aywaille, 296

Babcock, TSgt. George E. (G301), 96–97, 105
Backsteinfels Ridge, 194
Bailey, Sgt. Clifford G. (94 MP), 215
Baker, Lt. Claud W. (D376), 18, 20–21, 43
Baldringen, 241, 251, 278, 280
Bannholz Woods, 35, 61, 93–94, 96–99, 101, 103, 116, 118, 124–25, 131
Barrow, Lt Douglas A. (H302), 91
Basel, 6
Bastogne, 247
Battle Creek, 1
Baumgaertner, Lt. Carl J. (A302), 87, 89, 244
Baumholder, 294
Bawd, Sgt. Robert A. (I&R302), 274
Baxter, Pfc. William T. (M302), 284–85
Beardsley, Pvt. Albert J. (E376), 67
Becker, Maj. (I/GR 713), 18, 22
Beikert, Lt. (German Arty), 124
Belgium, 1, 296
Bender, Pfc. James M. (I302), 130, 272
Bendure, Lt. William (B376), 79
Berg, 28, 32, 46–47, 57, 67–70, 72, 78
Bergquist, Col. Earl C. (COS 94ID), 48, 126, 174
'Berlin Sally,' 47

Besch, 28, 30, 32, 44, 47–50, 57–60, 64, 66, 73, 77, 84, 96, 112

Beuren, 62, 116, 140

Beurig, 152, 197, 213, 217–18, 223, 225–26, 233–35

Beyer, 2nd Lt. Sylvester M. (356 Arty), 97, 100, 266

Bidwell, Lt. Col. James, W. (704 TDB), 104

Biedchen, 237

Billett, Capt. Omar M. (CCA 10AD), 258–59

Bilzingen, 139, 145

Bitburg, 21

Blakely, Capt. Larry A. (919 Arty), 18, 107–8, 110

Bloom, Lt. Edwin R. (B302), 83

Bock, Pfc. Stanley (F301), 98

Boggs, Lt. Andrew T. (7 AIB), 70

Boland, Lt. Paul (301 Arty), 231

Bolinger, Lt. James P. (D/18 TB), 81

Bondi, SSgt. Dominick, J. (I302), 273, 275

Borg, 12, 59, 83–84, 89, 91, 113–14, 116–17, 129, 131

Bouzonville, 294

Bowden, Capt. Harry C. (B376), 37, 44, 125, 131, 208, 219, 244, 249

Bowyer, 2nd Lt. Dale E. (I376), 33, 46, 73

Boyette, Sgt Woodrow J. (356 Fd Arty), 273, 287–88

Bradley, Lt. Gen. Omar N. (12 Army Gp), 83, 240, 293

Brehio, Capt. Edwin (1/376), 77, 249

Brendengen. Capt. Odin (A/18 TB), 77

Brenner, Maj. Gen. Karl Heinrich (GOC 6 SS MtnDiv), 267

Brewster, SSgt. (919 Arty), 132

Brightman, Capt. William A. (L376), 30–31, 46–47, 125–26, 157

Brimmer, Lt. Col. (Arty 376), 173

Brinkerhoff, SSgt. George L. (L302), 285

Brittany, 3, 4, 126

Brockmann, Lt. (SS Mtn Regt 12), 279–80

Brown, Capt. Raph T. (K376), 195, 208, 234, 250

Brown, Lt. (3/376), 253

Bruchsmühle, 266

Bruhl, Capt. (Arty), 173

Brumley, Maj. George W. (HQ 301), 201, 214, 232, 239, 245, 255, 267

Brusgard, Sgt. Andrew (1/376), 261

Bryant, Pvt. Russell (B376), 154, 195–96

Buchanan, Chaplain (1/376), 260–62

Buffalini, Pfc. Ernest L. (I301), 123

Buffington, Capt. Benjamin F. (390 Arty), 284

Bugel, Capt. Joseph (K302), 270, 272

Bulge, Battle of the, 1, 4, 5, 13, 71, 117, 153, 294

Bullard, Pfc. A. (A301), 84

Burdzy, Pvt. (A376), 42

Burgamy, Lt. Ravenl V. (I376), 45

Burke, Lt. William (356 Arty), 58

Burnett, SSgt. Robert E. (B376), 132

Burnshaw, Pfc. Edward C. (C302), 130

Buskager, Pvt. Vernon D. (3/302), 284

Butler, Lt./Capt. James W. (E302), 59, 114, 144, 146, 203

Butzdorf, 12–13, 18, 20–23, 27, 34, 37–38, 40–44, 50, 69, 72–73, 76, 83, 90, 94, 100, 118, 120, 122

Bybee, Lt. John W. (I302), 275, 277

Camp Forrest, 2

Campholz Woods, 12, 18, 21, 37, 62, 73–74, 83, 85–86, 89–92, 113–14, 118, 122

Camp Kilmer, 296

Camp Phillips, 2

Cancilla, Lt. Joseph E. (B301), 65, 120–21, 230

Capps, SSgt. James E. (L302), 143

Cardell, TSgt. Edward (I310), 123

Carpenter, Lt. (K302), 65, 68

Carr, Lt. James P. A. (88 CavRecceSqn), 70

Case, Tech-5, 287

Castanzo, Sgt. Joseph C. (A319 Engrs), 85

Castor III, Lt. Joseph P. (G302), 115–16

Caviness, Lt. Col. James M. (919 Arty), 94

Centrello, Tech-5 John J. (1/302), 86

Chalkley, Lt. Ben R. (C376), 20, 37, 39, 44, 157, 159, 163

Chamberlain, Lt. Col. Thomas C. (11 TB), 139, 247, 251

Chapman, TSgt. James T. (ATk 302), 284–85

Chapman, Pfc. Paul W. (M302), 276

Chapman, Pfc. Robert L. (I376), 167

Cheadle, Brig. Gen. Henry B. (HQ 94ID), 18, 43, 66, 69, 103

Christiansen, Lt. Arthur A (G301), 96, 104–6, 141, 212

Civil War, 155

Clapp, Lt. Col. Wadsworth P. (Engr 10AD), 153–54

Clark, Sgt. James E. (G302), 91

Clausi, Tech-5?SSgt Thomas M. (HQ 3/376), 46

Cleary, William L. (F376), 35

Clemens. Pvt. Irving S. (L301), 266

Climes, Pfc. Ernest E. (K301), 124

Cloudt, Lt. Col. Otto B., Jr. (3/302), 56–57, 64, 66, 78–80, 122, 130, 142, 145, 148, 174, 214, 223, 225, 231, 235, 241–42, 245, 254, 258, 270–71, 273–75, 277, 282, 284–85, 287–88

Cody, Lt. Joseph F. (H302), 113–14

Cohen, Pfc. Alvin (I301), 123, 130

Cole, Tech-5 Robert (G302), 92

Colgan, Capt. Charles B. (A301), 51, 122, 144, 230

Collier, Brig. Gen. William, A. (COS XX Corps), 49, 66, 93, 240

Collins, Pfc. James V. (I302), 65

Collins, TSgt. Raymond E. (E301), 100

Colson, Brig. Gen. Charles R. (CCA 8AD), 49, 66, 69–70

Colvin, Lt. Aaron L. (A376), 262

Concannon, Lt. Joseph F. (HQ 1/302), 89

Cook, Lt. (54 AIB), 252

Cornelius, Lt. James W. (B376), 37, 79, 125, 157

Cousineau, TSgt. James (C302), 63, 172–73

Cox, SSgt. Jack (C302), 87

Craddock, Capt. Henry (7 AIB), 70

Craig, Pvt. (A376), 42

Crandall, Lt. Col. (390 Arty), 94

Crandall, TSgt. Henry E. (B301), 121

Cranford, Sgt. Walter L. (M302), 276

Creighton, Lt. Richard L.(A376), 20

Crenshaw, Pfc. Eugene (L301), 102

Croan, Pvt. Charles F. (C376), 39

Crouse, Lt. Carl A. (B376), 283

Crutchfield, Sgt. Leon D. (B376), 244

Curi, Pfc. (G302), 92

Curler, Pvt. Howard (A376), 40, 42

Czechoslovakia, 296

Czerboskas, Lt. (C302), 59, 271, 274

Dadisman, Capt. Chester B. (A376), 76, 79, 125, 131, 196, 208, 218, 244

Daly, Lt. Thomas A. (K376), 31, 33, 46, 125–26, 206

Dansby, Lt. Cecil G. (I376), 126, 158

Darby, SSgt. Frederick R. (C302), 130

Darnell, Pfc. Curtis C. (F301), 98

Darrah, Capt. Simon D. (E376), 67–69, 78, 111, 233

Das Brüch Woods, 128, 141

Das Lee Woods, 103, 116, 120, 126, 128–29

Davis, Lt. Charles P. (F376), 115

Davis, TSgt. James A. (C302), 280

Decker, Lt. (HQ 376), 267

Degan, Maj. Gen. Hans (GOC 2d Mtn Div), 240

Delagoes, Sgt. Manuel M. (F376), 111

DeLibero, Pvt. Joe (A376), 42

Deller, Tech-5 John R. (356 Fd Arty), 273

Denmark, 15, 240

DePutron, Lt. Adrian B. (1/301), 54

Der Heidlich Hill, 18, 59, 62, 72

Derickson, Pvt. (A376), 42

Der Langen Woods, 118, 131–32

Devereauz, Capt. (CCB 10AD), 247, 256

Devine, Maj. Gen. John M. (GOC 8AD), 49, 70

Devizes, 3

Devonald, Lt. David H., II, (K301), 64, 120, 124, 128, 142, 210, 225, 228, 241

Dilmar, 116, 139

Dionne, Pfc. (C301), 121

Dittlingen, 140

Dodge, Lt. Maurice S. (F302), 74

Dodson, Lt. Arthur (E376)/Capt (G/376), 78, 138, 145, 190

Doherty, Lt. William J. (I376), 57

Dohs, Lt. Col. Francis H. (2/301), 85, 94,

96, 98–100, 102, 103, 126, 128, 141, 145, 199

Donkers, Lt. Harold J. (HQ 94), 149

Donovan, Capt. Charles W. (I301), 96, 128, 142, 167, 169, 242, 270, 282

Dossenbach, Maj. John R. (2376), 111, 219, 235, 249, 253–54, 258, 264

Douglas, Sgt. (C376), 20

Dreikopf Hill, 272–73, 275, 283, 285–88

Drenzek, Capt. (C301), 120–21

Dresser, Pfc. Johan A. (I376), 77

Dryland, 2nd Lt. Ernest N. (E376), 233

Duckworth, Capt. Edwin F.(C376), 16, 38, 79

Dudelange, 257, 266

Dumville, Lt. George L.(A376), 20–21

Dunn, Pfc. Warren (L301), 102

Durbin, Lt. Col. Rollin B. (G-3 94ID), 18

Durette, SSgt. Cecil F. (L302), 276

Dury, Sgt. (A376), 44

Düsseldorf, 295

Eardley, Capt. (A/61 AIB), 227

Earkley, Capt. R. V. (21 TB), 226

Eckstrom, Lt. Richard E. (B301), 230, 245

Edwards, Lt./Capt. Robert A. (I302), 57, 66, 123, 273, 275

Eft, 122, 139

Eggers, Pfc. William F. (L302), 143

Ehrenberg, Lt. Charles F. (301 Fd Arty), 87

Ehringer Berg Hill, 131

Eiderberg, 142

Eisberg, Capt. (20 AIB), 246, 257

Eisenhower, Gen. Dwight D., 2, 83, 117, 209, 291

Eisler, 1st Sgt. Jerome (C302), 86

Ellis, Pvt. Harry R. (L302), 277

Ellis, Lt. Col. Noel H. (Engr 94ID), 18, 171

England, 3, 296

English Channel, 27

Ernst, SSgt./TSgt. Arthur (G302), 91, 278–79

Ewasko, SSgt. Anthony S. (L302), 60–61

Faha, 118, 126, 128–29, 143

Fairchild, Lt. Thomas (G376), 34

Felicelli, SSgt. Bruno (HQ302), 274–75

Fell, SSgt. George F. (E301), 214

Fellerick, 139

Ferguson, Pvt. (3/302), 288

Fields, TSgt. Frank M. (K376), 31–32

Fikjs, Sgt. Otto H. (F376), 107

Filsch, 256

Finger, Sgt. John C. (H302), 278

Fink, Lt. Henry J. (K302), 58, 65–66, 68

Finkbone, Sgt. Richard W. (F302), 280

Finland, 240

Finlay, Capt. Joseph (A/7 AIB), 66

Fischönsdorf, 139

Fisher, 2nd Lt. John S. (E301), 99

Fisher, 2nd Lt. Arthur J. (7 AIB), 70

Fite, Pvt. (A376), 42

Flanagan, Capt. John (2/301), 99

Flanagan, Capt. Luis J. (1/302), 76

Fletcher, Lt. (CCA 10AD), 259

Flory, SSgt. Gladwin J. (3/376), 28, 33

Flower, Lt. James T. (I301), 282

Fluch, Sgt. Robert H. (1/302), 89

Foertsch, Gen. Hermann, 293

Fontaine, SSgt. Thomas W. (I302), 66

Forêt de Saarburg, 51, 55

Forêt de Trèves (Trier Forest), 225

Forsyth, SSgt. Murry W. (H301), 246

Fort Benning, 2

Fort Custer, 1, 2

Fort Jackson, 2

Fort Knox, 150–51, 220, 226

Fort McCain, 2

Fort Shanks, 3

Fortier, Brig. Gen. Louis J. (Arty Comd 94ID), 3, 118, 149

Foster, Lt. (L376), 195

Fox, Lt. Raymond G. (I376), 31, 32, 34, 36–37, 46, 58

Foxgrower, Sgt. Charles (D376), 40

Fraboni, Lt. John R. (L301), 102

France, 1, 3, 294

Franchino, Pfc. Frank A. (L301), 266

Frankenheim, 264

Franz, Maj. Gen. Gerhard (256 VGrDiv), 32, 112

Freeman, Pfc. Earl (L376), 77

French, Pvt. T. Jerome (B376), 155, 162–63

French Forces of the Interior, 4
Freudenburg, 128, 141–42, 145, 149, 153, 201, 226, 231
Friedrich, Maj. (FortInfRegt 'Merzig'), 15
Frierson, Capt. Paul E. (L301), 102, 120, 126, 141, 210, 235

Gaddis, Lt. Col. John W. (XO 302 Inf), 59, 143, 174
Gale, Lt. (CCB 10AD), 256
Gallant, Pfc. Wallace M. (M302), 276, 284
Gambosi, Lt. Louis J.(B/5 Rgrs), 202, 226, 237
Gass, Lt. Glenn H. (L301), 102–3
Gatchell, Col. Wade C. (CCR 10AD), 134
Gaynor, Tech-4 Joseph F. (HQ 3/302), 288
Gedaminski, Sgt. John (L302), 277
Geisbusch Woods, 104, 107–8, 125–26
Geizenburg, 149
Georgia, 2
Gerow, Gen. Leonard T. (GOC Fifteenth Army), 294
Gersbaugh, Sgt. Harry C. (356 Arty), 266
Ginsberg, Lt. Ralph E. (G302), 91
Glasgow, 3
Glass, Lt. H. (L302), 212
Glover, Lt. Jospeh E. (1/302), 86
Gobin, Lt. Robert E. (H302), 279
Godfrey, SSgt. David H. (E376), 67
Godwin, Lt. Peter F. (88 CavRecceSqn), 71
Goggins, Pfc. Thomas H. (C376), 125
Goldenschweig, Lt. William M. (I376), 31
Goodling, Lt. Rodney A. (Cannon Coy/ 376), 169
Goodrich, Col. (CCA 10AD), 77, 81
Graham, Sgt./SSgt. James A. (B301), 124, 213
Grant, Sgt. Philip D. (L302), 274
Green, SSgt. J. W. (E301), 100–101
Greene, Lt. James E, Jr. (E/5 Rgrs), 202
Grenada, 2
Grennock, 3
Griffin, Capt. James W. (G302), 59, 76, 80, 91, 144, 254, 277–78, 281
Grifford, TSgt. Elmer W. (E301), 100

Grose, TSgt. William B. (K302), 270, 274–75
Grossi, SSgt. Fred (K376), 32
Grzninski, Pfc. Felix J. (G376), 287
Guerrier, Pvt. James (G302), 81
Gutweiler, 268

Hachenberger, Col. (GrRegt 713), 15
Hack, Sgt. Eugene T. (Int/302), 274
Hager, SSgt. Carl W. (1/301), 214
Hagerty, Col. Roy N. (301 Inf), 51, 55, 72, 94, 112, 118, 126, 165, 199, 210, 226, 265, 282
Haggart, Capt. Jack P. (A301), 124
Hahn, Gen. Walther (GOC LXXXII Corps), 132, 169, 268, 293
Halderson, Capt. Paul R. (D/18 TB), 81
Halfway House, 20–22, 41, 76
Halle, TSgt. Ernest W. (HQ 301), 52
Hamilton, Pfc. Virgil E. (D376), 43
Hamm, 145, 148–49, 152, 203–4, 215–16, 245
Hammer, Lt. Mark (C302), 280–81
Hanover, Lt. (61 AIB), 227
Hardin, Lt. Col. Donald C. (HQ 301), 54–55, 235
Harmon, Maj. Gen. Ernest N., 294
Harrison, Pvt. A. Cleveland (B301), 52–55
Hardter Wald Woods, 277–78
Haskell, Maj. Waren B. (54 AIB), 247, 256
Hassett, Sgt. Patrick J. (H302), 276
Hawley, Lt. Richard A. (F376), 34, 107
Hayes, Maj. Samuel H. (HQ 376), 113
Heard, Pfc. James (H302), 144
Heath, Capt. John D. (G376), 68, 78, 107–8, 110–11, 192, 244, 250
Hebard, Tech-5 Harry E. (L302), 271
Heck, Cpl. Bernie H. (D376), 43
Heidelberger, Lt. Percy (2/376), 110, 259
Height 366, 142
Height 376 (Kesslinger Berg), 130
Height 387, 126, 128
Height 388, 129, 131
Height 398 (Ehringer Berg), 131
Height 405, 268
Height 406 (Alterberg), 128–29
Height 426 (Ockfener Berg), 234–35
Height 427, 253, 256, 268

Height 433, 253
Height 440 (Wäckseler Fels), 241
Height 463 (Hill 5), 241, 265
Height 464 (Hill 9), 241, 273, 276
Height 467, 278–79
Height 468 (Mühlenberg) (Hill 8), 241, 254, 277, 280–81
Height 471, 215
Height 472 (Hill 7), 241, 254, 280
Height 494 (Hill 4), 241
Height 495, 288
Height 500, 271, 274–76, 284, 287
Height 502 (Hill 3), 241, 250
Height 507, 282–83, 286–87
Height 508, 247
Height 536 (Hill 2), 241, 254, 258, 265
Henkel, Ernest (IR 481), 135–37
Henley, Lt. Robert H. (L301), 248, 265–66
Hentern, 172, 181, 241, 254, 278–79, 281
Herman, Capt. Grover B. (7 AIB), 70
Hermeskeil, 291
Highway 268, 246–47, 251, 254, 268, 272, 274, 280–81, 283, 285
Highway 407, 241, 247–48
Hill 1. See Hocker Hill
Hill 2 (Height 536), 241, 254, 258, 265
Hill 3 (Height 502), 241, 250
Hill 4 (Height 494), 241, 247–48, 250
Hill 5 (Height 463), 241–42, 247–48, 265
Hill 6 (Mühlenberg) (Height 468), 241–42, 247, 268, 282
Hill 7 (Height 472), 241, 251, 254, 280
Hill 8 (Height 468), 241, 254, 278, 280–81
Hill 9 (Height 464), 241, 258, 273, 276
Hill 10 (Height 500), 241, 258, 274
Hill 11, 241, 258
Hitler, Adolf, 10–11
Hobbs, Pvt. James C. (C376), 39
Hocker Hill (Höckerberg), 172–75, 202, 204–5, 214, 230–32, 239, 255
Hochweiler, 262
Hodges, Capt. Burgess G. (2/302), 62
Hodges, Lt. Gen. Courtney (GOC First Army), 290
Hodges, Lt. Jesse W. (L376), 206
Hodges, Lt. Tom (A376), 20, 44

Hodges, Maj. Arthur W. (1/301), 54, 56, 94, 96, 202, 205, 214, 225, 253, 255, 258
Hoelscher, Lt. Col. (GrRegt 712), 15
Hoffman, Maj. Albert F. (319 Engrs), 153, 205
Holbrook, Pvt. George (B301), 54
Holehouse, Capt. (A/20 AIB), 227–28
Honan, Lt. William J. (M302), 276–77, 284
Hoots, Tech-5 Robert (B302), 131
Hosea, Lt. Col. Silas W. (1/302), 49, 60, 89
Houston, Pop (A376), 40
Howard, Maj. Harold F. (HQ 301), 148, 164–65, 225, 232
Howenstine, Allen (H376), 35–36
Hubbard, Lt. Warren C. (3/302), 284
Hudson, TSgt. James E. (I301), 123
Hullender, Sgt. James C. (1/301), 214
Hunter, Lt. Charles A. (F302), 90, 146
Hurst, Capt. Francis M. (M302), 57, 174
Hürtgen Forest, 12
Huthnance, TSgt. Tom D. (C376), 164, 196

IG Farben Industries, 293
Indiana, 35
Irsch (Saarburg), 152, 209, 214, 221–23, 225–28, 234–35, 237, 241, 247–48, 251, 257, 265
Irsch (Trier), 257
Irminder Wald Ridge, 156, 158–59, 163–64, 192, 194, 202, 208–9, 235
Isaacman, TSgt. Nathaniel (E376), 67

Jacobson, Pfc. Orleane A. (E302), 82, 279
Jacques, Lt. William R. (I376), 158
Jaeger, Pvt. George (D376), 163
Janulis, Lt. Adolph A. (G376), 107
Jende, Sgt. Gerald W. (E376), 78
Jennings, SSgt. James L. (3/376), 45
Johnson, Col. Earle A. (302 Inf), 62, 72, 77, 118, 122, 129, 205, 226
Johnson, Lt. Leon P. (G301), 266
Johnson, SSgt. Henry (G376), 107
Johnson, 2nd Lt. Howard (C301), 121
Johnston, TSgt. William (G376), 107

Jones, Capt. William C. (919 Arty), 107
Jonscher, Lt. Robert W. (D301), 52, 55
Jurek, SSgt. Stanley K. (B302), 87

Kafkalas, Capt. (54 AIB), 251–52
Kaiserslautern, 291, 293
Kaiserslautern Gap, 291, 293
Kaiser-Wilhem-Brücke, 258
Kamins, Pfc. Richard J. (A376), 40–42, 132
Kansas, 2
Kansas City, 297
Kanzem, 134, 140, 147, 169
Karl, TSgt./1st Sgt. John (L302), 58, 60
Karlix, Pfc. Robert S. (G302), 143
Karthaus, 251, 257
Kastel (Rhine), 290
Kastel (Saar), 145, 148, 153, 165, 168–69, 201
Katzen, Pfc. Bennett P. (I301), 282
Kearns, Lt. Kenneth E. (1/301), 214
Kelley, 1st Sgt. William M. (B301), 145–46
Kelley, Maj. Thomas E. (2/376), 254
Kelly, SSgt./TSgt. Francis J. (L302), 61, 130–31, 285
Kelly, Lt. Peter R. (G302), 80
Kelsen, 141
Kesslingen, 129–31, 143
Kesslinger Berg, 130
Ketner, Sgt. Ray (E376), 69
Kettler, Pfc. K. O. (A376), 77
Keuchlingen, 15, 146, 148, 175
Kimball, Lt. Robert O. (HQ 302), 274
Kinateder, TSgt. Elmer H. (L301), 128, 266, 282
King, Lt. (K376), 33
King, TSgt. James L. (C302), 86
King, Pfc. Otis L. (F376), 108
Kinnan, SSgt. John H. (2/301), 214
Kinyon, Sgt. Gilbert E. (F302), 76
Kirf, 116, 128, 140–41
Klahn, Sgt. Robert A. (356 Fd Arty), 273
Klein, Pvt. (A376), 42
Klutsch, Lt. Joseph (I376), 73
Knadt, Maj. (GrRegt 714), 15
Kniess, Gen. Baptist (GOC LXXXV Korps), 293

Koblenz, 147
Koellhopper, SSgt. John R. (B301), 121–22
Kollesleuken, 141–42
Kommlingen, 254, 257
Konz, 157, 251, 258, 264
Kops, Capt. Herman, Jr. (F302), 59, 113–14, 144, 204, 244, 251, 254, 278–79
Korlingen, 268
Kornistan, Sgt. (C376), 20
Körrig, 139
Koshoffer, Lt. Joseph T. (A376), 283
Kovac, Pvt. (A376), 42
Kraft, Maj. (A & E Bn 416), 15, 22–23
Krefeld, 294
Kress, TSgt. Marvin L. (C302), 280
Kreuzweiler, 62, 116, 125, 137–39, 145
Krieger, Cpl. Donald W. (D376), 23
Krob, Lt. Norbert F. (A/778 TB), 280–81
Krupp Steel Works, 295
Krutweiler, 152, 165, 199, 212
Kuers, Lt. Marvin M. (G376), 287
Kummlerhof, 241, 277–78, 280–81

Laabs, Pfc. Raymond H. (L302), 143
Lampaden, 254, 257, 264, 270–73, 275–77, 283–87, 289
Lampadener Mühle, 272–73, 275, 283, 288
Land, Lt. William G. (B376), 283, 286
Lang, Capt. Steve (54 AIB), 252–53, 256
Larson, SSgt. Delbert A. (3/376), 45
Lateswald Wood, 31, 33
Ledesma, Sgt. Max A. (K302), 270–71
Lehman, SSgt. Robert G. (E301), 106
Leuk Branch, 134, 141–42, 144
Leverkusen, 295
Lewies, Lt. Harry J. (E302), 82, 91, 114
Lichirie, Lt. Col. Cornelius A. (90 CavRecceSqn), 150
Liège, 294, 296
Lindsay, Pfc. (A376), 40
Linerich, Pfc. James (A301), 124
Litka, Lt. Edward G. (G376), 47, 111
Long, Sgt. Flaud E. (K302), 271, 274–75
Lorient, 3
Loschenkopf Woods, 145
Love, Lt. Col. Robert L. (G-2 94ID), 18, 76

Luckridge. SSgt. Glenn (F376), 218–19
Ludwigshafen, 293, 295
Luxembourg, 1, 16, 22, 57, 257, 266–67, 282, 294
Luxembourg City, 293–94

Macon, Pfc., 287
Maculawicz, Pfc. Peter (L302), 142
Macumber, Pvt. Clifford R. (G302), 81
Maginot Line, 6
Magnuson, Pfc. Melvin C. (2/301), 239
Mahoney, Lt. Riggs (K302), 270
Mainz, 290
Maixner, Maj. Harold V. (2/302), 62, 80, 90–91, 113, 116, 122, 175, 203, 230–31, 241–42, 250, 254, 277–78, 281
Malinski, Capt. Frank (C376), 77, 219, 248
Mallard, Lt. Inman E. (3/376), 28
Mallich, Sgt. Samuel (I302), 272
Malloy, SSgt. William B. (G376), 107–8
Malony, Maj. Gen. Harry J. (GOC 94ID), 5–6, 16, 43–44, 48–49, 51, 66–67, 69–73, 83–84, 92–93, 107, 113, 117–18, 144, 149, 152, 212–13, 215, 220, 222–23, 240, 248, 282–83, 294–95
Maness, Lt. (F376), 190–91
Mannebach, 111, 139, 145, 155–56
Manning, Rev. Charles H. (H301), 297–303
Marek, Capt. Norman C. (C302), 60–62
Markowski, TSgt. Chester E. (L302), 58
Martin, Lt. Col. Olivius C. (2/376), 34, 43, 66, 69–70, 78, 106, 110–11, 138, 145, 190–91, 208, 219, 248, 233
Mason, Lt. Melvin I. (C376), 237
Mason, Lt. Stanley C. (F376), 34, 108–9
Matsuzawa, SSgt. Ichiro (A301), 122
Mauro, Pfc. John, Jr. (I376), 45
Mayfield, Pvt. Edward (C302), 130
McBride, Maj. Gen. Horace L. (GOC 80 ID), 290
McBride, Maj. William E. (1/301), 56
McCartney, Pvt. Charles F. (I302), 273
McClune, Col. Harold C. (376 Inf), 18, 72, 74, 78, 82, 112, 118, 131, 155–57, 160
McCormack, Pfc. Weldon J. (319 Engrs), 92
McCoy, Lt. James H. (K376), 30

McCullough, Lt. James C. (2/376), 110
McCumber, Pfc. Clifford R. (G302), 279
McElwee, Pfc. William B. (B302), 131
McIntyre, Pvt. (A376), 41
McKee, TSgt. Leland B. (I302), 275
McLoughlin, Lt. Harry W. (G376), 287
McNulty, Lt. Col. William A. (3/301), 72, 79, 94, 96, 107, 111–12, 120, 126, 141, 145, 165, 168–70, 223, 225, 235, 241
McPherson, SSgt. Leroy (M376), 33
McQuade, Sgt. William (D376), 43
Melksham, 3
Meneses, Pfc. James E. (I376), 77
Merlbach Stream, 52
Merschweiler, 139
Mertert, 150
Merzig, 149
Merzkirchen, 140
Mettlach, 15–16, 133, 146
Metz, 12, 21, 117, 154, 221
Metz, Sgt. (L302), 276
Meurich, 141
Meyer, Lt. L. A. (301 Arty), 114–15
Michigan, 1, 35
Michigan City, Indiana, 35
Middleton, Maj. A. H. (94 Arty), 286
Miller, Sgt. Domer V. (H303), 278
Miller, Lt. Col. George F. (1/301), 41, 51–54
Miller, Capt. George R. (D/5 Rgrs)), 202
Miller, Sgt. Marshall (B376), 161–62, 195
Miller, Capt. Russell D. (B/18 TB), 79–80
Miner, Lt. Col. Russell C. (1/376), 16, 18, 20–21, 37, 43–44, 73–74, 78–80, 84, 112, 125, 131, 159, 196, 208, 233–34, 244, 253, 257, 260, 262, 264, 283, 285–86, 288
Minich, Lt. Samuel T. (L301), 235, 242, 248
Minich, Ssgt. Ralph. O. (L301), 266
Misner, Lt. Charles C. (L302), 100
Mississippi, 2
Missouri, 297
Mitchigan, 1
Monkey Wrench Woods, 23, 33–36, 50, 59, 61, 72–73, 76
Monneren, 57, 67
Monroe, Sgt. Herbert L. (B376), 283
Montgomery, Fd. Marshal Sir Bernard L., 290, 293

Montgomery, TSgt. George (A301), 84

Moon, SSgt. William R. (G302), 116

Mooney, Sgt. Charles J. (HQ 3/302), 287–88

Moore, Tech-4 Mervin L. (3/376), 45

Morgan, Pfc. Morgan H. (G302), 278

Morris, Maj. Gen. William H. H. Jnr. (GOC 10AD), 12, 117, 150, 155, 209, 213

Morrison, Lt. (Arty), 43–44

Morrow, Lt. Col. Samuel L. (301 Arty), 55, 94

Morse, Lt. Dwight M. (K376), 30

Morton, TSgt. Howard J. (F302) 115, 278

Moscholz Woods, 131–32, 140

Moselle River, 1, 16, 21–22, 28, 57, 64, 68, 72, 84, 106, 117, 125, 134–37, 139–40, 144, 147–48, 250–51, 253, 257–58, 262–64, 282, 295,

Mousaw, Cpl. Earle F. (D376), 43

Moushgian, Maj. Richard (7 AIB), 70

Mühlenberg Hill (Hill 6), 241–42, 247, 268, 282

Munitions Assignment Board, 5

Münzingen, 93, 118, 120, 126, 128–29

Münzingen Ridge, 16, 38, 72, 76, 80, 85–86, 93–94, 96, 100, 102, 113, 117–18, 120, 123–24, 126, 128, 131, 144

Murphy, Lt. (376), 192

Murphy, SSgt. William J. (774 TDB), 271

Myers, Maj. Earl L. (3/302), 57

Myers. Lt. Richard H. (G301), 85

Nagy, TSgt. John F. (B376), 283, 286

Naha, 165

Nahe River, 290–91

Najjar, Lt. (A & P Pl/302), 273

Neff, Pfc. Leonard L. (F376), 108

Nennig, 46–50, 57–61, 64–9, 72, 77, 89, 96, 112–13, 124

Nettles, TSgt. Tommy (E302), 115

Neuman, Tech-4 Paul E. (356 Arty), 266

New Jersey, 296

New York, 3

Nichols, SSgt. Charles H. (B376), 132

Niedeleuken, 245

Niedermennig, 257

Niedersehr, 241, 251, 270, 272

Niederzerf, 237, 239

Nielson, Lt. (Cannon Coy, 376), 41

Nierstein, 293

Nohn, 90, 146

Norman, Lt. Col. Frank P. (2/302), 59–63, 72, 74, 78–80, 82

Normandy, 10, 154

Norquist, Lt. Samuel G. (A302), 76, 124

Norris, Lt. Col. Ned T. (CCA 10AD), 251, 257, 259

Oberemmel, 250, 254, 283

Oberhardt Woods, 130

Oberleuken, 13, 16, 52, 54, 85, 93, 115, 123, 126, 128–31, 143, 145, 170

Obersehr, 241, 251, 254, 257, 270–71, 274–76, 283, 286–88

Ober-Thünsdorf, 52

Oberzerf, 237, 239, 241

Ockfen, 151, 156, 163, 190–92, 194, 196–97, 208, 217–18, 221, 227, 234–35, 241

Ockfener Berg, 235, 242

Ockfener Domäne, 192

O'Grady, Capt. (CCA 10AD), 139–40, 246, 251, 257

O'Hara, TSgt. Frank (K302), 57–58

O'Hara, Lt. Col. James (54 AIB), 217, 247–48

O'Hara, TSgt. Robert (B301), 230

Olewig, 253, 257

Ollmuth, 241, 251, 264, 270

O'Neil, Maj. Gilbert N. (3/301), 228, 235, 247, 265–66

Oppenheim, 293

Oresko, TSgt. Nicholas (C302), 62–63

Orr, TSgt. Albert I. (L302), 271, 275–76

Orscholz, 16, 51–56, 67, 90, 116, 118, 122–23, 131, 143–46, 174, 202

Orscholz Switch, 1, 7, 12–13, 16, 22, 28, 33, 35, 38, 48, 51, 93, 107, 117, 124, 131, 139, 143, 150, 169, 295

Owings, Capt. Orville M. (H302), 459

Palet, Pfc. Francis A. (G302), 279

Palmer, Lt. Charles R. (391 Engrs), 28, 37

Paluszynski, TSgt. Leonard T. (C302), 280–81

Parker, Capt. Charles E. (A/5 Rgrs), 174, 213

Parkinson, TSgt. Tom R. (G301), 85, 96–97

Paschel, 241, 254, 258, 272, 288

Pash, SSgt. Daniel (L302), 271

Patch, Lt. Gen. Alexander M. (GOC Seventh Army), 290

Patton, Lt. Gen. George S., Jr. (GOC Third Army), 1, 6, 12, 48–49, 56, 71, 83–84, 93, 117, 135, 146–47, 152, 154–55, 157, 209, 240, 263, 267, 290–91, 293–94, 296

Paul, Maj. Gen. Willard S. (GOC 26 ID), 282

Pausner, Lt. Charles H., Jr. (Cannon/302), 284

Peace Monument, 123

Peck, Pvt. (A376), 42

Pellingen, 251, 260, 262, 268, 274, 283, 288

Penn, Lt. Frank A. (HQ Def Pl/376), 135

Pepper, Capt. Bernard M. (B/5 Rgrs), 202

Perl, 34, 45, 48–49, 57, 59, 85, 113, 122, 124, 126, 129, 131, 140

Peters, Lt.(C376), 40

Petri, Tech-5 Michael (K301), 170

Petry, Pvt. Jennings B. (F302), 74

Petry, TSgt Arnold A. (I376), 74, 77

Pfalzel, 149

Pfalzerwald, 293

Pflieger, Lt. Gen. Kurt (GOC 416 ID), 15, 54

Pflueger, SSgt. Paul (F302), 254

Phillips, Lt. Charles M. (778 TB), 284

Phillips, Lt. Col. John D. F. (G4 94ID), 231

Pierce, Lt. Robert C. (H376), 109

Pietrzah, Pvt. John F. (E376), 67

Piburn, Brig. Gen. Edwin W. (CCA 10 AD), 134, 209

Piotrzkowski, Pfc. Bernard (C302), 129–30

Pillingerhof, 84, 86–87

Pillow, SSgt. "The Rev" W. T. (A376), 40, 42, 249–50

Poinier, Lt. Col. Arthur D. (7 AIB), 66, 70–71

Porter, Lt. James W. (B/319 Engrs), 92

Potsdamer Platz, 129

Potthoff, SSgt. Brice P. (M302), 277

Poynter, Sgt. Harry J. (2/301), 104–5

Price, Sgt. Harold B. (C376), 44, 164

Prior, Lt. James E. (2/301), 99, 101

Queen Elizabeth, RMS, 3

Quentz, Sgt. Joseph J. (C376), 40

Quiberon Peninsular, 4

Raffesberger, Sgt. Clarence (K301), 124

Raley, Cpl. (I302), 277

Ramirez, Lt. Carmen L. (L302), 143, 271, 273, 285

Ramondini, Sgt. Frederick J. (HQ/301), 118

Ramsey, Tech-5 Paul E. (E376), 233

Rao, SSgt. Anthony S. (E376), 68

Redner, Pfc. (A376), 262

Regan, TSgt. Edward P. (G302), 81

Regan, Sgt. Johan A. (L302), 271

Reichley, TSgt. Ralph (B376), 195

Reims, 4

Remagen, 290

Remich, 16, 28, 31, 33, 47, 72–73, 78–80, 84, 94, 96, 99, 105, 107, 111, 124, 131

Rencavage, Sgt. Joseph (G301), 97

Renck, Lt. Donald L. (C302), 61

Reserve Officer Training Corps (ROTC), 2

Reudiger, Lt. (II/714 GrRegt), 38, 67

Reuter, Lt. Edmund G. (E301), 99, 214

Reynolds, Lt. Dale (H301), 101, 104–6

Reynolds, Pfc. Harvey J. (G302), 279

Rhine River, 21, 147, 264, 289–90, 293–95

Richards, Lt. Carl D. (C302), 61, 173

Richardson, Lt. Col. Jack J. (20 AIB), 209, 226, 237, 239, 253, 257–59

Riley, Lt., (CCB 10AD) 258–59

Riley, Lt. Col. John R. (CCA 10AD), 226–27

Ring, Lt. William (A376), 79

Risky, Tech-3 John F. (L302), 61

Rives, Lt. (D301), 255

Riviera, 296

Roberts, Col. William L. (CCB 10AD), 134

Robinson, Lt. (C302), 86, 129, 171–73

Rodt, 145

Roeschen, Lt. Col. Albrecht, 175–76

Romanowski, Sgt. Joseph A. (H302), 144

Römer Brücke, 258, 262–63

Roper, Maj. Benjamin S. (1/376), 73

Rosenberg Hill, 72

Routh, SSgt. John R. (I302), 276

Ruhr Pocket, 294–95

Runstedt, Fd. Marshal Gerd von, 12

Ruwer River, 240, 246, 250, 253–54, 258, 268, 270–72, 282

Ryan, Capt. John J. (3/376), 48, 57, 250

Saarbrücken, 293

Saarburg, 37, 85, 113, 124, 126, 129, 131, 133, 135, 140, 147, 149–50, 152, 155, 157, 165, 170, 174, 217, 223, 235, 245, 253, 257, 290

Saarburg State Forest, 51

Saarhausen, 205, 239, 241, 264

Saarlautern, 1, 267, 294

Saar River, 1, 15–16, 21–22, 38, 51, 67–68, 106, 117, 132, 140, 144–46, 147–49, 151–52, 154–56, 158, 160–62, 165, 167–71, 174–75, 191, 195, 197, 199, 203, 205, 208–9, 212, 215–16, 219, 221, 223, 239, 244, 249, 253, 257–58, 264, 282, 289–90, 295

Saarschleuse, 16

Sacco, Sgt. Vincent (G302), 278

Saint Nazaire, 3

Sanniac, Sgt. Joseph (A376), 77

Sauer River, 1, 154

Scales, Lt. Knox L. (G301), 96–97, 99–100

Schaefer, Lt. Carl (356 Arty), 102–3

Schaewen, SSgt. (IV/AR 416), 128–29

Scharfenberg Ridge, 156, 194–5, 197, 206, 208, 220–21, 227, 234–5, 242

Scharzberg Ridge, 250, 253

Schaub, Maj. John W. (94 MP), 216

Schloss Berg, 32–33, 48, 57, 65–66, 68–71

Schloss Bübingen, 30, 78, 84, 94

Schloss Saarfels, 201, 210, 226

Schloss Saarstein, 212

Schloss Thorn, 30, 50, 135–39

Schmidt. Sgt. Harry (A301), 85

Schoden, 197, 209, 217–18, 233, 244, 248–49, 253

Schofield, Lt. William W. (H301), 96, 99

Schömerich, 241, 254, 272, 277–81

Schrager, SSgt. Sidney (I302), 273

Schwarzbruch, 51

Schwarzwalder Hochwald, 291

Schweig, Pvt. Dick (A376), 40

Schwemer, SSgt. Frank (D302), 280–81

Scioli; Pfc. Michael A. (F302), 280

Scopoli, TSgt Mariano (F376), 108–9, 111

Scotland, 3

Seeby, Lt. Carl W. (K302), 57–58, 65–66

Sendric, Sgt. Simond J. (E302), 144

Serrig, 151–53, 165, 167, 169–70, 172–73, 175–76, 199, 201–3, 205–6, 210, 212–16, 223, 226, 230–31, 234, 237, 254

Shaddeau, Capt. (CCA 10AD), 139–40, 246, 251, 257

Shetler, Capt. Carl J. (A376), 16, 18, 20

Shocksnyder, Lt. Arthur A. (B301), 121, 245

Siegfried Line (Westwall), 1, 6–7, 10–11, 14, 23, 35, 90, 96, 100, 107–8, 110, 112, 114, 124, 130, 134, 138, 149–50, 152, 154, 156, 169, 197, 201, 290, 295

Sierck-les-Bains, 48, 57, 83

Simon, SS-Lt. Gen. Max (GOC XIII SS Korps), 293

Simuro, Lt. Bernard F. (E376), 68–69

Sinclair, Capt. Charles H. (F301), 96–98, 141, 145, 201

Sinclair, Pfc. Laverne (E302), 76

Singer, Tech-4 Adolph (919 Arty), 108

Sinz, 18, 30–31, 33, 37–38, 41, 62, 69, 72–73, 76, 78–82, 84, 90, 93–94, 96–107, 110–12, 118, 120, 122–25, 131, 138–40, 278

Slack, Brig. Gen. Julius E. (HQ XX Corps), 118

Smith, Capt. Cleo B. (C301), 52

Smith, Capt. John N. (L302), 57–59, 60–61, 174, 206, 210, 212, 242, 245, 274

Smith, Capt. Robert Q. (H376), 107, 190–92

Smith, Lt./Capt. Douglas LaRue. (M302), 57, 289

Smith, Lt. Oliver K. (G302), 91, 113–15
Smith, SSgt. John F. (C302), 171–72
Smith, Sgt. (A376), 42
Smythe, Lt. Henry J. (356 Arty), 97–98
Snyder, Capt. Emanuel P. (M376), 169
Synder, Capt. Jack A. (C/5 Rgrs), 202
Soka, Sgt. (C376), 37, 44
Sollenberger, Lt. William S. (G301),
    104–5
Söst, 140
Southampton, 3
South Carolina, 2
Springer, Lt. William P. (C376), 283
Staadt, 148, 152–53, 164–65, 168–69,
    197, 199, 201–2, 205, 209–10, 214–16,
    229, 235
Stafford, Lt./Capt. David F. (A376), 20,
    38, 43
Standish, Capt. Frederic D. (E376), 138,
    190–91, 208–9, 217–19, 244
Standish, Lt. Col. Miles L. (61 AIB), 217
Stanion, Maj. Warren F. (1/302), 89–90,
    112, 122, 124, 129, 143, 145, 170–72, 203,
    210, 244, 254–55, 258, 265
Steinbach, 246, 280–82, 284
Steinen, Capt. Otto P. (G301), 214,
    232, 246
Steinmühle, 51
Stempak, Lt. Walter M. (C301), 120
Stern, Sgt. Milton H. (G302), 278–79
Stevens, Capt. Clair H. (301 Arty), 91
Stinson, Lt. John D. (7 AIB), 71
Stockman, Sgt. George H. (L302), 274
Stockstad, Capt. Walter J. (E301), 99,
    100, 141, 214, 232
Straub, Capt. Herman C. (B301), 52–55
Strong, Sgt. Orville (C376), 164
Sullivan, Lt. Col. Richard P. (5 Rgrs),
    112, 122, 174, 202, 213, 237, 248, 250, 258
Summerford, Tech-4 Oscar E. (F302), 115
Susice, 296
Sweeney, Pfc. Ray (I376), 45
Swift, Pfc. Carl T. (G302), 278
Switzerland, 6

Tabel, Pfc. B. D. (A301), 85
Taben, 145, 148, 151, 153, 171, 174–76, 202,
    205, 209–10, 212–16, 223, 226, 231, 234,
    237, 239, 264
Tarforst, 256, 264
Tawern, 139–40, 148, 153
Tennesee, 2
Tettingen, 12–13, 18, 20–21, 23–27, 30–31,
    33–34, 37, 40–41, 44, 50–51, 58–62, 76–
    77, 83, 85, 87, 90–91, 94, 118, 123, 139
Thionville, 294
Thompson, Pfc. Kyle (I/02), 130
Thornton, Herman Pfc./Sgt. (C376),
    23–27
Thurston, Lt. Col. Benjamin E. (3/376),
    28, 32–33, 45–47, 57, 72–74, 79, 82, 84,
    112, 125–26, 139, 145, 157, 194–95, 206,
    220, 234–35, 242, 250, 253, 257, 264–67
Towers, Sgt. Jesse R. (319 Engrs), 37
Trassem, 54, 129, 202, 205
Travers, Lt. John R. (L302), 58–59, 77,
    130, 274, 277
Trefzger, Pfc./Sgt. Robert (C376), 23–27,
    160–61, 163–64, 196
Trier, 1, 12, 21, 83, 135, 146–50, 175, 209,
    237, 240, 246–47, 251, 253, 256–64, 268,
    274, 289–60, 295
Trinkline, Lt. Robert E. (E301), 214
Troupe, Pvt. David H. (B301), 246
Trowbridge, 3
Truels, Lt. John G. (F301), 98
Truss, Pfc. Joseph J. (I301), 123
Tullahoma, 2
Tywoneck, Pfc. Tyrone (A301), 124

Unsong Valor, 52
Unter den Eichen Woods, 16, 131, 143
Unterste Büsch Woods, 72, 78–81, 94, 96,
    99, 103, 107, 111, 125
Unter-Tünsdorf, 90
Urban, Sgt. (L301), 266
Utah Beach, 3

Van Dusen, Sgt. William D. (F376), 35
Vastola, SSgt. Salvatore (3/376), 73
Veckring, 44, 48, 83, 112
Vinue, Lt. Robert L. (K301), 241
Vogel, SSgt. Hans (HQ 94ID), 249, 261
Vulgamore, Cpl. Earl N. (D376), 43

Wackseler Fels Hill (Height 440), 232, 241, 245
Waldtresch Woods, 140
Walker, Lt. Harrison H. (A301), 84
Walker, Maj. Gen. Walton H. (GOC XX Corps), 1, 5–6, 12, 48–9, 71, 82–3, 92–3, 117–18, 126, 134, 144, 146–7, 152, 154–55, 267, 290–91
Walters, Pvt. (A376), 42
Wancio, Lt./Capt. Theo (B302), 89, 172–73, 281–82
Warren, Capt. William C. (K301), 111, 168, 242, 248
Wasserman, Pfc. Morris H. (HQ 1/302), 50
Watson, Sgt. Roy G. (K301), 124
Way, Capt. Julian M. (K376), 30–31
Wegand Line, 6
Wehingen, 90
Weiten, 142–45, 174
Wellman, Pfc. Russel E. (L302), 271–72
Wellom, Lt. T. J. (319 Engrs), 100
Welsch, Pvt. Milton A. (1/376), 23
Western Allies, 1, 11
Weston, Lt. Gordon A. (F376), 34, 108–9
West Point, 5
Westwall (Siegfried Line), 1, 6–7, 10–11, 14, 23, 35, 90, 96, 100, 107–8, 110, 112, 114, 124, 130, 134, 138, 149–50, 152, 154, 156, 169, 197, 201, 290, 295
Whitely, Lt. Col. (356 Arty), 94
Whiting, Charles (Historian), 154–55
Whitman, Capt. George P. (F376), 34–35, 107–11
Wicentwoski, Pvt. Whiz (A376), 40
Wichic, SSgt. Michael (G302), 81–82
Wies, 28, 30, 32, 38, 46–47, 57, 64–66, 68–69, 78, 84, 111
Wietersheim, Gen. Wend von (GOC 11 PzDiv), 21, 38, 106

Wilkins, Lt. Gus E. (E376), 67
Wiles, Sgt. Richard R. (G302), 277–78
Williams, Capt. Allan R. (I302), 57, 65, 123, 130, 142, 272
Willich, 294
Wilson, Lt. George B. (F376), 108–11
Wilson, Lt. Johan A. (356 Arty), 60
Wilson, Pvt. Tom (A376), 42
Wilson, Lt. Wilfred (F376), 34–35
Wiltingen, 134, 140, 148, 169, 249–50, 253, 264
Wiltshire, 3
Wincheringen, 135, 139, 145
Wiser, Sgt. (C376), 24
Wochern, 18, 21, 23, 34–35, 38, 44, 58–61, 63, 91, 126
Wolf, Lt. Robert H. (A301), 122, 205
Woodburn, Capt. Robert A. (A302), 50, 86, 172, 265
Woodrill, Capt. Gilbert S. (D301), 52
Woods, Capt. Altus L. Jr. (B302), 49, 60, 83, 87, 89, 131
Woodward, Lt. William C. (919 Fd Arty), 20
Woolman, Pfc. Wayne N. (E302), 115
Wuppertal, 295
Wylie, Pvt. (A376), 40

Yewell, Pfc. Edward D. (G302), 81
Young, Capt. John S. (S-2 302), 148

Zaring, Pfc. Paul L. (Cannon/302), 272
Zebin, Pvt. (A376), 40–41
Zerf, 152, 174, 202, 226, 237, 239, 241–42, 246–48, 253, 257, 264–66, 282, 288
Zimmerman, Maj. (1/376), 249, 260–62, 268
Zinny, Pvt. (A376), 42

Armed Forces Index

CZECH ARMED FORCES
1st Czech Armd Corps, 296

GERMAN ARMED FORCES
Army Group G, 132–33, 240
First Army, 106, 293
XIII SS Corps, 293
LXXXII Corps, 15, 22, 132, 169, 240, 267, 289, 293
—404 Volks Arty Corps, 12
—11th Pz Div, 21–22, 37–38, 48, 51, 64, 85, 106, 112, 169
    PzGren Regt 110, 21, 38, 41, 67–68
    PzGren Regt 111, 21, 38, 68, 204
    Pz Regt 15, 21, 38, 41, 67, 98, 106, 110, 112
    Pz Recce Bn 11, 21
    Pz Arty Regt 119, 21
    Army Flak Bn 277, 21
    Pz Sigs Bn 89, 21
    Pz Engr Bn 209, 21, 38
    Tk–Hunting Bn 61, 21, 38
    Pz Fd Trg & Rep Bn 61, 21
—21st Pz Div, 12
—416th Inf Div, 12, 15–16, 22, 32, 38, 54, 106, 132, 169, 227, 265
    Gren Regt 712, 15, 22, 53–54
    Gren Regt 713, 15, 18, 22, 112, 115, 143
    Gren Regt 714, 15, 22, 38, 67
    Fortress Inf Regt, "Merzig," 15
    Arty Regt 416, 15, 128–29
    Arty Bn 204, 15

Fortress Arty Regt 1024, 15, 133
Fortress Arty Regt 1025, 15, 155
Fd Trg & Rep Bn 416, 15, 22–23
—719th Inf Div, 12
—212th Volks Gen Div, 263
—256th Volks Gren Div, 32–33, 106, 112, 132, 141, 169, 265, 268
    Gren Regt 456, 33, 141
    Gren Regt 457, 33
    Gren Regt 458, 33
    Gren Regt 481, 135–37
    Arty Regt 256, 33
    Engr Bn 256, 33
    Fd Trg & Rep Bn 256, 33, 41
    Tk Hunting Bn 256, 33
    Fus Co 256, 33
—SS PzGren Bn 506, 231–32
—2nd Mtn Div, 240, 265, 268, 274
    Mtn Inf Regt 136, 240
    Mtn Inf Regt 137, 240, 248, 265, 282
    Mtn Arty Regt 11, 240, 270, 283–84
    Mtn Engr Bn 82, 240
    Tk Hunting Bn 55, 240
—6th SS Mtn Div "Nord," 267–68
    SS Mtn Inf Regt 11 "Reinhard Heydrich," 268, 272, 284, 287, 289
    IId Bn, SS Mtn Inf Regt 12, "Michael Gaismair," 268, 277, 279–81
    KG Brockmann, 279–80
    KG Dahne, 279
    SS Mtn Arty Regt 6, 268

SS Recce Bn 6, 268
SS Flak Bn 6, 268
SS Engr Bn 6, 268
LXXXV Corps, 293
9th Flak Div, 293

US ARMED FORCES
Combined Chiefs of Staff, 6
USAAF
—XII TAC, 293
—XIX TAC, 13, 116, 118
SHAEF, 4, 240, 263
12th Army Group, 263
First Army, 83, 153, 290
Third Army, 1, 4, 49, 83–84, 152–
    54, 296
Sixth Army, 71
Seventh Army, 117, 290
Ninth Army, 3, 153
Fifteenth Army, 294
—XXII Corps, 294
XII Corps, 1, 72, 83, 139, 263
—2nd Cav Gp, 1, 72, 139–40
—76 Inf Div, 263
XVIII Airborne Corps, 294
XX Corps, 1, 5, 43, 66–67, 71, 84, 93,
    112, 117–18, 138, 144, 147–48, 150,
    153–55, 174, 209, 213, 215, 223, 231,
    235, 240, 263, 267, 282, 290–91,
    294–95
—5 Fd Arty Gp, 150
—195 Fd Arty Gp, 150, 286
—1139, Cbt Engr Gp, 150, 153
    135 Cbt Engr Bn, 150, 153, 215,
    235, 245
—558 Fd Arty Bn, 84
101st Airborne Div, 71
8th Armd Div, 49, 70, 80, 82, 296
—CCA, 49, 66, 69–70, 72, 80, 82
    Task Force Goodrich, 77–81
    7th Armd Inf Bn, 66, 70–71, 77–
    78, 80–82
    18th Tk Bn, 66, 70, 77–79, 81
    88th Cav Recce Sqn, 66, 70–71,
    77–78
    53rd Armd Engr Bn, 70, 77–78

10th Armd Div, 3, 12–13, 117, 126, 132,
    134–35, 138–39, 144–45, 147, 149,
    151–52, 154–57, 159, 197, 209, 220–
    23, 228, 231, 235, 240–41, 251, 257,
    259, 263–64, 290–91, 295
—CCA, 12–13, 134, 139, 141–42, 162–
    64, 150, 226, 230, 237, 246
    Task Force Chamberlain, 139, 148,
    246–47, 251, 257
    Team Eisberg, 257
    Team Holehouse, 139–40
    Team O'Grady, 139–40, 246,
    251, 257
    Team Shaddeau, 139–40, 246,
    251, 257
    Task Force Richardson, 139–41,
    221, 246, 253, 257–61
    Team Billet, 140–41, 257
    Team Riley, 257
    Task Force Norris, 251, 257, 259
—CCB, 134, 139, 150, 226, 235, 237,
    247, 257
    Task Force O'Hara/Haskell, 221,
    247, 251, 253, 255–56, 259
    Team Devereaux, 247
    Team Lang, 252–53, 256
    Task Force Riley, 221–22, 226–28
    Team Holehouse, 227–28
    Team Kafkalas, 251
—CCR, 134, 139, 150, 253
    Task Force Cherry, 253
    Task Force Standish, 221, 226–27
    20th Armd Inf Bn, 209, 227–
    28, 237, 246
    54th Armd Inf Bn, 217, 221,
    237, 247, 256
    61st Armd Inf Bn, 217–18, 226–
    27, 233, 245
—21st Tk Bn, 226, 239
—609th TD Bn, 239
—90th Cav Recce Sqn, 150
—55th Armd Engr Bn, 247
12th Armd Div, 291, 294
5th Inf Div, 293
—11th Inf Regt, 293
8th Inf Div, 2

26th Inf Div, 112, 147, 264, 267, 282–83, 290, 296
—328th Inf Regt, 282
65th Inf Div, 267
66th Inf Div, 4
76th Inf Div, 263
77th Inf Div, 2
80th Inf Div, 290
83d Inf Div, 3
90th Inf Div, 1
—358th Inf Regt, 12–13
94th Inf Div
—301st Inf Regt, 4, 51, 54–55, 67, 72, 83, 93–94, 112, 118, 124, 126, 131, 148–49, 164–65, 201, 206, 210, 212, 225–26, 235, 237, 239, 258, 266–67, 282, 290–91, 294
　1st Bn, 51–56, 71–72, 83–85, 94, 96, 120, 126, 143–45, 165, 167, 170, 202, 205, 210, 214, 225–26, 230, 232, 253, 255, 258
　2d Bn, 52, 55, 71–72, 83, 85–86, 94, 96, 101, 104, 106, 112, 126, 128, 141, 145, 199, 201, 210, 214, 226, 232, 234, 239, 241, 245–46, 255
　3d Bn, 3, 51, 72, 79, 83–84, 94, 96, 101, 107, 111–12, 120, 126, 128, 141, 145, 170, 175, 197, 199, 201, 210, 212–13, 217, 223, 225–26, 228, 234–35, 241, 247, 250, 265–66, 282
—302d Inf Regt, 4, 15, 49, 62, 71–72, 77, 83, 93, 112, 118, 122–23, 129–31, 143, 148–49, 152–53, 174, 202, 205, 210, 226, 232, 282, 284, 286, 289–90
　1st Bn, 49–50, 59–63, 71–72, 76, 83–84, 86–87, 89–90, 112, 122, 124, 129, 131, 143, 145, 170–75, 199, 203, 210, 213, 226, 230–31, 241, 244, 254–55, 258, 265, 280–82, 284, 286–88
　2d Bn, 59–60, 62, 71–72, 74, 76–87, 89–91, 96, 113, 122, 143, 146, 148, 175, 203, 206, 210, 213, 215, 225–26, 230–32, 235, 241–42, 244, 250–51, 254, 267, 277–81

3d Bn, 56–57, 62–66, 68, 72, 78–80, 83, 112, 122, 129–31, 142, 144–45, 148, 174–75, 205–6, 210, 212, 214–15, 223, 225–26, 228, 231, 235, 241–42, 245, 254, 258, 270, 283, 287, 289
—376th Inf Regt, 3–4, 14, 18, 60, 72–74, 77–79, 82, 93, 112, 114, 118, 124, 131, 134, 139–40, 145, 149–50, 155, 175, 196–97, 206, 208–9, 217, 220, 222, 233, 264, 283, 290–91, 294
　1st Bn, 31–32, 34, 37–38, 44–45, 47–48, 59, 71–74, 76–78, 80–82, 112, 124–25, 131, 145, 156–63, 195–97, 208–9, 217–19, 233–34, 244, 248, 250, 253, 257, 260, 264, 283, 285–86, 288
　2d Bn, 16, 18, 20–27, 33–36, 43–45, 59–60, 66–70, 77–78, 82, 107, 111–12, 131, 138, 145, 156, 190–92, 194, 206, 208, 217–18, 233, 235, 249, 253–54, 258–59, 264, 286, 288
　3d Bn, 28, 30–34, 36, 45–48, 56–57, 72–74, 77, 79–80, 82, 112, 124–25, 139, 145, 156–59, 190, 192, 206, 208, 220, 234–35, 242, 250, 253–54, 257, 264–67
—Task Force Gaddis, 143–44
—5th Ranger Bn, 112, 114, 122–23, 126, 129, 146, 147, 152, 174, 202, 213–14, 226–28, 237, 241–42, 248, 250, 258, 267
—465th AAA Bn, 5, 89, 142, 149, 282
—248th Fd Arty Bn, 44, 110
—301st Fd Arty Bn, 4, 52, 54–55, 86, 90, 94, 114–16, 130, 143, 150, 231, 282
—356th Fd Arty Bn, 58, 60, 64, 94, 97, 100, 102, 106, 150, 214, 266, 273, 278, 285
—390th Fd Arty Bn, 4, 71, 110, 150, 284
—919th Fd Arty Bn, 4, 18, 44, 94, 107–8, 110, 132, 138, 244, 285
—7th Fd Arty Obs Bn, 149, 274–75